Learn SQL

Learn SQL

In a Weekend

DEANNA DICKEN

KEVIN THOMPSON

Premier
Press

Premier

Press ™

Publisher: Stacy L. Hiquet

Associate Marketing Manager: Heather Buzzingham

Managing Editor: Sandy Doell

Acquisitions Editor: Stacy L. Hiquet

Project Editors: Kezia Endsley, Estelle Manticas

Editorial Assistant: Margaret Bauer

Technical Reviewer: David Fields

Copy Editor: Laura Gabler

Interior Layout: Jill Flores

Cover Design: Premier Press, Inc.

Indexer: Sharon Shock

Proofreader: Kezia Endsley

ISBN: 1-931841-62-4

Library of Congress Catalog Card Number: 2001099846

Printed in the United States of America

02 03 04 05 RI 10 9 8 7 6 5 4 3 2 1

ACKNOWLEDGMENTS

First we would like to recognize the individuals who worked on this book. We want to thank Stacy Hiquet, Acquisitions Editor, for getting this book going. Estelle Manticas and Kezia Endsley, Project Editors, worked very hard to keep the book on schedule and looking good. We also need to thank Laura Gabler for her excellent work as copy editor and David Fields for his technical review.

We also want to thank our families for their understanding as we worked many nights and weekends over these past several months to get this book done. Thank you for your support and encouragement.

ABOUT THE AUTHOR

Deanna Dicken is a Microsoft Certified Solution Developer (MCSD). She has over 10 years experience in the computer industry, including six years as a consultant. During this time, she has worked on many large-scale, critical applications and has been involved in all phases of the life-cycle. She has also contributed to three SQL Server books for MCSE study guides and technical edited many other titles. Deanna lives on the outskirts of Indianapolis, Indiana with her husband, Curtis. They are expecting their first bundle of joy in May 2002, Kylee Marie Dicken.

Kevin Thompson is an independent contract developer in the Indianapolis area. He specializes in n-tier Internet/intranet and client/server application development. He has worked with SQL relational databases for the last 13 years. He has obtained several technical certifications including Microsoft SQL Server and Sybase Adaptive Server. He has also worked on several books on the topics of database development, database administration, and client/server programming. Kevin, his wife Lisa, and their children Alexandra, Davis, and Harrison live in Carmel, Indiana. Their dog Dakota enjoys eating sticks of butter, loaves of bread, and anything else that is left out overnight.

CONTENTS AT A GLANCE

CONTENTS

SUNDAY AFTERNOON
Security—Putting the Padlocks on 263

SUNDAY EVENING
SQL and the Application Developer 329

INTRODUCTION

In this age of information, many businesses live and die by the data they keep in databases. SQL is the gateway to that data. It gives you the capability to store, utilize, and analyze data.

Welcome to *Learn SQL in a Weekend*, your introduction to the powerful language known as SQL, Structured Query Language. In one short weekend, you will learn the skills necessary to take advantage of the information so vital to the productivity, strategy, and even survival of businesses in this day and age.

What This Book Is About

Learn SQL in a Weekend is an introduction to the widely used language of SQL. From this weekend course, you will learn

➤ Basic database terminology

➤ Data retrieval techniques

➤ Complex query creation and data summation

➤ Proper database design concepts

➤ Database object creation

➤ Data storage and manipulation commands

➤ Advanced database concepts such as views, triggers, and stored procedures

➤ Database security concepts

➤ How to use SQL with popular software packages and programming languages

Once you've completed this book, you will have an excellent foundation for using SQL with any RDBMS (relational database management system). Each RDBMS implements SQL in its own way, but the concepts covered here are fairly standard. We will point out differences between the major vendors as each topic is discussed. Therefore, this book makes an excellent stepping-stone toward more vendor-specific SQL topics.

Who Should Read This Book

Almost everyone in the world has been exposed to a database at some point in his or her life. Have you ever used an ATM, ordered something online, or bought groceries? Chances are your account balance, the description and price of the item you ordered, and the UPC and price of your groceries all came from a database. SQL is the standard by which people communicate with databases.

Whether you would like to build a database to store your record collection or perhaps someday work as a database administrator, *Learn SQL in a Weekend* is a great place to start to learn SQL. This book will guide you from the basic design of a database through more advanced techniques in communicating with one.

What You Need to Begin

All you really need to begin is this book. You can read through this book and get a feel for how SQL is used and why. If you'd like to be able to follow along with the examples, however, you will need an RDBMS to play with. This book provides a sample database and links to several free RDBMS trials on the Web. Once you download and install the trial software and sample database, you'll be ready to go. You will be able to try the examples in the book and check your results against the listings.

The Sunday Evening session provides listings to help you use SQL in conjunction with several popular software packages and programming languages. Should you wish to follow along with those examples, you will need a copy of that software.

How This Book Is Organized

➤ **Friday Evening: Introduction to SQL—Let the Weekend Begin!** introduces you to the hows and whys of SQL. The basic terminology of SQL and relational database management systems is described. The major RDBMS vendors, their products, and trial versions are discussed and links provided. Finally, this opening chapter walks you through setting up your sample database so you can follow along with the examples provided throughout the remainder of the book.

➤ **Saturday Morning: Selecting Data—How to See What's in There** gets you started communicating with a database. The most used SQL command, SELECT, is covered in this session along with several examples of uses for it and variations of it. You learn how to use the SELECT statement to find out what information is stored in the database.

➤ **Saturday Afternoon: Selecting Data—Bigger and Better** takes the SELECT statement several steps further. First this session covers several popular functions that can be used in the SELECT to perform arithmetic calculations, gather system information, format the results, and so forth. Next the session explores the benefits of grouping to summarize data. We then show you how to feed the results of one query into another. The nested SQL query is called a subquery. Finally, unions are covered. Unions allow you to combine the results of two or more queries to form a single result set.

➤ **Saturday Evening: Building a Home for Your Data** gets into the details of how you can put together your own database. It begins with a look at best practices for creating a relational database. You then move into the mechanics of creating a new database, filling it with your own tables, and relating the tables to one another. You then end the day by learning how to insert, modify, and delete data from these tables.

➤ **Sunday Morning: Optimization—Feel the Need for Speed?** kicks off the morning session. You discover many ways that you can get your database to perform at its highest level. The first and most basic way is through indexes. You learn how to create and use a few different kinds of indexes. Next, you see how you can use a little bit of programming to make high-performance stored procedures. Then, you learn about ensuring the integrity of your data with transactions. Finally, the session ends with a large variety of optimization tips and techniques.

➤ **Sunday Afternoon: Security—Putting the Padlocks On** is a session devoted to letting the right people see the right data and keeping everyone else out. You begin by discovering how to create accounts and groups for users. Next you see how these accounts can be given permission to certain parts of your database. Views are introduced, which provide you with the flexibility to let users see only what you want them to see. Lastly, you build some triggers that you can use to keep an eye on what data people are changing.

➤ **Sunday Evening: SQL and the Application Developer** ends the weekend with a look at how power-users and programmers can use SQL to make their jobs easier. The first part of the session tells how anyone can use applications such as Microsoft Excel and Word to directly access data in a SQL database. The remainder of the session is geared toward programmers. It discusses ways in which some of today's most popular programming languages can access your databases. The languages we cover are Visual Basic, Visual Basic .NET, Visual C++, Visual C# .NET, ASP, ASP .NET, and PowerBuilder. In these sections you'll find in-depth discussions about how each of the languages can connect to a database, retrieve data, and save changes. There is source code given for each so that you can follow along.

Special Features in This Book

Learn SQL in a Weekend contains lots of examples so you can follow along with the discussions. The example code and results are formatted differently than regular text so you can find them easily. The *In a Weekend* series also includes tips, notes, cautions, buzzwords, and Find It Online links to set apart important information.

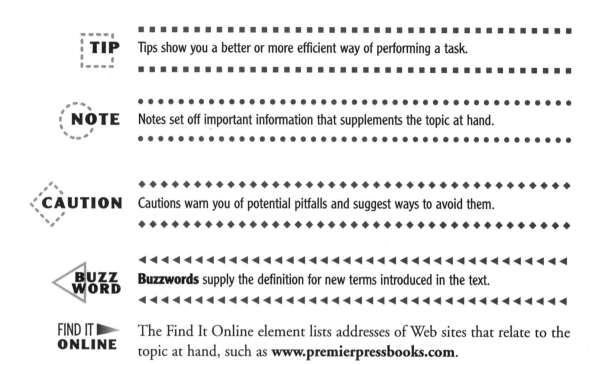

TIP

Tips show you a better or more efficient way of performing a task.

NOTE

Notes set off important information that supplements the topic at hand.

CAUTION

Cautions warn you of potential pitfalls and suggest ways to avoid them.

BUZZ WORD

Buzzwords supply the definition for new terms introduced in the text.

FIND IT ▶ ONLINE

The Find It Online element lists addresses of Web sites that relate to the topic at hand, such as **www.premierpressbooks.com**.

Introduction to SQL—Let the Weekend Begin!

- ➤ What Is SQL?
- ➤ Why Do You Need It?
- ➤ The 31 Flavors of SQL
- ➤ Where Do You Begin?
- ➤ The Anatomy of a Relational Database
- ➤ Setting Up the Sample Databases

It's Friday evening and you've had a long week. We're sure you can think of many things you'd rather be doing on a Friday night than reading a technical book. But you're doing it to better yourself, right? So tonight we'll take it fairly easy. We'll introduce you to SQL and how it is used. We'll define some terms and talk about some of the related vendors. Then we'll get everything ready for you to dig in deep tomorrow morning.

What Is SQL?

SQL, pronounced "sequel," is an acronym for *Structured Query Language*. A standards body called ANSI, the *American National Standards Institute*, maintains this language. Many vendors have created their own extensions to this standard while still maintaining their compliance to the standard. Therefore, SQL as it is defined by ANSI is referred to as ANSI SQL. We will delve into the topic of SQL extensions shortly.

First we'll tell you why SQL exists. SQL is a powerful query language that was created as a means to communicate with databases. Databases store data. SQL can be used to view, manipulate, and create this data. It can even define the structures that will hold the data. We are surrounded by information in this world. Knowing SQL gives you the edge to be able to collect, access, and analyze this information. Starting with the Saturday Morning session, we will show you how to use SQL to do these things and much more.

Because SQL is a standards-controlled language, it is reusable from database to database. You do not have to learn a different language if you need to get data from a contact database versus a recipe database or if you switched a database from one vendor to another. If each vendor created its own data access language, you couldn't jump from one vendor to another without learning a new language. With SQL, however, the basics are the same for every vendor that conforms to the standard. We mentioned that many vendors have their own extensions to SQL—but you don't have to learn these extensions unless you want to perform more complex operations against that database.

Why Do You Need It?

As mentioned previously, SQL is used to communicate with databases. Databases store information. If you know SQL and have access to a database, you can get the information out of that database or even put information in. If you use a computer, chances are you interact with databases. Many of the applications you have on your computer use a database to store the information you put into that application, such as contacts in your e-mail program. Businesses often use databases to store lists of and information on inventory, orders, employees, payroll, customers, and much more. Databases are everywhere. They are used to store your credit card transactions, phone calls, payment history, investment options, insurance claims, and criminal history, for example. You access a database when you check out at the grocery store, withdraw money from an ATM, call information, or conduct a search on the Internet. You didn't specifically request information from these databases using SQL, but someone did. They wrote the SQL, and your actions filled in a couple blanks and sent a request for information off to the database. Soon you will be the one writing the queries. This book will even show you how to write queries where unsuspecting individuals like yourself fill in the blanks and cause a SQL statement to retrieve information from a database.

If you are working with or planning to work with computers for a living, you need to learn SQL. Individuals whose career path is to develop software or e-commerce sites or administer databases someday especially need to learn SQL. Administrative assistants can benefit from learning SQL. They can create and maintain contact lists and other such information. It can also make filling out form letters and creating mailing labels a breeze. Executives can use SQL to perform ad hoc queries to gather the summary information they need to better drive the decisions that direct their company's future.

The 31 Flavors of SQL

Okay, maybe 31 is an exaggeration, but there are several. Let's look at the major vendors of *relational database management systems* (RDBMS) and the extensions to the standard they employ.

Oracle Corporation puts out a powerful RDBMS called (appropriately) Oracle. In its latest version, 9i, Oracle has several editions of its RDBMS aimed at various levels of user. They have an enterprise edition for very large database installations with hundreds or thousands of users. They also have a product called Personal Oracle aimed at the individual user. A free trial version of this product is available for download from the Web site. This requires you to have an Oracle Technology Network (OTN) password, but membership is free and you can sign up when you go to download.

Oracle uses an extension to SQL called PL/SQL. It allows the typical nonprocedural SQL to be used in a procedural manner. PL/SQL is like a programming language in that you can tell the database how to go about making the inserts or updates (or whatever SQL statements you want to perform) instead of just telling the database what you'd like to insert or update, for example. PL/SQL allows for procedure statements such as looping and IF-THEN statements.

FIND IT ▶
ONLINE
The Oracle Web site address is **http://www.oracle.com/**.

The free trial version of the DBMS is available at **http://otn.oracle.com/ software/products/oracle9i/content.html**.

Sybase and Microsoft collaborated on a product called SQL Server. They each release their own version of the product; however, they shared code and version numbers until a few years back anyway. When SQL Server was in version 4.2a, Sybase and Microsoft decided to go their different ways with the product. Microsoft started over and ended up with Microsoft SQL Server 6.0. Sybase arrived at System 10. Even though they are now very different products, they still share some similarities in both functionality and syntax.

Microsoft's current release is SQL Server 2000. It's a very powerful enterprise-level RDBMS with strong data-warehousing and analysis capabilities. SQL Server also has an assortment of editions of the product aimed at developers, personal users, embedded database needs, and also Windows CE-based handheld devices. SQL Server Enterprise edition runs on Windows 2000 Server, Windows 2000 Advanced Server, Windows 2000 Datacenter Server, Windows 2000 Professional, Windows NT 4.0, and Windows NT Workstation 4.0. Other versions are available that run on Windows 98, Windows Me, and Windows XP.

FIND IT ▶
ONLINE
The SQL Server home on Microsoft's Web site is **http://www.microsoft. com/sql**.

We highly recommend downloading the free 120-day evaluation version from **http://www.microsoft.com/sql/evaluation/trial/2000/default.asp**.

Sybase's product is now called Adaptive Server Enterprise (ASE). This is also an enterprise-level RDBMS (as if the name didn't give that away). Adaptive Server IQ is a similar product they have developed specifically for business intelligence. NT and Linux are the platforms of choice for the Sybase offerings. Their lightweight yet mighty RDBMS is called SQL Anywhere. Sybase is pushing hard to put SQL Anywhere at the top of the list of database management systems for mobile computing.

FIND IT ▶
ONLINE The Sybase Web site address is **http://www.sybase.com/**.

A 60-day trial of ASE 12.5 is available for download from the Sybase Web site at **http://www.sybase.com/ase_125eval**.

Both Sybase and Microsoft use T-SQL, or Transact-SQL, as their extension to ANSI SQL. T-SQL allows for similar procedural functionality; however, PL-SQL and T-SQL are very different in structure and syntax. Transact-SQL gets its name from the word *transaction*. A transaction is a unit of work performed by the database. It can be as small as a select statement, or, if prepared correctly, it can include hundreds of statements that are all interrelated. The statements grouped together in a transaction either all work or all fail as a unit. Transactions will be discussed in more detail in the Sunday Morning session.

The enterprise-level offering from IBM is DB2. DB2 holds the second-largest market share, squished between Oracle and SQL Server. The current release has been dubbed DB2 UDB (Universal Database). IBM developed the first relational database as well as the original version of SQL back in the 1970s. Much has changed since then, but IBM remains highly involved in the maintenance of the standards surrounding database technology.

FIND IT ▶
ONLINE The DB2 trial version is available at **http://www-4.ibm.com/software/data/db2/udb/downloads.html**.

The IBM Web site address is **http://www.ibm.com/**.

MySQL, pronounced "my S-Q-L," isn't listed as a top RDBMS, probably because it's free. Well, free if you accept the terms of their licensing agreement. Corporations can opt to pay for licenses of the product, which then gives them more flexibility. Even if you decide to pay for it, MySQL is very inexpensive comparatively. In addition to the software, you can even obtain the source code if you like. This gives you the ability to tweak the database management system to work just the way you need it to. This package supports many different operating systems:

Linux, Red Hat, Windows 95/98/NT/2000/XP, Solaris, FreeBSD, Mac OS X Server 1.1 and OS X 10.1.1, HP-UX 10.20, AIX 4.3, SCO, SGI IRIX, DEC OSF, and BSDi.

FIND IT ▶
ONLINE

The MySQL Web site address is **http://www.mysql.com/**.

MySQL can be downloaded at **http://www.mysql.com/downloads/index.html**.

There are also several smaller RDBMSs out there for the home user or the small business user. Microsoft has Access, which is part of the Office Suite of tools. They also make a product called Fox Pro. Both products are small RDBMSs with some programmability included for reporting and screen building. Sybase puts out SQL Anywhere, discussed earlier. Databases implemented on these products can have a limited number of users, usually fewer than 25.

Where Do You Begin?

We need to take the rest of this evening to establish a foundation for the discussion of the syntax of SQL. The first thing you need to do before you can start learning SQL is to understand the approach this book will take to presenting the topic. Then you will learn a little bit about relational databases so you can understand how SQL speaks to them. Lastly, we will show you how to establish your own sandbox (database) to play in. You will create some sample data and the structures that hold it so you can have something to work with first thing in the morning.

SQL is not tied to a particular product but instead is implemented as a standard by several products. Therefore, a single product must be chosen to present the information and test your SQL through. This book will use Microsoft SQL Server as the SQL interface. SQL Server is a very powerful database and yet is quick (relative to the others) to download and easy to get started on. And, well, we happen to think it's the best dang database management system out there. SQL Server can be set to run as ANSI compliant, which means all SQL statements issued against the database must conform to the standard. We won't be running SQL Server as ANSI compliant, however, because we will be covering non-ANSI statements and data types as well. For the most part, however, it does not matter what RDBMS you choose to use. The ANSI SQL presented in this book will work for any of them. We do realize that many of you already possess an RDBMS and will choose to use that instead of SQL Server. For this, we have provided the syntax for the sample database in the appendix for each major RDBMS. We will also point out differences in syntax between the vendors as that syntax is discussed. If you do not have an RDBMS to use to run the samples against, you can download a trial version of any of the database management systems discussed in the previous section, "The 31 Flavors of SQL."

The Anatomy of a Relational Database

To understand SQL, you must first understand relational databases. SQL is the mechanism by which users communicate with an RDBMS. RDBMSs store information in a relational manner. Relational means that one piece of information relates to another, which relates to another, and so forth, just like you are related to your parents, siblings, and cousins. A single RDBMS can hold many databases. Those databases do not have to be related, but the data inside of a single database is related to the rest of the data within that database.

◄◄
An **RDBMS** (*relational database management system*), also known as just DBMS, is the software that contains databases and provides an interface to those databases.
◄◄

Inside of a relational database, information is stored in tables. You can think of a table as a folder in a file cabinet, where the file cabinet is the database. Within a table (folder), you have several related pieces of information about the subject of the table (folder). Those pieces of information are called columns. Sometimes a piece of information from one folder leads you to look at another folder for more information. Similarly, in a relational database, the information in the column of a table can lead you to look at another table for more information. The table providing the additional information is referred to as the parent and the second table as the child. Thus the tables are related.

◄◄◄◄◄◄◄◄◄◄◄◄◄◄◄◄◄◄◄◄◄◄◄◄◄◄◄◄◄◄◄◄◄◄◄◄◄◄

A **database** is a container for related tables. It acts like a file cabinet containing many folders. It could hold all your customer and order information, for example.

◄◄◄◄◄◄◄◄◄◄◄◄◄◄◄◄◄◄◄◄◄◄◄◄◄◄◄◄◄◄◄◄◄◄◄◄◄◄

◄◄◄◄◄◄◄◄◄◄◄◄◄◄◄◄◄◄◄◄◄◄◄◄◄◄◄◄◄◄◄◄◄◄◄◄◄◄◄

A **table** stores pieces of related information like a folder in a file cabinet would. An example of a table would be a customer table, which would hold things like customer name, address, and phone number.

◄◄◄◄◄◄◄◄◄◄◄◄◄◄◄◄◄◄◄◄◄◄◄◄◄◄◄◄◄◄◄◄◄◄◄◄◄◄

◄◄◄◄◄◄◄◄◄◄◄◄◄◄◄◄◄◄◄◄◄◄◄◄◄◄◄◄◄◄◄◄◄◄◄◄◄◄◄

A **column** is a piece of information in a table, such as the address of your customer.

◄◄◄◄◄◄◄◄◄◄◄◄◄◄◄◄◄◄◄◄◄◄◄◄◄◄◄◄◄◄◄◄◄◄◄◄◄◄

To demonstrate this, say you want to track all your employees and the departments they work for. First you would need to gather up all the information you require about each employee. Secondly, you would then list all the departments in the company. Now you need to relate the two. Each employee works in a single department. Each department has many employees. This is considered a one-to-many relationship. Because each employee belongs to a single department, it only makes sense that you associate the department with the employee by storing the department name or identifier in the employee's file, or in this case, each employee's record or row in the Employee table. See Figure 1.1 for the visual representation of this relationship. Because each department has multiple employees, it is considered the parent table, and Employee is considered the child table. The Employee table depends on the Department table to fill in the department information for each employee row.

◀ ◀
A **row** represents a single entry within a table. For example, in your `Customer` table,
Billy Bob's Bait and Tackle would have its own entry, or row, separate from Little John's
Canoe Rental, because each one is an individual customer.
◀ ◀

Figure 1.1 displays a one-to-many relationship, but there are others. A
many-to-many relationship exists where one entity has many of another
and visa versa. An example of this would be between patients and doctors. A patient often sees many different doctors, and doctors treat many
different patients. Another type of relationship is one-to-one. Often with
this kind of relationship you will see the data stored together because each
of one entity belongs only to one of the other entity. An example of this
is person-to-spouse. Unless you are a bigamist, you will only have one
spouse at any given time, and that spouse will only have you as their
spouse. Finally, an unusual type of relationship is recursive. Recursive
means the relationship is from an entity back to itself. Figure 1.2 shows
this type of relationship by adding a manager to the model. A manager is
an employee, but at the same time, manager is an important piece of
information about an employee. At the same time that this relationship
is described as recursive, it is also proper to refer to it as a one-to-many
relationship. An employee has one manager, but a manager supervises
many employees.

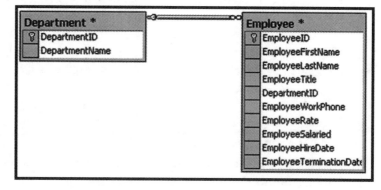

Figure 1.1

The relationship
between
`Employee`
and `Department`.

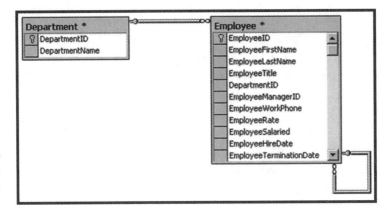

Figure 1.2

The recursive relationship of the `Employee` table.

In a relational table, there is always a column or set of columns that uniquely identify each row. The unique identifier is called a primary key. Primary keys are often denoted in a data model with a key symbol. For the Employee table in Figure 1.2, you can see that the primary key is `Employee_ID`. Each employee has an `Employee_ID`, and that ID will never belong to another employee. That makes this column an ideal primary key. Another important factor in choosing a primary key is that the value should be static. In other words, the unique value assigned to a row should never change. And, in fact, `Employee_ID` will never change for the employees in the table. This explains why `Employee_UserID` would not make a good choice for primary key. What if Sally Smith married Frank Fuller? Then her user ID would change from SSMITH to SFULLER. Now everything that relates to SSMITH is either lost or needs to be updated to follow this change of identification.

◄ ◄

A **primary key** is a column or set of columns that uniquely identify each row in the table.

◄ ◄

Because the primary key of a table uniquely identifies each row in the table, it also makes an excellent pointer from other tables. What we mean here is that a row in the table can be referenced from another table simply by referring to the primary key. No other information about the row is needed. As an example, look back at the `Employee` and `Department` tables. The `Department` table has a primary key of `Department_ID`. For each employee row to point to the correct department row, it need only have the `Department_ID`. A primary key from one table used as a pointer by another table is referred to as a foreign key. So whereas `Department_ID` is the primary key in the `Department` table, it is a foreign key in the `Employee` table.

◄◄◄

A **foreign key** is a column in the table used to point to the primary key of another table.

◄◄◄

Now that you have a basic understanding of relational database concepts, we'll apply these concepts to the sample database we will be using for this book. Don't worry if you don't follow fully at this point. In the Saturday Evening session, we'll be giving you a full explanation of how we arrived at this design. In Figure 1.3, you see the table layout of the sample database. This layout is called a data model. *Data models* are visual representations of the tables in a database and the relationships between those tables.

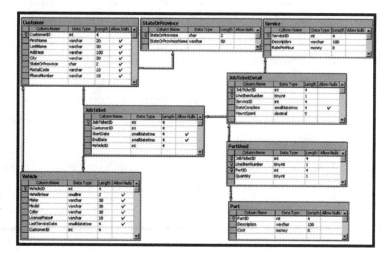

Figure 1.3

The data model for the sample database.

Figure 1.3 shows a database for a service-based company called The Slick Shop. They specialize in oil changes. As with most oil change companies, they also perform other minor maintenance to their customers' vehicles. They can replace air filters and windshield wipers, fill the various fluids in the engine, flush the radiator, and perform other such tasks. Most of what they do involves labor, but they also need to charge for parts that they replace or use up during service.

First and foremost, the Slick Shop needs to track their customers. The information they need to keep about their customers includes the customer's name, address, phone number, and vehicles they bring in for service. Because the customer only has one name, one address, and one phone number, you can put all that information together in the Customer table. The customer might bring in several vehicles, however, so you won't include this in the Customer table. It's a one-to-many relationship between vehicle and customer. Because the vehicle belongs to one customer but the customer can have many vehicles, you can reference the owner in the Vehicle table by including the CustomerID. The Slick Shop also needs to know certain information about the vehicle to easily identify it. They need to know the vehicle's year, make, model, color, and license plate number. They also like to track a vehicle's last service date so they know right away when the last time they serviced this vehicle was. Because the vehicle only has one of each of these things, we'll store them in the Vehicle table. The vehicle could have more than one owner over time, but The Slick Shop only cares about the current owner of the vehicle. Therefore, it'll be fine, for this purpose, to have CustomerID in the Vehicle table. The Slick Shop will just update this information if the ownership changes.

The company does all of their work by filling out job tickets. They fill out the start and end dates of the job, and the job gets a unique number so they can reference the jobs by number. They also have to know the customer requesting the work and the vehicle needing the work. CustomerID identifies the customers, and VehicleID identifies the vehicles, so you can include those columns in the JobTicket table as foreign keys to the Customer and Vehicle tables.

On the bottom part of the job ticket, the employees of The Slick Shop fill in the details of the work they are doing for the job. Because this information is related to the job ticket, but the number of lines in the detail varies, you need to make this a different table, called the JobTicketDetail table. You need the JobTicketID from the JobTicket table so you can relate the line items back to the job ticket. You will identify each row in the JobTicketDetail with its line item number. However, because more than one job ticket will have a line item number of one, we also need the JobTicketID to know which ticket the line item belongs to. Therefore, the primary key of the JobTicketDetail table is a combination of the JobTicketID and the LineItemNumber. Notice that JobTicketDetail is both a primary key and a foreign key in this instance.

Each item on the job ticket involves a service. The Slick Shop has to know what service was performed, how long it took, and when it was completed. Once they know all this, they can determine how much to charge the customer for the services they performed. Each service has a specific charge per hour. The Service table will hold this value. There is no reason to store it in the JobTicketDetail table every time the service is performed.

The last piece of information they need to total up the job ticket is the parts that were used to perform the service. Because a job ticket can involve multiple parts and a part can be used on many job tickets, there is a many-to-many relationship between JobTicketDetail and Part. Part is the table holding the list of available parts. Because of this relationship, there needs to be a third table. This third table is called PartUsed. There will be many parts used by a job ticket, but only one job ticket line item per part used. Therefore, the PartUsed table will need a foreign key from the JobTicketDetail table, which is JobTicketID and LineItemNumber. Similarly, a part will be used on many job tickets, so we need a foreign key to the Part table as part of the primary key for the PartUsed table. With JobTicketID, LineItemNumber, and PartID as the key to this table, it can hold a list of every part used on a job ticket and every job ticket that uses a particular part.

As you can probably see, this database could continue on and on. You could add in tables to control inventory by linking in with the `Part` table and the `PartUsed` table. The Slick Shop could keep track of accounts receivable and accounts payable if they wanted to by gathering information from the `JobTicketDetail` table. You could even add employee information into this database and store which employees performed which services on each vehicle. You could take that one step further and use the job ticket and employee information to schedule employee shifts or vehicle appointments based on the skills of the employees and the type of service the vehicle needs. But for the sake of simplicity, we'll stop with the data model we have. It will suffice to get the point across for the discussions to follow.

Setting Up the Sample Database

Now that the data model for The Slick Shop has been defined, you can use this model to create the database that will serve as your playground for the remaining chapters. Because we haven't discussed how to create a database or tables, for that matter, we will provide all the syntax for you here. The syntax can also be found in the appendix or downloaded from the Premier Press Web site. This way, you can cut and paste it into your favorite DBMS and save your fingers the workout. Each DBMS might require a slightly different syntax than provided here. The syntax for each specific DBMS we cover in this book has been provided in the appendix under the specific section for that particular DBMS.

Nothing else can happen until you create the database. This is, of course, assuming that you have already chosen and installed the DBMS you plan to use throughout this book. If you haven't, please do that now. Open your DBMS client software. In the case of SQL Server, you will open the Query Analyzer so you can type in the commands (or paste them in from the download)we need to issue to create the database. Please note that some DBMSs have graphical tools or wizards that help you perform such tasks without typing in the specific command, but you are here to learn

SQL, right? The following is the command you need to execute to create the sample database. Type the command as you see it here, and then click Execute or press Enter, whichever your DBMS prefers. If you aren't sure, refer to the appendix for the section on your DBMS.

```
CREATE DATABASE  SlickShop;
```

That was simple enough. Now you have a place to play. Let's create the structures that will hold the sample data. Before you can start adding tables, though, you have to tell the DBMS which database to use for the commands that you will be executing. Type the following and execute the command.

```
USE SlickShop;
```

Now you can create the table structures that you saw in Figure 1.3. We'll list the code to type here. The explanation of the syntax will come later. For now, type in (or paste in) each code listing and execute the command. By the way, the SQL syntax itself is not case sensitive nor does it care about spacing. For example, "CREATE TABLE" is the same as "create table". You can type this either in all uppercase or all lowercase and it would work the same. You can smush it all together (as long as you leave one space) and it will still work.

Again, we highly recommend that you download the syntax for the sample database from the Premier Press Web site instead of trying to type this in. You'll save yourself a lot of time and trouble. Should you make a mistake will typing this in, however, you can drop the database and start over. The statement you use to drop a database is as follows.

```
DROP DATABASE SlickShop;
CREATE TABLE StateOrProvince (
StateOrProvince       Char(2)      NOT NULL PRIMARY KEY CLUSTERED,
StateOrProvinceName   Varchar(50)  NOT NULL
);

CREATE TABLE Customer (
CustomerID      Integer       IDENTITY NOT NULL PRIMARY KEY CLUSTERED,
FirstName       Varchar(20)   NULL,
```

```
LastName            Varchar(30)   NULL,
Address             Varchar(100)  NULL,
City                Varchar(30)   NULL,
StateOrProvince     Char(2)       NULL REFERENCES StateOrProvince
                                  (StateOrProvince),
PostalCode          Varchar(10)   NULL,
PhoneNumber         Varchar(10)   NULL
);

CREATE TABLE Vehicle (
VehicleID       Integer       IDENTITY NOT NULL PRIMARY KEY CLUSTERED,
VehicleYear     SmallInt      NULL,
Make            Varchar(30)   NULL,
Model           Varchar(30)   NULL,
Color           Varchar(30)   NULL,
LicensePlate#   Varchar(10)   NULL,
LastServiceDate Smalldatetime NULL,
CustomerID      Integer       NOT NULL REFERENCES Customer (CustomerID)
);

CREATE TABLE Service (
ServiceID       Integer       IDENTITY NOT NULL PRIMARY KEY CLUSTERED,
Description     Varchar(100)  NOT NULL,
RatePerHour     Money         NOT NULL
);

CREATE TABLE Part (
PartID          Integer       IDENTITY NOT NULL PRIMARY KEY CLUSTERED,
Description     Varchar(100)  NOT NULL,
Cost            Money         NOT NULL
);

CREATE TABLE JobTicket (
JobTicketID Integer       IDENTITY NOT NULL PRIMARY KEY CLUSTERED,
CustomerID  Integer       NOT NULL REFERENCES Customer (CustomerID),
StartDate   Smalldatetime NULL,
EndDate     Smalldatetime NULL,
VehicleID   Integer       NOT NULL REFERENCES Vehicle (VehicleID)
);

CREATE TABLE JobTicketDetail (
JobTicketID Integer    NOT NULL REFERENCES JobTicket (JobTicketID),
```

```
LineItemNumber  TinyInt        NOT NULL,
ServiceID       Integer        NOT NULL REFERENCES Service (ServiceID),
DateComplete    Smalldatetime  NULL,
HoursSpent      Decimal(5,2)   NOT NULL DEFAULT 0,
CONSTRAINT PK_JobTicketDetail PRIMARY KEY (JobTicketID, LineItemNumber)
);

CREATE TABLE PartUsed (
JobTicketID     Integer        NOT NULL,
LineItemNumber  TinyInt        NOT NULL,
PartID          Integer        NOT NULL REFERENCES Part (PartID),
Quantity        TinyInt        NOT NULL,
CONSTRAINT PK_PartUsed PRIMARY KEY (JobTicketID, LineItemNumber,
PartID),
CONSTRAINT FK_JobTicketDetail_PartUsed FOREIGN KEY (JobTicketID,
    LineItemNumber) REFERENCES JobTicketDetail (JobTicketID,
    LineItemNumber)
);
```

Now that the structures are in place, you can fill them up with the sample data. We've included the following insert scripts. Simply type them in and execute them and you will have everything you need to get started tomorrow.

```
INSERT INTO StateOrProvince VALUES('AB','Alberta');
INSERT INTO StateOrProvince VALUES('BC','British Columbia');
INSERT INTO StateOrProvince VALUES('MB','Manitoba');
INSERT INTO StateOrProvince VALUES('NB','New Brunswick');
INSERT INTO StateOrProvince VALUES('NF','Newfoundland');
INSERT INTO StateOrProvince VALUES('NT','Northwest Territories');
INSERT INTO StateOrProvince VALUES('NS','Nova Scotia');
INSERT INTO StateOrProvince VALUES('NU','Nunavut');
INSERT INTO StateOrProvince VALUES('ON','Ontario');
INSERT INTO StateOrProvince VALUES('PE','Prince Edward Island');
INSERT INTO StateOrProvince VALUES('QC','Québec');
INSERT INTO StateOrProvince VALUES('SK','Saskatchewan');
INSERT INTO StateOrProvince VALUES('YT','Yukon Territory');
INSERT INTO StateOrProvince VALUES('AL','Alabama');
INSERT INTO StateOrProvince VALUES('AK','Alaska');
INSERT INTO StateOrProvince VALUES('AZ','Arizona');
INSERT INTO StateOrProvince VALUES('AR','Arkansas');
INSERT INTO StateOrProvince VALUES('CA','California');
INSERT INTO StateOrProvince VALUES('CO','Colorado');
```

```
INSERT INTO StateOrProvince VALUES('CT','Connecticut');
INSERT INTO StateOrProvince VALUES('DE','Delaware');
INSERT INTO StateOrProvince VALUES('DC','District of Columbia');
INSERT INTO StateOrProvince VALUES('FL','Florida');
INSERT INTO StateOrProvince VALUES('GA','Georgia');
INSERT INTO StateOrProvince VALUES('HI','Hawaii');
INSERT INTO StateOrProvince VALUES('ID','Idaho');
INSERT INTO StateOrProvince VALUES('IL','Illinois');
INSERT INTO StateOrProvince VALUES('IN','Indiana');
INSERT INTO StateOrProvince VALUES('IA','Iowa');
INSERT INTO StateOrProvince VALUES('KS','Kansas');
INSERT INTO StateOrProvince VALUES('KY','Kentucky');
INSERT INTO StateOrProvince VALUES('LA','Louisiana');
INSERT INTO StateOrProvince VALUES('ME','Maine');
INSERT INTO StateOrProvince VALUES('MD','Maryland');
INSERT INTO StateOrProvince VALUES('MA','Massachusetts');
INSERT INTO StateOrProvince VALUES('MI','Michigan');
INSERT INTO StateOrProvince VALUES('MN','Minnesota');
INSERT INTO StateOrProvince VALUES('MS','Mississippi');
INSERT INTO StateOrProvince VALUES('MO','Missouri');
INSERT INTO StateOrProvince VALUES('MT','Montana');
INSERT INTO StateOrProvince VALUES('NE','Nebraska');
INSERT INTO StateOrProvince VALUES('NV','Nevada');
INSERT INTO StateOrProvince VALUES('NH','New Hampshire');
INSERT INTO StateOrProvince VALUES('NJ','New Jersey');
INSERT INTO StateOrProvince VALUES('NM','New Mexico');
INSERT INTO StateOrProvince VALUES('NY','New York');
INSERT INTO StateOrProvince VALUES('NC','North Carolina');
INSERT INTO StateOrProvince VALUES('ND','North Dakota');
INSERT INTO StateOrProvince VALUES('OH','Ohio');
INSERT INTO StateOrProvince VALUES('OK','Oklahoma');
INSERT INTO StateOrProvince VALUES('OR','Oregon');
INSERT INTO StateOrProvince VALUES('PA','Pennsylvania');
INSERT INTO StateOrProvince VALUES('RI','Rhode Island');
INSERT INTO StateOrProvince VALUES('SC','South Carolina');
INSERT INTO StateOrProvince VALUES('SD','South Dakota');
INSERT INTO StateOrProvince VALUES('TN','Tennessee');
INSERT INTO StateOrProvince VALUES('TX','Texas');
INSERT INTO StateOrProvince VALUES('UT','Utah');
INSERT INTO StateOrProvince VALUES('VT','Vermont');
INSERT INTO StateOrProvince VALUES('VA','Virginia');
INSERT INTO StateOrProvince VALUES('WA','Washington');
```

```
INSERT INTO StateOrProvince VALUES('WV','West Virginia');
INSERT INTO StateOrProvince VALUES('WI','Wisconsin');
INSERT INTO StateOrProvince VALUES('WY','Wyoming');
INSERT INTO Customer (FirstName, LastName, Address, City,
    StateOrProvince, PostalCode, PhoneNumber )
Values ('John', 'Smith', '10341 Crestpoint Boulevard', 'North Beach',
    'VA', '10234', '1022341234');

INSERT INTO Customer (FirstName, LastName, Address, City,
    StateOrProvince, PostalCode, PhoneNumber )
Values ('Jacob', 'Salter', '234 North Main', 'Groveland', null,
    '45678', '7665554444');

INSERT INTO Customer (FirstName, LastName, Address, City,
    StateOrProvince, PostalCode, PhoneNumber )
Values ('Victoria', 'Smithe', '14301 Mountain Ridge Court',
    'Huntington', 'WV', '22211', '2175438679');

INSERT INTO Customer (FirstName, LastName, Address, City,
    StateOrProvince, PostalCode, PhoneNumber )
Values ('Bryce', 'Hatfield', '566 Pine Road', 'Marion', 'IN', null,
    null);

INSERT INTO Customer (FirstName, LastName, Address, City,
    StateOrProvince, PostalCode, PhoneNumber )
Values ('Kylee', 'Dicken', null, 'Upland', 'IN', '46905',
    '7654321098');

INSERT INTO Customer (FirstName, LastName, Address, City,
    StateOrProvince, PostalCode, PhoneNumber )
Values ('Alex', 'Thompson', null, null, 'IN', null, '3175551213');

INSERT INTO Customer (FirstName, LastName, Address, City,
    StateOrProvince, PostalCode, PhoneNumber )
Values ('Davis', 'Thompson', '298 North Broadway', 'Greensburg',
    'IN', '46514', '3175551214');

INSERT INTO Customer (FirstName, LastName, Address, City,
    StateOrProvince, PostalCode, PhoneNumber )
Values ('Harrison', 'Thompson', '345 Hawks Point Drive Apt B',
    'Indianapolis', 'IN', '46123', '3175551215');
INSERT INTO Vehicle (VehicleYear, Make, Model, Color, LicensePlate#,
    LastServiceDate, CustomerID)
```

```
VALUES ('2000', 'Chevrolet', 'S-10', 'Purple', 'TROJANS',
    '8-13-2001', 4);

INSERT INTO Vehicle (VehicleYear, Make, Model, Color, LicensePlate#,
    LastServiceDate, CustomerID)
VALUES ('1998', 'Ford', 'Mustang', 'Red', 'HH7832', '9-16-2001', 2);

INSERT INTO Vehicle (VehicleYear, Make, Model, Color, LicensePlate#,
    LastServiceDate, CustomerID)
VALUES ('2002', 'Pontiac', 'Grand Prix', 'Black', 'GOPRDUE',
    '5-21-2002v, 5);

INSERT INTO Vehicle (VehicleYear, Make, Model, Color, LicensePlate#,
    LastServiceDate, CustomerID)
VALUES ('1968', 'Chevrolet', 'Corvette', 'Black', 'KODIAK',
    '1-20-2002v, 1);

INSERT INTO Vehicle (VehicleYear, Make, Model, Color, LicensePlate#,
    LastServiceDate, CustomerID)
VALUES ('2002', 'Nissan', 'Altima', 'White', 'HEYDARE',
    '1-26-2002', 3);

INSERT INTO Vehicle (VehicleYear, Make, Model, Color, LicensePlate#,
    LastServiceDate, CustomerID)
VALUES ('2000', 'Chrysler', 'PT Cruiser', 'Black', 'ALEX T',
    '5-15-2002', 6);

INSERT INTO Vehicle (VehicleYear, Make, Model, Color, LicensePlate#,
LastServiceDate, CustomerID)
VALUES ('2002', 'Chevrolet', 'Trail Blazer', 'Green', 'I TRADE',
    '5-31-2001', 8);

INSERT INTO Vehicle (VehicleYear, Make, Model, Color, LicensePlate#,
    LastServiceDate, CustomerID)
VALUES ('2001', 'Ford', 'Expedition', 'Maroon', 'DAVIS T',
    '5-31-2001', 7);

INSERT INTO Vehicle (VehicleYear, Make, Model, Color, LicensePlate#,
    LastServiceDate, CustomerID)
VALUES ('1972', 'AMC', 'Gremlin', 'Pink', 'UGOGIRL', v2-17-2002', 4);

INSERT INTO Service (Description, RatePerHour)
VALUES ('Oil Change', 60.00);
```

```
INSERT INTO Service (Description, RatePerHour)
VALUES ('Replace Wiperblades', 10.00);

INSERT INTO Service (Description, RatePerHour)
VALUES ('Replace Air Filter', 10.00);

INSERT INTO Service (Description, RatePerHour)
VALUES ('Change PVC Valve', 10.00);

INSERT INTO Service (Description, RatePerHour)
VALUES ('Change and Flush Cooling System', 60.00);

INSERT INTO Service (Description, RatePerHour)
VALUES ('Change and Flush Differential', 60.00);

INSERT INTO Part (Description, Cost)
VALUES ('Protects 10w-30 Oil', 7.49);

INSERT INTO Part (Description, Cost)
VALUES ('Protects 10w-40 Oil', 7.49);

INSERT INTO Part (Description, Cost)
VALUES ('Black Gold 10w-30 Oil', 7.99);

INSERT INTO Part (Description, Cost)
VALUES ('Black Gold 10w-40 Oil', 7.99);

INSERT INTO Part (Description, Cost)
VALUES ('Motion Synthetic Oil 10w-30', 13.99);

INSERT INTO Part (Description, Cost)
VALUES ('Motion Synthetic Oil 10w-40', 13.99);

INSERT INTO Part (Description, Cost)
VALUES ('Texas Tea Economy Oil Filter', 3.99);

INSERT INTO Part (Description, Cost)
VALUES ('ACME Oil Filter', 4.99);

INSERT INTO Part (Description, Cost)
VALUES ('ACME Air Filter', 8.99);
```

```
INSERT INTO Part (Description, Cost)
VALUES ('ACME Wiper Blades', 9.99);

INSERT INTO Part (Description, Cost)
VALUES ('ACME Brake Fluid', 0.00);

INSERT INTO Part (Description, Cost)
VALUES ('ACME Transmission Fluid', 0.00);

INSERT INTO Part (Description, Cost)
VALUES ('ACME Coolant', 0.00);

INSERT INTO Part (Description, Cost)
VALUES ('ACME Windshield Fluid', 0.00);

INSERT INTO Part (Description, Cost)
VALUES ('ACME Differential Fluid', 0.00);

INSERT INTO Part (Description, Cost)
VALUES ('ACME PVC Valve', 12.99);

INSERT INTO JobTicket (CustomerID, StartDate, EndDate, VehicleID)
VALUES (1, '1-20-2002', '1-20-2002', 4);

INSERT INTO JobTicket (CustomerID, StartDate, EndDate, VehicleID)
VALUES (1, '7-20-2001', '7-20-2001', 4);

INSERT INTO JobTicket (CustomerID, StartDate, EndDate, VehicleID)
VALUES (2, '9-16-2001', '9-16-2001', 2);

INSERT INTO JobTicket (CustomerID, StartDate, EndDate, VehicleID)
VALUES (3, '1-26-2002', '1-26-2002', 5);

INSERT INTO JobTicket (CustomerID, StartDate, EndDate, VehicleID)
VALUES (5, '5-21-2002', '5-21-2002', 3);

INSERT INTO JobTicket (CustomerID, StartDate, EndDate, VehicleID)
VALUES (4, '8-13-2001', '8-13-2001', 1);

INSERT INTO JobTicket (CustomerID, StartDate, EndDate, VehicleID)
VALUES (4, '2-16-2002', '2-17-2002', 9);
```

```
INSERT INTO JobTicketDetail (JobTicketID, LineItemNumber, ServiceID,
    DateComplete, HoursSpent)
VALUES (1, 1, 1, '1-20-2002', .5);

INSERT INTO JobTicketDetail (JobTicketID, LineItemNumber, ServiceID,
    DateComplete, HoursSpent)
VALUES (2, 1, 1, '7-20-2001', .25);

INSERT INTO JobTicketDetail (JobTicketID, LineItemNumber, ServiceID,
    DateComplete, HoursSpent)
VALUES (2, 2, 3, '7-20-2001', .1);

INSERT INTO JobTicketDetail (JobTicketID, LineItemNumber, ServiceID,
    DateComplete, HoursSpent)
VALUES (2, 3, 4, '7-20-2002', .1);

INSERT INTO JobTicketDetail (JobTicketID, LineItemNumber, ServiceID,
    DateComplete, HoursSpent)
VALUES (3, 1, 1, '9-16-2001', .25);

INSERT INTO JobTicketDetail (JobTicketID, LineItemNumber, ServiceID,
    DateComplete, HoursSpent)
VALUES (4, 1, 1, '1-26-2002', .25);

INSERT INTO JobTicketDetail (JobTicketID, LineItemNumber, ServiceID,
    DateComplete, HoursSpent)
VALUES (5, 1, 2, '5-21-2002', .2);

INSERT INTO JobTicketDetail (JobTicketID, LineItemNumber, ServiceID,
    DateComplete, HoursSpent)
VALUES (5, 2, 1, '5-21-2002', .25);

INSERT INTO JobTicketDetail (JobTicketID, LineItemNumber, ServiceID,
    DateComplete, HoursSpent)
VALUES (6, 1, 5, '8-13-2001', 1.15);

INSERT INTO JobTicketDetail (JobTicketID, LineItemNumber, ServiceID,
    DateComplete, HoursSpent)
VALUES (7, 1, 1, '2-16-2002', .35);

INSERT INTO JobTicketDetail (JobTicketID, LineItemNumber, ServiceID,
    DateComplete, HoursSpent)
VALUES (7, 2, 3, '2-16-2002', .1);
```

```
INSERT INTO JobTicketDetail (JobTicketID, LineItemNumber, ServiceID,
    DateComplete, HoursSpent)
VALUES (7, 3, 4, '2-16-2002', .15);

INSERT INTO JobTicketDetail (JobTicketID, LineItemNumber, ServiceID,
    DateComplete, HoursSpent)
VALUES (7, 4, 6, '2-16-2002', 1.0);;

INSERT INTO JobTicketDetail (JobTicketID, LineItemNumber, ServiceID,
    DateComplete, HoursSpent)
VALUES (7, 5, 5, '2-17-2002', .5);

INSERT INTO PartUsed (JobTicketID, LineItemNumber, PartID, Quantity)
VALUES (1, 1, 4, 4);

INSERT INTO PartUsed (JobTicketID, LineItemNumber, PartID, Quantity)
VALUES (1, 1, 7, 1);

INSERT INTO PartUsed (JobTicketID, LineItemNumber, PartID, Quantity)
VALUES (1, 1, 11, 1);

INSERT INTO PartUsed (JobTicketID, LineItemNumber, PartID, Quantity)
VALUES (1, 1, 12, 1);

INSERT INTO PartUsed (JobTicketID, LineItemNumber, PartID, Quantity)
VALUES (2, 1, 5, 4);

INSERT INTO PartUsed (JobTicketID, LineItemNumber, PartID, Quantity)
VALUES (2, 1, 14, 1);

INSERT INTO PartUsed (JobTicketID, LineItemNumber, PartID, Quantity)
VALUES (2, 1, 8, 1);

INSERT INTO PartUsed (JobTicketID, LineItemNumber, PartID, Quantity)
VALUES (2, 2, 9, 1);

INSERT INTO PartUsed (JobTicketID, LineItemNumber, PartID, Quantity)
VALUES (2, 3, 16, 1);

INSERT INTO PartUsed (JobTicketID, LineItemNumber, PartID, Quantity)
VALUES (3, 1, 6, 4);
```

```
INSERT INTO PartUsed (JobTicketID, LineItemNumber, PartID, Quantity)
VALUES (3, 1, 7, 1);

INSERT INTO PartUsed (JobTicketID, LineItemNumber, PartID, Quantity)
VALUES (4, 1, 1, 4);

INSERT INTO PartUsed (JobTicketID, LineItemNumber, PartID, Quantity)
VALUES (4, 1, 8, 1);

INSERT INTO PartUsed (JobTicketID, LineItemNumber, PartID, Quantity)
VALUES (5, 1, 10, 1);

INSERT INTO PartUsed (JobTicketID, LineItemNumber, PartID, Quantity)
VALUES (5, 2, 3, 4);

INSERT INTO PartUsed (JobTicketID, LineItemNumber, PartID, Quantity)
VALUES (5, 2, 14, 1);

INSERT INTO PartUsed (JobTicketID, LineItemNumber, PartID, Quantity)
VALUES (5, 2, 12, 1);

INSERT INTO PartUsed (JobTicketID, LineItemNumber, PartID, Quantity)
VALUES (5, 2, 8, 1);

INSERT INTO PartUsed (JobTicketID, LineItemNumber, PartID, Quantity)
VALUES (6, 1, 13, 1);

INSERT INTO PartUsed (JobTicketID, LineItemNumber, PartID, Quantity)
VALUES (7, 1, 1, 4);

INSERT INTO PartUsed (JobTicketID, LineItemNumber, PartID, Quantity)
VALUES (7, 1, 8, 1);

INSERT INTO PartUsed (JobTicketID, LineItemNumber, PartID, Quantity)
VALUES (7, 1, 14, 1);

INSERT INTO PartUsed (JobTicketID, LineItemNumber, PartID, Quantity)
VALUES (7, 1, 12, 1);

INSERT INTO PartUsed (JobTicketID, LineItemNumber, PartID, Quantity)
VALUES (7, 2, 9, 1);
```

```
INSERT INTO PartUsed (JobTicketID, LineItemNumber, PartID, Quantity)
VALUES (7, 3, 16, 1);

INSERT INTO PartUsed (JobTicketID, LineItemNumber, PartID, Quantity)
VALUES (7, 4, 15, 1);

INSERT INTO PartUsed (JobTicketID, LineItemNumber, PartID, Quantity)
VALUES (7, 5, 13, 1);
```

What's Next?

Well, this is enough for a Friday night. Go have some fun or at least get a good night's rest. You have a lot to cover tomorrow. In the Saturday Morning and Afternoon sessions, we'll show you how to get information out of the sample database. This might not sound like much, but SQL is so powerful that there are many options available to you so you can get the data just the way you like it. It will take some time for this discussion. Following that, you will learn how to put data into the tables and how to manipulate that data. You will also learn how to create the structures that hold the data.

You might be wondering why you will be learning how to get information out before you learn to put information in. Well, there are several reasons. First of all, selecting information out of a database may be all some of you ever need to do, but if not, it will represent a majority of the tasks you will perform anyway. Secondly, the discussion of putting data into a database requires you to know how to get it back out so you know you did it correctly.

Tomorrow is going to be a busy day. Get some good sleep—you'll dig deep into SQL in the morning.

Selecting Data— How to See What's in There

- ➤ Using the SELECT Statement
- ➤ Sorting the Results
- ➤ Filtering the Results
- ➤ Joining Tables
- ➤ Creating Computed Columns

ood morning! We hope you slept well. We have quite a bit to cover today. Before the end of the day you will have all the information you need to use SQL to interact with relational databases. Today we'll show you how to get the information you want out of the database the way you want it. We'll also discuss database and table creation and show you how to put information into the database, change it, and delete it.

Using the SELECT Statement

We are willing to bet that once you start using SQL, the SELECT statement will be the command you use the most. The SELECT statement allows you to get information out of the database. Without it, you'd be able to put information into the database and manipulate it, but you'd never be able to see that information.

First we will examine the most basic SELECT statement. The full syntax will look different from vendor to vendor. Refer to your vendor's documentation if you would like to see the entire syntax offered for your database. You will be able to find vendor-specific commands and syntax in the appendix for everything covered in this book. We will go over the generic syntax here, which will be enough to do what is covered in this book. The SELECT statement has the following basic syntax.

```
SELECT column|expression [,n…]
FROM tablename {,n…};
```

Column refers to a column in a table. Expressions are not so straightforward and will be discussed in the next chapter. The [,n…] signifies that you can specify one or more of the previous item as needed. From this syntax, you can see that you are allowed to specify one or more columns or expressions to be selected from the database. The FROM clause then tells the database where to find the information being referenced in the SELECT clause. Here you can specify one or more table names.

◄◄◄

A **clause** is a portion of a statement. In the case of SQL, each clause is identified by a keyword. In the previous case, you have both a SELECT clause and a FROM clause. Notice that SELECT refers to the statement as well as a clause. The SELECT statement is the entire command, whereas the SELECT clause is everything from the keyword SELECT until the keyword FROM only.

◄◄◄

The most basic of SELECTs is to select a single column from a single table.

```
SELECT description
  FROM Part;
```

■ ■

Notice the indentation used in the previous statement. Keeping your clauses lined up in such a manner makes reading SQL statements much easier. This is especially true the longer the statement is. You will see this kind of indentation used throughout this book. It is standard practice to present SQL in this way and is of particular importance for SQL statements that are maintained or referenced often.

■ ■

This statement tells the RDBMS that you would like to see the contents of the Description column for every row in the Part table. As stated previously, every SELECT must have a FROM clause to tell the database where to find the data. In this case, the query looked in the Part table.

Without this piece of information, it would not have known where to look, especially considering there are two Description columns in the database. The Service table has a column called Description as well. Every table in a database has to have a unique name in the database, but column names need only be unique to the table.

The results of the previous query look like this:

```
Description
-----------------------------
Protects 10w-30 Oil
Protects 10w-40 Oil
Black Gold 10w-30 Oil
Black Gold 10w-40 Oil
Motion Synthetic Oil 10w-30
Motion Synthetic Oil 10w-40
Texas Tea Economy Oil Filter
ACME Oil Filter
ACME Air Filter
ACME Wiper Blades
ACME Brake Fluid
ACME Transmission Fluid
ACME Coolant
ACME Windshield Fluid
ACME Differential Fluid
ACME PVC Valve
```

What if you want to see the price for each of these parts, though? Well, now you need to ask the database for more than one column. Remember from the previous syntax that to specify more than one column in a SELECT, you just need to separate the columns with a comma. Here's what that query would look like:

```
SELECT Description, Cost
  FROM Part;
```

Results:

```
Description                        Cost
---------------------------        ----------
Protects 10w-30 Oil                 7.4900
Protects 10w-40 Oil                 7.4900
Black Gold 10w-30 Oil               7.9900
Black Gold 10w-40 Oil               7.9900
Motion Synthetic Oil 10w-30        13.9900
Motion Synthetic Oil 10w-40        13.9900
Texas Tea Economy Oil Filter        3.9900
ACME Oil Filter                     4.9900
ACME Air Filter                     8.9900
ACME Wiper Blades                   9.9900
ACME Brake Fluid                     .0000
ACME Transmission Fluid              .0000
ACME Coolant                         .0000
ACME Windshield Fluid                .0000
ACME Differential Fluid              .0000
ACME PVC Valve                     12.9900
```

The order in which you specify the columns is the order in which the columns are returned to you in the result set. In the previous case, Description was specified first and Cost second. Therefore, Description is the first column of the result set and Cost is second. If you reverse them, as in the following, they come back from the database in reverse order.

```
SELECT Cost, Description
  FROM Part;
```

Results:

```
Cost              Description
----------        ---------------------
 7.4900           Protects 10w-30 Oil
 7.4900           Protects 10w-40 Oil
 7.9900           Black Gold 10w-30 Oil
 7.9900           Black Gold 10w-40 Oil
13.9900           Motion Synthetic Oil 10w-30
13.9900           Motion Synthetic Oil 10w-40
 3.9900           Texas Tea Economy Oil Filter
 4.9900           ACME Oil Filter
 8.9900           ACME Air Filter
```

```
 9.9900                         ACME Wiper Blades
  .0000                         ACME Brake Fluid
  .0000                         ACME Transmission Fluid
  .0000                         ACME Coolant
  .0000                         ACME Windshield Fluid
  .0000                         ACME Differential Fluid
12.9900                         ACME PVC Valve
```

Another way of accomplishing similar results with less typing is to use the * expression. When you specify * in the SELECT, you are telling the database that you would like to see all of the columns of the specified table.

```
SELECT *
  FROM Part;
```

Results:

```
PartID       Description                         Cost
------       -------------------------           ---------
1            Protects 10w-30 Oil                 7.4900
2            Protects 10w-40 Oil                 7.4900
3            Black Gold 10w-30 Oil               7.9900
4            Black Gold 10w-40 Oil               7.9900
5            Motion Synthetic Oil 10w-30         13.9900
6            Motion Synthetic Oil 10w-40         13.9900
7            Texas Tea Economy Oil Filter        3.9900
8            ACME Oil Filter                     4.9900
9            ACME Air Filter                     8.9900
10           ACME Wiper Blades                   9.9900
11           ACME Brake Fluid                     .0000
12           ACME Transmission Fluid              .0000
13           ACME Coolant                         .0000
14           ACME Windshield Fluid                .0000
15           ACME Differential Fluid              .0000
16           ACME PVC Valve                      12.9900
```

Notice, not only are all the columns returned, but also they are returned in the order they exist in the table. This syntax is especially useful when you need to see all or most of the columns in the table and you don't want to take the time to type the column names.

What if you want to see what kind of prices you are charging for parts without seeing the part names? You can run the following query.

```
SELECT Cost
  FROM Part;
```

Results:

```
Cost
-----------
   7.4900
   7.4900
   7.9900
   7.9900
  13.9900
  13.9900
   3.9900
   4.9900
   8.9900
   9.9900
    .0000
    .0000
    .0000
    .0000
    .0000
  12.9900
```

This will do, but you really don't need to see all the duplicate prices. To eliminate the duplicate rows, SQL provides the keyword DISTINCT, which, when added to the SELECT statement just before the column list, lets SQL know you only want to see the unique rows retrieved from the query.

```
SELECT DISTINCT Cost
  FROM Part;
```

Results:

```
Cost
-----------
    .0000
   3.9900
   4.9900
   7.4900
   7.9900
   8.9900
   9.9900
  12.9900
  13.9900
```

That's nice, but how about something a little more useful? Say you want to find out what states your customers are coming from so you know where to target your marketing efforts.

```
SELECT DISTINCT StateOrProvince
  FROM Customer;
```

Results:

```
StateOrProvince
--------
NULL
IN
VA
WV
```

This is interesting. How'd that NULL get in there? Well, the Customer table does have one customer whose StateOrProvince value is unknown (NULL). Therefore, NULL is considered one of the unique values in the table for that column.

Sorting the Results

Well, you know how to get the information out. You even know how to order your columns, but what about ordering the rows? The SQL SELECT statement has a clause for just such an occasion. This clause is called the ORDER BY clause. No matter what you type in your SELECT statement or which clauses you include, the ORDER BY clause is always last.

```
SELECT column|expression [,n…]
    FROM tablename [,n…]
ORDER BY column|column_position [,n…] [ASC|DESC];
```

The ORDER BY clause requires at least one column name or column position. The column name is self-explanatory. Column position means the position of the column in the SELECT clause. If you were selecting Description and PartID, for instance, and wanted to see the rows in order by PartID, you could either use the column name, PartID, or use its position in the SELECT clause, which is 2. This query would resemble the following.

```
SELECT Description, PartID
    FROM Part
ORDER BY 2;
```

Results:

```
Description                         PartID
-----------------------             ------
Protects 10w-30 Oil                 1
Protects 10w-40 Oil                 2
Black Gold 10w-30 Oil               3
Black Gold 10w-40 Oil               4
Motion Synthetic Oil 10w-30         5
Motion Synthetic Oil 10w-40         6
Texas Tea Economy Oil Filter        7
ACME Oil Filter                     8
ACME Air Filter                     9
ACME Wiper Blades                   10
ACME Brake Fluid                    11
ACME Transmission Fluid             12
```

```
ACME Coolant                          13
ACME Windshield Fluid                 14
ACME Differential Fluid               15
ACME PVC Valve                        16
```

Notice that it sorted the rows by PartID, which is the second column in the query but the first column in the table. Now you might be wondering how SQL knew whether you wanted the PartID in ascending order (smallest to largest) or descending order (largest to smallest). As you can see, it listed the data in ascending order, which is the default sort order for the ORDER BY clause. You can also explicitly state that you want to see the results in ascending order by adding ASC to the end of the ORDER BY clause. Should you want to see the data in descending order, specify DESC at the end of the clause instead. The following query shows the same information as the previous one, only the results will be sorted in descending order by PartID. Also, this query will state the Sort column by column name instead of number.

```
SELECT Description, PartID
   FROM Part
ORDER BY PartID DESC;
```

Results:

```
Description                         PartID
------------------------            ------
ACME PVC Valve                        16
ACME Differential Fluid               15
ACME Windshield Fluid                 14
ACME Coolant                          13
ACME Transmission Fluid               12
ACME Brake Fluid                      11
ACME Wiper Blades                     10
ACME Air Filter                       9
ACME Oil Filter                       8
Texas Tea Economy Oil Filter          7
Motion Synthetic Oil 10w-40           6
Motion Synthetic Oil 10w-30           5
```

```
Black Gold 10w-40 Oil                    4
Black Gold 10w-30 Oil                    3
Protects 10w-40 Oil                      2
Protects 10w-30 Oil                      1
```

Here's an interesting question. What happens if you select all columns using * for the select list and a column position in the ORDER BY clause? SELECT * always returns the columns in the order in which they reside in the table, so the column position specified in the ORDER BY clause would correspond indirectly to the position of the column in the table. Take a look at the following to see an example of this.

```
SELECT *
    FROM Part
ORDER BY 3;
```

Results:

```
PartID    Description                     Cost
------    ---------------                 ----------
11        ACME Brake Fluid                  .0000
12        ACME Transmission Fluid           .0000
13        ACME Coolant                      .0000
14        ACME Windshield Fluid             .0000
15        ACME Differential Fluid           .0000
7         Texas Tea Economy Oil Filter     3.9900
8         ACME Oil Filter                  4.9900
1         Protects 10w-30 Oil              7.4900
2         Protects 10w-40 Oil              7.4900
3         Black Gold 10w-30 Oil            7.9900
4         Black Gold 10w-40 Oil            7.9900
9         ACME Air Filter                  8.9900
10        ACME Wiper Blades                9.9900
16        ACME PVC Valve                  12.9900
5         Motion Synthetic Oil 10w-30     13.9900
6         Motion Synthetic Oil 10w-40     13.9900
```

This query selects everything from the Part table and orders the results by Cost, which happens to be the third column in the table.

To further demonstrate the usefulness of the ORDER BY clause, say your boss asks you for a report on how much you charge for each part. He wants to see these parts in order from most expensive to least expensive. You would use the following query to obtain the results he wants.

```
    SELECT Description, Cost
        FROM Part
    ORDER BY Cost DESC;
```

Results:

Description	Cost
Motion Synthetic Oil 10w-30	13.9900
Motion Synthetic Oil 10w-40	13.9900
ACME PVC Valve	12.9900
ACME Wiper Blades	9.9900
ACME Air Filter	8.9900
Black Gold 10w-30 Oil	7.9900
Black Gold 10w-40 Oil	7.9900
Protects 10w-30 Oil	7.4900
Protects 10w-40 Oil	7.4900
ACME Oil Filter	4.9900
Texas Tea Economy Oil Filter	3.9900
ACME Brake Fluid	.0000
ACME Transmission Fluid	.0000
ACME Differential Fluid	.0000
ACME Coolant	.0000
ACME Windshield Fluid	.0000

Your boss is pleased with your report except for one little detail. He wants to see the parts that cost the same sorted in alphabetical order. You'll notice that the free parts are in random order by Description. To fix this, you need to first sort the list by Cost in descending order like you are already doing, and then sort by Description in ascending order within the first sort. SQL has taken this kind of scenario into account and provided ability to sort on several columns. The first column is the primary sort, the second column is the secondary sort, and so forth. Each additional column refines the order within the sort order already established from the preceding columns. To create the new report for your boss, you would type the following SQL SELECT.

```
SELECT Description, Cost
    FROM Part
ORDER BY Cost DESC, Description ASC;
```

Results:

Description	Cost
Motion Synthetic Oil 10w-30	13.9900
Motion Synthetic Oil 10w-40	3.9900
ACME PVC Valve	12.9900
ACME Wiper Blades	9.9900
ACME Air Filter	8.9900
Black Gold 10w-40 Oil	7.9900
Black Gold 10w-30 Oil	7.9900
Protects 10w-30 Oil	7.4900
Protects 10w-40 Oil	7.4900
ACME Oil Filter	4.9900
Texas Tea Economy Oil Filter	3.9900
ACME Brake Fluid	.0000
ACME Coolant	.0000
ACME Differential Fluid	.0000
ACME Transmission Fluid	.0000
ACME Windshield Fluid	.0000

The bossman seems pretty happy with this one. While he ponders the results of this report, he asks you if you could give him a list of customers by state and then by last name. "No problem," you say.

```
SELECT FirstName, LastName, Address, City, StateOrProvince,
    PostalCode
    FROM Customer
ORDER BY StateOrProvince, LastName;
```

Results:

First Name	Last Name	Address	City	StateOr Province	Postal Code
Jacob	Salter	234 North Main	Groveland	NULL	45678
Kylee	Dicken	NULL	Upland	IN	46905
Bryce	Hatfield	566 Pine Road	Marion	IN	NULL
Alex	Thompson	NULL	NULL	IN	NULL

```
Davis     Thompson  298 North Broadway    Greensburg   IN   46514
Harrison  Thompson  345 Hawks Point Drive Indianapolis IN   46123
                    Apt B
John      Smith     10341 Crestpoint      North Beach  VA   10234
                    Boulevard
Victoria  Smithe    14301 Mountain        Huntington   WV   22211
                    Ridge Court
```

There's something about this report that's bothering you. You notice that it's taking two lines to display each customer. Before you give your boss the chance to shoot it down, you want to go ahead and fix this. But how do you fit it all on the same line? As you examine the report, you notice that the column names StateOrProvince and PostalCode are longer than the data in those columns. Luckily, SQL allows you to name the resulting column anything you want. This is called an *alias*.

```
SELECT FirstName, LastName, Address, City, StateOrProvince AS
     State,
          PostalCode AS Zip
   FROM Customer
ORDER BY StateOrProvince, LastName;
```

Results:

```
FirstName LastName  Address               City         State Zip
-----     -----     --------------        ------       ---   -----
Jacob     Salter    234 North Main        Groveland    NULL  45678
Kylee     Dicken    NULL                  Upland       IN    46905
Bryce     Hatfield  566 Pine Road         Marion       IN    NULL
Alex      Thompson  NULL                  NULL         IN    NULL
Davis     Thompson  298 North Broadway    Greensburg   IN    46514
Harrison  Thompson  345 Hawks Point Drive Indianapolis IN    46123
                    Apt B
John      Smith     10341 Crestpoint      North Beach  VA    10234
                    Boulevard
Victoria  Smithe    14301 Mountain Ridge  Huntington   WV    22211
                    Court
```

So what's with this NULL in the state column? NULL means no value was entered into that column. It's like saying the value is unknown. An empty string ('') is different because a value was entered, but that value just happens to be empty. This would show up in the results as a blank instead of the word NULL. Notice that NULLs sort to the top in ascending order. They will sort to the bottom in descending order.

◄◄
A NULL value means no value has been entered for that column. It represents that the value for that column is not known.
◄◄

You hand this over to the boss and he asks you about these NULL things. So you confidently explain it to him. He decides he only wants to see customers who have complete address information. You not quite as confidently tell the boss, "Sure, I'll get that right to you." So far, you have no idea how to weed out those customers, so you read on.

Filtering the Results

Hmmm, the boss wants a subset of the customers. How are you going to remove the Customer rows without an address, a city, a state, or a postal code? Here comes the WHERE clause to the rescue.

```
SELECT column|expression [,n…]
  FROM tablename [,n…]
 WHERE condition [AND|OR] [n];
```

The WHERE clause allows you to filter out rows from the results set by stating, "I want this, this, and this, but only where this condition (or these conditions) is (are) true." So in the case of the report of customers with full addresses, you say, "I want the customer's first and last name, address, city, state, and postal code, but only where the address is not NULL and the city is not NULL and the state is not NULL and the postal code is not NULL."

Here's what that looks like in SQL:

```
SELECT FirstName, LastName, Address, City, StateOrProvince AS State,
       PostalCode
  FROM Customer
 WHERE Address is not NULL
   AND City is not NULL
   AND StateOrProvince is not NULL
   AND PostalCode is not NULL
ORDER BY StateOrProvince, LastName;
```

Results:

FirstName	LastName	Address	City	State	Postal Code
-----	------	---------------	------	---	-----
Davis	Thompson	298 North Broadway	Greensburg	IN	46514
Harrison	Thompson	345 Hawks Point Drive Apt B	Indianapolis	IN	46123
John	Smith	10341 Crestpoint Boulevard	North Beach	VA	10234
Victoria	Smithe	14301 Mountain Ridge Court	Huntington	WV	22211

Tada! All the incomplete addresses are gone and the boss is happy. Just in case he asks for something else, we're going to show you some other tricks you can do with the WHERE clause. Let's say you want to see only the customers who don't live in Indiana.

```
SELECT FirstName, LastName, Address, City, StateOrProvince, PostalCode
  FROM Customer
 WHERE StateOrProvince <> 'IN';
```

Results:

FirstName	LastName	Address	City	StateOr Province	Postal Code
-----	-----	---------------	-------	--------	-----
John	Smith	10341 Crestpoint Boulevard	North Beach	VA	10234
Victoria	Smithe	14301 Mountain Ridge Court	Huntington	WV	22211

You use IS NOT with NULL, but when you want to test inequality against a value, you use <>. If, instead, you want to test for equality, you use IS with NULL (as in WHERE City IS NULL) and = with a value as in the following:

```
SELECT FirstName, LastName, Address, City, StateOrProvince,
    PostalCode
  FROM Customer
 WHERE StateOrProvince = 'IN';
```

Results:

FirstName	LastName	Address	City	StateOr Province	Postal Code
Bryce	Hatfield	566 Pine Road	Marion	IN	NULL
Kylee	Dicken	NULL	Upland	IN	46905
Alex	Thompson	NULL	NULL	IN	NULL
Davis	Thompson	298 North Broadway	Greensburg	IN	46514
Harrison	Thompson	345 Hawks Point Drive Apt B	Indianapolis	IN	46123

IS, IS NOT, =, and <> are referred to as operators. They are not the only operators that SQL allows. Table 2.1 shows the types of operators you can use and what they mean.

TABLE 2.1 SQL COMPARISON OPERATORS

Operator	Description	Example	Meaning
IS	Equal (used with NULL)	City IS NULL	Where the City column contains a NULL
IS NOT	Not equal (used with NULL)	City IS NOT NULL	Where the City column does not contain a NULL
=	Equal	City = 'Chicago'	Where the City column contains 'Chicago'
<>	Not equal	City <> 'Chicago'	Where the City column does not contain 'Chicago'
<	Less than	Quantity < 5	Where the Quantity column contains a value less than 5
>	Greater than	Quantity > 5	Where the Quantity column contains a value greater than 5
<=	Less than or equal to	Quantity <= 5	Where the Quantity column contains a value less than or equal to 5
>=	Greater than or equal to	Quantity >= 5	Where the Quantity column contains a value greater than or equal to 5

Let's examine a few of these operators. Say you want to see a list of all the jobs your company worked beginning January 1, 2002. The following query would provide such a compilation.

```
SELECT *
  FROM JobTicket
 WHERE StartDate >= '1/1/2002';
```

Results:

```
Job     Customer  StartDate              EndDate                Vehicle
TicketID  ID                                                    ID
------  -----     ----------             ----------             ------
  1       1       2002-01-20 00:00:00    2002-01-20 00:00:00    4
  4       3       2002-01-26 00:00:00    2002-01-26 00:00:00    5
  5       5       2002-05-21 00:00:00    2002-05-21 00:00:00    3
  7       4       2002-02-16 00:00:00    2002-02-17 00:00:00    9
```

This query used >= because you wanted to see all jobs after and including January 1, 2002. What if you just want to see the jobs in January, though?

```
SELECT *
  FROM JobTicket
 WHERE StartDate >= '1/1/2002'
   AND StartDate <= '1/31/2002';
```

Results:

```
Job     Customer  StartDate              EndDate                Vehicle
TicketID  ID                                                    ID
------  -----     ----------             ----------             -----
  1       1       2002-01-20 00:00:00    2002-01-20 00:00:00    4
  4       3       2002-01-26 00:00:00    2002-01-26 00:00:00    5
```

This query combines less than or equal to January 31, 2002, with the previous query, which looked for job start dates greater than or equal to January 1, 2002. This results in a query that looks for job start dates between January 1, 2002, and January 31, 2002, inclusive.

Now you want to see all of those results plus the jobs started in May. Well, you can't look for the jobs between January 1, 2002, and May 31, 2002, which would give you jobs in February, March, and April as well. Instead, you need to use two sets of ranges to get the results you want.

```
SELECT *
  FROM JobTicket
 WHERE (StartDate >= '1/1/2002'
   AND StartDate <= '1/31/2002')
    OR (StartDate >= '5/1/2002'
   AND StartDate <= '5/31/2002');
```

Results:

Job TicketID	Customer ID	StartDate	EndDate	Vehicle ID
1	1	2002-01-20 00:00:00	2002-01-20 00:00:00	4
4	3	2002-01-26 00:00:00	2002-01-26 00:00:00	5
5	5	2002-05-21 00:00:00	2002-05-21 00:00:00	3

This query correctly displays the list of jobs started in January 2002 and May 2002.

CAUTION

◆◆◆◆◆◆◆◆◆◆◆◆◆◆◆◆◆◆◆◆◆◆◆◆◆◆◆◆◆◆◆◆◆◆◆◆◆

When combining AND and OR operators in the WHERE clause, it is important to use parentheses so it's clear which expressions are to be ANDed and which are to be ORed. If you fail to provide this type of information to the DBMS, you could get unexpected results. AND expressions are always evaluated before OR expressions.

◆◆◆◆◆◆◆◆◆◆◆◆◆◆◆◆◆◆◆◆◆◆◆◆◆◆◆◆◆◆◆◆◆◆◆◆◆

To demonstrate this caution, the following query will find all the vehicles in the Vehicle table whose Make is Chevrolet and VehicleYear is 2002 *or* whose VehicleYear is 2000 regardless of the value in Make.

```
SELECT VehicleYear, Make, Model
  FROM Vehicle
 WHERE VehicleYear = 2000
    OR VehicleYear = 2002
   AND Make = 'Chevrolet';
```

Results:

VehicleYear	Make	Model
2000	Chevrolet	S-10
2000	Chrysler	PT Cruiser
2002	Chevrolet	Trail Blazer

Notice that the order of precedence of the ANDs and OR in this query is what is causing these results. The AND expression is evaluated first, causing the DBMS to first find all vehicles with a VehicleYear of 2002 *and* a Make of Chevrolet, which gives you just one row. Next, the DBMS evaluates the OR, which says OR the vehicle can have a VehicleYear of 2000. This says nothing of the Make, so we get both vehicles having a VehicleYear of 2000. Thus the three rows in the result.

Now when you add parentheses to this query, it will evaluate differently.

```
SELECT VehicleYear, Make, Model
  FROM Vehicle
 WHERE (VehicleYear = 2000
   OR VehicleYear = 2002)
   AND Make = 'Chevrolet';
```

Results:

VehicleYear	Make	Model
2000	Chevrolet	S-10
2002	Chevrolet	Trail Blazer

Adding the parentheses around the OR causes these first two expressions to be evaluated first. So the DBMS looks for all the vehicles having a VehicleYear of 2000 *or* 2002. This intermediate result gives you five vehicles. Now the DBMS takes those rows and applies the AND, which says the vehicle also must have a make of Chevrolet, which narrows the result down to just the two vehicles.

From this, you can see the importance of using parentheses to clearly state the order of precedence when mixing AND and OR operators in your queries. Please do this if not for yourself, then for the unfortunate soul who has to maintain your queries long after you've forgotten why they were written.

While we are on the subject of operators, there are a few logical operators that we need to discuss here as well. These are IN, BETWEEN, and LIKE. IN is used to test for a list of values. An example of this is finding all customers who reside in a city from a certain list of cities.

```
SELECT FirstName, LastName, City
  FROM Customer
 WHERE City IN ('Marion', 'Upland', 'Indianapolis');
```

Results:

```
FirstName      LastName        City
------         -------         ---------
Bryce          Hatfield        Marion
Kylee          Dicken          Upland
Harrison       Thompson        Indianapolis
```

So the rows from the Customer table are filtered down to just those customers whose city is Marion, Upland, or Indianapolis. Notice that the list of values is contained within parentheses and that each string value is surrounded by single quotes. Numeric values would not be in single quotes unless you need to compare the numeric value to a numeric value stored in a string column such as PostalCode.

What about the customers who don't live in those cities? How do you find them? By simply adding a NOT before IN, you get the inverse of that result set.

```
SELECT FirstName, LastName, City
   FROM Customer
WHERE City NOT IN ('Marion', 'Upland', 'Indianapolis');
```

Results:

```
FirstName      LastName        City
------         ------          ---------
John           Smith           North Beach
Jacob          Salter          Groveland
Victoria       Smithe          Huntington
Davis          Thompson        Greensburg
```

Wait a minute! There are only four customers here. The Customer table has eight people. What happened to the fifth customer, whose city is not in the list? Well, the City column for that customer is NULL. It has no known value and is therefore not included in comparisons unless the comparison is explicitly matching on NULL.

```
SELECT FirstName, LastName, City
   FROM Customer
WHERE City NOT IN ('Marion', 'Upland', 'Indianapolis')
   OR City IS NULL;
```

Results:

FirstName	LastName	City
John	Smith	North Beach
Jacob	Salter	Groveland
Victoria	Smithe	Huntington
Alex	Thompson	NULL
Davis	Thompson	Greensburg

There. That looks much better.

If the list of values you want to match against is in a range, you could use BETWEEN instead. BETWEEN looks for a match against a range of values including the start and end of the range. If you need to find all the vehicles you've serviced that have a model year greater than 1997 and less than 2002, then BETWEEN is the best choice here even though you could get away with several options. All of the following queries give you the same results, but using BETWEEN is much more efficient and clean.

```
SELECT VehicleYear, Make, Model
  FROM Vehicle
 WHERE VehicleYear = 2001
    OR VehicleYear = 2000
    OR VehicleYear = 1999
    OR VehicleYear = 1998;

SELECT VehicleYear, Make, Model
  FROM Vehicle
 WHERE VehicleYear < 2002
    AND VehicleYear > 1997;

SELECT VehicleYear, Make, Model
  FROM Vehicle
 WHERE VehicleYear IN (2001, 2000, 1999, 1998);

SELECT VehicleYear, Make, Model
  FROM Vehicle
 WHERE VehicleYear BETWEEN 1998 AND 2001;
```

Results:

```
VehicleYear          Make                  Model
------               ---------------       ---------------
2000                 Chevrolet             S-10
1998                 Ford                  Mustang
2000                 Chrysler              PT Cruiser
2001                 Ford                  Expedition
```

As with IN, if you would like to see the opposite result set, specifying NOT before BETWEEN will provide that which you seek. Notice that the range is still inclusive even with the NOT.

```
SELECT VehicleYear, Make, Model
  FROM Vehicle
 WHERE VehicleYear NOT BETWEEN 1998 AND 2001;
```

Results:

```
VehicleYear          Make                  Model
------               ---------------       ---------------
2002                 Pontiac               Grand Prix
1968                 Chevrolet             Corvette
2002                 Nissan                Altima
2002                 Chevrolet             Trail Blazer
1972                 AMC                   Gremlin
```

Whereas BETWEEN helps you find values in a range, LIKE is used to find values matching a pattern. LIKE uses wildcard characters to act as placeholders for one or more characters in the pattern.

◄ ◄

BUZZ WORD A **wildcard** character is a character used to construct match expressions. Each wildcard character can represent one or more character positions in the match expression.

◄ ◄

What if you need to find only those customers whose last name starts with 'S'? You would write your query using LIKE and a match expression.

```
SELECT FirstName, LastName
  FROM Customer
 WHERE LastName LIKE 'S%';
```

Results:

```
FirstName          LastName
----------         ---------------
John               Smith
Jacob              Salter
Victoria           Smithe
```

The % in the pattern is used to match any character and any number of character positions. In the previous expression, it doesn't matter what the character is or how many characters come after the 'S'. The only requirement is that the first letter be a capital 'S'.

◆ ◆

If your database is set to be case sensitive, this query will only work if you use a capital 'S' in the pattern. If you use a lowercase 's', it will take you literally and not find a single row. Most DBMSs allow you to specify whether the database is case sensitive. Refer to the documentation for your DBMS.

◆ ◆

Now what if you want to find a string within a string? For instance, say you need to find a customer in the database, but the only thing you can remember about this person is that the address is something something Pine something.

```
SELECT FirstName, LastName, Address
  FROM Customer
 WHERE Address LIKE '%Pine%';
```

Results:

```
FirstName          LastName          Address
------             -------           -------------------
Bryce              Hatfield          566 Pine Road
```

But wait...there's more. Not only can you match multiple characters using %, but you can also match against any single character using the underscore character (_). The following query will find all customers whose first name is five characters long and ends in an 'e'.

```
SELECT FirstName, LastName
  FROM Customer
 WHERE FirstName LIKE '_ _ _ _ e';
```

Results:

FirstName	LastName
Bryce	Hatfield
Kylee	Dicken

Another thing you can do to create your match expression is specify a set of valid characters for a position in the string instead of accepting just any character when you use _. You create the list of acceptable characters by surrounding it with square brackets ([ ]). Inside the brackets, you can specify a list of characters ([abcde]) or a range of characters using – ([a-e]). The range is inclusive. Here you find all customers whose first name has a vowel as the second letter.

```
SELECT FirstName, LastName
  FROM Customer
 WHERE FirstName LIKE '_[aeiou]%';
```

Results:

FirstName	LastName
John	Smith
Jacob	Salter
Victoria	Smithe
Davis	Thompson
Harrison	Thompson

The _ finds anything for the first letter, the [ ] list finds a vowel in the second position, and the % finds the rest of the string no matter what the contents or the length. Now what if you want the opposite? Say you want to see only the first names that don't have a vowel in the second position. What if you just add a NOT to that LIKE statement?

```
SELECT FirstName, LastName
  FROM Customer
 WHERE FirstName NOT LIKE '_[aeiou]%';
```

Results:

FirstName	LastName
Bryce	Hatfield
Kylee	Dicken
Alex	Thompson

Hey, that worked! But be careful about just adding NOT. It won't work in most instances. If you had requested J for the first letter instead of _, then you'd get John and Jacob in your result set. Adding NOT in this case would give you all the other first names when all you really want is the names starting with J that do not have a vowel for the next letter. There aren't any of those in your Customer table. The better way to specify this query is using the wildcard character ^.

```
SELECT FirstName, LastName
  FROM Customer
 WHERE FirstName LIKE '_[^aeiou]%';
```

Results:

FirstName	LastName
Bryce	Hatfield
Kylee	Dicken
Alex	Thompson

Take a Break!

Take a few minutes here to get up and stretch. Maybe grab a cup of coffee. Try to absorb all that you've learned from the first part of this chapter. When you return, there is just as much information awaiting you in the second half. We'll show you the ins and outs of gathering information from multiple tables and then how to create computed columns in the result set.

Joining Tables

Welcome back! So you've learned how to select, sort, and filter, but only from a single table. What's the point of a relational database if you can't see how data relates between tables? That's where joins come in. As an example of why you'd want to join information together, we'd like you to take another look at the Vehicle table.

```
SELECT VehicleID, VehicleYear, Make, Model, CustomerID
  FROM Vehicle;
```

Results:

VehicleID	VehicleYear	Make	Model	CustomerID
1	2000	Chevrolet	S-10	4
2	1998	Ford	Mustang	2
3	2002	Pontiac	Grand Prix	5
4	1968	Chevrolet	Corvette	1
5	2002	Nissan	Altima	3
6	2000	Chrysler	PT Cruiser	6
7	2002	Chevrolet	Trail Blazer	8
8	2001	Ford	Expedition	7
9	1972	AMC	Gremlin	4

The problem with this information is that all you know about the owner of the vehicle is the CustomerID. To find out the customer's name, you have to query the Customer table. Instead of cross-referencing between the two lists, we'll show you how to write one query to get this information from both tables.

```
SELECT VehicleID, VehicleYear, Make, Model, FirstName, LastName
  FROM Vehicle, Customer
 WHERE Vehicle.CustomerID = Customer.CustomerID;
```

Results:

```
VehicleID VehicleYear  Make       Model        FirstName LastName
------    ------       -------    -------      -----     -----
1         2000         Chevrolet  S-10         Bryce     Hatfield
2         1998         Ford       Mustang      Jacob     Salter
3         2002         Pontiac    Grand Prix   Kylee     Dicken
4         1968         Chevrolet  Corvette     John      Smith
5         2002         Nissan     Altima       Victoria  Smithe
6         2000         Chrysler   PT Cruiser   Alex      Thompson
7         2002         Chevrolet  Trail Blazer Harrison  Thompson
8         2001         Ford       Expedition   Davis     Thompson
9         1972         AMC        Gremlin      Bryce     Hatfield
```

Now you can see the owner of each vehicle instead of just the CustomerID. All you had to do was add the Customer columns you wanted to see to the end of the SELECT statement, add the Customer table to the FROM clause, and join the two tables by the foreign key in the WHERE clause. CustomerID is the primary key in the Customer table and the Vehicle table's foreign key reference to the Customer table. Therefore, in the WHERE clause, you could join the two tables correctly by comparing the CustomerID in the Vehicle table to the CustomerID in the Customer table. However, because both columns have the same name, you have to make them unique by specifying the table they belong to. This is done using the syntax *tablename.columnname* (Customer.CustomerID, for instance).

CAUTION

◆ ◆

If you fail to join the tables in the FROM clause together in the WHERE clause, you end up with a Cartesian product. This means that every row from the first table is joined with every row in the second table and so forth until every possible combination is presented. In the case of the previous query, you would have received 72 rows back (9 Vehicle rows multiplied by 8 Customer rows) instead of just the 9.

◆ ◆

This kind of join only returns rows from both tables where those tables match on the columns equated to each other. This is also referred to as an INNER JOIN. SQL has two ways of specifying an INNER JOIN: in the

WHERE clause or in the FROM clause. The previous query shows the join in the WHERE clause. The following query shows you how to specify the join in the FROM clause.

```
SELECT VehicleID, VehicleYear, Make, Model, FirstName, LastName
  FROM Vehicle INNER JOIN Customer
    ON Vehicle.CustomerID = Customer.CustomerID;
```

Results:

VehicleID	VehicleYear	Make	Model	FirstName	LastName
1	2000	Chevrolet	S-10	Bryce	Hatfield
2	1998	Ford	Mustang	Jacob	Salter
3	2002	Pontiac	Grand Prix	Kylee	Dicken
4	1968	Chevrolet	Corvette	John	Smith
5	2002	Nissan	Altima	Victoria	Smithe
6	2000	Chrysler	PT Cruiser	Alex	Thompson
7	2002	Chevrolet	Trail Blazer	Harrison	Thompson
8	2001	Ford	Expedition	Davis	Thompson
9	1972	AMC	Gremlin	Bryce	Hatfield

As you can see, the result sets are the same. It's totally up to you as to which syntax to use. We personally use the WHERE clause to specify inner joins. You can choose for yourself.

When it comes to OUTER JOINS, however, you don't get a choice. Not if you want to stick to the standard, that is. Many DBMSs implement their own syntax for outer joins in the WHERE clause, however, the SQL standard only allows for outer joins in the FROM clause. Refer to the appendixes for alternate forms for outer joins under the DBMS you are using.

◆ ◆

CAUTION   If you decide to use the outer join syntax specific to your DBMS, you could get different results than you would using the standard. An outer join performed in the FROM clause could obtain a different intermediate result set that is then filtered by the WHERE clause.

◆ ◆

Unlike an INNER JOIN, an OUTER JOIN allows you to obtain the entire result set from one table regardless of its ability to find a match in the other table. For instance, take a look at the results of the following INNER JOIN query. This query will show a list of customers and the name of the state they live in.

```
SELECT FirstName, LastName, StateOrProvinceName
  FROM Customer INNER JOIN StateOrProvince
    ON Customer.StateOrProvince = StateOrProvince.StateOrProvince;
```

Results:

FirstName	LastName	StateOrProvinceName
John	Smith	Virginia
Victoria	Smithe	West Virginia
Bryce	Hatfield	Indiana
Kylee	Dicken	Indiana
Alex	Thompson	Indiana
Davis	Thompson	Indiana
Harrison	Thompson	Indiana

Notice that the previous query only gives you seven of the eight customers. Where is Jacob? Jacob's StateOrProvince value is unknown (NULL). Therefore, his row could not be joined to a row in the StateOrProvince table. Remember that a NULL is not equal to anything. If the StateOrProvince table had a NULL entry, the results would not have changed because a NULL in one column is not equal to a NULL in another column. The only way to get all the customers to display in the list is to use an outer join.

Outer joins have three types:

➤ A LEFT OUTER JOIN (or LEFT JOIN) specifies that you would like to retrieve all the rows from the left table regardless of its ability to match to a row in the right table.

➤ A RIGHT OUTER JOIN (or RIGHT JOIN) retrieves all the rows from the right table regardless of its ability to join to a row in the left table.

➤ A FULL OUTER JOIN (or FULL JOIN) gives you both. It retrieves all the rows from both tables regardless of the ability of either table to match the other.

Let's start by looking at a LEFT OUTER JOIN to solve the previous dilemma.

```
SELECT FirstName, LastName, StateOrProvinceName
   FROM Customer LEFT OUTER JOIN StateOrProvince
      ON Customer.StateOrProvince = StateOrProvince.StateOrProvince;
```

Results:

FirstName	LastName	StateOrProvinceName
John	Smith	Virginia
Jacob	Salter	NULL
Victoria	Smithe	West Virginia
Bryce	Hatfield	Indiana
Kylee	Dicken	Indiana
Alex	Thompson	Indiana
Davis	Thompson	Indiana
Harrison	Thompson	Indiana

Now you have all the customers from the Customer table and their matching entry from the StateOrProvince table. Jacob's row appropriately has NULL for StateOrProvinceName because his state of residency is unknown. What if you want to see all the states and provinces matched up against the customers who live there? Simply change the query to a RIGHT OUTER JOIN.

```
SELECT FirstName, LastName, StateOrProvinceName
   FROM Customer RIGHT OUTER JOIN StateOrProvince
      ON Customer.StateOrProvince = StateOrProvince.StateOrProvince;
```

Results:

FirstName	LastName	StateOrProvinceName
NULL	NULL	Alberta
NULL	NULL	Alaska
NULL	NULL	Alabama
NULL	NULL	Arkansas
NULL	NULL	Arizona
NULL	NULL	British Columbia
NULL	NULL	California
NULL	NULL	Colorado
NULL	NULL	Connecticut
NULL	NULL	District of Columbia
NULL	NULL	Delaware
NULL	NULL	Florida
NULL	NULL	Georgia
NULL	NULL	Hawaii
NULL	NULL	Iowa
NULL	NULL	Idaho
NULL	NULL	Illinois
Bryce	Hatfield	Indiana
Kylee	Dicken	Indiana
Alex	Thompson	Indiana
Davis	Thompson	Indiana
Harrison	Thompson	Indiana
NULL	NULL	Kansas
NULL	NULL	Kentucky
NULL	NULL	Louisiana
NULL	NULL	Massachusetts
NULL	NULL	Manitoba
NULL	NULL	Maryland
NULL	NULL	Maine
NULL	NULL	Michigan
NULL	NULL	Minnesota
NULL	NULL	Missouri
NULL	NULL	Mississippi
NULL	NULL	Montana
NULL	NULL	New Brunswick
NULL	NULL	North Carolina
NULL	NULL	North Dakota
NULL	NULL	Nebraska
NULL	NULL	Newfoundland

NULL	NULL	New Hampshire
NULL	NULL	New Jersey
NULL	NULL	New Mexico
NULL	NULL	Nova Scotia
NULL	NULL	Northwest Territories
NULL	NULL	Nunavut
NULL	NULL	Nevada
NULL	NULL	New York
NULL	NULL	Ohio
NULL	NULL	Oklahoma
NULL	NULL	Ontario
NULL	NULL	Oregon
NULL	NULL	Pennsylvania
NULL	NULL	Prince Edward Island
NULL	NULL	Québec
NULL	NULL	Rhode Island
NULL	NULL	South Carolina
NULL	NULL	South Dakota
NULL	NULL	Saskatchewan
NULL	NULL	Tennessee
NULL	NULL	Texas
NULL	NULL	Utah
John	Smith	Virginia
NULL	NULL	Vermont
NULL	NULL	Washington
NULL	NULL	Wisconsin
Victoria	Smithe	West Virginia
NULL	NULL	Wyoming
NULL	NULL	Yukon Territory

This gives you every row from the StateOrProvince table matched up with any rows in the Customer table having that StateOrProvince. As you can see, Indiana is listed five times because five customers reside there. Texas is only listed once and no customers live there, so the customer columns are filled with NULLs. Take note that Jacob is nowhere to be found in this list. Again, his StateOrProvince value is NULL, so none of the entries from the StateOrProvince table matched with him. To get a complete list of all the states and all the customers, you'd have to use a FULL OUTER JOIN, as in the following query.

```
SELECT FirstName, LastName, StateOrProvinceName
   FROM Customer FULL OUTER JOIN StateOrProvince
      ON Customer.StateOrProvince = StateOrProvince.StateOrProvince;
```

Results:

FirstName	LastName	StateOrProvinceName
Jacob	Salter	NULL
NULL	NULL	Alberta
NULL	NULL	Alaska
NULL	NULL	Alabama
NULL	NULL	Arkansas
NULL	NULL	Arizona
NULL	NULL	British Columbia
NULL	NULL	California
NULL	NULL	Colorado
NULL	NULL	Connecticut
NULL	NULL	District of Columbia
NULL	NULL	Delaware
NULL	NULL	Florida
NULL	NULL	Georgia
NULL	NULL	Hawaii
NULL	NULL	Iowa
NULL	NULL	Idaho
NULL	NULL	Illinois
Bryce	Hatfield	Indiana
Kylee	Dicken	Indiana
Alex	Thompson	Indiana
Davis	Thompson	Indiana
Harrison	Thompson	Indiana
NULL	NULL	Kansas
NULL	NULL	Kentucky
NULL	NULL	Louisiana
NULL	NULL	Massachusetts
NULL	NULL	Manitoba
NULL	NULL	Maryland
NULL	NULL	Maine
NULL	NULL	Michigan
NULL	NULL	Minnesota
NULL	NULL	Missouri
NULL	NULL	Mississippi
NULL	NULL	Montana

NULL	NULL	New Brunswick
NULL	NULL	North Carolina
NULL	NULL	North Dakota
NULL	NULL	Nebraska
NULL	NULL	Newfoundland
NULL	NULL	New Hampshire
NULL	NULL	New Jersey
NULL	NULL	New Mexico
NULL	NULL	Nova Scotia
NULL	NULL	Northwest Territories
NULL	NULL	Nunavut
NULL	NULL	Nevada
NULL	NULL	New York
NULL	NULL	Ohio
NULL	NULL	Oklahoma
NULL	NULL	Ontario
NULL	NULL	Oregon
NULL	NULL	Pennsylvania
NULL	NULL	Prince Edward Island
NULL	NULL	Québec
NULL	NULL	Rhode Island
NULL	NULL	South Carolina
NULL	NULL	South Dakota
NULL	NULL	Saskatchewan
NULL	NULL	Tennessee
NULL	NULL	Texas
NULL	NULL	Utah
John	Smith	Virginia
NULL	NULL	Vermont
NULL	NULL	Washington
NULL	NULL	Wisconsin
Victoria	Smithe	West Virginia
NULL	NULL	Wyoming
NULL	NULL	Yukon Territory

Now Jacob shows up on the very first line with a `StateOrProvinceName` of `NULL`, and you have all the same data from the previous query too.

Another type of join is called a self-join. What this means is that a table is joining to itself. Why would you want to do this? One very good reason to join a table to itself is in the case of a recursive relationship.

Remember from the Friday Night session that a recursive relationship occurs when a table is foreign keyed to itself. The example used to demonstrate this type of relationship was the manager of an employee. The manager of an employee is information about the employee and is therefore stored in the Employee table. At the same time, however, a manager is also an employee, who has a manager, who is an employee, and so forth—thus the need for the recursive relationship. How would you create a report of all the employees including their manager's name if the key to the Employee table was just EmployeeID? This is where you would use a self-join from the Employee table to itself to link the Employee.ManagerID to the Employee.EmployeeID to find the manager's row in the Employee table.

```
SELECT FirstName, LastName, FirstName, LastName
    FROM Employee INNER JOIN Employee
        ON ManagerID = EmployeeID;
```

Unfortunately, this syntax doesn't work. SQL requires each reference to a column in the SELECT clause to be unique. You know how to solve that by placing the table name in front of the column name. In this case, however, the table is the same. Similarly, SQL requires that each table name in the FROM clause be unique. How are you supposed to do this when joining a table to itself?

That's where aliases come to the rescue. As you learned earlier in this chapter, aliases can be used to provide a different name for an item in the query. You used them earlier to give a shorter name to the column StateOrProvince in the result set. You will use aliases here to give a unique name to the tables in the FROM clause. The new query, using aliases, will look like this:

```
SELECT e1.FirstName, e1.LastName, e2.FirstName, e2.LastName
    FROM Employee AS e1 INNER JOIN Employee AS e2
        ON e1.ManagerID = e2.EmployeeID;
```

SQL now knows that you want to join Employee to itself and which columns are coming from the Employee row (e1) and which columns are coming from the manager's row (e2). Note that AS is optional.

You could have also written the query as follows:

```
SELECT e1.FirstName, e1.LastName, e2.FirstName, e2.LastName
    FROM Employee e1 INNER JOIN Employee e2
        ON e1.ManagerID = e2.EmployeeID;
```

Another reason you would need a self-join is if you want to compare the contents of the table to itself. As an example, let's say you want to find all the customers that live in the same state. You could join the Customer table to itself on StateOrProvince to obtain this information.

```
SELECT c1.FirstName, c1.LastName, c1.StateOrProvince,
        c2.FirstName, c2.LastName, c2.StateOrProvince
    FROM Customer c1 INNER JOIN Customer c2
        ON c1.StateOrProvince = c2.StateOrProvince;
```

Results:

FirstName	LastName	State	FirstName	LastName	State
John	Smith	VA	John	Smith	VA
Victoria	Smithe	WV	Victoria	Smithe	WV
Bryce	Hatfield	IN	Bryce	Hatfield	IN
Kylee	Dicken	IN	Bryce	Hatfield	IN
Alex	Thompson	IN	Bryce	Hatfield	IN
Davis	Thompson	IN	Bryce	Hatfield	IN
Harrison	Thompson	IN	Bryce	Hatfield	IN
Bryce	Hatfield	IN	Kylee	Dicken	IN
Kylee	Dicken	IN	Kylee	Dicken	IN
Alex	Thompson	IN	Kylee	Dicken	IN
Davis	Thompson	IN	Kylee	Dicken	IN
Harrison	Thompson	IN	Kylee	Dicken	IN
Bryce	Hatfield	IN	Alex	Thompson	IN
Kylee	Dicken	IN	Alex	Thompson	IN
Alex	Thompson	IN	Alex	Thompson	IN
Davis	Thompson	IN	Alex	Thompson	IN
Harrison	Thompson	IN	Alex	Thompson	IN
Bryce	Hatfield	IN	Davis	Thompson	IN
Kylee	Dicken	IN	Davis	Thompson	IN
Alex	Thompson	IN	Davis	Thompson	IN
Davis	Thompson	IN	Davis	Thompson	IN
Harrison	Thompson	IN	Davis	Thompson	IN
Bryce	Hatfield	IN	Harrison	Thompson	IN

Kylee	Dicken	IN	Harrison	Thompson	IN
Alex	Thompson	IN	Harrison	Thompson	IN
Davis	Thompson	IN	Harrison	Thompson	IN
Harrison	Thompson	IN	Harrison	Thompson	IN

Uh, this is not quite what you want. You already know that John Smith lives in the same state as himself. So you need to tell SQL to eliminate the rows where the customer is equal to himself or herself.

```
Select c1.FirstName, c1.LastName, c1.StateOrProvince,
       c2.FirstName, c2.LastName, c2.StateOrProvince
  FROM Customer c1 INNER JOIN Customer c2
    ON c1.StateOrProvince = c2.StateOrProvince
   AND c1.CustomerID <> c2.CustomerID;
```

Results:

FirstName	LastName	State	FirstName	LastName	State
Kylee	Dicken	IN	Bryce	Hatfield	IN
Alex	Thompson	IN	Bryce	Hatfield	IN
Davis	Thompson	IN	Bryce	Hatfield	IN
Harrison	Thompson	IN	Bryce	Hatfield	IN
Bryce	Hatfield	IN	Kylee	Dicken	IN
Alex	Thompson	IN	Kylee	Dicken	IN
Davis	Thompson	IN	Kylee	Dicken	IN
Harrison	Thompson	IN	Kylee	Dicken	IN
Bryce	Hatfield	IN	Alex	Thompson	IN
Kylee	Dicken	IN	Alex	Thompson	IN
Davis	Thompson	IN	Alex	Thompson	IN
Harrison	Thompson	IN	Alex	Thompson	IN
Bryce	Hatfield	IN	Davis	Thompson	IN
Kylee	Dicken	IN	Davis	Thompson	IN
Alex	Thompson	IN	Davis	Thompson	IN
Harrison	Thompson	IN	Davis	Thompson	IN
Bryce	Hatfield	IN	Harrison	Thompson	IN
Kylee	Dicken	IN	Harrison	Thompson	IN
Alex	Thompson	IN	Harrison	Thompson	IN
Davis	Thompson	IN	Harrison	Thompson	IN

Hmmm. This is closer, but you still have a bunch of repeats. For each customer in table c1, this query gives the other four people that live in the same state. How do you eliminate the duplicates? It might seem a little strange, but the best way to do this is to only get the customers whose ID is greater than (or less than, if you prefer) the one being examined in table c1.

```
Select c1.FirstName, c1.LastName, c1.StateOrProvince,
       c2.FirstName, c2.LastName, c2.StateOrProvince
  FROM Customer c1 INNER JOIN Customer c2
    ON c1.StateOrProvince = c2.StateOrProvince
   AND c1.CustomerID > c2.CustomerID;
```

Results:

FirstName	LastName	State	FirstName	LastName	State
Kylee	Dicken	IN	Bryce	Hatfield	IN
Alex	Thompson	IN	Bryce	Hatfield	IN
Alex	Thompson	IN	Kylee	Dicken	IN
Davis	Thompson	IN	Bryce	Hatfield	IN
Davis	Thompson	IN	Kylee	Dicken	IN
Davis	Thompson	IN	Alex	Thompson	IN
Harrison	Thompson	IN	Bryce	Hatfield	IN
Harrison	Thompson	IN	Kylee	Dicken	IN
Harrison	Thompson	IN	Alex	Thompson	IN
Harrison	Thompson	IN	Davis	Thompson	IN

Finally, you have a list of customers who live in the same state as another customer. Another way to state this query is to move the CustomerID expression to the WHERE clause instead of the FROM clause:

```
Select c1.FirstName, c1.LastName, c1.StateOrProvince,
       c2.FirstName, c2.LastName, c2.StateOrProvince
  FROM Customer c1 INNER JOIN Customer c2
    ON c1.StateOrProvince = c2.StateOrProvince
 WHERE c1.CustomerID > c2.CustomerID;
```

You don't always have to join on equality. You can use inequality to join two tables as well. Say you want to find out all the vehicles whose model year is newer (greater than) the model year of the AMC Gremlin.

```
SELECT v2.*
  FROM Vehicle v1 INNER JOIN Vehicle v2
    ON v1.VehicleYear < v2.VehicleYear
 WHERE v1.Model = 'Gremlin';
```

Results:

Vehicle ID	Vehicle Year	Make	Model	Color	License Plate#	Last Service Date	Customer ID
1	2000	Chevrolet	S-10	Purple	TROJANS	2001-08-13 00:00:00	4
2	1998	Ford	Mustang	Red	HH7832	2001-09-16 00:00:002	2
3	2002	Pontiac	Grand Prix	Black	GOPRDUE	2002-05-21 00:00:00	5
5	2002	Nissan	Altima	White	HEYDARE	2002-01-26 00:00:00	3
6	2000	Chrysler	PT Cruiser	Black	ALEX T	2002-05-15 00:00:00	6
7	2002	Chevrolet	TrailBlazer	Green	I TRADE	2001-05-31 00:00:00	8
8	2001	Ford	Expedition	Maroon	DAVIS T	2001-05-31 00:00:00	7

One last type of join to look at is the CROSS JOIN. The CROSS JOIN joins everything from the first table to everything in the second table. If this type of join is used without a WHERE clause to relate the tables in some way, you will get a Cartesian product. If a relation is defined, then the CROSS JOIN acts the same as an INNER JOIN. Here's an example of a CROSS JOIN:

```
SELECT VehicleID, Customer.CustomerID
FROM Vehicle CROSS JOIN Customer;
```

Results:

```
VehicleID      CustomerID
------         ------
1              1
2              1
3              1
4              1
5              1
6              1
7              1
8              1
9              1
.
.
.
1              8
2              8
3              8
4              8
5              8
6              8
7              8
8              8
9              8
```

The entire result set isn't shown here because it's 72 rows. As explained earlier, a Cartesian product produces a result set containing the number of rows from the first table multiplied by the number of rows in the second table. In this case, you get all eight Customer table rows for each of the nine Vehicle table rows, resulting in 72 (8x9) rows. This result set is totally unusable. You have no idea which customer belongs to which vehicle. The two tables need to be related.

```
SELECT VehicleID, Customer.CustomerID
  FROM Vehicle CROSS JOIN Customer
 WHERE Vehicle.CustomerID = Customer.CustomerID;
```

Results:

```
VehicleID        CustomerID
------           ------
1                4
2                2
3                5
4                1
5                3
6                6
7                8
8                7
9                4
```

Now, as expected, you get just one customer, the right customer, for each vehicle in the result set. But all you have here is a simple INNER JOIN, which could be more simply represented with the following syntax.

```
SELECT VehicleID, Customer.CustomerID
  FROM Vehicle, Customer
 WHERE Vehicle.CustomerID = Customer.CustomerID;
```

That is all you need to know about joins to get started. You'll see a lot more examples of using joins in the chapters to come. Like we said, there's not much of a point in having a relational database if you can't use the relationships in your queries. This is what joins give you.

Creating Computed Columns

Computed columns are columns in your result set that are made up of one or more columns from the tables in the FROM clause of the query. They are also referred to as *expressions*. You can create these computed columns to show such things as the results of arithmetic operations or the combining of text fields.

Remember the customer list you created earlier today? Let's say the boss wants to see the customer's first and last name combined in one column. You can add these two columns to create a computed column called Customer Name.

```
SELECT FirstName + ' ' + LastName AS "Customer Name", Address, City,
       StateOrProvince AS State, PostalCode
FROM Customer;
```

Results:

Customer Name	Address	City	State	Postal Code
John Smith	10341 Crestpoint Boulevard	North Beach	VA	10234
Jacob Salter	234 North Main	Groveland	NULL	45678
Victoria Smithe	14301 Mountain Ridge Court	Huntington	WV	22211
Bryce Hatfield	566 Pine Road	Marion	IN	NULL
Kylee Dicken	NULL	Upland	IN	46905
Alex Thompson	NULL	NULL	IN	NULL
Davis Thompson	298 North Broadway	Greensburg	IN	46514
Harrison Thompson	345 Hawks Point Drive Apt B	Indianapolis	IN	46123

This query outputs a computed column that combines text columns from the Customer table. The text columns are combined using the + symbol. A space is used to separate the first and last name of the customer so the values will not run together. We have provided a name for this column using the alias "Customer Name". Notice that when an alias contains a space in the name, it must be surrounded by quotation marks.

You can create computed columns for numeric columns as well. For instance, say you want to find out the total cost for the part used for each line item in the PartUsed table. Rather than returning the information and getting out your calculator, you can use SQL to perform the calculations for you.

```
SELECT pu.JobTicketID, pu.LineItemNumber AS "Line#", p.Description,
       pu.Quantity, p.Cost, pu.Quantity * p.Cost AS "Part Total"
  FROM PartUsed AS pu INNER JOIN Part AS p
   ON pu.PartID = p.PartID;
```

Results:

Job Ticket ID	Line #	Description	Quantity	Cost	Part Total
1	1	Black Gold 10w-40 Oil	4	7.9900	31.9600
1	1	Texas Tea Economy Oil Filter	1	3.9900	3.9900
1	1	ACME Brake Fluid	1	.0000	.0000
1	1	ACME Transmission Fluid	1	.0000	.0000
2	1	Motion Synthetic Oil 10w-30	4	13.9900	55.9600
2	1	ACME Oil Filter	1	4.9900	4.9900
2	1	ACME Windshield Fluid	1	.0000	.0000
2	2	ACME Air Filter	1	8.9900	8.9900
2	3	ACME PVC Valve	1	12.9900	12.9900
3	1	Motion Synthetic Oil 10w-40	4	13.9900	55.9600
3	1	Texas Tea Economy Oil Filter	1	3.9900	3.9900
4	1	Protects 10w-30 Oil	4	7.4900	29.9600
4	1	ACME Oil Filter	1	4.9900	4.9900
5	1	ACME Wiper Blades	1	9.9900	9.9900
5	2	Black Gold 10w-30 Oil	4	7.9900	31.9600
5	2	ACME Oil Filter	1	4.9900	4.9900
5	2	ACME Transmission Fluid	1	.0000	.0000
5	2	ACME Windshield Fluid	1	.0000	.0000
6	1	ACME Coolant	1	.0000	.0000
7	1	Protects 10w-30 Oil	4	7.4900	29.9600
7	1	ACME Oil Filter	1	4.9900	4.9900
7	1	ACME Transmission Fluid	1	.0000	.0000
7	1	ACME Windshield Fluid	1	.0000	.0000
7	2	ACME Air Filter	1	8.9900	8.9900
7	3	ACME PVC Valve	1	12.9900	12.9900
7	4	ACME Differential Fluid	1	.0000	.0000
7	5	ACME Coolant	1	.0000	.0000

This query selects columns from the PartUsed and Part tables. Each row of the result set represents a part used on a line item on a job. It shows the quantity of each part used for the job and the cost of each part. The last column represents the total cost of that part for that line item on the job. The total is determined by multiplying the cost per part by the quantity used. This computed column was given the alias "Part Total". You can see from the query that * is used as the multiplication operator. Table 2.2 shows the arithmetic operators.

TABLE 2.2 SQL ARITHMETIC OPERATORS	
Arithemetic Operator	**Description**
+	Add
–	Subtract
*	Multiply
/	Divide
%	Modulo (remainder of a division operation)

We're sure you all are very familiar with add, subtract, multiply, and divide. We bet some of you, however, are wondering what the heck modulo means. Modulo acts like divide, but instead of giving you the entire result, it only gives you the remainder after whole number division. For example, 3 would divide into 22 seven times with 1 left over. That leftover piece (the remainder) is what modulo returns to you. We use modulo mostly to find out if a number is even or odd. If 2 divides into the number with no remainder, modulo is 0—and the number is even. Just for grins, let's see which vehicles in the Vehicle table have an even model year.

```
SELECT VehicleYear, Make, Model
   FROM Vehicle
  WHERE VehicleYear % 2 = 0
ORDER BY VehicleYear;
```

Results:

VehicleYear	Make	Model
1968	Chevrolet	Corvette
1972	AMC	Gremlin
1998	Ford	Mustang
2000	Chevrolet	S-10
2000	Chrysler	PT Cruiser
2002	Nissan	Altima
2002	Chevrolet	Trail Blazer
2002	Pontiac	Grand Prix

And conversely, if you want to see the odd-year vehicles, you would change the query slightly to the following.

```
SELECT VehicleYear, Make, Model
  FROM Vehicle
  WHERE VehicleYear % 2 = 1
ORDER BY VehicleYear;
```

Results:

VehicleYear	Make	Model
2001	Ford	Expedition

If you need to use more than one arithmetic operator in a single computation, then you need to be aware of operator precedence. Multiply, divide, and modulo operations are evaluated first. Addition and subtraction are evaluated second. If you have a tie—for instance, you have both a multiplication and a division operation in the same query—then the operations are evaluated from left to right. Consider the following expression.

```
2 * 6 / 3 + 1 - 3 % 2
```

With precedence in mind, the multiplication, division, and modulo operations will happen first and be evaluated from left to right. So first you get 2 * 6 = 12, leaving 12 / 3 + 1 - 3 % 2. Then it will evaluate the division, 12 / 3 = 4. This leaves 4 + 1 - 3 % 2. Modulo comes third instead of the addition, so 3 % 2 = 1 giving 4 + 1 – 1. Next you have a tie between addition and subtraction, so left-to-right evaluation gives you the addition first, 4 + 1 = 5. Finally, you have the subtraction, 5 – 1 = 4.

This is the default order of evaluation of an expression. If you would like more control over the order of evaluation, or would like to make your expression more readable (this is highly recommended), you can use parentheses to direct the order of evaluation. Let's tweak the expression a tad.

```
2 * 6 / (((3 + 1) – 3) % 2)
```

The innermost set of parentheses is evaluated first. So, 3 + 1 = 4, which leaves 2 * 6 / ((4 – 3) % 2). The next innermost parentheses contain 4 – 3. This gives 2 * 6 / (1 % 2). The last set of parentheses contains the modulo 1 % 2 = 1. This leaves 2 * 6 / 1. The multiplication ties in precedence with the division, but because of left-to-right order, it will be next. Thus 2 * 6 = 12, which leaves the division expression 12 / 1 = 12. See how radically different the answer is now simply because you added parentheses to direct the order of evaluation?

Computed columns allow you to push calculations off on the DBMS instead of returning the data and performing the calculations yourself. Just be aware of how you specify them.

What's Next?

So far this morning you have seen how to use SQL to get information out of a relational database. You know how to put the information in the order you choose and how to limit the result set to only the rows you are interested in. This afternoon, you will learn more advanced techniques to retrieve information. We've just scratched the surface here; read on to see just how powerful SQL is.

Selecting Data— Bigger and Better

➤ Using Functions
➤ Grouping the Results
➤ Filtering the Groups
➤ Using Subqueries
➤ Creating Unions

In this chapter, we are going to build on what you learned this morning. We're going to show you even more ways you can customize the results you obtain from the database. You'll learn how to put the power of the database to work to perform tasks for you that you may be doing now by hand. The queries in this chapter are going to become increasingly complex. Don't feel bad if you have to read a section a couple times to grasp the concepts. That's why we saved these topics for the advanced chapter on selecting data.

Using Functions

SQL has built-in functions available for your use, just like in application development tools like Visual Basic, C, Delphi, PowerBuilder, and the like. These functions allow you to extend your productivity on the database server and not rely as much or at all on an application tool to perform these tasks. This means you can get the results you want straight from the server without having to write code in another language to manipulate that data to see those results.

Unfortunately, the functions supported by each DBMS vary quite a bit. Many of the aggregate functions like MIN, MAX, COUNT, SUM, and AVG are standard throughout the various implementations. Other functions that operate on strings, numeric values, or date and time values are not so standard. You can get the gist of what these types of functions can do for you, but you will need to refer to your DBMS's documentation to find out exactly which types of functions are implemented and what they are named. Fortunately, most vendors have structured their documentation in a similar fashion so that you can simply search for functions and then search under the type of function, date time for instance, to find a list of supported functions and a description of each.

Here's the kicker, though. As you read earlier, one of the best things about SQL being a standard is that if you stick to the standard you can port (move) your code from vendor to vendor and it'll work. Well, because most functions are not standard, using them makes your code less portable (moveable) between vendors. All this means is if you need to use functions to get the job done, and chances are you will, you just need to modify those queries before porting the code to the new vendor. In many cases, the new vendor will have a similar function—it'll just have a different name.

Now that the disclaimer is out of the way, let's start exploring some of these functions and how they help get the job done quicker. There are several types of functions you are going to examine in turn. These are aggregate, mathematical, string, conversion, date time, and system.

Aggregate Functions

Aggregate functions give you a single answer based on a set of data passed into the function. These functions provide a particular statistic about the data set.

COUNT

For instance, a very highly used aggregate function is COUNT. COUNT takes a set of data and counts the number of items in the set. It returns a single value, the count. Consider the following example.

```
SELECT COUNT(StateOrProvince)
  FROM Customer;
```

Result:

```
------
7
```

Essentially, COUNT returned the number of rows in the Customer table. You didn't specify a WHERE clause to eliminate any rows from the result set, so the entire list of states from the Customer table was fed into the COUNT function, which returned 7, the number of states in the StateOrProvince column of the Customer table. Hold on! There are only three states in the StateOrProvince table. Why did SQL return 7? Well, COUNT asked it to count them, not to distinguish one from the other. To get the count of unique states in the StateOrProvince column, you have to add DISTINCT to the query as follows.

```
SELECT COUNT(DISTINCT StateOrProvince)
  FROM Customer;
```

Result:

```
------
3
```

Ah, now you get just a count of the distinct (unique) values in the requested column. One more question, though. Why isn't there a column name? Well, this is an expression and we didn't assign the expression a name, so it left it blank. You can assign the expression a name, if you'd like, using the AS keyword that we discussed in the Saturday Morning session.

Another thing you can do with COUNT is count all the rows of the result set without specifying a column name. You do this by using *. This is used quite often to determine how many rows are in a particular table.

```
SELECT COUNT(*) AS CountAll
  FROM Customer;
```

Result:

```
CountAll
------
8
```

Notice this gives you the same result as specifying a column without using DISTINCT. What would happen if you used DISTINCT here? Absolutely nothing would be different. Why is that? That is because a row in a table is unique by definition, so specifying DISTINCT against every column in the row (*) does not change a thing. What it will do, though, is return an error. COUNT(DISTINCT *) is not a valid request.

SUM

What if instead of counting the values in a column, you want to add them together? The SUM function does that for you. Similarly, you pass it a result set (a column name or expression) and it returns the sum of the values in that set. DISTINCT can be used with SUM to compute the total of only the unique values, should you need it. However, * will not work with SUM as it would not know what exactly you would like to add together.

```
SELECT SUM(Cost)
  FROM Part;
```

Result:

```
----------
99.8900
```

```
SELECT SUM(DISTINCT Cost)
  FROM Part;
```

Result:

```
 - - - - - - - - - -
70.4200
```

Adding DISTINCT to the query causes it to throw out all the duplicate values in the Cost column of the Part table before adding the remaining values together. Therefore, you get a completely different answer from the second query versus the first query.

MAX and MIN

MIN and MAX are short for minimum and maximum. Given a list of values, they return the smallest value or the biggest value, respectively.

If you want to determine the most expensive and least expensive parts in the Part table, you can use the following query.

```
   SELECT Cost
      FROM Part
ORDER BY Cost;
```

Results:

```
Cost
 - - - - - - - - - -
.0000
.0000
.0000
.0000
.0000
3.9900
4.9900
7.4900
7.4900
7.9900
7.9900
8.9900
9.9900
12.9900
13.9900
13.9900
```

As you can see, a tie exists for the least expensive parts, which are displayed at the top of the list. There is also a tie for most expensive, which are shown at the bottom of the list. A more efficient way to determine the cost of the most and least expensive parts is to execute the following query using the MAX and MIN functions.

```
SELECT MAX(Cost) AS "Most Expensive", MIN(Cost) AS "Least Expensive"
  FROM Part;
```

Results:

```
Most Expensive          Least Expensive
----------              ---------------
13.9900                     .0000
```

As you can see, the MAX function returned the maximum Cost value and MIN returned the minimum Cost value. Also notice that you can use multiple functions in a single SELECT statement.

AVG

Another aggregate function is the AVG function. This function averages the values passed in to it. So, using the Part table again, let's find the average cost of the parts in the table.

```
SELECT AVG(Cost) AS "Average Cost"
  FROM Part;
```

Result:

```
Average Cost
----------
6.2431
```

STDEV and VAR

The last two aggregate functions covered here are STDEV and VAR, which stand for standard deviation and variance. We don't know about you, but we are rarely asked to find the standard deviation for a set of data. Regardless, we'll provide a couple examples here in case your job is a little more statistical in nature than ours.

```
SELECT STDEV(Cost) AS "Standard Deviation"
  FROM Part;
```

Result:

```
Standard Deviation
-----------
5.1502449375409984
```

```
SELECT VAR(Cost) AS "Variance"
  FROM Part;
```

Result:

```
Variance
-----------
26.525022916666678
```

You will find aggregate functions used quite a bit during your stint with SQL. Aggregate functions tend to be standard among the major vendors. The functions you've learned here should serve you well no matter what DBMS you are querying against.

Mathematical Functions

Along the same lines as the aggregate functions, there are the mathematical functions. What's the difference? Whereas both types of functions return a single value as the result, mathematical functions operate on a single value instead of a set of values like aggregates. Every function discussed from here forward is a nonaggregate.

◄ ◄
An **aggregate function** is a function that operates on a set of values to determine the single value to return. Examples of aggregate functions include AVG, MIN, MAX, COUNT, and SUM.
◄ ◄

Grouped under mathematical functions there are functions for doing trigonometry, such as SIN, COS, TAN, COT, ACOS, ASIN, and ATAN. These stand for sine, cosine, tangent, cotangent, arccosine, arcsine, and arctangent, respectively. We don't do a whole lot with the trig we learned in high school nor do we know many people that do, so we're going to skip these and dig into some of the more widely used mathematical functions.

ABS

ABS is a function used to return the absolute value of the passed-in column value or expression. Unlike the aggregate functions used previously, this function and all the functions from here forward will return a value for every value that is in the result set passed in. This means that if you ask for the absolute value of every row in the Part table, you would get 16 rows back, one for each row in the Part table. This doesn't make much sense, though, because all the values in the Cost column are positive, so ABS does nothing for you. Instead, you can use the following query to demonstrate the ABS function. You'll see that positive values come out positive, zero values come out zero, and negative values come out positive.

```
SELECT ABS(35.31), ABS(0), ABS(-35.31);
```

Results:

```
------      --------     ------
35.31       0            35.31
```

CEILING (or CEIL) and FLOOR

The CEILING and FLOOR functions can be used to find the nearest integer above or below the supplied value. This works like rounding except you specify which direction the value will round.

```
SELECT CEILING(35.31) AS RoundUp, FLOOR(35.31) As RoundDown;
```

Results:

```
RoundUp     RoundDown
-------     ---------
36          35
```

CAUTION   ◆◆◆

CEILING is not named the same in every DBMS. Oracle, for instance, names their function CEIL.

◆◆◆

ROUND

Speaking of rounding, let's see what the actual ROUND function will do. ROUND is used to round a value to the precision specified. If you specify a negative number for the precision, it counts off that value left from the decimal point. If you specify a positive number, it counts off right from the decimal point. A value of zero places the precision at the decimal point. If a negative number is specified that is greater than the number for digits left of the decimal, 0 is returned. The following query demonstrates several results from specifying different precisions.

```
SELECT ROUND(35.31, -1), ROUND(35.31, -3), ROUND(35.31, 1),
ROUND(35.31, 0);
```

Results:

```
-----     ---     -----     -----
40.00     .00     35.30     35.00
```

SIGN

If you just want to find out if a value is positive or negative, you can use the SIGN function. If the value is zero, it returns 0. If the value is positive, it returns 1. If the value is negative, it returns −1.

```
SELECT SIGN(35.31) AS Positive, SIGN(0) AS Zero, SIGN(-35.31) AS
    Negative;
```

Results:

```
Positive    Zero        Negative
------      ------      -------
1.00        0           -1.00
```

SQUARE and SQRT

You can square a value using SQUARE or find the square root using SQRT. These are straightforward, so we'll just show you an example.

```
SELECT SQUARE(2) AS SquareOfTwo, SQRT(4) AS SquareRootOfFour;
```

Results:

```
SquareOfTwo     SquareRootOfFour
------------    ----------------
4.0             2.0
```

There are several other mathematical functions. The ones we've discussed here are the more common ones. The type of functions you can use depends on your DBMS. Refer to the documentation for a complete list.

String Functions

Oh, where to begin? So many string functions, so little time. Again, as with the mathematical functions, we will not be able to cover them all, but we will give you a taste of the more important ones, and you can use your system documentation to find out about any others you want to use.

UPPER and LOWER

We're sure you've already figured out that string functions operate on string data such as char and varchar data types. Two of the things you'll want to do the most with string data is change the characters to either all uppercase characters or all lowercase characters. UPPER is used for the former and LOWER for the latter. As with all expressions, these can be used in any part of the statement that supports expressions. Therefore, if you use it in the SELECT clause, you get the data back with the altered case.

```
SELECT UPPER(Model) AS AllUp, LOWER(Model) AS AllLow
   FROM Vehicle;
```

Results:

AllUp	AllLow
S-10	s-10
MUSTANG	mustang
GRAND PRIX	grand prix
CORVETTE	corvette
ALTIMA	altima
PT CRUISER	pt cruiser
TRAIL BLAZER	trail blazer
EXPEDITION	expedition
GREMLIN	gremlin

If you use it in the WHERE clause, the case of the data is altered for the purposes of the comparison. This is very important when your database is set to be case sensitive. If the column has mixed-case strings in it, the value you are comparing it to has to match the case of every letter exactly to be equal. If the Slick Shop's database is case sensitive, the following query would not find the row you are looking for because the case does not match. Instead, you'd have to use the second query to be sure that the database gave us every possible case-insensitive match.

```
SELECT *
  FROM Vehicle
 WHERE Model = 'Grand prix';
SELECT *
  FROM Vehicle
 WHERE UPPER(Model) = UPPER('Grand prix');
```

In a case-sensitive database, the first query would not find the row in the Vehicle table. The second query would convert the columns data to all uppercase as well as the constant you are comparing it to. LOWER would work just as well here, by the way. You just need to be consistent with the function used on both sides of the equation.

LTRIM and RTRIM

Another very useful function pair is LTRIM and RTRIM. These guys trim spaces off the left or right side of the column or expression passed in. LTRIM trims the left side, whereas RTRIM does the right side. This becomes important when working with columns of the data type char. The char data type pads the data in the column with spaces until it is the exact size of the column definition. In other words, if you have a column defined as char(20) but the value you want to store in it is only 12 characters long, the database will add eight spaces at the end of the data so it will be exactly 20 characters long. varchar columns do not do this. They only store what they are given. Don't misunderstand, though. There are still many good reasons for using a char versus a varchar. You'll read all about that later tonight in the Saturday Evening session. Regardless, if you need to compare a value to a char type column, it is best to trim the information first in the WHERE clause.

As with other functions, you can also use these trim functions in the SELECT. For instance, consider that you are working on mailing labels from a database that has a column called City as a char(30), a State column as char(2), and a Zip column as char(5). To make the concatenation of city, state, and ZIP code look right on the mailing labels, you'll want to trim the `City` column first. You don't need to trim the other two columns because `State` is supposed to be exactly two characters and `Zip` is supposed to be exactly five characters.

```
SELECT RTRIM(City) + ', ' + State + ' ' + Zip
   FROM Contacts;
```

So you can visualize this, let's plug in values instead of columns.

```
SELECT RTRIM ('Columbus                         ') + ', ' + 'OH' +
     ' ' + '32109';
```

Results:

```
---------------------
Columbus, OH  32109
```

LEFT, RIGHT, and SUBSTRING (or SUBSTR)

The LEFT and RIGHT functions return the specified number of characters from the left or right side of the string. Similarly, SUBSTRING retrieves the requested number of characters but takes a starting position as a parameter. This allows users to retrieve a portion of a string from the middle. To demonstrate this, we're going to use the `PhoneNumber` column from the `Customer` table. The following query will break the phone number into its respective parts and add formatting.

```
SELECT '(' + LEFT(PhoneNumber, 3) + ')' + SUBSTRING(PhoneNumber, 4,
     3) + '-' + RIGHT(PhoneNumber, 4) AS "Formatted Phone"
   FROM Customer;
```

Results:

```
Formatted Phone
----------------
(102)234-1234
(766)555-4444
(217)543-8679
NULL
```

```
(765)432-1098
(317)555-1213
(317)555-1214
(317)555-1215
```

This query first adds the open parenthesis and then finds the area code by getting the left three characters of the PhoneNumber column. Next it adds the close parenthesis and looks for the phone prefix by using SUBSTRING to find the middle three characters of the prefix, which begin at position four in the PhoneNumber string. Next it adds the dash and finishes it off by obtaining the right four digits of the PhoneNumber column. The result is a nicely formatted phone number. Notice that the NULL was left alone appropriately.

NOTE SUBSTRING is shortened to SUBSTR in some databases. Oracle and DB2, for instance, use SUBSTR. SQL Server, MySQL, and Sybase use SUBSTRING.

LEN (or LENGTH or DATALENGTH)

LEN is a function you can use to find the length of a column of expression. It is sometimes named LENGTH (Oracle and DB2) or DATALENGTH (Sybase) as well. The following query returns the length of the customer's first name from the Customer table.

```
SELECT LEN(FirstName) AS Length, FirstName
  FROM Customer;
```

Results:

```
Length       FirstName
-------      ----------
4            John
5            Jacob
8            Victoria
5            Bryce
5            Kylee
4            Alex
5            Davis
8            Harrison
```

SPACE

Now how about making all first names the same length. Hmmm. We'll use the SPACE function to fill them all to 10 spaces. To do this, you have to subtract their current length from 10 to get the number of spaces to pad. So you can see that it worked, we add the LastName column to the end of the string.

```
SELECT FirstName + SPACE(LEN(FirstName)* -1 + 10) + LastName
  FROM Customer;
```

Results:

```
-------   -------
John      Smith
Jacob     Salter
Victoria  Smithe
Bryce     Hatfield
Kylee     Dicken
Alex      Thompson
Davis     Thompson
Harrison  Thompson
```

REPLACE

REPLACE is another handy string function. It can be used to replace a portion of a string with another value. You use this function by specifying, first, the string that contains the value you'd like to replace. Then specify the portion that needs replacing. Finally, give it the string to use as the replacement. This function would be very useful for situations such as a change to the area code containing the majority of your customers. You wouldn't want to go update these by hand. You'd want to run one SQL statement to update them all and be done with it. Here is an example of what the SELECT would look like. Keep in mind, however, that SELECT statements never modify the underlying data. We haven't shown you how to do that yet. You'll read about that shortly in the Saturday Evening session.

```
SELECT PhoneNumber AS 'Old Number',
       REPLACE(PhoneNumber, '317', '111') AS 'New Number'
  FROM Customer;
```

Results:

```
Old Number      New Number
------------    --------------
1022341234      1022341234
7665554444      7665554444
2175438679      2175438679
NULL            NULL
7654321098      7654321098
3175551213      1115551213
3175551214      1115551214
3175551215      1115551215
```

SOUNDEX

If you want to look for matching strings by sound rather than a straight character match, you can use SOUNDEX. SOUNDEX converts the string into a number representing its sound value. It ignores vowel sounds. When you compare the SOUNDEX results of two strings, you are essentially asking if they sound the same regardless of whether they are spelled the same. The following is an example using the Customer table.

```
SELECT c1.LastName, c2.LastName
  FROM Customer AS c1, Customer AS c2
 WHERE SOUNDEX(c1.LastName) = SOUNDEX(c2.LastName)
   AND c1.LastName <> c2.LastName
   AND c1.CustomerID < c2.CustomerID;
```

Results:

```
LastName        LastName
-----------     --------------
Smith           Smithe
```

This query selects back the last names from the Customer table where the last names have the same sound but not the same spelling. Also, to avoid duplicate comparisons, make sure the CustomerID from the first instance of the table is always less than the CustomerID of the second instance of the Customer table.

DIFFERENCE

Similar to SOUNDEX is the function DIFFERENCE. DIFFERENCE is used to determine just how closely two strings sound like each other. Instead of looking for a direct match, you are looking for a value from 1 to 4, with 4 representing the best match.

```
SELECT DIFFERENCE('Grey', 'Gray') AS Difference;
```

Result:

```
Difference
----------
4
```

CONCAT (||)

As you've seen, the plus operator (+) is used to concatenate strings in SQL Server. In some DBMSs, such as ORACLE and DB2, you must use the function CONCAT or the symbol || to concatenate strings. The following is an example of both in Oracle.

```
SELECT 'This is a way to do concatenation ' || ' in Oracle',
       CONCAT ('This is another way to do concatenation', ' in
           Oracle')
  FROM DUAL
```

These are some of the more widely used string functions. There are many more available. The documentation for your particular DBMS will show you the other functions supported by that vendor.

Conversion Functions

Conversion functions allow you to change a value from one data type to another, apply formatting, or in some cases change the value itself. This section looks at a few of the more common conversion functions.

CAST

To convert data from one data type to another, you can use the CAST function. For instance, if you need to concatenate a money value with a varchar, you can cast that money column or expression as a string first to allow the concatenation to work.

Fortunately, most data types can be automatically converted from one data type to another by the DBMS. These are referred to as *implicit conversions*. Conversions that will not take place without using a conversion function are referred to as *explicit conversions*.

◄◄
An **implicit conversion** is one that the DBMS can perform without specific instruction to do so. For example, SQL Server will automatically convert an integer value to a string if it is used in a string function. SQL Server cannot convert a SMALLINT to a string without being told to, however.
◄◄

◄◄
An **explicit conversion** requires the user to tell the DBMS that the value needs to be converted and what data type it needs to be.
◄◄

The example used previously, money to varchar, requires an explicit conversion. In the first SELECT that follows, we attempt an implicit conversion and get denied. In the second SELECT, we tell the DBMS that we'd like the money column cast as a varchar(10) and the query works beautifully.

```
SELECT 'The price of ' + Description + ' is ' + Cost
   FROM Part;
```

Results:

```
Server: Msg 260, Level 16, State 1, Line 1
Disallowed implicit conversion from data type varchar to data type
      money, table 'SlickShop.dbo.Part', column 'Cost'. Use the CONVERT
      function to run this query.
```

```
SELECT 'The price of ' + Description + ' is ' + CAST(Cost AS
    VARCHAR(10)) + '.'
  FROM Part;
```

Results:

```
-------------------------------------------
The price of Protects 10w-30 Oil is 7.49.
The price of Protects 10w-40 Oil is 7.49.
The price of Black Gold 10w-30 Oil is 7.99.
The price of Black Gold 10w-40 Oil is 7.99.
The price of Motion Synthetic Oil 10w-30 is 13.99.
The price of Motion Synthetic Oil 10w-40 is 13.99.
The price of Texas Tea Economy Oil Filter is 3.99.
The price of ACME Oil Filter is 4.99.
The price of ACME Air Filter is 8.99.
The price of ACME Wiper Blades is 9.99.
The price of ACME Brake Fluid is 0.00.
The price of ACME Transmission Fluid is 0.00.
The price of ACME Coolant is 0.00.
The price of ACME Windshield Fluid is 0.00.
The price of ACME Differential Fluid is 0.00.
The price of ACME PVC Valve is 12.99.
```

CONVERT

CONVERT works similarly to CAST; however, it allows the users to specify a style or format to use in converting the data. Again, it only needs to be used for conversions that need to be explicitly defined. Because this function allows the users to specify a style or format, it can make your conversions customizable. Next we combine several columns from the Vehicle table to form a sentence regarding the last service date of each vehicle. You can see that the VehicleYear column, a SMALL-INT, needs to be CAST as a char(4) to be combined with the string. The LastServiceDate, we want to see with the format mm/dd/yyyy applied. There are several format codes. Refer to your DBMS's documentation for the applicable codes.

```
SELECT 'The last service date of the ' + CAST(VehicleYear AS CHAR(4)) +
       ' ' + Make + ' ' + Model + ' was ' +
       CONVERT(VARCHAR(10), LastServiceDate, 101) + '.'
  FROM Vehicle;
```

Results:

```
---------------------------
The last service date of the 2000 Chevrolet S-10 was 08/13/2001.
The last service date of the 1998 Ford Mustang was 09/16/2001.
The last service date of the 2002 Pontiac Grand Prix was 05/21/2002.
The last service date of the 1968 Chevrolet Corvette was 01/20/2002.
The last service date of the 2002 Nissan Altima was 01/26/2002.
The last service date of the 2000 Chrysler PT Cruiser was 05/15/2002.
The last service date of the 2002 Chevrolet Trail Blazer was
      05/31/2001.
The last service date of the 2001 Ford Expedition was 05/31/2001.
The last service date of the 1972 AMC Gremlin was 02/17/2002.
```

ASCII and CHAR

The ASCII function provides the numeric ASCII value for a character.
Conversely, CHAR is used to get the character value for an ASCII value.

```
SELECT ASCII('A') AS A, ASCII('a') AS a;
```

Results:

```
A          a
-------    --------
65         97
```

```
SELECT CHAR(65) AS 'ASCII 65', CHAR(97) AS 'ASCII 97';
```

Results:

```
ASCII 65    ASCII 97
----        -----
A           a
```

Other Conversion Functions

Some databases have specific functions for certain conversion types. For example, Oracle has three such functions: TO_DATE, TO_CHAR, and TO_NUMBER. As you can guess, these functions convert data from one data type to date, char, or number, respectively. The three work similarly, so we'll just show you the syntax for TO_DATE.

```
SELECT TO_DATE('12-JUN-1999', 'mm/dd/yyyy')
   FROM DUAL;
```

 NOTE In Oracle, you always have to have a FROM clause. If you are not selecting from a particular table, as in the case of variable assignment or selecting back the current date, you have to use the dummy table DUAL.

Date and Time Functions

Date and time functions vary in name quite a bit from vendor to vendor. We will present the more common ones here. Refer to your system documentation for other date and time functions available in your DBMS.

Date and time functions allow you to perform many types of tasks on these data types. For instance, there are functions that perform mathematical type tasks, some that are used for formatting, and others that allow you simply to obtain the current date and/or time.

GETDATE (or SYSDATE)

Let's start with the basics. How do you find out what today is? In SQL Server, the function you use is called GETDATE. This is also true of MySQL and Sybase. Oracle and DB2, however, call this function SYSDATE. The first example is from SQL Server. The second is the Oracle syntax.

```
SELECT GETDATE();
SELECT SYSDATE()
  FROM DUAL;
```

DATEADD and DATEDIFF

Two of the mathematical date and time functions are DATEADD and
DATEDIFF. DATEADD adds a particular value to part of the date. In
other words, you can use it to add two days to the original date, or maybe
you would like to add 32 weeks. Similarly, DATEDIFF is used to find the
interval between two dates given the part of the date you are interested
in. Table 3.1 shows the various date parts that can be specified.

TABLE 3.1 DATA PARTS FOR USE WITH DATEADD AND DATEDIFF

Date Part	Format
Days	dd, d
DayofYear	dy, y
Hours	hh
Milliseconds	ms
Minutes	mi, n
Months	mm, m
Quarters	q, qq
Seconds	s, ss
Weeks	wk, ww
Years	yy, yyyy

Let's say the boss wants you to start printing labels for the next service date of the vehicles when they come in for an oil change. You can use DATEADD to add three months to the current date to find out when the vehicle should be due back. Let's assume the vehicle is brought in on June 1, 2002.

```
SELECT DATEADD(mm, 3, GETDATE()) AS NextServiceDate;
```

Results:

```
NextServiceDate
---------------------------
2002-09-01 00:00:00.000
```

A good use of DATEDIFF is to find out how many weeks it's been since a vehicle was last worked on by the shop. The vehicle table has a column called LastServiceDate that will work nicely for this query. The results assume today's date is June 1, 2002.

```
SELECT Make, Model, DATEDIFF(wk, LastServiceDate, GETDATE()) AS Weeks
  FROM Vehicle;
```

Results:

Make	Model	LastServiceDate	Weeks
Chevrolet	S-10	2001-08-13 00:00:00	41
Ford	Mustang	2001-09-16 00:00:00	36
Pontiac	Grand Prix	2002-05-21 00:00:00	1
Chevrolet	Corvette	2002-01-20 00:00:00	18
Nissan	Altima	2002-01-26 00:00:00	18
Chrysler	PT Cruiser	2002-05-15 00:00:00	2
Chevrolet	Trail Blazer	2001-05-31 00:00:00	52
Ford	Expedition	2001-05-31 00:00:00	52
AMC	Gremlin	2002-02-17 00:00:00	14

This information is specific to SQL Server (but also applies to Sybase). Other DBMSs have similar functionality but under different function names. For instance, to add three months to a date as you did earlier, you would use the function ADD_MONTHS in Oracle.

DATEPART

DATEPART allows you to obtain the value of a specific piece of the date-time value. You can obtain information on all the same date parts listed previously in Table 3.1. The following is an example of some of the date parts that are available.

```
SELECT DATEPART(qq, '5/21/2002') AS Quarter,
       DATEPART(wk, '5/21/2002') AS Week,
       DATEPART(dw, '5/21/2002') AS DayofWeek,
       DATEPART(mm, '5/21/2002') AS Month,
       DATEPART(ms, '5/21/2002  13:12:11:120') AS Milliseconds;
```

Results:

Quarter	Week	DayofWeek	Month	Milliseconds
2	21	3	5	120

DATENAME

If you prefer to see the name of the date part instead of the number of the date part, use the function DATENAME in place of DATEPART. As you can see from the following example, it's really only useful for the parts of the date that have a corresponding name.

```
SELECT DATENAME(qq, '5/21/2002') AS Quarter,
       DATENAME(wk, '5/21/2002') AS Week,
       DATENAME(dw, '5/21/2002') AS DayofWeek,
       DATENAME(mm, '5/21/2002') AS Month,
       DATENAME(ms, '5/21/2002  13:12:11:120') AS Milliseconds;
```

Results:

Quarter	Week	DayofWeek	Month	Milliseconds
2	21	Tuesday	May	120

DAY, MONTH, and YEAR

DAY, MONTH, or YEAR functions provide the same results as using the DATEPART function for the day, month, or year, respectively. The following example shows the syntax.

```
SELECT DAY('5/21/2002') AS Day,
       MONTH('5/21/2002') AS Month,
       YEAR('5/21/2002') AS Year;
```

Results:

```
Day         Month       Year
------      --------     -------
21          5           2002
```

System Functions

The functions discussed in this section allow you to access system information or provide decision type functionality. There are several system functions, but they vary widely from vendor to vendor. Please refer to the documentation for your DBMS to learn more about the system functions available to you.

USER_NAME

The USER_NAME function finds either the name associated with a user ID or the current user's name. If an ID is passed in, the associated name is returned. If nothing is passed in, the current user's name is returned.

```
SELECT USER_NAME(2) AS 'USER ID 2', USER_NAME() AS 'Current User';
```

Results:

```
USER ID 2    Current User
---------    -------------
guest        dbo
```

DATALENGTH

If you need to determine how much space (bytes) a value or expression will use, the DATALENGTH function can provide this information. If you remember our earlier discussion of the string function LEN, it returned the length of a string value. This is the same as determining the storage requirements for a `char` or `varchar` column because every character occupies a single byte of storage space. Therefore, some DBMSs do not have a LEN function but instead rely on the DATA-LENGTH function to obtain this information. Unlike LEN, DATA-LENGTH can evaluate all data types, not just string equivalents. If you want to know how much space a mathematical expression will consume, you can do the following.

```
SELECT DATALENGTH(10* PI()/68);
```

Result:

```
--------
8
```

Or what if you just want to know how much room each row of the vehicle table is taking up in the database? If you add up the data length of each of the columns in the row, you will get the entire storage requirement of that row of data.

```
SELECT DATALENGTH(VehicleID) +
       DATALENGTH(VehicleYear) +
       DATALENGTH(Make) +
       DATALENGTH(Model) +
       DATALENGTH(Color) +
       DATALENGTH(LicensePlate#) +
       DATALENGTH(LastServiceDate) +
       DATALENGTH(CustomerID) AS 'Storage in Bytes'
   FROM Vehicle;
```

Results:

```
Storage in Bytes
---------
40
34
43
42
38
43
47
41
35
```

Notice that each row does not consume the same amount of space. How can that be? Whereas most data types always occupy the same amount of storage space in the database no matter what their value, varchar columns (and varchar columns) occupy only the space needed to hold the value stored in that column on that row. This is another advantage of using the varchar data type over the char data type.

ISNULL (or NVL)

There is a predicament that comes up from time to time when using SQL. We're sure you'll run into it at least once yourself. It occurs when you need to return a set of data, but one of the columns has NULL for some of the rows and that is not acceptable. For instance, it might be preferable to see a value of 0 rather than a NULL for an entry on an accounting report. Another common occurrence is the user wanting to see Unknown (or similar) in place of NULLs. The ISNULL function allows you to replace NULLs found in a column or an expression with a value of your choosing. In the sample database, a customer doesn't have a value for StateOrProvince, so you can replace it with Unknown. You need to cast StateOrProvince as a varchar(10) first, however, or only Un will fit in the char(2) column as it stands.

```
SELECT FirstName, LastName,
ISNULL(CAST(StateOrProvince AS Varchar(10)), 'Unknown')
  FROM Customer;
```

Results:

FirstName	LastName	
John	Smith	VA
Jacob	Salter	Unknown
Victoria	Smithe	WV
Bryce	Hatfield	IN
Kylee	Dicken	IN
Alex	Thompson	IN
Davis	Thompson	IN
Harrison	Thompson	IN

CASE

CASE evaluates a value or an expression to determine the appropriate result. It can compare values to a column or evaluate several Boolean expressions. For instance, if you have a column in your table that has only a code in it, you can use CASE to return the meaning instead of the value. There isn't one in the sample database, so let's make one up.

```
SELECT ProjectName, Priority =
      CASE PriorityCode
         WHEN 'H' THEN 'High'
         WHEN 'M' THEN 'Medium'
         WHEN 'L' THEN 'Low'
         ELSE 'Invalid priority code'
      END
  FROM Projects;
```

This second example, however, uses several Boolean expressions to determine the appropriate comment for each vehicle in the Vehicle table of the sample database.

```
SELECT VehicleYear, Make, Model, Comment =
      CASE
         WHEN VehicleYear > 2001 THEN 'New Car'
         WHEN VehicleYear > 1999 THEN 'Fairly New Car'
         WHEN VehicleYear > 1995 THEN 'Not too old'
         WHEN VehicleYear > 1980 THEN 'A car'
         ELSE 'An antique!'
      END
FROM Vehicle;
```

Results:

VehicleYear	Make	Model	Comment
2000	Chevrolet	S-10	Fairly New Car
1998	Ford	Mustang	Not too old
2002	Pontiac	Grand Prix	New Car
1968	Chevrolet	Corvette	An antique!
2002	Nissan	Altima	New Car
2000	Chrysler	PT Cruiser	Fairly New Car
2002	Chevrolet	Trail Blazer	New Car
2001	Ford	Expedition	Fairly New Car
1972	AMC	Gremlin	An antique!

Take a Break!

Whew! That's a lot of functions. You did all that reading on just one section. Well, you've earned yourself a break. We'll mix it up a little in the second half of this chapter. When you pick this book back up, you'll discover how to group your results together and even how to eliminate certain groups. After that, the chapter discussed just what the heck a subquery is and why you might want to use one. Finally, you'll learn how to obtain a combined result set from multiple queries.

Grouping the Results

You've learned how to select information back from the tables in your database and you know how to use aggregate functions to obtain statistics on that data. What if you want to categorize that data and get statistics on the categories instead of the whole? We're going to show you how to use a new clause in the SELECT statement to do just this. The GROUP BY clause allows you to combine the rows being selected into logical groups. It is normally used when one or more aggregate functions are used in the SELECT clause. Every column or expression in the SELECT clause, except the aggregate(s), is usually included in the GROUP BY clause. This allows the DBMS to provide the statistics requested via the aggregates on each of those groups.

All columns or expressions in your SELECT clause should be included in the GROUP BY clause except for any aggregates. You can receive unexpected results if you leave one out. Some DBMSs will not process the query unless you conform to this rule.

The best way to explain the usefulness of this clause is to show you some examples. In this first example, you find out how many customers you have from each state.

```
SELECT StateOrProvince, COUNT(*)
    FROM Customer
GROUP BY StateOrProvince;
```

Results:

```
StateOrProvince
-------         -----
NULL             1
IN               5
VA               1
WV               1
```

The GROUP BY caused each row in the Customer table to be included in a group based on the values in its StateOrProvince column. It then counts the customers in each group and returns a list of the states found in the table and the number of rows having that value for StateOrProvince. Notice that even the NULL values are categorized together and counted. In this case there is one customer with a NULL value in StateOrProvince. If you don't want the NULLs included, simply add a WHERE clause. Note that the WHERE clause always comes before the GROUP BY clause.

```
SELECT StateOrProvince, COUNT(*)
    FROM Customer
   WHERE StateOrProvince IS NOT NULL
GROUP BY StateOrProvince;
```

Results:

```
StateOrProvince
-------         -----
IN              5
VA              1
                1
```

The WHERE clause is evaluated first, which eliminates the rows not meeting the criteria specified. Then the GROUP By clause takes the remaining rows and groups them. If you want all the groups to show up in the results even if all the rows for that group were eliminated by the WHERE clause, use the ALL keyword.

```
SELECT StateOrProvince, COUNT(*)
    FROM Customer
   WHERE StateOrProvince IS NOT NULL
GROUP BY ALL StateOrProvince;
```

Results:

```
StateOrProvince
---------        -------
NULL             0
IN               5
VA               1
WV               1
```

NULL shows up again. This time, however, it has no rows in its group because the WHERE clause eliminated the one customer with a NULL in StateOrProvince.

As mentioned before, you can have multiple aggregate functions in the SELECT clause. Because most of the aggregate functions work best with numeric data, we'll use the Quantity column from PartUsed.

```
SELECT PartID,
        Avg(Quantity) AS Average,
        Sum(Quantity) AS Sum,
        Count(Quantity) AS Count
    FROM PartUsed
GROUP BY PartID;
```

Results:

PartID	Average	Sum	Count
1	4	8	2
3	4	4	1
4	4	4	1
5	4	4	1
6	4	4	1
7	1	2	2
8	1	4	4
9	1	2	2
10	1	1	1
11	1	1	1
12	1	3	3
13	1	2	2
14	1	3	3
15	1	1	1
16	1	2	2

The previous query evaluated each row in the PartUsed table to group them by the PartID. Then it calculated each one of the aggregates for each of the groups independently to return the result set.

Not only can you have multiple aggregates with a GROUP BY, but you can also have no aggregates in the SELECT clause. If you go back to the StateOrProvince query and take off the aggregate, you get the following.

```
SELECT StateOrProvince
   FROM Customer
  WHERE StateOrProvince IS NOT NULL
GROUP BY StateOrProvince;
```

Results:

```
StateOrProvince
--------
IN
VA
WV
```

This just tells you what the unique values are in the StateOrProvince column that passed the WHERE clause condition. You can receive the same results using the DISTINCT keyword and leaving off the GROUP BY.

```
SELECT DISTINCT StateOrProvince
  FROM Customer
 WHERE StateOrProvince IS NOT NULL;
```

If you include a value in the SELECT clause that is unique to every row in the result set after the WHERE is applied, then you'll get just as many rows when the GROUP BY is applied. This is because the GROUP BY cannot find any nondistinct rows to group. So if you add CustomerID, the key to the Customer table, to the StateOrProvince query you've been using, you will get just as many rows back as you would without the GROUP BY. Be cautious of what columns you include in your SELECT clause and how they can affect the results of the grouping.

```
SELECT CustomerID, StateOrProvince
  FROM Customer
 WHERE StateOrProvince IS NOT NULL
GROUP BY CustomerID, StateOrProvince;
```

Results:

```
CustomerID      StateOrProvince
--------        ----------
1               VA
3               WV
4               IN
5               IN
6               IN
7               IN
8               IN
```

Filtering the Groups

Just like you've learned to use the WHERE clause to eliminate unwanted rows from your result set, here you'll learn to use the HAVING clause to eliminate unwanted groups from the results of the GROUP BY clause.

Because the HAVING clause always operates on the GROUP BY clause, it always immediately follows the GROUP BY clause. In the HAVING clause, you can use the same operators you can use in the WHERE clause.

As an example of using the HAVING clause, let's revisit the query you used earlier to find the number of customers in each state. This time, however, you only want to see the states that have more than one customer in them.

```
SELECT StateOrProvince, COUNT(*)
   FROM Customer
  WHERE StateOrProvince IS NOT NULL
GROUP BY StateOrProvince
HAVING COUNT(*) > 1;
```

Results:

```
StateOrProvince

-------       -------
IN            5
```

You can see from these results that the HAVING clause removed the groups for the states of Virginia and West Virginia because they only had one customer each. They needed two or more to make it into the final result set.

As mentioned earlier, you can use the ALL keyword in the GROUP BY clause to allow groups to show up in the result set even if they have no rows matching the WHERE clause conditions. With the HAVING clause, however, those groups can still be eliminated from the final result set if they don't match the conditions of the HAVING clause.

You can use columns or expressions in the HAVING clause that were not requested in the SELECT clause. The following query uses the PartUsed table to demonstrate this.

```
SELECT PartID,
       Avg(Quantity) AS Average,
       Sum(Quantity) AS Sum
   FROM PartUsed
GROUP BY PartId
  HAVING Count(Quantity) > 1;
```

Results:

PartID	Average	Sum
1	4	8
7	1	2
8	1	4
9	1	2
12	1	3
13	1	2
14	1	3
16	1	2

Notice that all the groups in which the part was not used for more than one job were eliminated. You know this because if they hadn't been, the Average and the Sum columns would contain the same value for those parts used only once. This query shows that an aggregate not defined in the SELECT is perfectly legal in the HAVING clause.

Okay, but what about using just a column in the HAVING clause instead of an aggregate? How about listing only parts that contain the word Oil? This works for some DBMSs but does not work in all, so check your documentation for compatibility.

```
SELECT pu.PartID,
       p.Description,
       Avg(Quantity) AS Average,
       Sum(Quantity) AS Sum
  FROM PartUsed AS pu, Part AS p
 WHERE pu.PartID = p.PartID
GROUP BY pu.PartID,
       p.Description
 HAVING p.Description LIKE ('%Oil%')
ORDER BY pu.PartID;
```

Results:

PartID	Description	Average	Sum
1	Protects 10w-30 Oil	4	8
3	Black Gold 10w-30 Oil	4	4
4	Black Gold 10w-40 Oil	4	4
5	Motion Synthetic Oil 10w-30	4	4
6	Motion Synthetic Oil 10w-40	4	4
7	Texas Tea Economy Oil Filter	1	2
8	ACME Oil Filter	1	2

Using Subqueries

Now that you know all the pertinent clauses of a SELECT statement, let's do it all over again. Won't that be fun? What we mean is, we're going to show you how to place a query within a query. And somewhere along the way, we'll try to tell you why you'd want to do such a thing. These queries within a query are referred to as *subqueries*. They are found not only in SELECT statements but also in INSERT, UPDATE, and DELETE statements, which you'll learn about shortly.

◄◄◄◄◄◄◄◄◄◄◄◄◄◄◄◄◄◄◄◄◄◄◄◄◄◄◄◄◄◄◄◄◄◄◄◄

A **subquery** is a SELECT statement nested inside another query. It returns a value to the containing query for evaluation. The query containing the subquery is referred to as the outer query. A subquery is often referred to as an inner query, inner select, subselect, or nested query.

◄◄◄◄◄◄◄◄◄◄◄◄◄◄◄◄◄◄◄◄◄◄◄◄◄◄◄◄◄◄◄◄◄◄◄◄

In a SELECT statement, subqueries can appear in the SELECT, WHERE, and HAVING clauses. In some DBMSs, using more advanced techniques, you might even find them in the FROM clause, but we're going to leave that one alone for the purpose of this book.

Subqueries within the WHERE Clause

By far the most popular place to find a subquery is in the WHERE clause. You can use this nested query to go off and execute another SELECT statement, whose result will then be evaluated with the remainder of the Boolean expression on that line. For example, if you want to retrieve a list of customers who live in the same state as Kylee Dicken, you can use the following query.

```
SELECT FirstName, LastName, StateOrProvince
  FROM Customer
WHERE StateOrProvince = (SELECT StateOrProvince
                            FROM Customer AS c2
                          WHERE c2.FirstName = 'Kylee'
                            AND c2.LastName = 'Dicken');
```

Results:

FirstName	LastName	StateOrProvince
Bryce	Hatfield	IN
Kylee	Dicken	IN
Alex	Thompson	IN
Davis	Thompson	IN
Harrison	Thompson	IN

When this subquery is evaluated, it gives back a single result, which is IN. The rows from the Customer table are checked for the same StateOrProvince, and the matching rows are returned in the result set. This could have been done with a simple SELECT, as shown here:

```
SELECT c1.FirstName, c1.LastName, c1.StateOrProvince
  FROM Customer AS c1, Customer AS c2
WHERE c1.StateOrProvince = c2.StateOrProvince
  AND c2.FirstName = 'Kylee'
  AND c2.LastName = 'Dicken';
```

Notice that in the earlier subquery, we had to identify the Customer table with an alias. Even though it was referenced in two SELECT statements, the second query is still part of the first, so the tables need to be distinguished. This is particularly important for correlated subqueries. These are subqueries that must be evaluated for every row because the tables in the outer query (the query containing the subquery) are referenced by the subquery.

◄◄

A **correlated subquery** is a subquery that references the tables of the outer query. Because of this reference, the subquery must be reevaluated for every row examined by the outer query.

◄◄

EXISTS

To help demonstrate correlated subqueries, we'd like to introduce you to the EXISTS keyword. EXISTS tests a subquery for the existence of rows that meet the conditions of the subquery. The subquery does not need to return any columns, so most people use an * in the SELECT clause (we prefer to use 1, but that's just us). The subquery is evaluated, and if there are rows that match the condition, `true` is returned. If no rows match, `false` is returned. Here is an example of a subquery being tested by EXISTS. It also happens to be a good example of a correlated subquery.

```
SELECT VehicleYear, Make, Model
FROM Vehicle AS v
WHERE EXISTS (SELECT *
              FROM JobTicket AS jt
              WHERE jt.VehicleId = v.VehicleId);
```

Results:

VehicleYear	Make	Model
2000	Chevrolet	S-10
1998	Ford	Mustang
2002	Pontiac	Grand Prix
1968	Chevrolet	Corvette
2002	Nissan	Altima
1972	AMC	Gremlin

The previous query uses the subquery to check the `JobTicket` table to see if the vehicle is on any of the job tickets created thus far. Only six of the nine vehicles have a job ticket. To find this out, the subquery had to know which rows from the outer query were being scrutinized. Therefore, in the WHERE clause of the subquery you see a join from the table in the inner query to the table declared in the outer query. That makes this a correlated subquery.

But what if you want to find the vehicles that aren't on a job ticket? After all, why are these vehicles in the system if you haven't or aren't planning on working on them? Stay tuned.

NOT EXISTS

The EXISTS keyword helped you find the vehicles that have at least one job ticket. How do you go about finding the opposite result, the vehicles without a job ticket? Well, you simply reverse your existence test to make it a nonexistence test. You do this by using NOT EXISTS.

```
SELECT VehicleYear, Make, Model
FROM Vehicle AS v
WHERE NOT EXISTS (SELECT *
                  FROM JobTicket AS jt
                  WHERE jt.VehicleId = v.VehicleId);
```

Results:

VehicleYear	Make	Model
2000	Chrysler	PT Cruiser
2002	Chevrolet	Trail Blazer
2001	Ford	Expedition

Now when the subquery returns a `true` because there is a matching row in the `JobTicket` table, the row from the outer join is thrown out because the NOT causes the `true` to become a `false`. And likewise, if no row is found in `JobTicket`, a `false` is returned by the subquery. The NOT makes the `false` a `true`, and that `Vehicle` row from the outer query becomes part of the result set.

ANY

Up until now, the subqueries you've looked at have either returned a single value or, in the case of EXISTS and NOT EXISTS, `true` or `false`. The ANY keyword, however, allows you to perform a comparison against a list of values. The subquery following the ANY keyword can return a single column. If the value being compared to the subquery fulfills the comparison against any value in the list returned by the subquery, that expression evaluates to true. You can use any comparison operator (such as >, <, <>, and =) with the ANY keyword.

In the following sample, we are looking for all vehicles whose date of last service matches any `StartDate` in the `JobTicket` table. Although this query is not terribly useful, it does show how the expression is set up. You can see that you do find out from the data that follows that one of the six vehicles that have job tickets was not finished on the same day as any of the start dates in the `JobTicket` table.

```
SELECT VehicleYear, Make, Model, LastServiceDate
  FROM Vehicle AS v
 WHERE LastServiceDate = ANY (SELECT StartDate
                               FROM JobTicket AS jt);
```

Results:

VehicleYear	Make	Model	LastServiceDate
2000	Chevrolet	S-10	2001-08-13 00:00:00
1998	Ford	Mustang	2001-09-16 00:00:00
2002	Pontiac	Grand Prix	2002-05-21 00:00:00
1968	Chevrolet	Corvette	2002-01-20 00:00:00
2002	Nissan	Altima	2002-01-26 00:00:00

IN

The IN operator provides another way to look for a match against a list of values returned from the subquery. Again, the subquery can only return one column of data. The value in the expression is then evaluated against the column of data returned from the subquery to look for a match. If a match is found, the expression evaluates to `true`, otherwise `false`.

For an example of this, you can search for all customers whose StateOrProvince matches a StateOrProvince in the StateOrProvince table. It should be a given that all the values will match because a foreign key exists between Customer and StateOrProvince. The only row that won't match is the customer without a value in the StateOrProvince column (it contains NULL).

```
SELECT FirstName, LastName, StateOrProvince
  FROM Customer
 WHERE StateOrProvince IN (SELECT StateOrProvince
                             FROM StateOrProvince);
```

Results:

```
FirstName        LastName           StateOrProvince
---------        ---------          -----------
John             Smith              VA
Victoria         Smithe             WV
Bryce            Hatfield           IN
Kylee            Dicken             IN
Alex             Thompson           IN
Davis            Thompson           IN
Harrison         Thompson           IN
```

NOT IN

If you just add a NOT before IN, you completely reverse the results of the previous query using IN. With NOT IN, only the rows that don't match will be returned. This will give you a list of customers who do not have a StateOrProvince value matching one of the values in the StateOrProvince table.

```
SELECT FirstName, LastName, StateOrProvince
  FROM Customer
 WHERE StateOrProvince NOT IN (SELECT StateOrProvince
                                 FROM StateOrProvince);
```

Results:

```
FirstName          LastName          StateOrProvince
---------          ----------        -----------
```

Zero rows are returned. How can this be? There is a customer with NULL for the StateOrProvince column in the Customer table. NULL doesn't match a value in the StateOrProvince table, so why isn't it returned here? That is because NULL neither matches nor fails to match, it is simply unknown. Therefore, if you want to see the customers with an unknown StateOrProvince value, you have to explicitly check for NULL in the WHERE clause.

```
SELECT FirstName, LastName, StateOrProvince
  FROM Customer
 WHERE StateOrProvince NOT IN (SELECT StateOrProvince
                                 FROM StateOrProvince)
    OR StateOrProvince IS NULL;
```

Results:

```
FirstName          LastName          StateOrProvince
---------          ---------         -----------
Jacob              Salter            NULL
```

There's the missing customer. By adding an OR condition, searching specifically for NULL values, to the previous query, you were able to find the last remaining customer.

Using Aggregates

One other condition we'd like to cover here is returning an aggregate from your subquery. So for instance if you want to know which vehicles are newer (have a greater VehicleYear) than the average vehicle in the Vehicle table, you can use the following query.

```
SELECT VehicleYear, Make, Model
  FROM Vehicle
 WHERE VehicleYear > (SELECT AVG(VehicleYear)
                        FROM Vehicle);
```

Results:

VehicleYear	Make	Model
2000	Chevrolet	S-10
1998	Ford	Mustang
2002	Pontiac	Grand Prix
2002	Nissan	Altima
2000	Chrysler	PT Cruiser
2002	Chevrolet	Trail Blazer
2001	Ford	Expedition

First the query finds the average VehicleYear from all the rows in the Vehicle table, which is 1993. It then plugs that value into the outer query to find all the vehicles with a VehicleYear greater than 1993. Seven of the nine vehicles have a greater VehicleYear value.

Subqueries within the HAVING Clause

Very similar to using subqueries with the WHERE clause is using them with the HAVING clause. Remember that the HAVING clause is to the GROUP BY clause what the WHERE clause is to the SELECT clause. Because of this, we will not go into great detail here. We will show you an example, however.

```
SELECT VehicleYear, Count(*)
   FROM Vehicle
GROUP BY VehicleYear
  HAVING VehicleYear > (SELECT AVG(VehicleYear)
                         FROM Vehicle);
```

Results:

VehicleYear	Count
1998	1
2000	2
2001	1
2002	3

The subquery is evaluated to find the average VehicleYear value is 1993. That value is then plugged into the HAVING clause expression, and all VehicleYear groups with a value greater than 1993 are returned in the result set.

Subqueries within the SELECT Clause

Subqueries used in the SELECT clause look similar to the ones you just saw. Subqueries in the SELECT clause can only return a single value, however. This is because the result of the subquery becomes a value in the result set and not just a value or set of values that are plugged into an expression to be evaluated as is the case with the subqueries in the WHERE clause.

We'll examine both a correlated and noncorrelated subquery in the examples that follow. First, here is the noncorrelated subquery.

```
SELECT VehicleYear, Make, Model, (SELECT AVG(VehicleYear)
                                  FROM Vehicle) AS Average
   FROM Vehicle;
```

Results:

VehicleYear	Make	Model	Average
2000	Chevrolet	S-10	1993
1998	Ford	Mustang	1993
2002	Pontiac	Grand Prix	1993
1968	Chevrolet	Corvette	1993
2002	Nissan	Altima	1993
2000	Chrysler	PT Cruiser	1993
2002	Chevrolet	Trail Blazer	1993
2001	Ford	Expedition	1993
1972	AMC	Gremlin	1993

Notice that the noncorrelated subquery is evaluated once for the entire query and that result is plugged into the Average column for each row in the result set.

A correlated subquery, as you know, will be evaluated once for every row in the result set and has the potential to return a different value for each row in that result.

```
SELECT VehicleYear, Make, Model, (SELECT MAX(EndDate)
                                  FROM JobTicket AS jt
                                  WHERE jt.VehicleID =
                                      v.VehicleID) AS EndDate
    FROM Vehicle AS v;
```

Results:

VehicleYear	Make	Model	EndDate
2000	Chevrolet	S-10	2001-08-13 00:00:00
1998	Ford	Mustang	2001-09-16 00:00:00
2002	Pontiac	Grand Prix	2002-05-21 00:00:00
1968	Chevrolet	Corvette	2002-01-20 00:00:00
2002	Nissan	Altima	2002-01-26 00:00:00
2000	Chrysler	PT Cruiser	NULL
2002	Chevrolet	Trail Blazer	NULL
2001	Ford	Expedition	NULL
1972	AMC	Gremlin	2002-02-17 00:00:00

In this case, the subquery is joined to the outer query on VehicleID, thus making it a correlated subquery. This forces the query to be evaluated once for every row in the result set. Therefore, as you can see, each vehicle in the previous list has its very own maximum EndDate from the JobTicket table. This represents the last day the vehicle was worked on.

Subqueries within Subqueries

You've seen a query within a query, but it's also possible to place a subquery within a subquery. This is called *nesting*. The outermost query is the first level, and each level of query below that is a nested level. You can go several levels deep with nested queries. The breaking point is determined by how complex the query is and how powerful a system you are using for the DBMS. (We have never had a problem nesting as far as we want. We're fairly certain you won't either.)

Why would you want to nest a query within a subquery? Good question; glad you asked. Well, every query you write has the potential to be used as a subquery to another query and so on. The best way to write complex queries is to break it apart into smaller chunks. First you make each chunk work. Then you can attempt to combine the queries until you get the results you want.

For example, to find a list of vehicles that have a combined part cost on the job ticket greater than $40, first you find the combined part cost for each job ticket.

```
SELECT JobTicketID, SUM(p.cost * pu.Quantity)
   FROM PartUsed AS pu,
         Part AS p
   WHERE pu.PartID = p.PartID
GROUP BY JobTicketID;
```

Results:

```
JobTicketID
-------      ---------
1            35.9500
2            82.9300
3            59.9500
4            34.9500
5            46.9400
6              .0000
7            56.9300
```

It looks like three of the job tickets have a combined part cost of greater than $40. Next you need to find which vehicles are on those tickets.

```
SELECT JobTicketID, VehicleID
  FROM JobTicket As jt
 WHERE 40 < (SELECT SUM(p.cost * pu.Quantity)
               FROM PartUsed pu,
                    Part p
              WHERE pu.PartID = p.PartID
                AND pu.JobTicketID = jt.JobTicketID);
```

Results:

```
JobTicketID     VehicleID
------          -----
2               4
3               2
5               3
7               9
```

Just as predicted, four of the job tickets appear with their associated vehicle. All you had to do was take the first query and add it to the WHERE clause of the new query. Notice the GROUP BY had to be removed as well as the JobTicketID column because subqueries can only return a single result or column of results. Because of the manner in which you are referencing this subquery, you have to return the sum by JobTicketID, so you have to make this a correlated subquery by joining to the outer query's JobTicketID.

Now then, lastly, you need to gather the pertinent information about the vehicles revealed in the previous query. To do this, you can modify the new query to return just the list of vehicle IDs because the vehicle information is your ultimate goal.

```
SELECT VehicleYear, Make, Model
  FROM Vehicle
 WHERE VehicleID IN (SELECT VehicleID
                       FROM JobTicket AS jt
                      WHERE 40 < (SELECT SUM(p.cost * pu.Quantity)
                                    FROM PartUsed pu,
                                         Part p
                                   WHERE pu.PartID = p.PartID
                                     AND pu.JobTicketID =
                                   jt.JobTicketID));
```

Results:

```
VehicleYear     Make            Model
--------        -------         ---------
1998            Ford            Mustang
2002            Pontiac         Grand Prix
1968            Chevrolet       Corvette
1972            AMC             Gremlin
```

By breaking the query down into logical chunks, you can not only test your results along the way but also make the task of creating this complex query a lot less daunting. These same results can be achieved without nesting queries three levels deep, but it makes for a nice example of how to nest a subquery within a subquery.

Creating Unions

The UNION operator allows you to combine two or more similar SELECT statements. It takes the results of each query, eliminates the duplicates, and returns the list as a single result set. The queries have to have the same number of columns. The data types of those columns have to be either the same type, implicitly convertible, or be explicitly converted to a compatible type. Finally, the columns must be in the same order because the data will be combined in the order defined in the first query. The columns themselves do not need to be the same column or even come from the same set of tables.

The following query is an example of a simple UNION to bring together two result sets. In this case, the columns are the same, but remember that they do not need to be the same columns. The first result set brings back all the Ford vehicles, and the second result set brings back all the Chevrolet vehicles. The UNION combines the two queries, eliminates the duplicates (there are none here), and returns the list as a single result set.

```
SELECT VehicleYear, Make, Model
  FROM Vehicle
 WHERE Make = 'Ford'
UNION
SELECT VehicleYear, Make, Model
  FROM Vehicle
 WHERE Make = 'Chevrolet';
```

Results:

VehicleYear	Make	Model
1968	Chevrolet	Corvette
1998	Ford	Mustang
2000	Chevrolet	S-10
2001	Ford	Expedition
2002	Chevrolet	Trail Blazer

We're going to make it a bit more elaborate so you can see more interesting results. This will also find all vehicles with a VehicleYear less than 1995 in both queries.

```
SELECT VehicleYear, Make, Model
  FROM Vehicle
 WHERE Make = 'Ford'
    OR VehicleYear < 1995
UNION
SELECT VehicleYear, Make, Model
  FROM Vehicle
 WHERE Make = 'Chevrolet'
     OR VehicleYear < 1995
ORDER BY VehicleYear;
```

Results:

VehicleYear	Make	Model
1968	Chevrolet	Corvette
1972	AMC	Gremlin
1998	Ford	Mustang
2000	Chevrolet	S-10
2001	Ford	Expedition
2002	Chevrolet	Trail Blazer

Notice that we now have an extra row. The AMC Gremlin snuck into the list because of the OR we added to each query. We really only needed to add it to one or the other because the UNION eliminated the duplicate row. The Corvette would have been listed twice as well because it matched the newly added condition, too.

Also notice that we added an ORDER BY clause. You can only have an ORDER BY clause on the final query. It will affect the entire result set, however. If you were to have an ORDER BY clause for each query, it could get very confusing.

If you want to see all the duplicate rows generated by combining multiple queries, you must use the ALL keyword. Take the previous query, which would have had two rows for the Gremlin and the Corvette had the UNION not filtered out the duplicates. Let's see it again here with the ALL keyword included.

```
SELECT VehicleYear, Make, Model
   FROM Vehicle
 WHERE Make = 'Ford'
    OR VehicleYear < 1995
UNION ALL
SELECT VehicleYear, Make, Model
   FROM Vehicle
 WHERE Make = 'Chevrolet'
      OR VehicleYear < 1995
ORDER BY VehicleYear;
```

Results:

```
VehicleYear     Make          Model
--------        ----------    ---------
1968            Chevrolet     Corvette
1968            Chevrolet     Corvette
1972            AMC           Gremlin
1972            AMC           Gremlin
1998            Ford          Mustang
2000            Chevrolet     S-10
2001            Ford          Expedition
2002            Chevrolet     Trail Blazer
```

Now we have the entire result set from both queries. You might be wondering why the Corvette doesn't show up three times in the list because it is a Chevrolet and is less than a 1995, which is a condition in both the first and second queries. The answer is the Corvette matched the `Make` condition in the second query, so the OR condition was never evaluated. It already passed the first condition and therefore made it into the result set for the second query. It passed the `VehicleYear` condition of the first query and thus the two occurrences in the final result set.

What's Next?

This afternoon, you learned about several functions and how they can simplify your life. You also discovered the GROUP BY and HAVING clauses, which help you logically categorize your results and remove the groups you don't need. Finally, you explored queries within queries, called subqueries, and the many possibilities they open up for you. Now that you've studied so much about using SQL to get information out of the database, the next chapter will show you how to put information into the database.

Building a Home for Your Data

- ➤ How to Design a Normalized Database
- ➤ How to Create and Modify Your Database
- ➤ About Data Types You'll Use in Your Database
- ➤ How to Create and Modify Tables
- ➤ How to Insert, Update, and Delete Data

So now you know how to get data out of your database. But how did it get in there in the first place? Not surprisingly, this is your job too. It's actually not very difficult for you to put data into a database. The tricky part is getting it in there in such a way that it's easy for you to get it back out. Throw the data in haphazardly and you'll have a tough time maintaining it or even finding it again. Kind of like when you throw papers and notes into various piles on your desk. Good luck trying to find that one certain memo from last month. Organize and sort them out later? Forget about it! Don't let your first SQL database look like your desk. Read through this chapter and by the end of the evening you'll be ready to design and populate a clean, logical database.

Using Normalization

Making your database easier to manage, maintain, and query from involves a fair amount of planning on your part. We know—you hate the planning part. "Just get me to the fun stuff," you say! Sure, you can skip over this part of the chapter to learn how to create your database and insert your data, but we think you'll be sorry later. As with most things in life, a little planning up front will pay off in the long run. In the world of relational databases, this planning is known as *normalization.*

For this discussion about normalization, we'll show you how to design that sample database that you worked with in the prior chapters. In the Friday Evening session, we gave you a brief overview of the database. Now we'll take you back to square one and show you the steps you have to go though to arrive at this design.

The Slick Shop needs a database that will help keep track of customers who have automotive work done, what that work is, and how much it costs them. The first steps, long before you can even think about designing the database, involve project planning. Project planning includes important steps such as gathering requirements, documenting a statement of work, budgeting, documenting function specifications, estimations, and documenting the project plan.

NOTE Although these are all very important steps that should not be ignored, they are the subjects of an entire book in themselves. For this book, we will assume that you have already completed these steps and are ready to design the database.

After meeting with the users and project sponsors, you grab a copy of one of their invoices (see Figure 4.1).

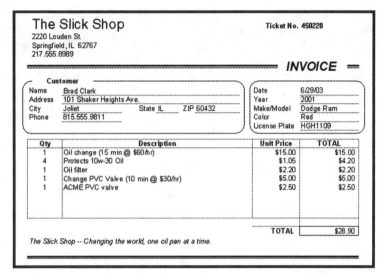

Figure 4.1

The Slick Shop invoice. This is the information that the database will need to store.

Based on this invoice, you draw up a list of the basic pieces of information that need to be stored.

➤ Customer's name

➤ Customer's address

➤ Customer's vehicle information

➤ Invoice (or job ticket) number

➤ The date of the job

➤ The cost of the labor

➤ What services were performed

➤ How long was spent on each service

➤ What parts were used

➤ The cost of the parts

➤ The total cost of the job

Next you can take your first cut at creating a table for this data (see Table 4.1).

TABLE 4.1 FIRST DESIGN	
Column Name	**Sample Data**
CustName	Brad Clark
CustAddress	101 Shaker Heights Ave. Joliet, IL 60432
CustPhone	8155559811
Vehicle	2001 Dodge Ram, Red, HGH1109
JobTicket	450228
StartDate	06/29/03
EndDate	06/29/03
LaborCost	$60.00/hr, $30.00/hr
TimeSpent	0.25 hours, 0.16 hours
Services	Oil change, Change PVC value
PartUsed	4 quarts Protects 10w-30 oil, Oil filter, ACME PVC valve
PartsCost	$4.20, $2.20, $2.50
TotalCost	$28.90

Without having to try too hard, you probably can spot many problems with this table design. First of all, with this design, you're going to have trouble searching for customers by last name or customers who live in a certain state. The first and last name fields should be separated, as should the different parts of the address and vehicle information. The other big problem is keeping the services, parts used, and costs in long lists. Storing them this way will make it very difficult to get them back out of the database. What are you going to do, search the Services, PartUsed, and PartsCosts columns for the positions of the commas? Then what, try to match them together based on their order? Can you already see a problem? The oil change service uses two parts, oil and an oil filter. Clearly, you need to separate this information. Keeping these decisions in mind, you can take another shot at the table design, shown in Table 4.2.

That's a little better. It solves the set of concerns raised earlier. But you can do better. Now you'll begin the formal process of normalization. This process uses a series of steps known as Normal Forms. They are appropriately named First, Second, and Third Normal Form.

First Normal Form

The rules of First Normal Form are as follows:

➤ Eliminate repeating groups of data in individual tables.

➤ Create a separate table for each set of related data.

➤ Identify each set of related data with a primary key.

The first rule has you looking for groups of repeating data. A quick look at the table so far reveals several data items that are repeated. The services, labor costs, time spent, parts, and part costs are each repeated three times. The obvious problem here is, what happens if a car needs more than three services or more than three parts replaced? You can solve this problem by putting each service, time, part, and cost in its own row. This way, every time a new service or part is needed, you can just add a new row. This will allow for any number of services or parts to be used on the same car.

Based on the second rule, look at the data to see if it can be broken into distinct sets of related information. It looks like there are three basic types of data: customer information, vehicle information, and details about the job. So separate these into different tables, calling the new tables Customer, Vehicle, and Job. But once you separate them, how will you know what work was performed for which customer and on which vehicle? To solve this problem, you need to take a look at the third rule.

Column Name	Sample Data	Column Name	Sample Data
	TABLE 4.2 SECOND DESIGN		
FirstName	Brad	Service2	Change PVC value
LastName	Clark	Service3	
Address	101 Shaker Heights Ave.	LaborCost1	$60.00 per hour
City	Joliet	LaborCost2	$30.00 per hour
StateOrProvince	IL	LaborCost3	
PostalCode	60432	TimeSpent1	0.25 hours
PhoneNumber	8155559811	TimeSpent2	0.16 hours
Year	2001	TimeSpent3	
Make	Dodge	Part1	4 quarts Protects 10w-30 oil
Model	Ram		
Color	Red	Part2	Oil filter
LicensePlate#	HGH1109	Part3	ACME PVC valve
JobTicket	450228	Part1Cost	$4.20
StartDate	06/29/03	Part2Cost	$2.20
EndDate	06/29/03	Part3Cost	$2.50
Service1	Oil change	TotalCost	$28.90

The third rule is suggesting that you take each one of these tables and create a primary key for them. Remember in the Friday Evening session you learned that a primary key was a way to uniquely identify each row in your table. You'll start with the `Customer` table. Now you could make the customer's first and last name the primary key. However, sooner or later you'll end up with two customers named John Smith. How about including the address, city, state, and ZIP code as part of the primary key? Well, it's true that this would make it unique, but there are a couple of problems with this. First, when John Smith moves, the Slick Shop will want to update his address, which means they'll be updating the primary key. Remember when we talked about primary keys, we told you that you should choose columns that will never have to be changed. Also, although it's okay for you to have six columns in the primary key if you need to, it will be cumbersome when you start to relate this table to others.

For these reasons, what you'll do is create a unique identifying number for each customer. You'll simply assign a sequential number to each customer. This will be your primary key on the `Customer` table. You'll do the same for the `Vehicle` table. The Job table already has a natural candidate for the primary key. The Slick Shop is already in the practice of assigning a unique number to each job ticket. You'll just use this as your primary key.

TIP Just because you create a column in a table does not mean that you have to reveal it to the customers or even your users. The column can be used just to make your life as a SQL programmer easier. Your new surrogate key, the customer number, will just be used to relate tables together. You will not print the number on the customer's invoice or even display it to the users.

◄ ◄

A **surrogate key** is data that by itself has no meaning, like a name or an address does. This data uniquely identifies each row in a table. A sequentially increasing number is an example of a surrogate key. A car's VIN, although unique, is not a surrogate key because it means something. The numbers and letters of a VIN tell about the year, manufacturer, and make of the car.

◄ ◄

Now you're ready to return to the problem of how to relate the jobs to the correct customers and vehicles. To solve this, you'll create a foreign key column in the Job table to hold the customer number. Every row in the Job table will have a customer number. Remember in the Friday Evening session when we told you about one-to-many relationships? Well, this is one of them. On the "one" side is Customer—there can only be one row for each customer. On the "many" side is Job—each customer can have many jobs related to him. Likewise, you'll create another foreign key column in the Job table to hold the vehicle number. This is another one-to-many relationship. Over time, a vehicle can have many jobs performed on it.

Now that you've removed the repeating data, separated it into three tables, related the tables together, and assigned primary keys, it's time to see what they look like so far. Figures 4.2, 4.3, and 4.4 show the Customer, Vehicle, and Job tables, respectively.

Figure 4.2

This is the Customer table separated from the service data. The first column is now the primary key.

CustomerID	FirstName	LastName	Address	City	StateOrProvince	PostalCode	PhoneNumber
243	Brad	Clark	101 Shaker Hei...	Joliet	IL	60432	8155559811

Figure 4.3

This is the Vehicle table. Note that a LastServiceDate column has been added.

VehicleID	CustomerID	VehicleYear	Make	Model	Color	LicensePlate#	LastServiceDate
11	243	2001	Dodge	Ram	Red	HGH1109	6/29/2003

Figure 4.4

This is the Job table. The service, time, parts, and cost information are stored in this table.

JobTicketID	VehicleID	CustomerID	Service	HoursSpent	RatePerHour	Part
450228	11	243	Oil Change	.25	60.00	4 Quart
450228	11	243		.00	.00	Oil Fi
450228	11	243	Change PVC valve	.16	30.00	ACME P

ur	Part	PartCost	StartDate	EndDate
	4 Quarts Protects 10w-30	1.05	06-29-03	06-29-03
	Oil Filter	2.20	06-29-03	06-29-03
	ACME PVC valve	2.50	06-29-03	06-29-03

NOTE You might have noticed that the total cost has been left out. An examination of the data shows that you can compute the total cost in a query by looking at the cost of parts, quantity of parts used, cost of labor, and labor hours. You can make this calculation and print the total when an invoice is requested.

Second Normal Form

The rules of Second Normal Form are as follows:

➤ Remove subsets of data that apply to multiple rows of a table and place them in separate rows.

➤ Create relationships between these new tables and their predecessors through the use of foreign keys.

The first rule is again having you seek out and eliminate duplicate data. Only this time instead of looking for data that is repeated among similar columns, you're looking for identical data that is repeated in separate rows. Looking at the Job table, you can see that the job ticket number and job dates are repeated. So what's wrong with that? Well, what happens if, after your users enter all this data, they find out they entered one of the dates wrong? They will have to find and change each row in the table that has the wrong date and fix it. If you took this information and put it in its own table, then you would only have to store each job ticket number and date one time. That would make data entry and maintenance a lot easier.

What you should do is split the Job table in two. Make a table called JobTicket to hold the common information about a job, such as the ticket number, start date, and end date. Then make another table called JobTicketDetail. This one will store an individual row for each different labor item that makes up the job, such as changing the oil, the oil filter, and PVC valve. The relationship between tables such as these is often called a header-detail relationship.

The second rule is similar to one of the rules applied during First Normal Form. It wants you to create a relationship between the new tables that you just split out. You need to make sure that each row in the JobTicketDetail table stays related to the correct row in the JobTicket table. This will keep the header and details together. The way that you'll keep them related is to add the job ticket number as a column in the JobTicketDetail table. This column now becomes a foreign key.

As you're progressing along with your normalization, it is important that from time to time you go back and revisit the Normal Forms that you already completed to make sure that the tables still comply. For example, the new JobTicketDetail table does not yet have a primary key, as First Normal Form requires. You can just create another surrogate key and start assigning sequential numbers to each row. However, because you already have the job ticket number as a column, maybe you should make use of it. The job ticket number alone cannot be the primary key because there will be several detail rows for the same ticket. So what you should do is add a line item number column. This will be a number that starts at 1 for each job ticket and increases with each new detail row that is added. This column cannot be the primary key on its own either because the values will not be unique. However, the combination of the job ticket number and the line item number will uniquely identify exactly one row in this table.

Now it's time to step back and take a look at these tables so far. The Customer table remains the same as that shown in Figure 4.2, and Vehicle remains the same as in Figure 4.3. The JobTicket table is shown in Figure 4.5 and JobTicketDetail in Figure 4.6.

Third Normal Form

The rule of Third Normal Form is as follows:

➤ Remove columns that are not dependent on the primary key.

Third Normal Form can be a little trickier than First and Second. What this rule means is that you should look at each column in each table and ask yourself if it directly relates to the primary key. Apply this question to the Customer table first. Remember, the primary key on this table, CustomerID, identifies a unique individual. So do the FirstName and LastName columns directly relate to the CustomerID? Yes, that is the

Figure 4.5

This is the JobTicket table. It contains only the data that applies to the job ticket as a whole.

JobTicketID	VehicleID	CustomerID	StartDate	EndDate
450228	11	243	06/29/2003	06/29/2003

Figure 4.6

This is the JobTicketDetail table. It has one row for each job that is performed on a car or for each part that is used.

JobTicketID	LineItemNumber	Service	HoursSpent	RatePerHour	Part	PartCost
450228	1	Oil Change	.25	60.00	4 Quarts Protec...	1.05
450228	2		.00	.00	Oil Filter	2.20
450228	3	Change PVC ...	.16	30.00	ACME PVC valve	2.50

name of that individual. What about the `Address`, `City`, `StateOr-Province`, and `PostalCode`? Yes, they do too. They tell the one and only place that this person lives.

Now you can skip ahead and apply the question to the `JobTicketDetail` table. When you do this you can see that the `HoursSpent` column directly relates to the line item on a job ticket. It tells how long that line item took. However, the `Service` and `Part` columns do not. This is not data that is unique to just one line item of just one job ticket. The Slick Shop will perform oil changes for many customers, each on a different job ticket. They will also use oil filters and PVC valves on many job tickets.

What you'll do then is very similar to what you've done before. You'll remove the service tasks and parts from `JobTicketDetail` and put them into separate tables. You'll create primary keys for the new tables. Then you'll relate the `JobTicketDetail` to them by creating foreign keys.

Separating the services and parts gives you a couple of nice advantages. If the name of a part ever changes, it will only have to be updated in one place. It also allows the users to keep a master list of available services and parts. Later when a customer drives in for some work, the users can simply choose the services and part from lists.

Take a look at the change to the `JobTicketDetail` table in Figure 4.7 and the two new tables, `Service` in Figure 4.8 and `Part` in Figure 4.9. The `Customer`, `Vehicle`, and `JobTicket` tables have not changed.

Figure 4.7

This is the `JobTicketDetail` table. Two foreign keys, `PartID` and `ServiceID`, have been added, and `Quantity` is its own column.

JobTicketID	LineItemNumber	ServiceID	PartID	Quantity	DateComplete	HoursSpent
450228	1	1	1	4	06/29/2003	.25
450228	2	1	8	1	06/29/2003	.25
450228	3	4	16	1	06/29/2003	.16

ServiceID	Description	RatePerHour
1	Oil Change	60.00
2	Replace Wiperblades	10.00
3	Replace Air Filter	10.00
4	Change PVC Valve	30.00
5	Change and Flush Cooling System	60.00
6	Change and Flush Differential	60.00

Figure 4.8

The Service table.

PartID	Description	Cost
1	Protects 10w-30 Oil	1.05
2	Protects 10w-40 Oil	1.10
3	Black Gold 10w-30 Oil	7.99
4	Black Gold 10w-40 Oil	7.99
5	Motion Synthetic Oil 10w-30	13.99
6	Motion Synthetic Oil 10w-40	13.99
7	Texas Tea Economy Oil Filter	3.99
8	Oil Filter	2.20
9	ACME Air Filter	8.99
10	ACME Wiper Blades	9.99
11	ACME Brake Fluid	2.62
12	ACME Transmission Fluid	3.15
13	ACME Coolant	7.49
14	ACME Windshield Fluid	1.25
15	ACME Differential Fluid	5.25
16	ACME PVC Valve	2.50

Figure 4.9

The Part table.

In most cases a database that is in Third Normal Form will suffice. However, Fourth and Fifth Normal Forms have been defined as well. These are more complex and are outside the scope of this book.

A Couple of Final Changes

There is one additional change that you should make to the database. As you look back at the JobTicketDetail table in Figure 4.7, you will see that there is some duplicate data that could be refined a little more. Notice how the first two line items are actually part of the same service task—the oil change. It took two rows because there were two parts involved, the oil and the oil filter. In fact, there may be some service tasks that take several parts. This means that the ServiceID, HoursSpent, and DateComplete will be repeated several times within the same service task. What you'll do then is introduce a new table that will go between JobTicketDetail and Part. It will be dedicated to storing the parts that are used on a given detail row. After you remove the part information from JobTicketDetail, this table can focus on the service task and will only need to store one row per task. Because the new table will be related to both JobTicketDetail and Part, it will need to include the primary key columns from both. You will also move the Quantity column to this table because it directly relates to parts. Call the new table PartUsed.

Now for a peek at what the tables look like. The modified JobTicketDetail is shown in Figure 4.10 and the new PartUsed table in Figure 4.11. The Part table has not changed but is displayed in Figure 4.12 to show its relation to PartUsed. The Customer, Vehicle, JobTicket, Part, and Service tables remain unchanged as well.

Figure 4.10

The JobTicketDetail table is the same except that PartID and Quantity have been removed.

JobTicketID	LineItemNumber	ServiceID	DateComplete	HoursSpent
450228	1	1	06/29/2003	.25
450228	2	4	06/29/2003	.16

Figure 4.11

This is the new
PartUsed table. It
links a single part
to a single job
ticket line item.

JobTicketID	LineItemNumber	PartID	Quantity
450228	1	1	4
450228	1	8	1
450228	2	16	1

PartID	Description	Cost
1	Protects 10w-30 Oil	1.05
2	Protects 10w-40 Oil	1.10
3	Black Gold 10w-30 Oil	7.99
4	Black Gold 10w-40 Oil	7.99
5	Motion Synthetic Oil 10w-30	13.99
6	Motion Synthetic Oil 10w-40	13.99
7	Texas Tea Economy Oil Filter	3.99
8	Oil Filter	2.20
9	ACME Air Filter	8.99
10	ACME Wiper Blades	9.99
11	ACME Brake Fluid	2.62
12	ACME Transmission Fluid	3.15
13	ACME Coolant	7.49
14	ACME Windshield Fluid	1.25
15	ACME Differential Fluid	5.25
16	ACME PVC Valve	2.50

Figure 4.12

The Part table has
not changed but is
displayed here to
show its relation to
PartUsed.

This gives you some nice separation between the services that are being performed and the parts that are being used.

You may be thinking that the DateComplete column in the JobTicketDetail table looks like duplicate data. That's not necessarily so. This column was designed because the Slick Shop wanted to keep track of completion dates for individual line items. They often have large repair jobs that take two or more days to complete.

Finally, you'll add a lookup table called StateOrProvince. This is a simple table that has just two columns, one for the two-character state or province abbreviation and one for the full name. A foreign key is also added to the StateOrProvince column in the Customer table that references the new table. The main purpose of having a lookup table like this is for user convenience. This allows you to display the full state or province name to users in pick lists. The table can also be used in a join with Customer, to print the full name and address on reports or invoices.

Advanced Design

This sample database is straightforward and fairly simple, yet involved enough for you to practice some meaningful SQL. You could carry the design of the database much farther, and indeed, for a real-life business you would need to do so. We'll finish this section by giving you a couple of quick ideas on how the design could be improved.

One of the problems with the current design will surface when a user tries to print an invoice for work that was done a year or two ago. It is likely that the price of the parts and labor will increase over time. The SQL SELECT command will join the tables together and use whatever amount it finds in the RatePerHour and part Cost columns. So what will happen is that the invoice will show the correct work that was done, but it will be shown at today's prices. This will not be an accurate reflection of the history of that invoice.

A common way of solving this problem is to redesign the Service and Part tables to include historical prices. In the Part table, for example, you could add a column called EffectiveDate, the date on which the price for the given part goes into effect. Then you could change the primary key to be both PartID and EffectiveDate. This would allow you to, over time, save several different prices for each part. You could even enter price changes that will take effect in the future. If you think about it for a minute, this will really mess up the SQL SELECT command that figures out the total cost of the job. No longer can you simply use a PartID to join to the `Part` table. Doing this will give you the price history for that part, which may be dozens of rows. The SELECT command will have to be rewritten to compare today's date to the `EffectiveDate`.

CAUTION

◆ ◆
Changing the primary key of table after your design is complete and SQL has been written can cause you to have to make many other changes as well. If the primary key was used as a foreign key in any other table, that will have to be changed as well. Any INSERT or UPDATE commands that modify the table will have to be changed. Also most if not all SELECT commands that involve the table will have to be changed.
◆ ◆

Now for one more example of an improvement that could be made to the design. Let's say the database has been in use for a couple of years now at all 1,800 Slick Shops nationwide, each with its own database. Now the corporate headquarters would like you to combine all of the data nightly and create some SQL queries that will give them a better idea of how the business is doing nationally. They will not create new data or change it but will only run queries. This means that you have to create a separate corporate database just for them. Your first inclination might be to copy the same design used by the Slick Shop and load it nightly from each of the 1,800 databases. However, you'll quickly discover some reasons why this might not be a good choice. One worry is that there might be so much data in this corporate database that queries will run too slowly. A bigger problem is that each Slick Shop gets to set their own prices for their labor and parts. This means that the corporate database cannot simply keep labor and part costs in the Service and Part tables as they are designed today.

A solution is to denormalize the corporate database. Denormalize? After you've spent all this time learning how to normalize, we're saying to turn around and undo it? Well, yes, but there's a very good reason. Many of the reasons for normalizing a database center on making it easier to maintain the data. Your corporate users are not going to be allowed to change the data, only run SELECT commands. The way to do this is to revert the database back to one that is closer to the First Normal Form design. Look back at Figure 4.4. All of the data about the job is back in one table, including the prices. The actual price that each Slick Shop charged will be in this table, along with exactly which service and parts were used. Because no data is modified on this table, it can be heavily indexed for maximum query performance.

NOTE We'll be covering indexes in the Sunday Morning session.

Your head is probably aching after that discussion! But we hope you have an appreciation for how important database design can be. The good news is that once you've done this a few times, you'll start to get good at it. Soon you won't have to take your tables through so many steps to arrive at your final design. The important points to remember about normalization are highlighted here:

➤ Separate distinct data items into different tables.

➤ Eliminate repeating and duplicate data by creating separate tables.

➤ Make sure all tables have primary keys.

➤ Relate tables together with foreign keys.

Creating Databases

Okay, now that you have planned out all of your tables, it's time to build them. But first you'll need a place for these tables to live. All of your tables will exist within a database. A single database can house many tables. Some DBMSs allow you to store up to 255 tables inside your database. Many of them, especially the enterprise versions, still have limits, but they are very high. SQL Server, for example, allow you to create millions of tables in a single database. A table, however, can only exist in one database at a time. If you need the same table in two databases, you will have to maintain two separate copies of the table.

TIP

■ ■

An alternative to creating a second copy of the same table is to use a view. The first data-base contains the table with the data. Meanwhile, the second database contains a view that points to the table in the first database. See "Creating and Using Views" in the Sunday Afternoon session for more on views.

■ ■

Not only does the database contain the tables that hold your data, but it also holds the information about the tables themselves—information such as the names and data types for each column in the table, default values, and whether or not the column allows NULL values. The database stores this information in catalog or system tables. These are special tables that the DBMS creates and maintains on its own.

CAUTION

◆ ◆

Normally, you should just leave the system and catalog tables alone. Modifying these tables directly is risky business and could cause your data to become corrupted or lost.

◆ ◆

Other special items or objects that are stored in your database include stored procedures, triggers, views, key definitions, indexes, and database users. Your DBMS probably supports several other unique features, many of which are stored in the system tables within your database.

The method and command used to create your database will vary depending on the DBMS you are using. The commands are different because each DBMS has options allowing you to specify the database size and file location. There are also a variety of options specific to each DBMS. In addition to written commands, some DBMSs also include a graphical interface to make creating your database even easier. The SQL Server graphical window for creating a database is shown in Figure 4.13.

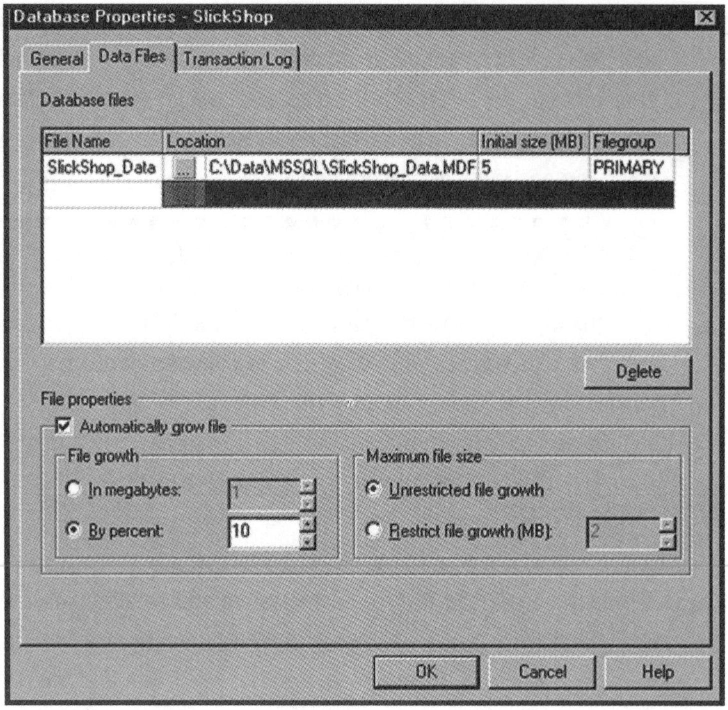

Figure 4.13

Not only does this SQL Server create a database dialog that allows you to specify the name and size of the database file, but it also has options to automatically increase the size as needed.

In general, the command to create your database will look like this:

```
CREATE DATABASE dbname [options];
```

The options may let you tell the DBMS such information as where the database files should be located, the size of the files, how much memory to use, the size and location of log files, language choice, and sort order. Your DBMS has many other options that are worth taking some time to review. Most times, however, the default options have been carefully set for most small to medium-sized databases. Large or mission-critical databases deserve careful review of all of the available options.

Data Types

Okay, there's just one more topic that you need to understand before jumping in and creating your first table. You're going to need to know your available data types. Yes, it's back to the planning thing again! But just like before, a little planning can pay off big. This time the benefits will come in the form of saving disk space and increasing performance.

Every column in every table must be assigned a data type. This allows you to earmark a column for a certain kind of data, such as text, numbers, or dates. As you are selecting data types for each column, you will also be determining their size. The choices you make for the data type and size are very important. Making the wrong choice might cause problems, such as users not being able to enter data, large amounts of disk space going to waste, or even reduced performance.

We'll give you a couple of examples now to illustrate the importance of data type choices and a couple examples later in this section. For the first example, consider the `Customer` table, which stores names and addresses. When you come to the column that will store the ZIP codes, you decide to make it an integer column. After all, ZIP codes are either five- or nine-digit numbers, right? After just a few weeks, however, the Slick Shop gets a customer who is passing through from Vancouver. His postal code is V6Z 1P5. Now the database refuses to allow his postal code because it is not a number.

As a second example, remember that in the `Customer` table you have separate columns for the customers' first and last names. You make them character columns each of size 10. Fate strikes again when a new customer named Jackqueline Hollingsworth shows up. Neither her first or last name will fully fit into the defined columns. The Slick Shop manager is embarrassed to have to hand her an invoice that says Jackquelin Hollingswo.

You get the idea. The data types and sizes that you choose might come back to haunt you, so choose wisely. The best way to do this is to know all of your available choices. Let's take a look at them now.

Just as the CREATE DATABASE command varies from one DBMS to the next, so do the data types. Later when we show you how to create tables, we will be using standard SQL syntax. For the data types, however, you'll have to learn the types that are available in your particular DBMS.

Regardless of the DBMS you are using, there are some very basic categories of data types that they all share. They are as follows:

➤ Strings

➤ Numbers

➤ Dates and times

➤ Booleans

➤ Binary data

String data types include any character, number, or symbol that can be typed in with a keyboard. String data types can be either fixed in length or variable. Numeric data types include whole, decimal, positive, and negative numbers. Date and time are special data types that are intelligent enough to know how clocks and calendars work. For example, a date data type will not let you store the date February 29, 2003, because it is not a leap year. Boolean data types allow for the storage of yes/no, on/off, or 1/0 data. Finally, binary data types can store data such as graphics or encrypted files.

The first example involving the ZIP codes pointed out that the choice of a numeric data type was not appropriate. The second example about the first and last name fields demonstrated that while the data type may have been correct, the size was not. For every single column that you create, you will have to make two decisions, type and size.

String Data Types

The string or character data types allow you to define the maximum number of characters that they will hold.

```
CHAR(25)
```

This notation is specifying that a column can hold no more than 25 characters. This would have probably been a better choice for the first and last name columns. This notation is also saying that the column is going to be fixed width. If you store the last name Smith in this column, it will still occupy 25 bytes in the database. The last 20 bytes will be wasted space.

Let's say that you change the first and last name fields to a fixed length of 25 characters. After a couple of years, your database now has 100,000 customers saved. The average length of the first names is six, and the average length of the last names is eight. These two fields alone take up 5,000,000 bytes, of which 3,600,000 contain absolutely nothing. These fields would be good candidates for variable length character types.

VARCHAR(25)

The VARCHAR data type will only use as much space as it needs. The last name Smith will only take five bytes. However, if you change the name from Smith to Smithsonian, it will expand to now use 11 bytes. Now, in the example, the first and last name column will only occupy a little more than 1,400,000 bytes.

NOTE To be totally accurate, it would take a little more than 1,400,000 bytes. This is due to the overhead storage required by the VARCHAR data type. More about this later.

Your DBMS will have a limit on how big you can define CHAR and VARCHAR fields. This is usually anywhere from 2,000 to 8,000 characters. Most DBMSs have another character data type to store even more.

TEXT, MEMO, LONG VARCHAR

The TEXT, MEMO, or LONG VARCHAR data types can store much more than any CHAR and VARCHAR. Each DBMS has a different maximum, from 64,000 to more than 2 billion characters! This is also a variable sized field but will include more storage overhead than the VARCHAR.

Which String Data Type Should You Choose?

First of all, the text, memo, and LONG VARCHAR data types should be used sparingly. They do contain more overhead than the other data types but often have limitations. These data types probably cannot be indexed, probably cannot be used in joins, and will likely be slower as searching or sorting columns. These data types are most useful for storing miscellaneous information and notes. Very lengthy data that will be viewed and printed but not normally searched on or sorted is a good candidate for these types. In the sample database, you could add a TEXT, MEMO, or LONG VARCHAR column to the `JobTicket` table. It would be a good place to type notes about what was wrong with the car when it came in and what special tasks were performed during the service.

Ordinarily your choice will be between the CHAR and VARCHAR data types. A rule of thumb that we suggest is to always try to use VARCHAR and fall back to CHAR when necessary. As demonstrated earlier, using VARCHAR is a great way to conserve space in your database. So when is the right time to fall back to CHAR? If your string data is going to be either very short or always be the same length. If you create a column for the customers' middle initials and define it as VARCHAR(1), you will actually end up wasting space. The DBMS is going to use one or two bytes of overhead in addition to the middle initial. So storing the letter 'R' will really take two or three bytes. You'd be better off defining it as CHAR(1). This will always use just one byte. Now say you want to create a column for the status of each job. The status values will be WAITING, WORKING, and ALLDONE. Each of these is seven characters long. There is no need to make this a variable length column, because the data does not vary. You'd simply make it CHAR(7).

Numeric Data Types

In similar fashion to the string data types, you will get to choose the size of the numeric data types as well. This is where you will really have to pay attention to your DBMS manual or online help. One vendor's integer may take up four bytes, whereas another's takes only two. Following are some of the most typical numeric types that store whole numbers.

```
INTEGER, INT, SMALLINT, TINYINT, NUMBER(x)
```

These data types will not store any decimal places. They will only store positive and negative numbers. If your vendor's integer data type is 4 bytes, it will store whole numbers anywhere in the range of −2,147,483,648 to 2,147,483,647. However, if your vendor's integer data type is two bytes, it will only store whole numbers from −32,768 to 32,767.

TIP

If you have a column that will never need negative numbers, check to see if your DBMS supports unsigned data types. If so, this would make the range of a 4-byte integer 0 to 4,294,967,295.

NOTE

Some databases now support 8-byte integers, called `bigint` or `int8`. This data type can store numbers as high as 9,223,372,036,854,775,807! That would be useful if your database was going to keep track of the exact amount of the national debt. By the way, that number is called 9 quintillion.

Other data types are available to hold decimal data.

```
FLOAT, REAL, NUMERIC, DECIMAL, NUMBER(x,y), DOUBLE
```

Although you can often use these data types without specifying a size, you will usually want to do so. So that you don't just get the default, you should specify both a size and precision, like

```
DECIMAL(7, 2)
```

The 7 indicates that the total size of the number including digits on the left and right of the decimal point cannot exceed seven. The 2 indicates that there will be no more than two digits on the right of the decimal point.

Floating point data types such as float and real only require you to specify the size. The precision will vary.

Your database may also include data types called money, smallmoney, or currency. These are really the same as a decimal, numeric, or double data type only they are predefined. These types will always have two decimal places and by default will be displayed with a leading currency symbol.

Which Numeric Data Type Should You Choose?

The strategy for choosing your numeric data type should be the same as the strings. Choose one that is big enough to hold your data now and in the foreseeable future, but don't choose them so big that you waste a lot of space. When defining the Cost column in the Part table, you could have made it decimal(12, 2). This would correctly allow the part cost to use two decimal places; however, it would also allow parts to be priced at well over a billion dollars each! A better choice would be decimal(6, 2). This would allow for a total of six digits including the decimals, so part prices could go into the thousands; however, this only takes half the space of the first choice.

Another strategy you should use is to try to select whole number data types, like integer, as often as possible. Whole numbers are easier to work with and are not subject to rounding errors like decimal numbers sometimes are. The choice between decimal and whole number data types is usually pretty easy to make. The Cost column in the Part table needs to be a decimal because a quart of oil sells for $1.05. The CustomerID column in the Customer table will be an integer because no decimals are required. Decimal values would only make the CustomerID more awkward to work with. But what about the RatePerHour column in the Service table? Is the Slick Shop always going to set its rates at whole numbers such as $60, $62, and $78? If they are, then you could use an integer data type. Better yet a smallint or even a tinyint if your database supports it. The danger here is that one day the Slick Shop might want to set the rate to $69.50 per hour. Then you'd be in trouble.

Whole number data types such as integer are one of the most basic and widely supported data types. This makes it one of the easiest to use when you start accessing data from programming languages and query tools. If you're sure you don't need decimals, go with an integer data type. If there's a chance that you'll need decimals later, bite the bullet now and set it up right the first time. Finally, if this is a column that is intended to hold an amount of money, your best bet is usually to go ahead and make it a decimal.

Date and Time Data Types

Your database will provide you with data types that store dates and times. Behind the scenes, your database will actually store the dates and times as numbers. This is not something that you have to worry about, though. Whenever you view one of these data types, it will automatically be displayed in a familiar date or time format. Likewise, when you are inserting or updating one of these columns, you can use these same familiar formats. As mentioned earlier, these data types are smart enough to understand invalid dates and times. Your database, for example, will not allow you to save the value 12:73 in a time column.

Most databases have one data type for dates and another for times. Some, however, combine the date and time into a single data type. Following are some of the data types that are in this category.

```
DATE, TIME, DATETIME, SMALLDATETIME, TIMESTAMP
```

As with the other data types discussed so far, it will be important here as well to choose an appropriate size. Many of the databases do not give you a choice. If you want to store a date, you must use the DATE data type. Others give you a size choice such as DATETIME versus SMALL-DATETIME. Either way, you need to be aware of the storage limitations. Just as the numeric data types have upper and lower boundaries, so do the date and time data types. Actually, the time data type is nothing to worry about. It will cover all of the hours, minutes, and seconds in a day. The only thing to note here is how precisely it can store time. Some databases will only go as low as seconds, whereas others will keep track down to the thousandths of a second.

Date data types, on the other hand, do have definite upper and lower limits. These limitations are usually not an issue for most columns that you will create. Ordinarily these columns store dates that are relatively close to today, such as invoice dates, birth dates, and due dates. Date data types can go much farther into the past and the future if you have that need. Some go back as far as 4700 B.C. and as far ahead as A.D. 9999. You might need this if you are storing dates related to ancient Roman history or the date you predict the Cubs will win their next World Series.

NOTE Be sure to note these limitations especially if your database offers a type such as SMALLDATETIME. This kind of data type is a great way to save space but may be too restricting. In the Sybase and Microsoft databases, SMALLDATETIME only covers dates from 1900 to 2079 and only keeps time to the nearest minute.

One more note on date and time data types. These tend to be the most temperamental types to work with. Some databases are very strict about the format used to insert dates and times. It might, for example, demand that your date be formatted as yyyy-mm-dd, with dashes between the numbers, not slashes. Other databases will be more flexible, allowing either the month or the year to be first and allowing the use of either dashes or slashes. Some databases even understand if you use the format 10-DEC-03. Another thing to watch out for is the use of quotes around the date. Some databases do not need any delimiters surrounding dates and times. Others will try to interpret 10-19-03 as 10 minus 19 minus 3 and give you a nasty error message. These databases probably demand that delimiting characters surround the dates and times. The delimiters will be either single quotes, double quotes, or pound signs.

Boolean Data Types

There are many cases when you might need a column to store simple yes/no data. In the sample database, you could create a `PreferredCustomer` column in the `Customer` table. You could also have a `GenericBrand` column in the Part table. Using a Boolean data type for these would give you a quick and simple way to flag questions with a yes or no answer. Many of the DBMSs have special Boolean data types available.

BIT, YES/NO

TIP   If your DBMS does not provide a special Boolean data type, you can simply use the one character string data type, CHAR(1). Then you can store values like Y, N, 1, or 0.

Binary Data Types

Binary types are not as frequently used as the ones that we've talked about so far, but they can be very useful. Here are some of the binary types that are used by the different DBMSs.

BLOB, IMAGE

Some DBMSs simply use the types previously discussed, whereas others will allow you to specify a size. These sizes go as high as 4 gigabytes in some DBMSs. Although these binary types can store ordinary text strings, they are typically used to store the contents of binary files. Many times graphics, photos, documents, or scanned images are stored in a binary data type column. On a previous real-life project, we used two separate binary columns in a customer table to store the photo and signature of each customer. Later we were able to have our application retrieve these images and print them on demand.

Another typical use of a binary column is to store sensitive data. Plain text data can be run through encryption software and then stored in the binary column. When it is needed again, the encrypted data can be selected and decrypted for use.

Like the text and memo data types discussed earlier, your DBMS might put restrictions on the use of binary data types. It might be unavailable or limited for searching, sorting, indexing, or joining.

Creating Tables

All right, now that you are armed with all of that design information, it's time to create some tables! Actually, compared to normalization and determining the appropriate data types, creating the tables is going to be pretty easy.

First take a look at the basic syntax to create a new table.

```
CREATE TABLE tablename
(colname1 datatype,
 colname2 datatype,
 ...
);
```

All you really need to do is give the table a name and list all of the columns with their data types. Table and column names need to begin with a letter but can contain numbers and a few special characters, such as the underscore. A naming convention using names that are all one word with the first letter of each word in uppercase, like PartUsed and LineItemNumber, will be used for the sample database. Other people like to put underscores between the words, such as part_used and line_item_number. It really doesn't matter as long as you find something that you're comfortable with.

◄◄◄

A **naming convention** is an agreed-upon standard for giving names to all objects within a database. The standard might dictate the case, tense, punctuation, and abbreviations that should be used when naming new objects.

◄◄◄

The command to create the `Part` table looks like this:

```
CREATE TABLE Parts
(PartID integer,
 Description varchar(100),
 Cost decimal(6,2)
);
```

Note that the entire list of columns is enclosed within parentheses and commas separate each column. This is just the very basic syntax. You could stop here with this much information and begin creating all of your tables. There are, however, several other options that you can use while creating a table.

Column-Level Constraints

There are many options that let you customize how each column responds to data. An expanded CREATE TABLE syntax is shown in the following:

```
CREATE TABLE tablename
(colname1 datatype [NULL | NOT NULL] [UNIQUE]
[CHECK(expression)] [DEFAULT value]
[IDENTITY | AUTO_INCREMENT]
[PRIMARY KEY] [REFERENCES othertable (othercol)],
 colname2 datatype [NULL | NOT NULL] [UNIQUE]
[CHECK(expression)] [DEFAULT value]
[IDENTITY | AUTO_INCREMENT]
[PRIMARY KEY] [REFERENCES othertable (othercol)],
 ...
);
```

Notice that there are square brackets around each of the options. The square brackets indicate that this feature is optional and can be left out entirely. These options are called constraints and can be specified for each individual column.

▲▲

A **constraint** is an option that further defines a table or a column. It will either add more information to or put certain restrictions on the table or column.

▲▲

The first constraint is NULL or NOT NULL. This allows you to specify whether or not a column accepts NULL values. If a column is defined as NOT NULL, some value has to be assigned to that column or else the database will produce an error. If you do not specify one of these two constraints, the database will assign its default, which is usually NULL. For the Part table created earlier, you are going to specify that none of the three columns can contain a NULL value. All three of these are important enough that you are going to demand that the user not leave any of them blank. It would not do the Slick Shop any good to have a NULL value, for example, in the Description column. They would look at it one day and see that part number 101 costs $15.50 but not know what that part is. A good example of where it would make more sense would be if you added a Color column to this table. For a few of the parts the Slick Shop sells, the color matters, such as fuzzy dice. However, most of the items, like oil and air filters, do not have color choices. These products would have a NULL value in the Color column.

▲▲

NULL is the absence of data. It is not the same thing as zero (0), nor is it the same thing as an empty string (' '). It is often used in databases to represent "not applicable" or "I don't know."

▲▲

Placing the UNIQUE constraint after a column's name and data type will ensure that there will be no duplicate values entered into that column. In the database, you may choose to add this constraint to the Description column in the Part table so that no two products end up getting the same exact name.

The CHECK constraint lets you include some data validation directly into the table. You can assign an expression to a column that will be validated before the data is inserted or modified. If the expression turns out to be false, the data will not be inserted or changed. For example, on the Part table, you might want to add a CHECK constraint to make sure that no one sets a value in the Cost column to a negative number. The expression is just like an expression that you would use in a WHERE clause. The expression must be placed in parentheses after the keyword CHECK.

When the DEFAULT constraint is specified, you do not have to insert a value for that column even if it is defined as NOT NULL. In the case where a value is not provided, the default value will be used. You may want to use this constraint as well for the Cost column in the Part table. You could make the default value $0.01. That way, if a Slick Shop employee needs to enter a part but does not know the price, it will get entered anyway with a price of one cent. Hopefully, the employee will return later and update it to the correct price.

Take a look at the CREATE TABLE command now making use of these four column constraints.

```
CREATE TABLE Part
(PartID integer NOT NULL,
 Description varchar(100) NOT NULL UNIQUE,
 Cost decimal(6,2) NOT NULL CHECK(Cost >= 0.00) DEFAULT 0.01
);
```

The IDENTITY or AUTO_INCREMENT constraint will define a numeric column that will automatically populate itself with incrementing numbers. This can be an extremely useful feature when creating ID numbers, especially numbers that have no real meaning. You might have noticed that several of the tables that you created last night, such as `Customer`, used the IDENTITY constraint. You might have also noticed the INSERT commands for those tables did not include a value for those particular columns. The DBMS will automatically populate the column with the next available number. You don't really care what a new customer's number is, you just want the customer to have one that is unique.

NOTE Not all DBMSs support auto-numbering as a constraint. In Access, for example, you define the data type of the column as `'AutoNumber'`. Still other DBMSs require you to write your own auto-numbering code in a trigger.

There are also constraints available that will define primary keys and foreign key relationships. Using these while creating tables will enable your database to enforce referential integrity.

◄◄◄

Referential integrity is the concept of keeping a database's tables properly related to one another. If two tables are related in a database, there should not be missing or undefined data in any of the columns that make up the relationship.

◄◄◄

Using the PRIMARY KEY constraint after a column will designate that column, and that column alone, as the primary key. Some databases will also go ahead and create an index on this column as well. You'll add this constraint to the `PartID` column.

```
CREATE TABLE Part
(PartID          integer       NOT NULL PRIMARY KEY,
 Description     varchar(100)  NOT NULL UNIQUE,
 Cost            decimal(6,2)  NOT NULL CHECK(Cost >= 0.00)
                               DEFAULT 0.01
);
```

As you learned earlier, a primary key column will uniquely identify each row of data in a given table. The database will not allow you to enter the same value in the primary key column on two separate rows. This sounds just like the UNIQUE constraint, doesn't it? Well, yes, it is very similar. In the preceding code, you already had a UNIQUE constraint set up on the `Description` column. Couldn't `Description` just be used as the primary key? Yes, it could. This just wouldn't really be the best choice, however. Because the `Description` column has meaningful data, it will be subject to change. It is very likely that one day the part descriptions will need to be changed. Because the primary key column of the `Part` table is used as a foreign key in another table, changes like this would have to be synchronized. A surrogate key like `PartID` is a better choice. Because the number doesn't mean anything, it probably will never change. Plus, remember that you don't have to show this number to the users, so they will not even be tempted to change it.

The REFERENCES constraint is used to create foreign key relationships. You will remember that in the `PartUsed` table there is a `PartID` column that is a foreign key to the `PartID` in the `Part` table. This relationship can be defined when you create the `PartUsed` table.

```
CREATE TABLE PartUsed (
JobTicketID             integer,
 LineItemNumber         integer,
 PartID                 integer REFERENCES Part(PartID),
 Quantity               integer
);
```

After the keyword REFERENCES, specify the name of the table and column to which this is a foreign key. The PRIMARY KEY and REFERENCES constraints can be used as we've described them here only if the primary and foreign keys are made up of just one column. If two or more columns make up the key, a table-level constraint must be used.

NOTE The tables that you created in the Friday Evening session included one other column constraint, CLUSTERED. This refers to the way the column's data will be indexed. We'll cover this in the Sunday Morning session.

Table-Level Constraints

For a table like `PartUsed` that has more than one column in its primary key, the CREATE TABLE command will not allow you to use the PRIMARY KEY constraint beside each column. Instead, you must use a table-level constraint that is specified below all of the columns. The syntax for table-level constraints is given in the following:

```
CREATE TABLE tablename (
colname1  datatype,
 colname2 datatype,
 ...
 [, PRIMARY KEY (colname1, colname2)]
 [, FOREIGN KEY (colname1, colname2) REFERENCES othertable(col1,
    col2)]
 [, UNIQUE (colname1, colname2)]
);
```

NOTE Be sure to take note of the commas before the keywords PRIMARY KEY and FOREIGN KEY. Some databases do not like it when you forget these commas and will produce cryptic error messages that will leave you scratching your head.

The `PartUsed` table needs to make use of two of these table-level constraints. First the primary key includes three columns: `JobTicketID`, `LineItemNumber`, and `PartID`. Next the foreign key that references the `JobTicketDetail` table uses two columns: `JobTicketID` and `LineItemNumber`. Take a look at the CREATE TABLE command.

```
CREATE TABLE PartUsed(
JobTicketID          integer,
LineItemNumber       integer,
PartID               integer REFERENCES Part(PartID),
Quantity             integer,
PRIMARY KEY (JobTicketID, LineItemNumber, PartID),
FOREIGN KEY (JobTicketID, LineItemNumber) REFERENCES
JobTicketDetail(JobTicketID, LineItemNumber)
);
```

Notice how you can use a table-level constraint to create the foreign key reference to JobTicketDetail. However, at the same time, you can use a column-level constraint to create the foreign key reference to Part. This key could have been defined at the table level as well. The command that follows will produce identical results to the one just preceding it.

```
CREATE TABLE PartUsed
(JobTicketID integer,
 LineItemNumber integer,
 PartID integer,
 Quantity integer,
 PRIMARY KEY (JobTicketID, LineItemNumber, PartID),
 FOREIGN KEY (JobTicketID, LineItemNumber) REFERENCES
     JobTicketDetail(JobTicketID, LineItemNumber),
 FOREIGN KEY (PartID) REFERENCES Part(PartID)
);
```

By creating the PartUsed table with these two foreign keys, you've just related three tables together. Figure 4.14 has a diagram that shows the relationships.

The first thing we'd like you to notice are the little keys to the left of some of the column names. These show columns that make up the primary key. Now look at the lines between the tables. Each line indicates a foreign key

Figure 4.14

The relationship between JobTicketDetail, PartUsed, and Part.

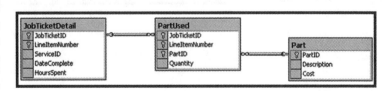

relationship between two tables. One side of the line has a picture of a key. This is the primary key side. The other, the foreign key side, has a picture of a little chain link. From Figure 4.14 you can also see the one-to-many relationships. The primary key side (with the key) is the "one" side. The foreign key side (with the chain link) is the "many" side. Think about the Part and PartUsed tables. There will only be one PartID 501 in the Part table. However, over time, there will be several rows in PartUsed that have a PartID of 501.

It's easy to see which columns are related to each other in Figure 4.14 because the same column names have been used. The columns that store part numbers are called PartID in both the PartUsed and Part tables. However, you do not have to use matching names to relate columns together. Consider the tables in Figure 4.15.

This is a simplified example of tables that hold package shipment information. Say you have a small customer table called Cust and one for the parcels called Package. You can see that you need two foreign keys in Package that reference Cust, one for the sender and one for the recipient. It would be nice if you could put two columns called CustomerID in the Package table so that they matched Cust. Of course, you can't do this. Instead, you create column names that make sense to you, SenderID and ReceiverID. You then create a foreign key from each one of these to CustomerID in the Cust table. SQL will treat these foreign keys the same as if they had matching column names.

Figure 4.15

Column names do not have to match to set up foreign key relationships.

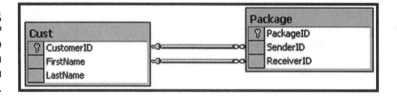

Primary and foreign key definitions are not required in a database. If they are not created, you will still be able to join tables together with a SELECT command. However, having the keys does provide you with some nice features. It will ensure that you do not enter any data that violates the relationship. For example, the foreign key between PartUsed and Part ensures that no PartID is added to PartUsed that does not first exist in Part. In other words, the Slick Shop cannot use a part until it has been entered first. The foreign key will also prevent someone from deleting a row in the Part table if it has already been used in the PartUsed table. This will prevent orphaned data.

◄◄

An **orphaned data** item is one that cannot be traced back to its parent. It is data in a foreign key column that should exist as a primary key in another table but does not. This is often the result of the row in the primary key table being deleted.

◄◄

Your database might provide some other useful constraints related to foreign keys. It might allow you to define cascading updates or cascading deletes.

◄◄◄

A **cascading update** will handle the situation when a primary key value is updated. The cascading update will automatically update any related foreign key values in other tables to match the new value.

◄◄◄

◄◄◄

A **cascading delete** will handle the situation when a primary key row is deleted. The cascading delete will automatically delete the related foreign key rows in other tables. An alternative action might also be available to update the foreign key values to NULL instead of deleting the row.

◄◄◄

Another benefit of taking the time to define the primary and foreign keys is that many external software packages will take advantage of this information. Software such as data-modeling packages will read all of the table information including the keys and create an Entity Relationship Diagram (ERD). The diagrams in Figures 4.14 and 4.15 earlier came from a data-modeling software package. The key definitions are also used by graphical query tools to automatically create the joins for SELECT statements.

The final table-level constraint that was shown in the syntax was UNIQUE. Use this at the table level if you want the combination of two or more columns to be unique. You might want to use the UNIQUE constraint on the Customer table to ensure that you don't enter the same person twice. The combination of FirstName, LastName, and City is unique in the CREATE TABLE command that follows:

```
CREATE TABLE Customer (
  CustomerID        Integer IDENTITY(1,1) NOT NULL PRIMARY KEY CLUSTERED,
  FirstName         Varchar(20)  NULL,
  LastName          Varchar(30)  NULL,
  Address           Varchar(100) NULL,
  City              Varchar(30)  NULL,
  StateOrProvince   Char(2)      NULL,
  PostalCode        Varchar(10)  NULL,
  PhoneNumber       Varchar(10)  NULL,
  UNIQUE (FirstName, LastName, City)
);
```

This means that the database will not allow you to add two people with the same name from the same city. However, it will allow people to have the same first and last names as long as they have different cities.

TIP That scenario was just for example purposes. That would actually not be a very good way to make sure the same customer did not get entered twice. It is certainly possible that two different people with the same name live in the same city. The approach that we've taken to this requirement in the past is to perform a check in the application that inserts new customers. We had the program search for existing customers with the same name as the one being added. If there were any matches, we had a window pop up displaying the matched names with addresses and let the user either choose one or continue with the insert.

Take a Break!

Okay, time for a break! Don't doze off now. In the next half of this chapter, you'll get to start plugging in some data and making that database work for its money. But first, all that talk about data types got us thinking of a little quiz for you. The answers are at the end of the chapter.

1. Which data type would you use to store the number of miles the moon is from the earth? (Hint: The moon is about 239,000 miles from the earth.)

    A. 1-byte unsigned integer

    B. 2-byte unsigned integer

    C. 4-byte integer

    D. 8-byte integer

2. Which data type would you use to store the number of miles from the earth to the sun? (Hint: The sun is about 92 million miles from the earth.)

3. Which data type would be best to store the entire text of Lincoln's Gettysburg Address? (Hint: It contains just under 1,500 characters, including spaces.)

    A. CHAR(1500)

    B. VARCHAR(8000)

    C. MEMO

    D. IMAGE

All right, enough of that. Let's get back to business!

Modifying and Dropping Tables

So now you know enough to create your own tables, and assuming you build them right the first time, you're all set. But you know as well as we do that tables will need to be changed, maybe even removed.

Modifying Tables

When we talk about modifying tables in this section, we mean changing the structure of the table, not the data inside the table. We'll talk about modifying the data later in this chapter in the section called "Updating Data."

Modifying the structure of a table is done with the ALTER TABLE command. There are three basic things that can be modified: columns, column constraints, and table constraints.

Columns can be added to a table, given a new name, given a new type, or removed from the table. The syntax to add a column is as follows:

```
ALTER TABLE tablename
ADD colname datatype [constraints];
```

You simply give the new column a name and a data type. If you want to add a column to hold part colors, use the following command:

```
ALTER TABLE Part
ADD Color varchar(15)
```

This will add the column Color to the end of the table. Remember, though, that SQL does not care about the order of the columns. It's important to note that this command can be executed to add the new column even if there is already data in the table. The values for the new column will all be set to NULL. You can then use UPDATE commands to set the values if you want.

TIP

Although the order of the columns does not matter, you might want to add your new column in a logical position rather than at the end. Check to see if your DBMS supports an option to add the column at any spot in the table.

You probably also noticed that after the data type you get to specify column-level constraints. These will be the same ones that are available with the CREATE TABLE command, such as NULL/NOT NULL, CHECK, and DEFAULT. For the new Color column, you could have defined it to be NOT NULL. The problem with this is what value would be given to the existing rows? It's for this reason that your database will not allow you to add a NOT NULL column unless you also define a default value.

```
ALTER TABLE Part
ADD Color varchar(15) NOT NULL DEFAULT 'Blue';
```

This will add the Color column, and every row that previously existed will now have the value 'Blue' in this new column.

There is also the following syntax to remove a column from a table.

```
ALTER TABLE tablename
DROP COLUMN colname;
```

Any data that is in that column, of course, will be gone as well as constraints assigned to that column. Also, if the column is referenced in an index, view, stored procedure, or trigger, one of two things will happen. Either your database will not allow you to drop the column or the index, view, stored procedure, or trigger will not function properly anymore.

Following is an example showing how to remove the `Color` column. Indexes, views, triggers, and stored procedures will be covered in Sunday's chapters.

```
ALTER TABLE Part
DROP COLUMN Color
```

NOTE Not all DBMSs allow you to drop a column. If yours does not, your only way to do this is to drop the entire table and re-create it without the column you don't want. Of course, as you'll see in the next section, dropping a table will delete all of its data, so you'll want to save your data first. See the sidebar called "Using the INSERT Command to Help Remove a Column" in the "Inserting Data" section of this chapter for one method of dropping a column without losing all of your data.

There are many other DBMS-specific uses of ALTER TABLE. The following list includes some of the things that can be done with ALTER TABLE.

➤ Change a column's data type.

➤ Rename a table.

➤ Add primary or foreign keys.

➤ Create or drop indexes.

➤ Enable or disable triggers.

➤ Add column constraints such as `DEFAULT`, `CHECK`, `UNIQUE`, and `NULL`.

Dropping Tables

This probably goes without saying, but *be careful!* There is no recycle bin where you can go back and restore a table after it's gone. Even if you do have a full database backup, it is not easy to get just one single table restored apart from the rest of the database.

Deleting or dropping a table will delete almost everything that is connected to it. Most important, all of the data in that table will be gone. The table structure, indexes, triggers, constraints, and privileges will be deleted as well. Some DBMSs will delete the views associated with the table; however, most will not. In this case, the view will be left sitting there without its associated table and will no longer work. The same is true of a stored procedure that references the dropped table. We'll cover stored procedures in the Sunday Morning session and we'll talk about views in the Sunday Afternoon session.

The syntax for dropping a table is pretty basic.

```
DROP TABLE tablename
```

It's a simple little command but a powerful one! SQL will not stop to ask you, "Are you sure?" It will just drop the table with no regrets. The DROP TABLE command, however, is nice enough to prevent orphaned data. It will not let you drop a table if another table has referenced it in a foreign key.

Take, for example, the `Customer` and `JobTicket` tables. For right now, assume that these are the only two tables in the database. The `JobTicket` table has a foreign key on its `CustomerID` column that references the same column in the `Customer` table. It's okay to drop the `JobTicket` table because this will simply leave a list of people in the `Customer` table. The DBMS will not let you drop the `Customer table`, though. If it did, all that would be left would be a bunch of `CustomerID` numbers in the `JobTicket` table that do not relate to anyone.

If you really do want to drop the `Customer` table, you have a couple of choices. You can drop the tables in the correct order, first `JobTicket`, and then `Customer`. Your other option is to remove the foreign key constraint and then drop the `Customer` table. Of course, by doing this, you will leave orphaned data in `JobTicket`.

Remember when we asked you to assume that those were the only two tables in the database? Well, they're not, are they? In fact, you would not be able to drop `JobTicket` because `JobTicketDetail` references it in a foreign key. You can't drop `JobTicketDetail` either because `PartUsed` references it in a foreign key. In order to drop the `Customer` table without removing the constraints, you would have to drop tables in this order: `PartUsed`, `JobTicketDetail`, `JobTicket`, and finally `Customer`.

Just one more reason why your mother stresses the importance of good planning and doing the job right the first time!

Inserting Data

So what good is a table without data? None. After all this planning, creating, altering, and dropping, it's high time to store some real data. SQL uses the INSERT command to put a new row of data into a table. Take a look at the syntax:

```
INSERT INTO tablename [(colname1, colname2, ...)]
VALUES (value1, value2, ...);
```

It's really a pretty easy command. Simply list the column names you want to put data in, and then list the values in the same order. Your database will validate the command for you. It will make sure that you've specified the same number of columns as values. It will also see to it that the values are of the same data types as the columns. Of course, any problem with these validations will be reported as an error and no data will be inserted.

Here's a sample INSERT command:

```
INSERT INTO Customer
  (FirstName, LastName, Address, City, StateOrProvince, PostalCode)
VALUES
  ('Christian', 'Badar', '8007 Landover Rd.', 'Indianapolis', 'IN',
     '46000');
```

This command will insert a new person into the `Customer` table. Notice how all of the values use quotes around the data. This is because all six of the columns are character data types. If you are inserting data into a numeric column, however, do not use quotes. Notice also how the order of the values matches the order of the column names. A mistake that your database will not be able to catch for you will be if you mix up values of the same data type. In the preceding command, if you switched 'IN' and '46000', that is the way they would be stored. They are both character data going into character columns. The only thing that may save you is if '46000' was too long to fit in the StateOrProvince column (which it is). In this case, your DBMS will either generate an error or truncate the data and store as much as will fit in the column.

What about the CustomerID column? Why not include that column? You'll recall that earlier in this chapter we pointed out that the CustomerID column in the Customer table is auto-numbered. Because of this you are not allowed to specify a value for this column. The database will automatically find the highest number used so far, increment it by one, and use it in your new row.

Now consider this INSERT statement:

```
INSERT INTO Customer
 (City, PostalCode, Address, FirstName, StateOrProvince, LastName)
VALUES
 ('Indianapolis', '46000', '8007 Landover Rd.', 'Christian', 'IN',
    'Badar');
```

This will produce identical results as the previous command. This example demonstrates that you do not have to list columns in the same order as they were created. Again just make sure that the values appear in the same order as the column names.

Not all of the columns in the table have to be included in the INSERT command. Any column that allows NULL values or has a default defined does not have to be specified. In the Customer table, most of the columns are defined to allow NULLs. If a customer came to the Slick Shop but did not want to divulge her address, she could still be entered with this command:

```
INSERT INTO Customer (FirstName, LastName)
VALUES ('Mona', 'Lambdin');
```

This will leave the remaining fields with NULL values. They could later be changed with an UPDATE command. If any of the columns that are left out of the INSERT command have a default defined, the default value will be inserted. If instead a value is provided, the value will supersede the default.

If you look back at the syntax of the INSERT command, you'll see that the list of columns is actually optional. You could write your INSERT command list this:

```
INSERT INTO JobTicketDetail
VALUES (1, 2, 2, '5/18/2003', 0.25);
```

If you leave off the list of columns, the INSERT command assumes that you are providing a value for every column and that they are in the correct order. If you want to leave any of the columns out or use a different order, you must include the list of column names.

◆◆◆◆◆◆◆◆◆◆◆◆◆◆◆◆◆◆◆◆◆◆◆◆◆◆◆◆◆◆◆◆◆◆◆◆◆◆

CAUTION It is not a good practice to leave out the column list, especially for INSERT statements that are executed within a stored procedure, a trigger, or an external program. If someone ever adds new column, removes a column, or changes their order within the table, this kind of INSERT will no longer work. An INSERT statement that explicitly names its columns will most likely continue to function properly.

◆◆◆◆◆◆◆◆◆◆◆◆◆◆◆◆◆◆◆◆◆◆◆◆◆◆◆◆◆◆◆◆◆◆◆◆◆◆

Here's a useful variation of the INSERT syntax:

```
INSERT INTO tablename [(colname1, colname2, ...)]
SELECT colname1, colname2, ...
  FROM othertable
[WHERE whereclause];
```

Instead of explicitly entering the values, this syntax allows you to get the data from another table. This will work as long as the SELECT command returns the same number of columns as is specified in the column list and they are of the correct data type and size.

Try this out with the Customer table. Say that the Slick Shop of Peoria is closing and will be referring all of their customers to the Slick Shop of Springfield. Now assume that Peoria's Customer table has been put in the Springfield database and named PeoriaCustomer. You can copy all of the Peoria customers into Springfield's Customer table with this command:

```
INSERT INTO Customer (FirstName, LastName,
    City, StateOrProvince, Address, PostalCode, Phone)
SELECT FirstName, LastName,
        City, StateOrProvince, Address, PostalCode, 'REQUEST'
  FROM PeoriaCustomer
 WHERE City <> 'Springfield';
```

There are several things to take note of in this command. Again you can see that columns are not inserted in their defined order, but the order specified does match the column list. Next the phone numbers are not copied. Instead, the word 'REQUEST' is used to remind the employees to ask each customer for his or her phone number. Finally, a WHERE clause is included on the SELECT command. This will only copy the customers from PeoriaCustomer who do not live in Springfield.

Unlike the standard INSERT command, which would only load one row at a time, this one has the potential to load hundreds or thousands of rows at the same time.

USING THE **INSERT** COMMAND TO HELP REMOVE A COLUMN

A few pages back when we were talking about using the ALTER TABLE command to remove a column, we mentioned that not all DBMSs support this syntax. As we said, the only way to remove a column in that case is to drop the entire table and re-create it without the unwanted column. The problem here is that all of the data will be lost. We'll show you one solution to this problem here using the INSERT command with SELECT.

con...

For this example, let's say you're working with a table called Department. You want to remove the Location column, but you want to be sure to keep all of the rest of the data. First you'll create a table to use temporarily that has the same columns and data types as the Department table.

```
CREATE TABLE DeptTemp
(DeptID Integer,
 DeptName Varchar(50),
 ProfitCenterNum Integer,
 Location Varchar(20)
);
```

You can just create this table without any constraints. You especially do not want any auto-numbered columns, because you want to retain all of the original data. Now you'll copy all of the data from Department into this table.

```
INSERT INTO DeptTemp (DeptID, DeptName, ProfitCenterNum,
     Location)
SELECT DeptID, DeptName, ProfitCenterNum, Location
  FROM Department;
```

Next drop the Department table and re-create it without the Location column.

```
DROP TABLE Department;
CREATE TABLE Department (
(DeptID           Integer,
 DeptName         Varchar(50),
 ProfitCenterNum Integer
);
```

Now you can populate the new Department table using the data in the temporary table.

```
INSERT INTO Department (DeptID, DeptName, ProfitCenterNum)
SELECT DeptID, DeptName, ProfitCenterNum
  FROM DeptTemp;
```

Finally, after verifying that the data was copied correctly, you can get rid of the temporary table.

```
DROP TABLE DeptTemp;
```

Before the INSERT statement adds rows to a table, it will first validate all of the table- and column-level constraints. It will make sure that you are not adding a duplicate primary key or duplicate data that violates a UNIQUE constraint. It will make sure none of the CHECK constraints are violated. It will also make sure you are not adding data to a foreign key that does not exist in the referenced table. An example of this would be if you tried to insert a new row into `JobTicket` with the `CustomerID` set to `500`, when there is no `CustomerID` of `500` in the `Customer` table. This is where the strength of the relational database comes into play. This kind of referential integrity validation will help to ensure that you are not creating bad data. It will force you to create the customer row first and then the job ticket.

Updating Data

Modifying data in SQL is accomplished by using the UPDATE command. The syntax for the command is as follows:

```
UPDATE tablename
    SET colname1 = expression1, colname2 = expression2, ...
[WHERE whereclause];
```

An example of a very simple UPDATE command follows. Using this command, you'll change every row in the `Customer` table to have the same state.

```
UPDATE Customer
    SET StateOrProvince = 'IL';
```

This will change every single state to Illinois because you did not include a WHERE clause at the end of the command. This is the same as running a SELECT without a WHERE clause—all rows are affected. Most times this is not what you will want to do. Usually you will want to include a WHERE clause in order to perform a more selective update.

CAUTION

◆ ◆

Take extra care when issuing an UPDATE command. It is easy to get so caught up with the columns and values you're setting that you forget to add the WHERE clause. We've done that before on a live production database. Believe us—that can ruin your day!

◆ ◆

Besides the WHERE clause, the syntax also shows that more than one column can be updated at the same time. Let's try the UPDATE command again, this time changing the city and state of everyone who has certain ZIP codes.

```
UPDATE Customer
   SET City = 'Springfield', StateOrProvince = 'IL'
 WHERE PostalCode IN ('62701', '62702', '62703', '62704', '62707');
```

This command will set both the `City` and `StateOrProvince` columns at the same time. Notice how the WHERE clause is identical to one that you would use in a SELECT command. Nearly any WHERE clause that you can use with a SELECT command can also be placed in an UPDATE.

TIP

■ ■

Before executing an UPDATE command, you might want to test it first. To do this, write a SELECT command and paste in the exact WHERE clause that you are planning on using in the UPDATE. You can then examine the rows that are returned. These will be the very same rows that you are getting ready to update.

■ ■

So UPDATE can use the same WHERE clauses as the SELECT statement. What about that cool subquery you learned about this afternoon? Yes, that will work too! A subquery can be used in the WHERE clause of an UPDATE. Let's say that you have several jobs that are backlogged in the `JobTicket` table. They are scheduled to start over the next two weeks. You already have rows for them in `JobTicket`. However, you want to schedule all the customers from Peoria to have their service start this Tuesday. You could use a subquery to look at the `City` column in the `Customer` table even though you're updating `JobTicket`.

```
UPDATE JobTicket
   SET StartDate = '2003-02-04'
 WHERE CustomerID IN
 (SELECT CustomerID
    FROM Customer
   WHERE City = 'Peoria' AND StateOrProvince = 'IL')
   AND EndDate IS NULL;
```

You've taken care in the WHERE clause of the subquery to make sure that you're updating the customers from Peoria, IL (not the ones from Peoria, AZ). You're also being careful to only update the jobs that are not already done, by looking for end dates that are NULL.

A nice feature of the UPDATE command is that the expression to which you set the column does not have to be a hard-coded value. It can be based on the value of another column or even based on its own value. If you want to increase the cost of all of the filters the Slick Shop sells by 5 percent, you can use the following UPDATE:

```
UPDATE Part
   SET Cost = Cost * 1.05
 WHERE Description LIKE '%filter%';
```

The UPDATE command will even let you use the result of a query to set the new column value. Study the next command for a minute.

```
UPDATE Vehicle
   SET LastServiceDate = (SELECT MAX(jtd.DateComplete)
                            FROM JobTicketDetail jtd
                            JOIN JobTicket jt
                              ON jt.JobTicketID = jtd.JobTicketID
                           WHERE jt.VehicleID = 4)
 WHERE VehicleID = 4;
```

In this example, you're updating the LastServiceDate column in the Vehicle table for vehicle number 4. You're making sure that its LastServiceDate matches the latest DateComplete for that same vehicle in the JobTicketDetail table. Look at the SELECT command first. It joins JobTicket and JobTicketDetail so that it can find the maximum DateComplete value for vehicle number 4. It's important to note that this query will return only one column and one row. You've then taken that SELECT command and placed it in an otherwise ordinary UPDATE statement.

As with the INSERT statement, UPDATE will verify all table and column constraints to make sure there are no violations. If there are violations, the UPDATE will be cancelled and an error message will be returned. A foreign key relationship is one of the most important constraints verified. Your database will ensure that these relationships remain valid. Any attempt to violate a foreign key relationship will result in an error and the data will not be updated. Say, for example, you want to update the CustomerID in the JobTicket table because you think that the customer is incorrect for job ticket 4051. Run the following UPDATE statement:

```
UPDATE JobTicket
   SET CustomerID = 22018
 WHERE JobTicketID = 4051;
```

This statement will run fine if there really is a CustomerID of 22018 in the Customer table. If there is not, then the UPDATE will fail and you will get an error message explaining that you were trying to violate a foreign key relationship. If the UPDATE command were to allow you to do this, you would be creating bad data. You would have a job ticket that could not be traced back to a customer.

What if you tried to update the CustomerID in the Customer table instead? Let's say you get the wacky idea that you want to change a customer's ID number from 1 to 101. Now you're entering a dangerous area, because you're thinking about updating a primary key.

```
UPDATE Customer
   SET CustomerID = 101
 WHERE CustomerID = 1;
```

This command will work as long as CustomerID 1 has not been used as a foreign key value in any other table. In this case, that means as long as there are no vehicles or job tickets assigned to this customer.

NOTE In the sample database, this UPDATE will not work even if the `CustomerID` has not been used as a foreign key. This is because the `CustomerID` is an auto-numbered column. An auto-numbered column does not allow updates.

Earlier in the chapter, we talked about and defined cascading updates. If you were allowed to update the `CustomerID` column and had defined a cascading update to take place, then you would not have received an error. Instead, when you issued the previous UPDATE command, it would have updated the customer number to 101 in all three tables: `Customer`, `Vehicle`, and `JobTicket`.

Deleting Data

We've talked about inserting and updating, so it must be time for deleting. When you use the SQL DELETE command, you will be removing an entire row of data at the same time. If you really just want to delete the values from a few of the columns but leave the rest of the row, then you should use the UPDATE command instead.

The syntax for the DELETE command is as follows:

```
DELETE FROM tablename [WHERE whereclause];
```

It's a pretty easy command. Simply name the table and specify which rows you want to delete. Just like the UPDATE command, DELETE uses a WHERE clause to specify which rows will be deleted. Again, this WHERE clause is the same as you would use in a SELECT statement. The WHERE clause is optional, so the most simple form of DELETE would be like this example:

```
DELETE FROM PartUsed
```

Because you did not use a WHERE clause, this command will delete all of the rows in the table. Remember the caution we gave you in the last section about forgetting the WHERE clause on an UPDATE? How bad would it be to forget it on a DELETE? There's no easy way to get those rows back. If you don't have a copy or backup of that data, it's gone forever. We're happy to report that we haven't made this mistake on a production database (yet).

Using the DELETE command to delete all of the rows from a large table may take a long time. If your database is using a transaction log, each and every row deleted must have information written to the log. Some DBMSs offer the TRUNCATE TABLE command as an alternative to DELETE.

```
TRUNCATE TABLE tablename;
```

This command will very quickly delete all rows from the table. The trade-off is that this command does not store any information in the transaction log. This means that if you have to restore transactions from backup, there will be no record of this action. Your DBMS might also prevent you from using TRUNCATE on tables that are referenced by other tables as a foreign key.

Although there are many perfectly valid reasons to delete all of the rows from a table, most of the time you'll find yourself deleting only a few rows at a time. In fact, it is very common to use the primary key column or columns in the WHERE clause to delete just one row. Following is an example showing how to remove an obsolete part from the Part table.

```
DELETE FROM Part WHERE PartID = 323;
```

Because PartID is the primary key of the Part table, you are ensuring that only one row will be deleted. To delete just one row from a table that has more than one column in the primary key such as JobTicketDetail, you use this command:

```
DELETE FROM JobTicketDetail
 WHERE JobTicketID = 4039 AND LineItemNumber = 3;
```

Just like SELECT and UPDATE, the WHERE clause can get more sophisticated. It can include subqueries that reference other tables. You'll use a subquery to modify the earlier example where you deleted an obsolete part.

```
DELETE FROM Part
 WHERE PartID IN
 (SELECT PartID
    FROM Part
   WHERE PartID NOT IN (SELECT DISTINCT PartID FROM PartUsed));
```

This DELETE command actually uses a subquery within a subquery. If you examine it closely, you'll see that the second SELECT gets a list of all parts that have been used. The first SELECT gets a list from the Part table of everything that is not in the list of used parts. This list of unused parts is then deleted from the Part table.

Just like the tip that we gave you in the "Updating Data" section, it is also a good idea to test the WHERE clause with a SELECT before running the DELETE. Because the preceding command to delete unused parts is a little involved, you would probably want to test it first this way:

```
SELECT PartID, Description, Cost
   FROM Part
 WHERE PartID IN
 (SELECT PartID
    FROM Part
   WHERE PartID NOT IN (SELECT DISTINCT PartID FROM PartUsed));
```

This will show you the list of products that are unused. If this looks good, you can then run the DELETE. The DELETE command will indicate that it succeeded, and most DBMSs will even tell you how many rows were deleted. If you used the same exact WHERE clause for the SELECT and DELETE, the number of rows should match. Just to be sure, you could run the SELECT once again. This time it should not return any rows, meaning that now all of the parts in the Part table have been used at least once.

It is perfectly safe to issue a DELETE command with a WHERE clause that does not find any rows. For example, nothing will happen if the Part table has PartID values from 1 to 100 and you issue the following command:

```
DELETE FROM Part WHERE PartID = 323;
```

This makes it convenient to run a recurring DELETE job and not have to worry about whether or not the WHERE clause found any rows. You could run the earlier DELETE command every couple of months to find and delete all unused parts. If it runs when there are not unused parts to be deleted, then no harm done!

The DELETE command is also subject to referential integrity checks. In the preceding examples, you have been deleting rows from the Part table. Every time you do this, your database is going to check to make sure that the PartID you're deleting is not used as a foreign key value in the PartUsed table. If it has been used, the delete will not be allowed. Were it to allow this delete, you would be leaving orphaned data in PartUsed.

Remember the discussion earlier in this chapter about dropping tables, and how because of the foreign keys they had to be dropped in a certain order? For the same reason, this applies to DELETE as well. If you really want to delete a part that has been used already, you will first have to delete all of the PartUsed rows that reference that PartID. However, once you delete rows from PartUsed, you may have just left some of the line items in JobTicketDetail without parts. You may want to delete those line items as well. Finally, because you've now deleted some line items from a job ticket, you may want to just go ahead and delete the whole thing from JobTicket. So this is just an example that shows you should not take deletes lightly in a relational database. Stop first and think about the consequences a delete will have on the related tables.

REFERENTIAL INTEGRITY SEEMS LIKE A
PAIN—SHOULD YOU SKIP IT?

You're probably guessing that we'll answer that with, "No! Don't ever skip it! Are you nuts?" Actually, the answer is that there are pros and cons of both sides of this question.

We've discussed many good reasons to build referential integrity into your database. These reasons include ensuring that no orphaned data is created by INSERTs, UPDATEs, or DELETEs and keeping primary and foreign key relationships linked at all times. It is because of this referential integrity, for example, that you can be confident that when you look at a job ticket, you will be able to trace it back to a valid customer and a valid vehicle.

We also discussed earlier the fact that you don't have to define primary and foreign keys if you don't want to, thus removing the referential integrity. If you are in a database design phase or very early in an application development stage, you might want to temporarily go without the referential integrity. During these periods, the table structures are often subject to frequent changes. Columns may be added, removed, and shifted to other tables as you are trying to come up with the best design.

Let's say that you've just finished your database design and created all of your tables. You then discover that you need to add a column to hold a second customer address line and that you don't need the phone number column after all. Your DBMS may be one that doesn't allow you to delete columns, so you have to drop the table and re-create it. Earlier in this chapter, we talked about the effect that referential integrity has on dropping tables. If you have all of the foreign keys defined, you would have to first drop three other tables in the correct order before you could drop the Customer table. Then, of course, you would have to

con...

re-create all four tables. To make matters worse, what if those tables had data in them that you didn't want to lose? Without the foreign keys, however, you could have just worked with the `Customer` table alone.

One strategy is to leave the foreign keys off until the database design is nailed down tight. This strategy does come with its dangers, though. Many times, especially on large projects, the goal of finalizing a design is a moving target. We've been on projects where application development gets fully under way while the table structures are still changing on a daily basis. The application developers might be completely unaware that the foreign keys are missing. This can lead to big mistakes.

Let's say that you've decided to leave your foreign keys off until you're sure the table structures are 100 percent correct. Meanwhile developers begin coding and you eventually forget to create the keys. Several weeks later, after an application is in production, you discover that the database has a whole bunch of job tickets with `NULL` values in the `CustomerID` column—some even have invalid numbers. The developers didn't know that a job ticket always had to have a customer assigned to it. They also wrote code that deletes customers without regard for whether there are any job tickets or vehicles related to that customer. The database allowed them to write these INSERTs and DELETEs, so they figured they must be okay. Now you not only have bad data that must be cleaned up but the developers have to rewrite their code.

Another situation where leaving referential integrity off is common is on data warehouse databases. These databases are typically built for reporting purposes. Often they are tuned such that they are no longer fully normalized. Also some or all of the tables may have their data completely deleted and reloaded on a routine basis. Because these kinds of tables are not being used as the primary data entry destination, they don't need the benefits of referential integrity. It would also be a huge hassle to delete and reload the tables in the proper order.

con...

> Naturally, the decision to use referential integrity will rely on your
> unique situation. As you can tell from the preceding discussion, it is
> there to help you keep a nice orderly database but at times can be an
> administrative pain. Our recommendation is that you plan to use refer-
> ential integrity for active data entry and transaction processing data-
> bases. Also make it a priority to get it in place as soon as possible.
> However, if you have a data warehouse or reporting database, you
> might be better off without the referential integrity.

If your DBMS provides for cascading deletes, you might find this to be a
handy feature. A cascading delete is specified while defining a foreign key.
The following code shows the CREATE TABLE statement for the
Vehicle table used in last night's session. This one is modified to include
a cascading delete action on the foreign key that references Customer.

```
CREATE TABLE Vehicle (
  VehicleID        Integer IDENTITY(1,1) NOT NULL PRIMARY KEY
                   CLUSTERED,
  VehicleYear      SmallInt NULL,
  Make             Varchar(30) NULL,
  Model            Varchar(30) NULL,
  Color            Varchar(30) NULL,
  LicensePlate#    Varchar(10) NULL,
  LastServiceDate  Smalldatetime NULL,
  CustomerID       Integer NOT NULL
                   REFERENCES Customer (CustomerID) ON DELETE CASCADE
);
```

With this cascading delete in place, if you delete a customer from the
Customer table, all vehicles that customer owns will be deleted as well.
This is a powerful feature that can be a nice time-saver. It can also be confusing for people who don't realize the database has cascading actions and
can't figure out why certain rows sometimes disappear.

Cascading deletes can involve more than just two tables. The preceding example might not work so smoothly in the Slick Shop database because the `VehicleID` column is used as a foreign key in the `JobTicket` table. This means that you could not delete a vehicle if it had one or more job tickets created for it. You could, however, set up a cascading delete on `JobTicket`. In fact, you might want to set up cascading deletes all the way down the chain of tables. If you did this, when you deleted a row from `Customer`, not only would all related rows from `Vehicle` be deleted but so also would related rows from `JobTicket`, `JobTicketDetail`, and `PartUsed`. This cascading delete is depicted in Figure 4.16. In effect, you'd be erasing all traces of that customer ever existing. What power you now possess!

Figure 4.16 shows how this one command

```
DELETE FROM Customer WHERE CustomerID = 247;
```

can actually delete 16 rows.

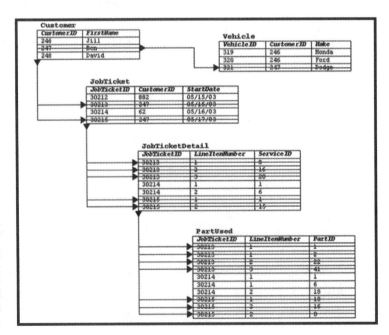

Figure 4.16

The effects of a single DELETE command, when all of the tables have cascading delete actions defined.

Modifying and Dropping Databases

The ALTER DATABASE or SET command is available to make changes to a database, and the DROP DATABASE command will delete the whole thing.

Modifying Databases

Your DBMS will provide you with one or more methods of changing its characteristics. It might provide SQL commands such as these two:

```
ALTER DATABASE dbname [options];
SET option = value;
```

In addition to or in place of these, you might also have a graphical interface available to make database changes. These are changes or settings that affect the entire database. They include such things as

➤ Adding, deleting, or resizing database storage files

➤ Specifying backup drives or tapes

➤ Specifying the use of transaction logs

➤ Setting backup and recovery options

➤ Changing sort options

➤ Changing character sets

➤ Setting the behavior of transactions

➤ Setting cache options

This merely names a few of the things that can be changed. When we talked about creating databases earlier, we said that creating a database with its default options is sufficient for most databases. These settings and options will let you fine-tune your databases after development is well under way or even complete.

Dropping Databases

DROP DATABASE is the granddaddy of all DROP commands. Issuing this command will wipe out everything—tables, data, indexes, triggers, stored procedures, and permissions. Not your everyday kind of command.

```
DROP DATABASE dbname;
```

Depending on your DBMS and even the version you are using, DROP DATABASE might not actually remove the database files. It might just remove all references to the database, so that the DBMS no longer knows anything about it, and no one can access it. The files might be left there for you to back up or delete as you see fit. Be sure to determine whether your DBMS leaves the files. Unused database files could be left consuming a lot of valuable disk space.

What's Next?

That is definitely enough for today, wouldn't you agree? You've been through all the fundamentals of SQL. You're now equipped to handle a large percentage of the SQL tasks that you'll need to do on a day-to-day basis. Tomorrow morning, you'll be digging deeper by taking a look at how you can fine-tune your tables and SQL. You know how to put data in and get it back out. But is it fast enough for you? Is it fast enough for your end users? Hint: It's never fast enough for your end users.

Until then, get up and have a good night. Rent a movie, reintroduce yourself to your family, or take yourself to dinner. See you in the morning!

Oh, the answers to the quiz?

1. The moon is about 239,000 miles from the earth. You would need a 4-byte integer to store this number. A 2-byte unsigned integer will only hold 65,536. A 4-byte signed integer will hold more than 2 billion.

2. The sun is about 92 million miles from the earth. So the same 4-byte integer could be used.

3. The Gettysburg Address contains just under 1,500 characters including spaces. So you would really only need the CHAR(1500).

Optimization— Feel the Need for Speed?

- ➤ Understanding Indexes
- ➤ Creating Stored Procedures
- ➤ Understanding Transactions
- ➤ Optimizing Your Database

Relational database management systems are good. Most have been around for years and have been fine-tuned by their vendors for optimal performance. You've already learned enough this weekend to create a database, say to catalog your home DVD collection. This database would perform very nicely too. However, if your database is supporting a business, you'll want to begin investigating some performance enhancements. These will help ensure that the database users get the best response time possible.

Understanding Indexes

The number one performance booster in a relational database is the use of indexes. Indexes provide fast access to data. Like many of the SQL language features we've talked about so far, indexes have a very basic form and syntax. However, you can benefit even further from learning about their inner workings.

A SQL index is very similar to the index in the back of a book. If you want to find pages in this book that talk about the SELECT command, you *could* start at the beginning and flip through page by page looking for it. Every time you found a page that talked about the SELECT command, you could dog-ear that page and continue searching. You'd have to search all the way to the end of the book because you never know where we'll talk about SELECT next. Well, you've read enough books to know that's not the way to do it. This book has an index, so you can just go back there, look up SELECT, and note all of the pages next to it. This is much faster, especially because the index is in alphabetical order.

A SQL index works the same way. If you ask your database to find all of the customers who have the last name Hatfield, you don't want it to have to look at every single customer. It would be faster if it could look at an index like this book has so that it would be able to quickly find every Hatfield. That's just what we're going to show you how to do.

Creating an Index

A SQL index is created on a column or a group of columns within a table. A table can also have more than one index, a nice feature that this book does not have. To get started, take a look at the syntax to create an index.

```
CREATE [UNIQUE] INDEX indexname
    ON tablename (columnname [ASC | DESC] [,…n]);
```

This will build a single index on one or more columns on a single table. A minute ago we were talking about finding customers with the last name Hatfield. We said that it would be faster if you could use an index to look up last names. So that's just what you'll do—create an index on the last name column of the Customer table.

```
CREATE INDEX idx_LastName
    ON Customer (LastName);
```

That's all you need to do. When you execute this CREATE INDEX command, after a few seconds it will be done. The index will be created and available for use. Now the really nice thing about the index is that you don't have to worry about explicitly using it because your DBMS will do that for you. If you're ready to do a last name search, just submit a SELECT command.

```
SELECT FirstName, LastName, City
  FROM Customer
 WHERE LastName = 'Hatfield';
```

This is no different than the basic SELECT that you learned about in the Saturday Morning session. Only now it will return results faster. The DBMS automatically recognizes that you are searching based on the LastName column. It also knows that an index is available for that column. So in the same way you quickly find things in this book with its index, the DBMS looks at the index named idx_LastName and knows right where to find Hatfield. You didn't even have to specify the name of the index— the DBMS just knew it was there and used it!

So you had to *give* the index a name but didn't have to *use* it. Will you ever use the name? Rarely, if at all. An index is a database object, just like a table, a column, a stored procedure, and a trigger. All database objects must have a name, so that's why you need to come up with one. We're going to use a naming convention of idx_ followed by the column name. You can call it whatever you want, but be aware that you might occasionally see this name pop up in places. These object names are stored in the system or catalog tables, and your DBMS has commands that can list the objects. Also sometimes when there is a problem a SQL error message might include the name of an index. The idx_ naming convention will help you quickly identify that the object name you're looking at is an index on the LastName column.

When new customers come into the Slick Shop, they most certainly will not arrive in alphabetical order. This means that they will be inserted into the Customer table in a random, unsorted order. This is fine because, as Figure 5.1 shows, the index will be sorted and will point to the data rows.

NOTE A SQL database will not actually store the index entries in a top-to-bottom alphabetized list like this. The DBMS will key the index in a hierarchical format called a *B-Tree*. This provides even faster lookups than an alphabetized list would. Fortunately, you never have to worry about how indexes are internally stored. So for this book, we'll just keep it simple and continue to show indexes as a sorted list like the one shown in Figure 5.1.

Figure 5.1

Figure 5.1

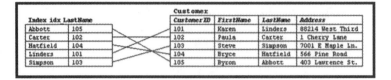

Sorted index
entries point to the
data rows.

So do you have to create an index before you can search on a particular column? No, you can search using a WHERE clause on any column, indexed or not. However, if you search on a column that has no index, it will be the same as flipping through this book page by page. The SELECT command will have to look at every single row for the matching value. This kind of search is called a table scan.

BUZZ WORD

◄ ◄

A **table scan** is the process of a SQL command looking at every row in a table one by one in order to test the values of one or more columns.

◄ ◄

A table scan is the kind of activity that you will want to try to avoid. The sample database only has a handful of customers right now. Any DBMS will be able to easily look up a customer from this list in the blink of an eye, even without an index. Someday, though, the Slick Shop expects to get more than 100,000 customers in their database. Every time a new customer gets added, the SELECT command will get a little bit slower. It will be hard to notice at first, but soon the users will realize that your database is not as speedy as it once was. Then they'll call you, and you will be forced to feel their pain.

With an index, however, queries will seem to run as quickly with 100,000 rows as they did with 10. A well-indexed table can produce excellent response times even after millions upon millions of rows have been inserted. Now we're not going to lie to you and tell you that a query on a 10-row table will perform the same as on a 10 million-row table. We will, however, say that performance will degrade an order of magnitude faster on a table without an index. The DBMS stores the index information so efficiently that even with 10 million entries it will only have to look at a few index entries before it finds the one you want.

What about when you add new customers or change some last names? How do you update the index? Good news—you don't have to! The DBMS will constantly watch the INSERT and DELETE commands that you perform and accordingly add or remove entries from the index. It will also watch for UPDATE commands that affect the index, such as a change to a last name. In this case, the index entry will be re-sorted to its proper place. Figure 5.2 shows how the index from earlier is affected by such changes.

So you just worry about maintaining the data and the DBMS will worry about maintaining the index. One thing you might want to think about, however, is whether updating an indexed column will cause too much of a strain on the database. As you saw, when the LastName column was updated, the index had to be rearranged. This operation will occur very quickly. But what if data from this column were being updated hundreds of times per day, or even per hour? This process of re-sorting the index might begin to contribute to poor performance. More about this later when we talk about performance and optimization.

Figure 5.2

We added a new customer, 106, which has caused a new index entry. We also updated Paula's last name from Carter to Zimmer, which has caused her index entry to move to the bottom of the list.

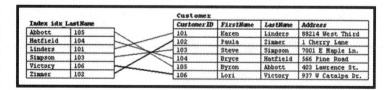

In the Saturday Morning and Saturday Afternoon sessions, you learned how to perform some more advanced WHERE clauses. You saw the use of ranges with BETWEEN, lists with IN, and wildcards with LIKE. The database can use an index for any of these types of queries. The next three SELECT commands that follow will make use of the index on the LastName column.

```
SELECT FirstName, LastName, City
  FROM Customer
 WHERE LastName BETWEEN 'Abbott' AND 'Hatfield';
```

Because the DBMS stores the index entries in order, it just has to find the last name Abbott and then return all of the rows in index order until it finds Hatfield.

```
SELECT FirstName, LastName, City
  FROM Customer
 WHERE LastName IN ('Abbott', 'Hatfield', 'Carter');
```

This is very similar to the query earlier that looked for Hatfield. Only this time the database will use the index to locate three different names.

```
SELECT FirstName, LastName, City
  FROM Customer
 WHERE LastName LIKE 'H%';
```

This query too will use the index. It's the same idea as you using a phone book to point out all the last names that start with H. You would be able to quickly open the phone book and find the first name that starts with H, and then run your finger down all of the names until you hit the last one starting with H. Now imagine someone asking you to point out all of the last names in the phone book that *end* with the letter S. That would be much more difficult. In fact, you would just have to start from the beginning and examine every name in the book. A SELECT command would have to do the same thing. It would have to perform a full table scan to get this list of names.

You would write the SELECT command like this:

```
SELECT FirstName, LastName, City
  FROM Customer
 WHERE LastName LIKE '%S';
```

This query will work and will return the correct results—it will just be much slower than the previous one. When wildcard characters are used in queries, the indexes will only be used if the wildcard characters come at the end of the comparison string.

As you saw in the Saturday Morning session, the WHERE clause of a SELECT is likely to contain more than one comparison. Consider the following query:

```
SELECT FirstName, LastName, City
  FROM Customer
 WHERE LastName = 'Thompson'
   AND FirstName = 'Davis';
```

If you still only have the one index on the LastName column, will this query be able to use it? Yes, it will. The DBMS's optimizer will recognize that the LastName column has an index and use it to find all of the people with the last name Thompson. That will take care of most of the work. Then it will just need to scan through the Thompsons one by one looking for everyone with the first name Davis. So because the FirstName column is not indexed, it still has to do a little bit of scanning, but it's minimal compared to a full table scan.

◀◀◀◀◀◀◀◀◀◀◀◀◀◀◀◀◀◀◀◀◀◀◀◀◀◀◀◀◀◀◀◀◀◀◀◀◀◀◀
An **optimizer** is programming logic that is built into the DBMS. Its purpose it to investigate SQL commands before they are executed and determine the best and fastest way to execute the command.
◀◀◀◀◀◀◀◀◀◀◀◀◀◀◀◀◀◀◀◀◀◀◀◀◀◀◀◀◀◀◀◀◀◀◀◀◀◀◀

As mentioned at the beginning of this section, you can create more than one index on a table. You could create one index on the LastName column, one on the FirstName column, and one on the Address column. In fact, you could create an index on every single column if you wanted to. We don't recommend that you do this though. Just as the index for this book takes up a certain amount of space, so do database indexes. Indexes can also hamper performance in some areas. Later in this chapter, we'll talk about the space consumed by indexes, performance issues, and strategies for determining which columns to index.

For now, you should just think about what makes sense. You know that the optimizer will look at the WHERE clauses for indexed columns. So ask yourself which columns you most commonly use in WHERE clauses. You might not know yet if this is a brand new database. If not, you'll have to take your best guess for now. You can always add or remove indexes later as development progresses. In the Customer table, you think you'll be doing a lot of searching by the customer's last name. You also know that you're going to have a report that looks up all customers in a given ZIP code. Knowing this, you'll create an index on the LastName column and another one on PostalCode. Remember this does not limit you to querying on those two columns alone. You might need to occasionally search on the PhoneNumber column. That's okay—it will just be a little slower than searching on the LastName or PostalCode columns. If you find yourself doing frequent searches on PhoneNumber, it probably makes sense to index that column too.

The primary key column is always a good choice for an index as well. In fact, many DBMSs will automatically create an index on this column when you create the table and indicate that it is the primary key. If this is not done automatically, you will want to go ahead and create it on your own. There are two reasons for this. First, the primary key of a table ends up getting frequently used in WHERE clauses. Second, the primary key will be used in joins. When two tables are joined together, the query will benefit greatly if the columns involved in the join are indexed. The DBMS is actually performing a lookup based on the joined columns, the same as if you had put them in the WHERE clause. The following query joins Customer and Vehicle to get a list of each customer and the customer's related cars.

```
SELECT LastName, FirstName, VehicleYear, Make, Model
  FROM Customer INNER JOIN Vehicle
    ON Customer.CustomerID = Vehicle.CustomerID
 ORDER BY LastName, FirstName, VehicleYear DESC;
```

The CustomerID column from Customer is being used in the join and so is the CustomerID from Vehicle. The query can run faster if both of these columns are indexed. The CustomerID column is a foreign key in the Vehicle table. As a rule of thumb, all primary and foreign key columns are excellent candidates for indexes.

Indexes are not used exclusively by SELECT statements. Inserts, updates, and deletes will benefit from them as well. As we showed you in the Saturday Evening session, the INSERT, UPDATE, and DELETE commands can each make use of a WHERE clause. For example, if you create an index on the VehicleYear column, the following UPDATE command will use it.

```
UPDATE Vehicle
   SET LicensePlate# = NULL
 WHERE VehicleYear = 2004;
```

The index will be used to find the correct rows to update in the same way a SELECT command would use the index to find the rows to display.

Composite Indexes

Now recall that the JobTicketDetail table has two columns in its primary key. Also recall that earlier in this chapter we mentioned that an index could be created on more than one column. The syntax for creating an index on the primary key of JobTicketDetail then looks like this:

```
CREATE INDEX idx_JobID_LineNum
      ON JobTicketDetail (JobTicketID, LineItemNumber);
```

This one index, idx_JobID_LineNum, has the index information for both columns. An index that is made up of two or more columns is called a *composite index*. Your new composite index is perfect because it includes both columns that define the primary key. Often these two columns will be used in the join of a query, like the following SELECT.

```
SELECT j.HoursSpent, p.PartID, p.Quantity
  FROM JobTicketDetail AS j INNER JOIN PartUsed AS p
    ON j.JobTicketID = p.JobTicketID
   AND j.LineItemNumber = p.LineItemNumber
 WHERE j.HoursSpent < 0.50;
```

This query lists all of the PartIDs that have been used on a line item task that took less than a half hour. Notice that the joined columns are JobTicketID and LineItemNumber, the same ones on which you built your new index.

There are many other cases where you can use a composite index other than primary and foreign keys. Let's say that you've found out that the Slick Shop often queries for vehicles based on their make, model, and color. For example, it's common for them to need to look for a red Ford Mustang.

```
SELECT VehicleID, CustomerID, VehicleYear, Make, Model, Color
  FROM Vehicle
 WHERE Make = 'Ford'
   AND Model = 'Mustang'
   AND Color = 'Red';
```

You might want to create a composite index on all three of these columns: Make, Model, and Color.

```
CREATE INDEX idx_Make_Model_Color
    ON Vehicle (Make, Model, Color);
```

Now when you execute that query to look for all red Ford Mustangs, the optimizer will use this one index to quickly find each of those rows. This index will also get used when a query uses only Make and Model in the WHERE clause. The same is true if only Make is in the WHERE clause. The optimizer can use the index if the columns in the query come from the first part, or left side, of the index. Figure 5.3 shows a representation of the index just created on the Vehicle table.

Index idx_Make_Model_Color

AMC	Gremlin	Pink	9
Chevrolet	Corvette	Black	4
Chevrolet	S-10	Purple	1
Chevrolet	Trail Blazer	Green	7
Chrysler	PT Cruiser	Black	6
Ford	Expedition	Maroon	8
Ford	Mustang	Red	2
Honda	Accord	Blue	10

Figure 5.3

A composite index on the `Vehicle` table.

The index is sorted first by `Make`; then `Model`; then `Color`. From this figure you can see that it will be easy for the DBMS to look at the index and find all Chevrolet S-10s regardless of color. It would also be easy to find all of the Chevrolets since the index is sorted first by the `Make` column. However, a query that asks for all of the black cars will not be so easy.

```
SELECT VehicleID, CustomerID, VehicleYear, Make, Model, Color
  FROM Vehicle
 WHERE Color = 'Black';
```

This query will not be able to use the index. Just like you would have to search down the list one by one looking for "Black", so does this query. This query will perform a table scan. Now if you find that this kind of query is also very common, you could simply create an index on the `Color` column as well.

```
CREATE INDEX idx_Color
    ON Vehicle (Color);
```

The `Color` column is now used in two separate indexes.

Indexes are also used to speed up sorting. Because the column data is already stored as sorted information in the index, the DBMS can take advantage of this if it's used in an ORDER BY clause. Because the Vehicle table now has the new ind_Color index, the following query will use it.

```
SELECT VehicleID, CustomerID, VehicleYear, Make, Model, Color
  FROM Vehicle
 ORDER BY Color;
```

Sorted Indexes

In the CREATE INDEX syntax you also saw the optional keywords ASC and DESC. These refer to the order in which the index stores its data. By default, index data is stored in ascending order. So the command used to create the idx_Color index is the same as this one:

```
CREATE INDEX idx_Color
    ON Vehicle (Color ASC);
```

You might find that certain data is viewed in reverse order most often. This might be the case with the VehicleYear column. You might often sort it descending so that the newer cars are always at the top. In this case, you could make use of the following index:

```
CREATE INDEX idx_Year
    ON Vehicle (VehicleYear DESC);
```

A descending sort index like this will only help you out when sorting data. If the index is being used for a WHERE clause for searching purposes, the optimizer does not really care if it is sorted ascending or descending. It can find the data just as easily either way. Most people just create their indexes with the default ascending order unless they have special sorting requirements.

Unique Indexes

A unique index will prevent duplicate values from being entered within the same column. The syntax for this option uses the UNIQUE keyword.

```
CREATE UNIQUE INDEX idx_License
    ON Vehicle (LicensePlate#);
```

This index will not allow any duplicate license plate numbers to be entered into the Vehicle table. If any INSERT or UPDATE command tries to set the LicensePlate# column to a value that already exists, the command will be cancelled and will fail. If there is already data in the table, the CREATE UNIQUE INDEX command will first check to see that the values of the column are already unique. If they are not, the index cannot be created. A NULL is considered a value, so a uniquely indexed column cannot have more than one row with a NULL value.

You might recognize this as being very similar to the UNIQUE constraint covered in the Saturday Evening session. That's because it is. The UNIQUE constraint and the unique index perform the same job, making sure that duplicate values do not get into the same column or group of columns. The difference, of course, is that the index not only does that job but performs the duties of an index as well.

Clustered Indexes

Indexes fall into two general categories, clustered and nonclustered. So far we've discussed only nonclustered indexes.

◄◄◄
A **clustered index** is one that will actually keep the physical order of the data rows sorted. A **nonclustered index** does not affect the physical order of the data.
◄◄◄

All indexes, clustered or nonclustered, keep their own index information sorted. But only a clustered index affects the order in which the data is stored.

You're going to revisit an index created a few pages back. Remember the index on the LastName column of the Customer table? It's shown in Figure 5.2. This is a nonclustered index. The last names are sorted within the index, but the data rows are not. You'll make this a clustered index instead.

```
CREATE CLUSTERED INDEX idx_LastName
    ON Customer (LastName);
```

When a clustered index is created on a table that already has data in it, the existing data will be re-sorted. The data and the index will now be in the same order. Figure 5.4 shows the result on the Customer table after creating this clustered index. Notice how the data rows have been reordered by the last name and now match the index order.

Because the rows can only be sorted one way at a time, there can only be one clustered index per table. There can still be other nonclustered indexes at the same time.

The benefit of a clustered index is shorter response time on queries that access the data in this particular order. For example, the clustered index on the LastName column will benefit from this query:

```
SELECT CustomerID, FirstName, LastName, City
  FROM Customer
 ORDER BY LastName;
```

The query wants to return the customers sorted by last name. Because of the clustered index, the data does not have to be sorted. It is already stored in the right order. Some WHERE clauses will also benefit from a clustered index. This query is asking for all of the customers whose last name is in the last half of the alphabet.

Figure 5.4

A clustered index keeps the data physically sorted.

Index idx LastName			Customer			
			CustomerID	FirstName	LastName	Address
Abbott	105		105	Byron	Abbott	403 Lawrence St.
Hatfield	104		104	Bryce	Hatfield	566 Pine Road
Linders	101		101	Karen	Linders	88214 West Third
Simpson	103		103	Steve	Simpson	7001 E Maple Ln.
Victory	106		106	Lori	Victory	937 W Catalpa Dr.
Zimmer	102		102	Paula	Zimmer	1 Cherry Lane

```
SELECT CustomerID, FirstName, LastName, City
  FROM Customer
 WHERE LastName >= 'N';
```

All the optimizer will have to do is find the first name that starts with N and then just return the rows in order until the end of the table is reached.

Clustered indexes will maintain the sorted order of the data even as rows are added, changed, and deleted. So there is an extra processing cost involved with them.

The Cost of Indexes

A while ago we mentioned that you could create an index on every single column in a table if you wanted to. This would mean that an index would be available for any query or join that you come up with. Although this is true, indexes do come at a price. There is no free lunch. Indexes consume disk space and processing time.

As you saw back in Figures 5.1 and 5.3, an index stores a copy of the data from the column or columns that are indexed. An index also has some overhead bytes as well. If you indexed every column of a table, you would be doubling the amount of storage space used. In fact, given the overhead, you would more than double the space. Besides filling up a server's disk quicker, this can have side effects such as longer backup cycles and increased backup media requirements.

If you feel that disk space is relatively cheap and the extra storage requirements don't concern you, performance certainly should. The server will be able to perform only a certain number of operations per second. If it's spending too much of its time updating indexes, you could start to see slow response time from queries and data modification commands. Every time a row is inserted into a table, all indexes on that table must be modified and re-sorted so that the new values can be added. Likewise, every time a row is deleted, all indexes need to remove the deleted values. When data is updated, indexes will need to be adjusted if any of their columns were changed.

You've probably visited a Wal-Mart store in the middle of December. There are a dozen or more checkout lanes, each beeping away as items are scanned. Well, every time you hear a beep, a row is being inserted into a table somewhere with the information about the product that was just scanned. Think of the volume of data that is being inserted. They cannot afford to have their database get bogged down by constantly re-sorting indexes to accommodate this new data. This is a good example of a table that should have as few indexes as possible.

Which of your columns should be indexed? This is another one of those design questions that has no easy answers. You will need to examine each table individually and weigh its potential performance gains against its potential performance hindrances. The example of the Wal-Mart transaction table is a case where the speeds of the inserts are the top priority. If customers have to wait in line too long because of slow scanners, Wal-Mart will start losing business. In this case, the fewer indexes the better. The obvious trade-off will be that without indexes, getting data out of such a table will take a long time. This might need to be an operation that occurs by long-running jobs during off-peak hours.

The Slick Shop, on the other hand, has a fairly low-volume database. Let's say they average nine jobs per hour. So there are usually several minutes between database entries. This should allow plenty of time for the database to maintain its indexes. As you start looking at each table, you might want to go ahead and create indexes on all the columns you think might be queried one day. So in the `Customer` table you create indexes on `CustomerID`, `FirstName`, `LastName`, `City`, `StateOrProvince`, and `PostalCode`. All of the columns except `Address` and `PhoneNumber` because you figure that it's not likely someone will query on these two. You'll then continue with each table in the same way, indexing every column that is even a remote candidate. Even though you have the luxury of a low-volume processing system, you should not neglect the storage space required for all of these indexes. Many of the Slick Shops across the country have older database servers that don't have much in the way of disk space. Creating indexes in a careless manner like this could eat up all of their disk space in a hurry.

A better approach to take is to start conservatively. Begin by building indexes on the primary and foreign keys of each table. Next create indexes for only those columns that you know *for sure* will be used heavily in WHERE clauses. This is a good point to step back and watch as development or usage of the database begins. If a front-end application is being developed for this database, some clues will begin to surface. For example, a search window might be developed for the Slick Shop application to look up parts by their description. Is this a special-duty feature that is only used once a month, or is it the main method of assigning parts to a job and used several times an hour? If the latter is true, this column is a good candidate for an index.

For each table, you will also want to decide if there is a good candidate for a clustered index. Remember that this kind of index has even more processing overhead than a nonclustered index, so you might not want one on every table. A search window that displays parts sorted by description could benefit from a clustered index on the `Description` column. This is not data that changes frequently, so the cost of reordering rows is not a concern. A large, high-volume table, however, might have trouble keeping up with not only sorting its indexes but also sorting its data.

The nice thing about indexes is that they are more forgiving than tables and columns. If you find that you've put a column in the wrong table or chosen the wrong data type for a column, this could be a costly mistake. Developers will have likely written a lot of SQL that will no longer work after you correct your mistake. Indexes, on the other hand, can be added and dropped virtually at will. Even after a database is being used in production, an index can be added and immediate performance gains can be accomplished. What if you discover the index is worthless or takes up too much space? Drop it at any time. Creating and dropping indexes will not affect the SQL code that has been written. Remember that the optimizer determines whether indexes are available—the SQL commands do not vary.

◆◆◆◆◆◆◆◆◆◆◆◆◆◆◆◆◆◆◆◆◆◆◆◆◆◆◆◆◆◆◆◆◆◆◆◆◆

Some DBMSs have a very advanced feature called *optimizer hints.* This is a feature in which the SQL command can name the particular index that it wants the optimizer to use. This is a case where dropping an index could cause a query to stop working. This feature is seldom used because the optimizers are very good at choosing the indexes on their own. You should, however, be aware that this option exists because someone might one day use it without your knowledge.

◆◆◆◆◆◆◆◆◆◆◆◆◆◆◆◆◆◆◆◆◆◆◆◆◆◆◆◆◆◆◆◆◆◆◆◆◆

Dropping an Index

Aha! Finally, a use for that index name! You'll need to know an index's name if you ever want to get rid of it.

```
DROP INDEX tablename.indexname;
```

This command will, of course, delete the index from the table. No data will be lost from the table, and the index can be re-created at any time. So this is a fairly safe command. When the index is dropped, the space that it was consuming will be immediately freed. The trade-off is that the moment the index is gone, the optimizer can no longer use it to speed up queries.

Creating Stored Procedures

Many of the database systems that we've discussed in this book support the creation and use of *stored procedures.* A stored procedure is a set of one or more queries or commands that are saved and can be executed later. In fact, there's a lot more to them than that. Stored procedures can include command logic that performs loops, conditional statements, and can run external processes.

How Can Stored Procedures Speed Things Up?

Stored procedures should always be a consideration if you are concerned about database performance. They can improve performance for the following reasons:

➤ They are precompiled.

➤ They can perform complex, multistep operations.

➤ Smaller requests are sent to the server.

You can think of a stored procedure as very similar to a function or subroutine in a programming language. It is simply a series of commands that get executed when called. Like programming languages, a stored procedure can accept arguments and return values. The procedures also get compiled, just as most languages do. The biggest difference is that within a stored procedure, you can include SQL commands and have it return rows and columns.

Earlier in this chapter, we talked about how the optimizer looks at queries and examines the tables, columns, and indexes to determine the best plan of attack. This optimization process will occur every time the query is run. This will happen even if the very same query gets run hundreds of times a day. If this query were in a stored procedure, the optimizer would only have to determine its plan one time, when the procedure is first created. The information the optimizer puts together is compiled into the procedure. When it's run, the optimization step will be skipped, and the query can begin immediately. Naturally, because a step is being removed from the process, the query will run faster.

Now, before you get your hopes up too high, let us adjust your expectations. The optimizers in today's DBMSs are very good at what they do. They are very fast too. If you take a SELECT command and place it in a stored procedure, you might not be able to tell any difference in speed. You most certainly will not see any difference in the Slick Shop sample database—it's just too small. In fact, even with many large databases, you might have a hard time seeing a difference. The optimization process many times takes less than a second in the first place. But don't stop reading! This is a very real benefit. Stored procedures can include any number of SQL commands, each one precompiled and preoptimized. Begin combining these and the speed difference will start to surface. Don't forget also that a multiuser database will have dozens or even hundreds of users executing the same queries all day long. Multiply the time savings by the number of times the procedure is executed and you start to see its worth.

Writing a Procedure

Before showing you a few stored procedure examples, we want to explain one thing. When you write a stored procedure, you can use programming code in addition to SQL commands. This code can do looping, do branching, make use of variables, and so on. The programming languages are unique to each database system. Oracle's language is called PL/SQL, whereas SQL Server and Sybase use Transact-SQL. The vendors don't even pretend to follow any kind of standard. In fact, they are each very proud of their language and its individual capabilities. As we said in the first chapter, we are showing most examples from SQL Server and will do so here. We will not, however, get into the details of Transact-SQL. We'll just show and explain enough so you can understand the things stored procedures are capable of doing.

Okay then, with that disclaimer out of the way, let's take a look at a simple stored procedure.

```
CREATE PROCEDURE GetCustomerVehicleData
  AS

SELECT c.FirstName, c.LastName, v.VehicleYear, v.Make, v.Model
  FROM Customer AS c
  JOIN Vehicle AS v
    ON c.CustomerID = v.CustomerID
ORDER BY c.LastName, c.FirstName, v.VehicleYear;

GO
```

This procedure simply contains one SELECT command that returns a sorted list of all customers and their vehicles. The first line gives the procedure a name, `GetCustomerVehicleData`. When the preceding statements are run, the procedure will be created in the current database. It is also compiled at the same time. This means that just like any other programming language compiler, the syntax will be checked. Not only are the keywords checked for spelling and proper usage, but the query is analyzed as well. It will be checked to make sure that valid table and column names have been used and that the query is otherwise written correctly. The optimizer will also examine the query at this time and store its execution plan. The only thing that does not happen is the running of the SELECT command itself. When you create the procedure, if all goes well, you will just get a simple message returned to you that says something like "The command completed successfully."

In order to run the procedure, you just need to call it by name.

```
EXECUTE GetCustomerVehicleData;
```

This will run the precompiled procedure and return a result set like the following:

```
FirstName   LastName     VehicleYear   Make        Model
---------   ----------   -----------   -------     --------
Kylee       Dicken       2002          Pontiac     Grand Prix
Bryce       Hatfield     1972          AMC         Gremlin
Bryce       Hatfield     2000          Chevrolet   S-10
Jacob       Salter       1998          Ford        Mustang
John        Smith        1968          Chevrolet   Corvette
Victoria    Smithe       2002          Nissan      Altima
Alex        Thompson     2000          Chrysler    PT Cruiser
Davis       Thompson     2001          Ford        Expedition
Harrison    Thompson     2002          Chevrolet   Trail Blazer
```

It's the same exact output that you would get if you had just run the SELECT outside of the stored procedure.

As we said, procedures can accept arguments. This is where you'll begin to see some more possibilities. The `GetCustomerVehicleData` procedure is fine, but you could make it more dynamic by allowing the user to get filtered results. Modify the procedure a little bit to accept an argument, a vehicle year. Then you can have the procedure return the same data but only restrict it to return vehicles that are the same year the user specifies.

NOTE In order to modify a procedure, you will have to drop it first. Because a procedure is another object in a database like tables, columns, and indexes, no two procedures can have the same name. In this case, you will need to execute the following command before you can create the procedure again.

```
DROP PROCEDURE GetCustomerVehicleData;
```

```
CREATE PROCEDURE GetCustomerVehicleData
  (@Year int)
  AS

SELECT c.FirstName, c.LastName, v.VehicleYear, v.Make, v.Model
  FROM Customer AS c
  JOIN Vehicle AS v
    ON c.CustomerID = v.CustomerID
 WHERE v.VehicleYear = @Year
ORDER BY c.LastName, c.FirstName, v.VehicleYear;

GO
```

You've now added two things to the procedure. At the beginning, you specified that the procedure will accept an integer argument into the variable called @Year. Then you added a WHERE clause that looks for vehicles that match the year passed into that argument. Now when you execute this procedure, you're required to pass it one argument.

```
EXECUTE GetCustomerVehicleData 2002;
```

This gives you only the rows that you want.

FirstName	LastName	VehicleYear	Make	Model
Kylee	Dicken	2002	Pontiac	Grand Prix
Victoria	Smithe	2002	Nissan	Altima
Harrison	Thompson	2002	Chevrolet	Trail Blazer

Now you have a flexible, preoptimized query. You can give users access to this query, and off they go! They don't even have to know how to write a SELECT query. They'll just have to know the name of the procedure and any arguments that are required. This can be a useful method of separating front-end development from the back-end development.

◄◄◄
In terms of application development, **front-end** refers to the programs that the users interact with. **Back-end** refers to the database.
◄◄◄

Using Stored Procedures to Divide Up Your Work

In the Sunday Evening session, we're going to discuss the use of SQL in front-end programming languages and development tools, such as Visual Basic and ASP.NET. You'll see examples there of SQL that is embedded into the front-end code. This means that the developer who is writing a front-end application would have to know SQL well and be able to write good SELECT, INSERT, UPDATE, and DELETE commands. As an alternative, you could use stored procedures to divide this workload among two groups of developers. Back-end developers or database administrators (DBAs) could be in charge of creating and maintaining stored procedures that handle all data access. Front-end developers would then be free to concentrate more on data collection and presentation.

Some people say that this separates the ones who do the real work from those who merely point and click. We're not going to get in the middle of that argument. We will say, however, that this method does have many benefits. The front-end application developers would technically only need to know the procedure name and its arguments. They could then call the procedure from their program and work with the results that are returned. If any changes are needed, say a new column needs to be added, the stored procedure developers could make them. Once changes have been made, the application developers don't have to worry about what the specific SQL change was. They simply have to adjust their code to reflect any input or output changes. For example, the application developer might be receiving a new column in the output or be expected to pass a new argument.

This division of labor comes in very handy when a stored procedure is required to handle some pretty complex logic. A back-end stored procedure developer can spend days writing a procedure that is several hundred lines long. At the same time, the application developer could be getting the code ready to call the procedure and work with the results that will be returned. The application developer doesn't have to worry about how complex the procedure is but instead just needs to know the inputs and the outputs. In fact, the front-end developer doesn't have to know SQL at all.

If you think this division of labor seems a little too utopian, you're probably right. Although the development environment being described is utilized by many projects at many companies, it's not as ideal as it sounds. We do highly recommend that the front-end developers not only know SQL but also have at least some active participation in the back-end development. An application developer will be able to write a much better system with the knowledge of things like primary keys, foreign keys, indexes, cascading actions, triggers, and table joins. Keep in mind that the front-end and back-end developers that we've described can actually be the same person. Whether it's one person or two separate developers, you'll still get many benefits from having the SQL written outside of the front-end application.

You probably recognize this development model. Many times in the programming world one person will write a function that is used by someone else. In fact, the function might be used by several people for several different projects. In the same way, a stored procedure can serve as common code that can be used in many different places. A single procedure could be called from more than location in the same application. It could also be called by several different applications. This provides some nice reusability.

Multistep Stored Procedures

All right, it's time to turn your attention back to the specifics of the stored procedures. We've mentioned a few times that you can benefit from the capabilities of a complex procedure. Let's take a look at one now.

```
CREATE PROCEDURE PartUsageByState
   (@Part int, @BeginDate smalldatetime, @EndDate smalldatetime,
      @State char(2))
   AS

IF @BeginDate < '2000-01-01'
    RETURN -1;

-- create the working table
CREATE TABLE #temp
  (JobTicketID int);

-- get a list of all JobTicketIDs that used the given
-- part between the given dates.
INSERT INTO #temp
(JobTicketID)
SELECT jt.JobTicketID
  FROM JobTicket AS jt
  JOIN JobTicketDetail jtd ON jt.JobTicketID = jtd.JobTicketID
  JOIN PartUsed AS pu ON jtd.JobTicketID = pu.JobTicketID
                    AND jtd.LineItemNumber = pu.LineItemNumber
                    AND pu.PartID = @Part
 WHERE jt.StartDate BETWEEN @BeginDate AND @EndDate;

-- join in the temporary table and return the vehicles owned
-- by customers who live in the given state or province.
SELECT c.FirstName, c.LastName, v.VehicleYear, v.Make, v.Model
  FROM Customer AS c
  JOIN Vehicle AS v ON c.CustomerID = v.CustomerID
  JOIN JobTicket AS jt ON c.CustomerID = jt.CustomerID
  JOIN #temp ON jt.JobTicketID = #temp.JobTicketID
 WHERE c.StateOrProvince = @State;

-- remove the temporary table
DROP TABLE #temp;

GO
```

NOTE The lines that begin with two dashes are comments.

Because this is not an extensive book about Transact-SQL, we will not go into great detail about this procedure—we'll just point out the highlights. First of all, the purpose of this procedure is to return a list of vehicles that were serviced with certain parts between two given dates. Furthermore, the vehicle's owner must live in a certain state. The way that this procedure accomplished its task is to divide the work into two separate queries. A temporary table is created to hold an intermediate result set. The temporary table gets populated with the `JobTicketID` numbers for jobs that used the given part between the two dates. This temporary table is then joined into the second SELECT, which looks for customers who live in a certain state. It is this second SELECT that actually returns the rows. Finally, before the procedure exits, the temporary table is dropped.

This procedure shows a common example of how an intermediate result set can be stored and then later used. This is the kind of processing that is not very conducive to front-end programming. It is much more convenient and concise to put all of this work into one stored procedure.

NOTE If you're really on the ball and not too sleepy from reading late last night, you might be asking why you didn't just perform that task all in one query. Good question! Actually, you could have. There are two reasons that we didn't have you do that. First, we wanted to demonstrate to you a more complex query that used an intermediate result set. Second, and more important, this is a technique that you should consider when dealing with large SELECT commands. Sometimes, when too many tables get joined into a query, it can actually get bogged down and perform badly. Breaking a query into separate steps like this might increase performance. Even if you don't see a significant performance gain, writing a query this way will often help you and your stored procedure heirs to understand it better.

Cursors and Looping

Another advanced feature that stored procedures can take advantage of is the cursor. A *cursor* is a mechanism that will hold the rows and columns of a result set so that they can be processed in some way. Often this processing involves looping through each row one by one, examining the data, and performing some action. You can think of the cursor as a pointer to a given row in a result set. Using commands, you can move the cursor down the list. The row that the cursor is pointing to is referred to as the current row. You are not limited to using cursors only in stored procedures. However, because there are several commands involved with cursor use, it is most common and convenient to write them into a stored procedure.

For database systems that support cursors, the syntax is pretty standard. First the cursor must be defined. A SELECT statement is part of the definition. This will be the basis for the result set.

```
DECLARE cursor_name CURSOR FOR select_statement;
DECLARE CURSOR cursor_name IS select_statement;
DECLARE CURSOR cursor_name FOR select_statement;
```

The first DECLARE syntax is for Sybase and Microsoft, the second is for Oracle, and the third is Informix. You can see that they all have the same requirements, a cursor name and a SELECT command. At the end of the DECLARE command, a full SQL SELECT is expected. It can be any valid SELECT, complete with joins and WHERE clauses if you need them. The following command defines a new cursor with a two-table query.

```
DECLARE vehicle2002 CURSOR FOR
SELECT c.FirstName, c.LastName, v.VehicleYear, v.Make, v.Model
  FROM Customer AS c
  JOIN Vehicle AS v
    ON c.CustomerID = v.CustomerID
 WHERE v.VehicleYear = 2002
ORDER BY c.LastName, c.FirstName, v.VehicleYear;
```

At this point, however, the command has not run. First it must be opened.

```
OPEN cursor_name;
```

This causes the SELECT defined in the cursor to be executed. The result set is stored in memory—it will not be returned to the screen or to a front-end application. You must use further cursor commands to access it. At this point you can begin to move the cursor through the result set.

```
FETCH cursor_name INTO variable1 [, variable2...];
```

The FETCH command will first move the cursor so that it points to the next row. It will then populate the variables with the data from the columns of the current row. The number of variables that you name in the FETCH command must match the number of columns in the SELECT. If the cursor is pointing to the last row in the result set when the FETCH command is issued, a special error code or flag will be set so that you'll know you're at the end.

When you're finished with the cursor, be sure to close it:

```
CLOSE cursor_name;
```

For the cursor example, you're going to create a stored procedure called DeleteOldJobs, which will look for jobs that are more than two years old and delete them.

```
CREATE PROCEDURE DeleteOldJobs AS
DECLARE @Ticket int

-- define the cursor
DECLARE c1 CURSOR FOR
 SELECT JobTicketID
   FROM JobTicket
  WHERE StartDate <= DATEADD(yy, -2, getdate( ));

-- open the cursor actually runs the query
OPEN c1;

-- put the first JobTicketID into the variable
FETCH c1 INTO @Ticket;

WHILE @@FETCH_STATUS = 0
   BEGIN
```

```
     -- delete the old job data
     DELETE FROM PartUsed
      WHERE JobTicketID = @Ticket;

     DELETE FROM JobTicketDetail
      WHERE JobTicketID = @Ticket;

     DELETE FROM JobTicket
      WHERE JobTicketID = @Ticket;

     -- move the cursor to the next JobTicketID, and put
     -- the ID in the variable.
     FETCH c1 INTO @Ticket;
   END

-- close the cursor and free up memory
CLOSE c1;
DEALLOCATE c1;

GO
```

Notice that the standard cursor commands like DECLARE, OPEN, and FETCH are combined with a Transact-SQL command such as WHILE. This is where you will have to learn your DBMS's language if you want to do something like loop through a cursor.

With this procedure in place, it can be run every now and then to purge the old data.

```
EXECUTE DeleteOldJobs;
```

Data-Modification Procedures

Stored procedures are not only good for data retrieval, but they can also be very useful for data modification. A stored procedure does not have to return a result set. If you have a stored procedure whose purpose it is to insert new customers and vehicles, there is really no need to return anything. Why would you want to write a procedure to handle simple INSERT commands? For just the same reasons already discussed. Even procedures that perform INSERT, UPDATE, and DELETE commands receive a performance gain from being precompiled. Also you can take advantage of the database system's language capabilities to perform several tasks from just one procedure call.

As an example, you're going to create a procedure that will add a new customer and the customer's vehicle to the database at the same time. This is a procedure that would be used when a new customer comes to the Slick Shop.

```
CREATE PROCEDURE        AddCustomerVehicle
  (@FirstName            varchar(20),
   @LastName             varchar(30),
   @Address              varchar(100),
   @City                 varchar(30),
   @StateOrProvince      char(2),
   @PostalCode           varchar(10),
   @PhoneNumber          varchar(10),
   @Year                 smallint,
   @Make                 varchar(30),
   @Model                varchar(30),
   @Color                varchar(30),
   @LicensePlate#        varchar(10))
AS

DECLARE @CustID int

-- insert a new customer row
INSERT INTO Customer
  (FirstName, LastName, Address, City,
   StateOrProvince, PostalCode, PhoneNumber)
VALUES
  (@FirstName, @LastName, @Address, @City,
   @StateOrProvince, @PostalCode, @PhoneNumber);

-- save the new CustomerID number that was auto-generated
SELECT @CustID = @@identity;

-- insert a new vehicle row
INSERT INTO Vehicle
  (VehicleYear, Make, Model, Color,
   LicensePlate#, LastServiceDate, CustomerID)
```

```
VALUES
  (@Year, @Make, @Model, @Color,
   @LicensePlate#, NULL, @CustID);
```

```
GO
```

Yes, this procedure does have a lot of arguments that you have to pass it. However, it is doing two jobs at once. First it inserts a new row into the Customer table. No big deal there. But look at what it does next. It saves the value of a special Transact-SQL variable called @@identity. This variable contains the auto-number that was just assigned to that new customer. This is valuable because you need it to make the insert into the Vehicle table. So that's what you have it do next.

These are basically the same two steps that you would have to perform if you were not using a stored procedure. Here, though, you've combined them into one call. As a matter of fact, without the procedure this task would be even more involved than just two INSERT commands. Think about this—after you do the first INSERT, how would you know what CustomerID the database just assigned to the new row? You need to know this so that you can use it for the INSERT to the Vehicle table. After the INSERT, you could SELECT the row back out by using the FirstName and LastName in the WHERE clause. But what if it returns more than one person with the same name? Alternatively, you could query for the highest CustomerID like this:

```
SELECT MAX(CustomerID)
  FROM Customer;
```

This would usually work. However, what happens if in the split second between your INSERT and this SELECT, someone else inserts a row into Customer? In that case, your SELECT command will actually return the number that the other user just generated. Not good! Even if you do find a reliable way to discover the new CustomerID, it will still be at least a three-step process: an INSERT, one or more SELECTs, and the final INSERT.

The stored procedure, on the other hand, is one simple call like this:

```
EXECUTE AddCustomerVehicle 'Junior', 'Richardson',
    '404 West Pine Ave.',
    'St. Louis', 'MO', '20115', '3135550987', '2002', 'Lincoln',
    'Continental', 'Blue', '38XP2JR';
```

Again, don't expect a result set to be returned from this procedure call. At the most you'll probably get two separate messages informing you that a row has been inserted.

Network Traffic

One last performance benefit of stored procedures that we stated was that smaller requests are sent to the server. Even if you just look at the small procedure GetCustomerVehicleData, you can see the difference. If a program were issuing that same SELECT command, it would be sending about five times as many characters over the network as it would if it just called the procedure. Once again, this is not the kind of thing you will notice when you are working on a database by yourself. But don't forget about the multiplying effect of all of the other users that will be sending SQL back and forth over the network when the database is in production. It's also worth noting that SQL database commands might not be the only traffic competing for the network. The network can have many types of data floating around, such as files being retrieved, output being sent to printers, e-mails being exchanged, and sports Web sites being downloaded.

The more your SQL commands can be condensed, the quicker they will make it to the server for execution. One of the best ways to do this is to package SQL commands into stored procedures.

Take a Break!

Okay, time to slow down for a minute and take a break. Kind of ironic that we'd tell you to slow down in the middle of a chapter on speed, isn't it? Do you think people will ever perform as relentlessly as computers?

Perhaps so if everybody had all kinds of performance optimization techniques like those we've been presenting.

Then again, people do have several. People can learn speed-reading, go speed-walking, send instant messages to friends, have a power lunch, get abs of steel in 15 minutes, get instant credit approval, grab some fast food, take a shot at being an instant winner, attend a fast-track training course, phone home while driving, fast forward through the commercials, and when it's all done take a power nap.

Wow, that should buy you enough time to finish reading this chapter before noon!

Understanding Transactions

Ready to get back to it? All right then, let's tackle the subject of transactions. In a nutshell, a *transaction* is one or more operations combined to form a single unit of work. An example would be when you say to your spouse in the morning, "I'm going to work now." That sounds like you're doing just one single thing. In reality you're going to work on a proposal, write several e-mails, code a program, attend a meeting, secure the company Web site, and on and on. You're bundling all of these activities into one thing you call "work."

Now, if you fail at one of your tasks during the day, you'll still go home and say, "I'm home from work!" This is where there is a major difference with a database transaction. A transaction in a relational database will not accept any failures at all.

One of the classic examples of a database transaction comes from the world of banking. Let's say you walk up to your bank's ATM and choose to make a transfer. You elect to transfer $100 from your savings account to your checking account. Now everybody knows that there is no real cash involved in this transfer—it's all done electronically. Your savings account balance will be reduced by $100, and your checking account balance will be increased by the same amount. This is an oversimplification, but for the purpose of this example, assume that there is a table called Checking and another called Savings. Let's also say that your account number is 1234.

In terms of SQL then, the ATM needs to make the following two updates in order to process your transfer.

```
UPDATE Savings
   SET Balance = Balance - 100
 WHERE AccountNbr = 1234;

UPDATE Checking
   SET Balance = Balance + 100
 WHERE AccountNbr = 1234;
```

Two quick updates, the ATM spits out a receipt, and you're on your way. But what if the second UPDATE fails for some reason? What if, in the fraction of a second between the first UPDATE and the second, the bank's database server crashes? We'll tell you what happens—you just lost $100! The first UPDATE reduced your savings balance, but the second one either failed or never got the chance to run. You could switch the order of these two commands, but you'd essentially have the same problem. This time the problem would go in your favor, so you might not mind, but the bank sure will!

This example presents a scenario where it is critical that both steps in the process must succeed. If it's not possible that they both succeed, they both must fail. This is what transactions are all about. They define a unit of work and ensure that every command within the unit succeeds. If just one thing in the transaction fails, everything must be put back the way it was at the beginning.

The way this is done is to begin a transaction before the first command and then check each command along the way. As soon as you detect that one of them has failed, cancel the transaction. If you reach the end without any failures, end the transaction normally. There are three commands you'll use to accomplish this.

```
BEGIN TRANSACTION;
COMMIT TRANSACTION;
ROLLBACK TRANSACTION;
```

Place the BEGIN TRANSACTION command before the first SQL command that modifies any data. This acts as a bookmark. If all goes well and all of your commands succeed, you issue a COMMIT TRANSACTION command at the end. This will make all changes permanent and allow the database to forget about that bookmark. If you find that a command has failed, you execute the ROLLBACK TRANSACTION command. This will cancel every command that was executed all the way back to the bookmark, the BEGIN TRANSACTION. After a ROLLBACK you cannot tell that anything happened. The database will be in exactly the same state as it was before you executed the BEGIN TRANSACTION.

NOTE The ROLLBACK TRANSACTION command will only reverse changes made in the current user's session. In other words, if you issue a ROLLBACK command, this will not affect the data that other users are changing at the same time.

Let's return back to the banking example now and look at the flowchart in Figure 5.5. This demonstrates the error checking that must be performed within a transaction. It shows that if either step fails, a ROLLBACK TRANSACTION command is immediately issued. Only if every single step succeeds should a COMMIT TRANSACTION be performed.

Let's turn our attention back to the Slick Shop database now. One place that you might want to use a transaction is when you add a new job ticket with all of its detail and part information. Assume that the Slick Shop has a front-end application that allows the employee to enter all of the job ticket information including the parts that will be used. This application has a Save button that will send all of this data to the database at the same time. It will insert one row into `JobTicket`, one or more rows into `JobTicketDetail`, and one or more rows into `PartUsed`. This is a good situation where you'll want to use a transaction. If there is ever an error

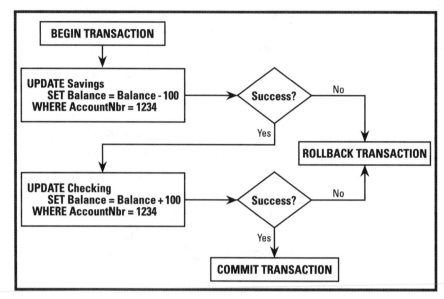

inserting into the `JobTicketDetail` table, you don't want to leave the successfully inserted row in `JobTicket`. If you did, you would have a job ticket sitting in the database without any related details.

Here's an example of a full transaction to handle the task of inserting a job ticket with all of its details. For this example, you're going to be sending each individual command one at a time from a front-end application. This application will perform some tasks and error checking that will be shown in parentheses.

```
BEGIN TRANSACTION;

INSERT INTO JobTicket
   (CustomerID, StartDate, VehicleID)
VALUES
   (3, '2002-12-22', 5);

(Application checks for an error, if there is an error...)
   ROLLBACK TRANSACTION;

(Application retrieves the new JobTicketID and finds that it is 13)
```

```
INSERT INTO JobTicketDetail
  (JobTicketID, LineItemNumber, ServiceID, HoursSpent)
VALUES
  (13, 1, 1, 0.5);

(Application checks for an error, if there is an error...)
  ROLLBACK TRANSACTION;

INSERT INTO PartUsed
  (JobTicketID, LineItemNumber, PartID, Quantity)
VALUES
  (13, 1, 2, 1);

(Application checks for an error, if there is an error...)
  ROLLBACK TRANSACTION;

INSERT INTO PartUsed
  (JobTicketID, LineItemNumber, PartID, Quantity)
VALUES
  (13, 1, 8, 1);

(Application checks for an error, if there is an error...)
  ROLLBACK TRANSACTION;

(If the application determines there were no errors at all...)
  COMMIT TRANSACTION;
```

Notice how the application meticulously checked for errors after every INSERT. Even if the first three had worked and the fourth had failed, the ROLLBACK would put the database back in its original state. No part of this job ticket would be in the database. This keeps the integrity of the data intact.

Sending each command separately from an application is usually not the best way to handle this situation, however. Doing it this way risks adversely affecting other users. When you begin a transaction, you're telling the database that you want to reserve the right to roll back the changes later if necessary. In order to ensure this capability, the database will place locks on your data and possibly other data that shares the same page. Some DBMSs work with data in 8K or 16K pages. Each page will contain several rows of data. When you insert or update a row, the database system can put a lock on the entire page until you are done. In the case of a transaction, you are not considered done until a COMMIT or ROLLBACK command has been issued.

NOTE Check the documentation for your DBMS. Each has its own locking schemes. Some lock pages, some lock a single row, whereas others lock an entire table. Your database system might even have commands or settings that you can use to fine-tune the type of locks that it will use.

The more commands that are in your transaction, the more locks you'll be creating. And the more locks you create, the better chance you have of blocking another user. You will block another user if your transaction has a lock on some data that another user needs to access. Whatever command the other user has run will just sit and wait until your transaction is done. This is why it's critical in a multiuser database that transactions run as quickly as possible. The transaction that you created sends all of its commands from an application. This will require a lot of interaction between the database and the application. This will naturally be slower than running the whole transaction on the database server. How can you do that? With a stored procedure, of course. With just a few changes, you can rewrite this transaction as a stored procedure.

```
CREATE PROCEDURE AddOilChangeJobTicket
   (@Cust int, @Start smalldatetime, @Vehicle int,
    @OilType int, @Quarts tinyint, @FilterType int, @Hours
      decimal(5, 2))
AS

DECLARE @TicketID int

BEGIN TRANSACTION;

INSERT INTO JobTicket
   (CustomerID, StartDate, VehicleID)
```

```
VALUES
  (@Cust, @Start, @Vehicle);

IF @@ERROR <> 0
  BEGIN
    ROLLBACK TRANSACTION;
    RETURN -1;
  END

SELECT @TicketID = @@IDENTITY;

INSERT INTO JobTicketDetail
  (JobTicketID, LineItemNumber, ServiceID, HoursSpent)
VALUES
  (@TicketID, 1, 1, @Hours);

IF @@ERROR <> 0
  BEGIN
    ROLLBACK TRANSACTION;
    RETURN -1;
  END

INSERT INTO PartUsed
  (JobTicketID, LineItemNumber, PartID, Quantity)
VALUES
  (@TicketID, 1, @OilType, @Quarts);

IF @@ERROR <> 0
  BEGIN
    ROLLBACK TRANSACTION;
    RETURN -1;
  END

INSERT INTO PartUsed
  (JobTicketID, LineItemNumber, PartID, Quantity)
VALUES
  (@TicketID, 1, @FilterType, 1);

IF @@ERROR <> 0
  BEGIN
    ROLLBACK TRANSACTION;
    RETURN -1;
  END
```

```
COMMIT TRANSACTION;
RETURN 0;

GO
```

NOTE   As before, this procedure is written in SQL Server's Transact-SQL language. If you're using a different DBMS, you'll have a couple of differences, such as the way you determine whether there was an error and the way you retrieve the auto-generated `JobTicketID`.

This procedure, `AddOilChangeJobTicket`, is designed to add a new job ticket, add one line item for the oil change, and use two parts: oil and an oil filter. As discussed earlier in the stored procedure section of this chapter, there are several advantages to having these commands combined in one procedure. The command sent to the database is much smaller, the code is combined into one neat package, and you have your database system's language available to use. As far as transactions go, having these commands in a stored procedure means that they will be executed quicker and therefore hold locks open for a shorter time period.

One of the keys, then, to writing good transactions is to get them to do their job as quickly as possible. We've just suggested that a stored procedure is one way to do this. Another is to try to keep the transaction as short as you can. If it has to include 15 different commands, that's okay. But if it can get the same thing done in only 10 commands, that's the way to go. The fewer the number of commands, the more likely the transaction will run quicker, which means holding fewer locks open for less time.

If for some reason you cannot use a stored procedure (maybe your DBMS doesn't support them), by all means never stop in the middle of a transaction for user interaction. After the BEGIN TRANSACTION has been sent, never prompt the user for information or stop to display a message. Once a prompt or message like this pops up, there's no telling how long it will be before the user responds to it. They might leave for their lunch break. Meanwhile the transaction will be half complete and might be holding locks open that are blocking other users.

A nice feature of a transaction is that other database users will not be able to see any of your changes until the transaction is committed. If another user happens to run a SELECT command while your transaction is still running, their results will not reflect your changes. They will see the data the way it was before you changed it. This prevents them from seeing incomplete or inconsistent data. If you were running the AddOilChangeJobTicket stored procedure at the same time someone else was selecting job ticket data, they would not want to see incomplete data. If they could see your changes as you made them, they might see a JobTicket row without any matching details. Another reason for not letting them see your changes is because you might perform a ROLL-BACK. You don't want another user to see data changes that may end up getting cancelled. They would be left looking at rows that don't really exist. Now the instant that you perform a COMMIT TRANSACTION, your changes will be made permanent and all users will see them.

One more thing—you will always be able to see your own changes even before they are committed. If in the middle of a transaction you need to select some data, your changes will be visible to you. You will be the only user to whom the database shows your changes until they are committed.

Optimizing Your Database

The optimization techniques talked about so far this morning will go a long way toward putting your database in high gear. In this final part of the chapter, we'll give you some advanced tuning options and ideas. They will be most useful to you if you are developing a large-scale, high-volume, or mission-critical database. These databases usually have higher expectations placed on them and excellent performance is a top priority. That's not to say that your smaller, low-volume databases cannot use the techniques as well. It's just that it may not be worth the time and effort involved. You might only end up gaining a few milliseconds of speed from your small database. A large database with dozens or hundreds of users, on the other hand, might be able to gain several seconds per transaction.

Fine-Tune Your Queries

There are many things that can be done to speed up the SQL that you write. This section presents many different ideas for writing queries, returning results, and debugging applications.

Use Those Indexes

We started this chapter talking about the importance of indexes. So by now it goes without saying that you'll want to try to get as many queries as possible to use one or more indexes. That's what they're there for! Set aside a few different points during each project to review the types of queries that are being used. Use this time to determine whether there need to be more indexes or whether some are going unused. You'll take your best guess when you first create the database and then reevaluate as development progresses. Often you'll find out that a new index is needed after the database is being used in a production environment.

So how will you know when a new index is needed? You'll usually find out from someone else with a not-so-subtle clue like, "Hey, why is this thing so slow?" If an end user or a developer can show you a screen or an operation that seems to take too long, this will give you a good starting place. For example, a user complains that it used to take about one second for the customer search list to pop up, but now it takes 10 seconds. The first thing to do is to look for the query that generates that list. Maybe the query looks like this:

```
SELECT FirstName, LastName, Address,
       City, StateOrProvince, PostalCode, PhoneNumber
  FROM Customer
 WHERE StateOrProvince = 'IL';
```

The problem might be that over time, more and more customers have been added to the `Customer` table and that the `StateOrProvince` column is not indexed. If there's no index, this query will have to perform a table scan every time it runs. The solution could be as simple as creating an index on this column.

What if, in a situation like this, there was already an index on the column or creating one didn't seem to help? In this case, it could be a problem with the way an application is interacting with the database. To find out for sure, first eliminate the application from the equation. Copy the query from the application and run it in your DBMS's query editor or Interactive SQL (ISQL) environment. This will show you how well the query performs without any overhead or strange things that may be happening inside an application. If you still consider the query to be slow in this environment, you know that there is fine-tuning work to be done. This could be anywhere from creating a simple index to restructuring the tables involved in the query. There are many other options that will give you some ideas in the remainder of this chapter.

Avoid Large Result Sets

If you find that the query is running much quicker outside of the application, you've already made some progress. One problem might be that the query is just returning too much data. The example query for a customer search list returns all of the customers who live in Illinois. An example of this customer search is shown in Figure 5.6.

If there are thousands of customers in this state, it might take a while for the application to receive that many rows. Sure the query might run quickly, but getting all of those bytes from the database over to the application might be the slow part. If you could reduce the number of bytes being transferred, that might improve performance. There are two ways to do this: bring back fewer rows or bring back fewer columns. Is it really necessary to return seven columns in this customer search list? Maybe it could be split up. The query could select just the `FirstName`, `LastName`,

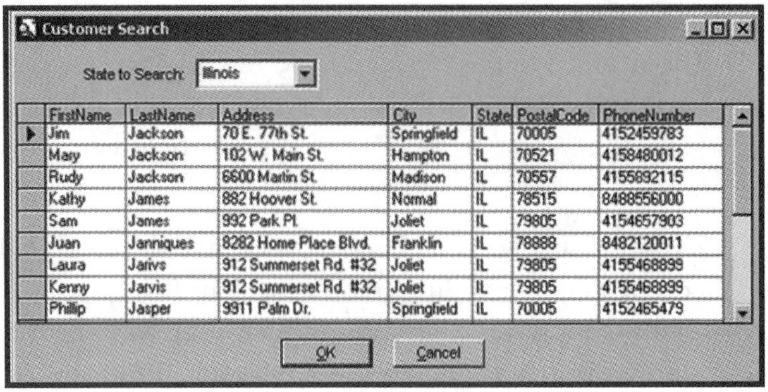

Figure 5.6

A customer search window that returns a lot of columns and rows.

and Address columns and display them in a list. A customer could be selected, and further details could be displayed on demand. This could significantly reduce the amount of data being pulled from the database.

Limiting the number of rows returned can be a big help as well. The search window allows the user to select a state and will return all customers who live in that state. If this still returns hundreds or thousands of rows, you might want to include an addition search condition. You could add a last name or city search option. Either one of these will significantly reduce the number of rows that are returned. Not only will this allow the data to be displayed faster, but the data will also be more manageable for the user to browse through. This type of customer search is displayed in Figure 5.7.

Sorting Data

If you must return a large result set, consider its sort order. Is it being sorted by the database server or the client PC? Does it need to be sorted at all? Although database servers are very good at sorting, there may be times

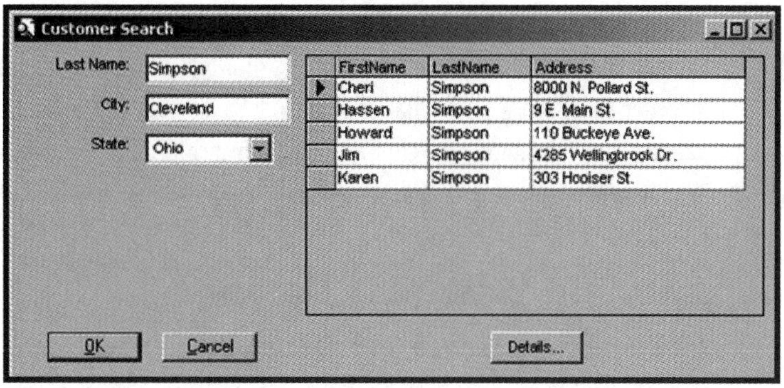

Figure 5.7

This search window
returns fewer
columns and fewer
rows. A button is
provided to view
the full details of a
selected customer.

when you find it better to issue a SELECT command without an
ORDER BY clause. If the database has very heavy simultaneous usage,
you might want your queries to get on and off the server as quickly as
they can. One way to do this is to skip the sorting step. If this sounds
good, but you really need sorted data, you have a couple of options. If
you want the data in the same order as a clustered index, you're in luck.
The data is already sorted and will be returned that way. If not, you could
have the client PC sort it. This is a definite part of the equation that you'll
want to consider. Sorting data at the client means it will not have to con-
tend with any other database processes during the sort. Most sort routines
that are built into programming and reporting tools are very quick. On
the downside, this might hinder users who are stuck with PCs that are
underpowered. The question of whether to perform sorts at the client or
the server is often one that can only be answered by observing production
database usage or by stress testing.

◄◄◄◄◄◄◄◄◄◄◄◄◄◄◄◄◄◄◄◄◄◄◄◄◄◄◄◄◄◄◄◄◄◄◄◄◄

Stress testing is the process of running multiple database operations at the same time in order to observe performance. Often a stress test will attempt to duplicate or even exceed the maximum expected load of its future production environment.

◄◄◄◄◄◄◄◄◄◄◄◄◄◄◄◄◄◄◄◄◄◄◄◄◄◄◄◄◄◄◄◄◄◄◄◄◄

Load Up Your Test Database

It's best if you can load up your development database with a lot of sample data. Put as much data in as you expect there to be when the database goes live. This will help performance problems to surface long before it gets into the user's hands. It will point out slow queries, the need for indexing, or inappropriate use of front-end applications. However, loading sample data is often a step that gets skipped by developers and DBAs. Why? It's a pain and it takes a long time. No one is going to sit and type in hundreds of thousands of rows of test data. So most of the time developers are writing SQL for tables that have only a dozen or so rows. Tables that small will always perform fabulously! It's worth the effort to spend a few hours or even a few days to get some good sample data created.

Creating test data doesn't have to be hard. Here are a few options. First, if the database you are creating is replacing another, draw your data from the old database. This is the best possible situation. You'll have real data complete with its real-life quirks and anomalies. Your DBMS might have tools that can directly copy data from the old database to the new one. If not, it will have a way to import data from a file. One of the issues that you'll probably face here is that an old database and a new one often are far from identical. It will take some work on your part to get the right columns into the right tables.

If you don't have the luxury of an existing database to draw your data from, you could write a program. A small program or stored procedure could be written to perform inserts into your tables. Programs like this often have a base set of data that they draw from to create the INSERT commands. For example, when building an INSERT command for the

`Customer` table, the program might randomly choose a last name from a file, then randomly choose a first name, then randomly choose an address, and so on. This method lets you loop as many times as you want to create the number of rows you need. The data that you'll end up with will be a little redundant, but you'll have the volume that you need.

One final option we'll discuss for loading sample data is to use a commercially available test-data-generation tool. You or your company might already own one of these. Many data-modeling tools already include this as a feature. Check the help file or product documentation if you're not sure. It might be a feature that's buried deep in a menu somewhere. If you don't have one, there are several companies that market these kinds of products. One such product is called WinSQL from IndusSoft Technologies. Although this product's main function is to edit and execute SQL, it also includes a data generation feature. It can create realistic data by reading from files or by getting data from other tables. It can also quickly create random data by matching a pattern or by simply generating meaningless garbled text. Figure 5.8 shows this tool being used to generate some customer data.

Following is some of the sample data that this tool generated:

Customer ID	FirstName	LastName	Address	City
41	Kyle	Buscavage	12011 Sunset Valley Rd	Bohemia
42	Evangelos	Antonini	11606 Vantage Hill Rd	Green Bay
43	Melvin	Bird	8 W 36th St	Fort Lauderdale
44	Lauren	Bowling	231 Old Tower Hill Rd	Cincinnati
45	Lucien	Cantey	356 Chebacco Rd	Auburndale
46	Nathan	Bushek	515 N Sam Houston Pkwy	Huntingdon Valley
47	Nakhle	Barge	5218 S Westnedge Ave	Cambridge
48	Cesario	Adonizio	4199 Campus Dr Ste 550	Irvine
49	Gilbert	Bonner	910 Duncan Ln APT 44	Chicago Heights
50	Andrea	Ash	9030 W Sahara Ave 340	Beaverton

Figure 5.8

WinSQL is one
tool that can
quickly create a
large amount of
test data.

A more expensive but possibly more robust tool is called DataFactory from Quest Software. Like WinSQL, it will display the tables and columns from your database and allow you to define how each column is to be loaded. DataFactory, however, is keenly aware of foreign key references and will create valid data between tables with correct referential integrity.

Information about WinSQL can be found at **http://www.indus-soft.com/**, and the Web site for DataFactory is **http://www.quest.com/**.

Limit Your Use of Grouping Commands

Although GROUP BY and HAVING clauses are very nice features, they, too, take extra time to process. Once again if you find yourself developing on a multiuser database that you expect to be heavily used, you might want to reconsider these two clauses. As you can imagine, there are several steps that the DBMS must take to group, summarize, and refilter a GROUP BY, HAVING query. Every step that a query must perform will not only take longer but is an extra opportunity to get stuck waiting in line for another process to complete. Results that have to be grouped and summarized many times can have this performed by a client application. Development tools such as Visual Basic and PowerBuilder, for example, have built-in graphical tools that can easily handle data grouping and summarization. In fact, reporting tools such as Crystal Reports and Cognos Impromptu do not want you to use GROUP BY and HAVING clauses. One of the strongest suits of these tools is their ability to crunch, combine, rotate, and drill down into data. Using these clauses would actually take away much of the flexibility of these types of reporting tools.

Drop Indexes before Bulk Loads

Earlier in this chapter, we talked about the fact that indexes will actually cause more work for INSERT, UPDATE, and DELETE commands. Most of the time this will not even be noticeable, especially when you're inserting just a row here and a row there. But when you're trying to load hundreds or thousands of rows at the same time, the performance hit can be all too visible. The indexes will be constantly reordering themselves over and over again for every new row that is inserted. There are two things that can help speed bulk loads. First try dropping all of the indexes before loading the data. Without any indexes you'll see the data load much quicker. You will, of course, have to spend some time re-creating the indexes after the data is loaded. However, many times this two-step process is much faster than loading with the indexes still on the table. If you find that it's not practical to drop the indexes for a short time, try sorting the data before loading it. If the data is sorted the same way as one of the indexes, that index will have much less work to perform when each new row comes in. The best choice, if possible, is to have the data presorted the same as the clustered index.

Avoid Table Scans

When we talked earlier about table scans, we practically called them evil. Well, if you're dealing with a large table, they are evil. Nothing will make a query crawl slower than having it table scan 500,000 rows.

Imagine what the following SELECT command must go through to find matching rows on a 500,000-row table with no indexes.

```
SELECT FirstName, LastName
  FROM Customer
 WHERE City = 'Springfield'
   AND (StateOrProvince = 'AZ' OR StateOrProvince = 'NV')
   AND LastName LIKE '%z%';
```

The poor database will have to examine every single row and look for the city of Springfield. Then it will check for either of two states. Finally, the killer, it will have to scan through every last name looking for the letter z. This is a fairly simple query to investigate. It is easy to see the three columns that are being used and which ones could benefit from an index. The City column could and possibly StateOrProvince as well. A more complex query, however, like the next one might not be so easy to figure out.

```
SELECT v.VehicleYear, v.Make, v.Model, p.Cost, pu.Quantity
  FROM Vehicle AS v
  JOIN JobTicket AS jt
    ON v.VehicleID = jt.VehicleID
   AND jt.StartDate > '2002-01-01'
  JOIN JobTicketDetail AS jtd
    ON jt.JobTicketID = jtd.JobTicketID
  JOIN PartUsed AS pu
    ON jtd.JobTicketID = pu.JobTicketID
   AND jtd.LineItemNumber = pu.LineItemNumber
  JOIN Part AS p
    ON pu.PartID = p.PartID
   AND p.Cost > 5.00
 WHERE v.VehicleYear > 1969;
```

This query joins five tables together in order to show parts that cost more than $5.00 used in jobs after January 1, 2002, in cars built after 1969. If this were a query that you found to be running slowly, it might not be easy to know where to start looking. The first step, though, would be to look at each column that is involved in a join and make sure that it is indexed. So you'd check columns such as VehicleID, JobTicketID, and LineItemNumber. If this doesn't help or the indexes were already in place, it might be time to dig deeper.

Examine the Execution Plan

Some of the database systems have analysis tools built into them to help debug queries like this. Each DBMS has its own syntax for turning this feature on. Oracle's command, for example, is EXPLAIN PLAN, whereas SQL Server uses SET SHOWPLAN_TEXT ON. Each DBMS will also have its own way of displaying the results. When this option is turned on and the query is executed, instead of ordinary rows and columns returned, an execution plan will be displayed. You'll see the optimizer's plan of attack. Now, looking into a computer's brain is not always pretty. Take a look at SQL Server's SHOWPLAN_TEXT for a five-table query:

```
Nested Loops(Inner Join, OUTER REFERENCES:([pu].[PartID]))
    Nested Loops(Inner Join, OUTER REFERENCES:([jtd].
        [LineItemNumber],
                    [jtd].[JobTicketID]))
        Nested Loops(Inner Join, OUTER REFERENCES:([jt].
            [JobTicketID]))
            Nested Loops(Inner Join, OUTER REFERENCES:
                        ([jt].[VehicleID]))
                Clustered Index Scan
                    (OBJECT:([SlickShop].[dbo].[JobTicket].
                    [PK__JobTicket__7F60ED59] AS [jt]),
                    WHERE:([jt].[StartDate]>'Jan  1 2002
                        12:00AM'))
                Clustered Index Seek
                    (OBJECT:([SlickShop].[dbo].[Vehicle].
                    [PK__Vehicle__78B3EFCA] AS [v]),
                    SEEK:([v].[VehicleID]=[jt].[VehicleID]),
                    WHERE:([v].[VehicleYear]>1969)
                        ORDERED FORWARD)
            Clustered Index Seek
                (OBJECT:([SlickShop].[dbo].[JobTicketDetail].
                [PK_JobTicketDetail] AS [jtd]),
                SEEK:([jtd].[JobTicketID]=[jt].[JobTicketID])
                ORDERED FORWARD)
        Clustered Index Seek
            (OBJECT:([SlickShop].[dbo].[PartUsed].[PK_PartUsed]
                AS [pu]),
```

```
                    SEEK:([pu].[JobTicketID]=[jtd].[JobTicketID] AND
                    [pu].[LineItemNumber]=[jtd].[LineItemNumber])
                    ORDERED FORWARD)
     Clustered Index Seek
          (OBJECT:([SlickShop].[dbo].[Part].[PK__Part__7D78A4E7]
               AS [p]),
          SEEK:([p].[PartID]=[pu].[PartID]),
          WHERE:(Convert([p].[Cost])>5.00) ORDERED FORWARD)
```

Yikes! We weren't kidding when we said that it was not going to be pretty. Don't worry, though, we're not going to get into the full details of this output. We just want to point out some of the key things you'll want to look for in an execution plan output like this. The plan will show indexes that are going to be used to fetch the data. It will often also show the order in which it will process the query. The biggest thing that you'll be looking for is some kind of reference to a table scan. In the output, there are several lines that say Clustered Index Seek, but notice the one near the top that says Clustered Index Scan. That keyword *scan* is the clue you're looking for. It tells you that at least one table scan is going to be performed. If you read down a couple lines farther, you'll see the culprit behind the table scan: WHERE:([jt].[StartDate]>'Jan 1 2002 12:00AM').

Based on this execution plan, the first thing that you should try is to create an index on the StartDate column in the JobTicket table. Indeed, after you create this index and rerun the SHOWPLAN_TEXT, you get slightly different output from the execution plan. This time instead of reporting a scan, it says Index Seek and then names the new index. It looks as though that will resolve the table scan problem. Of course, the true test will be to run the query in its normal environment and see how long it takes.

Deadlocks

Deadlock situations will not only slow users down, but they will also stop users in their tracks. A deadlock occurs when two users are each waiting to access data that the other has locked. Figure 5.9 helps explain deadlocking.

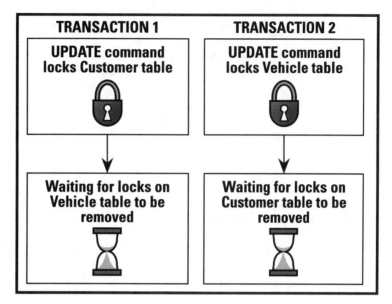

Figure 5.9

A deadlock occurs when two users are waiting for each other to release their locks.

In this example two users have each started a transaction. They are both updating the Customer and Vehicle tables. The first transaction updates Customer and locks a part of that table. Before the first transaction does anything else, the second transaction updates Vehicle and locks part of that table. Now the first transaction wants to update the Vehicle table but must wait until the lock is released. Likewise, the second one wants to update the Customer table but must wait for that lock to be released. So like two stubborn mules, neither one wanting to budge, they have a deadlock. Both transactions will just sit there and wait. Eventually, one of them will time out, fail, and get rolled back, allowing the other one to proceed.

One way to help avoid deadlocks is to write the transactions so that they access the tables in the same order. If you could rewrite the second transaction to update Customer first and Vehicle second, this will help. Figure 5.10 shows how the scenario looks when the transactions update in the same order.

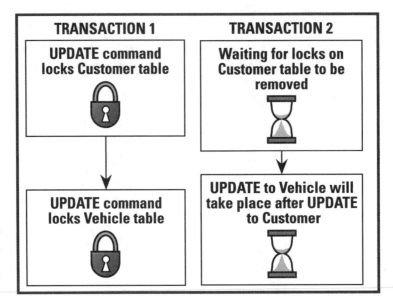

Figure 5.10

The transactions access the tables in the same order to avoid a deadlock.

This way these two transactions will never be waiting for each other to release locks. One of them might have to wait a short time for the other to commit. As Figure 5.10 shows, if the second transaction tries to begin while the first one is running, it will get stopped right away. It will be freed to continue as soon as the first transaction is either committed or rolled back.

Set Up a Database Trace

Many times it's difficult to determine the cause of a performance problem because a front-end application hides all of the SQL commands that it uses. When you press Search, Save, or OK in an application, what is SQL sending to the database? Is it just one simple SELECT or is it a half-dozen complex queries? Sometimes it's hard to determine even when you wrote the program's source code. One way to look under the covers is to put a *trace* between your front-end application and your database. A trace will allow you to view SQL commands and data that are passing to and from the database.

There are a few different ways you can capture this information. Your database system might come with this feature. If it does, you'll probably have to log on as the administrator and turn this feature on. If it does not have this feature, you might be able to set up a trace using Open Database Connectivity (ODBC). If your front-end application runs on Windows and uses ODBC to connect to the database, you can open the ODBC administrator and turn on tracing. A log file will be created containing all SQL commands that your application sends while it runs. When the application is finished, you can review the log file. If neither of these is an option, you could use a network packet-sniffer. This kind of program will intercept all of the traffic that is passing through a network, not just SQL commands.

◆ ◆

Unless you or someone you know is experienced at sniffing network packets, you might want to leave this option alone. There are a lot of bytes passed back and forth on a network, and you'll be seeing all of them. Most of what you'll see will be confusing binary data. Unless you or your friend knows what you're doing, it could turn out to be a frustrating experience.

◆ ◆

If none of the tracing options are available, you can just do it from within the application. This suggestion assumes that you have access to the source code or access to someone who does. Go to the part of the application where you suspect the performance problem. Modify the program such that either before or after each SQL command is sent, output is also sent to a log file. This can just be a plain file that will contain one SQL command after the next. You could even make the application a little fancy and create a switch that will turn this feature on only when you need it.

Fine-Tune the Database

A big consideration when you are designing a database for performance is its main role. Does the database fit the mold of an online transaction processing (OLTP) database or online analytical processing (OLAP) database? An OLTP database is one that is most heavily involved with data entry and modification. As its name suggests, its job is to process transactions. It expects to deal with inserts, updates, and deletes all day long and possibly in high volumes. This is not to say that queries cannot be run against an OLTP database. However, because its main focus is data collection, queries and reports might be limited. An OLAP database, on the other hand, is made for reporting. It will have tables specifically built to serve up a wide variety of reports quickly. This type of database will usually not have any data entry taking place. New or updated data is fed to it in batches hourly, daily, or weekly.

The type of database that you are building will have an effect on the way you design your tables and indexes. If you are building an OLTP database, you will want to normalize the tables in order to reduce entry and maintenance of redundant data. Normalization will also help keep the integrity of the data intact. Because an OLTP database is not as concerned with reporting, it will benefit from fewer indexes. Remember that indexes will actually slow down data modification commands. An OLAP database is built for reporting speed. Because it will not be accepting data entry, it can be loaded up with indexes. Several index combinations can be built to aid a variety of queries. The table structure will be much different too. These tables can actually be denormalized. When two or more tables are brought together, there will be fewer tables involved in the query. Fewer tables mean fewer joins, and fewer joins mean quicker results. Remember these tables are not going to accept data entry, so the fact that they have redundant data no longer matters.

The OLAP database is actually a copy of the OLTP, except it's just shaped or stored differently. A typical scenario is that the OLTP database works hard all day receiving new data and modifications. Later, in the middle of the night, jobs are run that extract data from this database and load it into the OLAP database. Before the data can be loaded, it might have to be joined or summarized in order to fit the table structures. The next morning both databases are ready to begin their day. The OLTP is ready for more data, and the OLAP is ready to run reports.

The Slick Shop database is an OLTP database. You've normalized it and created only a few indexes. What would its sister database, the OLAP, look like? First of all you'd identify some tables to denormalize. Let's say you're planning to do a lot of reporting on job ticket data. To show all details of a job ticket, you'd have to query JobTicket, JobTicketDetail, PartUsed, Part, and Service. That's five tables and several columns to be joined. Instead, you'll build one single table to hold this information.

```
CREATE TABLE          JobTicketCombined
  (JobTicketID        int,
   CustomerID         int,
   StartDate          smalldatetime,
   EndDate            smalldatetime,
   VehicleID          int,
   LineItemNumber     tinyint,
   ServiceDesc        varchar(100),
   RatePerHour        money,
   HoursSpent         decimal(5, 2),
   DateComplete       smalldatetime,
   PartDesc           varchar(100),
   PartCost           money,
   Quantity           tinyint);
```

This table has a lot of columns, and it will have a lot of rows too. Look how the table not only has a separate row for every line item but also has a separate row for every part used. Much of the data in this table, such as JobTicketID, CustomerID, and StartDate, will be repeated over and over again. That's okay, though, because this database will not be used to update data. You don't have to worry about finding all of the copies of the same data and getting them updated. This is especially true if your nightly batch loading jobs remove all of the data before reloading the tables. In this case, the tables would get a fresh start every night.

As mentioned earlier, indexing is a big part of an OLAP database. You would start placing indexes on this table with very little worry. You don't have to be as cautious as before because the goal here is quick output. But data does have to get into the tables at some point, doesn't it? It might be nightly or weekly, but whenever it happens all of those indexes are going to slow down the load. This is something that you'll have to measure. If it takes four hours to fully reload your heavily indexed OLAP database, is this okay? It might be, especially if it's during a time period in which no one uses this database. If your office is closed at night, there should be plenty of time for this nightly update. If this nightly job, however, is taking 15 hours, it's time for a new plan. One idea mentioned before is to load the tables without their indexes. Drop all of the indexes, load the data, and then re-create them. This will allow the data to be loaded much faster as it eliminates the needless index reorganization. When the indexes are created as the last step, they only have to do their thing one time.

The OLAP table you just built is at the detail level. In it you'll be able to find all details from every job. You might want to build summary level tables as well. These will have data that has already been totaled up and stored into neat categories such as weekly or monthly totals. This would save even more time when reports are being generated. If you had people who were interested in the Slick Shop's monthly statistics, you'd build another table, like this one:

```
CREATE TABLE          JobTicketMonthly
   (Month             tinyint,
    Year              smallint,
    NumOfJobs         int,
    LineItemsPerJob   tinyint,
    AvgRatePerHour    money,
    AvgHoursSpent     decimal(5, 2),
    AvgPartCost       money,
    TotalRevenue      money);
```

This is a very different kind of table. It has just one row for every month of every year. On that row, you'll be able to see the number of jobs that were performed, average hours and costs, as well as the total revenue for the month. These are all numbers that might take a while to generate, but they only need to be done one time. A program or stored procedure that runs at the end of every month can summarize the data and insert a new row into this table. Now whenever someone needs monthly data, it's a lightning-quick query away.

Fine-Tune the Server

Another opportunity to gain some performance is to place data and indexes on separate disk controllers. This means that one physical read/write device will access data whereas another accesses indexes, so you can have two controllers that are working simultaneously. The time to set this up actually comes way back at the time the database is created. There are a couple of requirements to make use of this feature. First and foremost, your server must have at least two separate hard drives. Second, your DBMS must allow you to store data and indexes on separate drives. The first thing to do is to allocate space for the data when you first create the database. Remember in the last chapter when we talked about creating a database, we said that you can usually accept the default options. This is a case where you will want to find the syntax for your database system's CREATE DATABASE command. It will show you how to specify a particular drive that the data and indexes will be stored on. The next step comes when you are creating tables and indexes. When creating them, you will have the opportunity to specify the drive where the data will reside. The same goes for indexes. By carefully separating them like this, you can nicely divide the work across two or more drives.

Another option you might have available to you is called *striping*. This is the practice of taking a single table and spreading its data out over two or more disks. This will also be an option when creating your table. You can specify multiple disks on which to store the data. The database system will then take care of spreading out (striping) the data equally across each of the disks. The advantage will be in both queries and data modification commands. Each disk controller can work for you at the same time when accessing this table. A possible disadvantage, however, is that unless these drives are dedicated to this one table, they'll be competing with activity from other tables. Striping is most often used with very large tables.

What's Next?

Armed with all of these good optimizing ideas, you're probably all set to drive over to the office and start tuning all of your databases, right? Okay, okay, we know it's still Sunday. Don't go back any sooner than you have to.

After lunch we'll pick it up again and talk about security. We'll show you how to let the people in who should be there and how to keep everyone else out. You'll be able to do this with password protection on a few different levels. We'll also introduce you to the stored procedure's first cousin, the trigger.

Security— Putting the Padlocks on

➤ Considering Database Security

➤ Creating and Using Views

➤ Using Triggers

It's hard to forget about security. Everywhere you turn, you're reminded of it. You're prompted for several passwords each day, viruses occasionally fill up your mailbox, and every few weeks news breaks that a hacker has breached yet another security hole. Hollywood even produces a new movie every so often that glamorizes the world of hacking. Your concern, as far as SQL goes, is how you can secure this database that you've spent all this time on. This afternoon's session is going to focus on just that topic, database security. We'll break down this broad category and take a look at security from several angles.

Considering Database Security

It will probably be no surprise to you to hear that database security via SQL is password based. Like us, you no doubt have dozens of usernames and passwords that you have to keep track of. This seems to be the most accepted form of security right now. The basic protection model of a relational database comes in two layers. A username and a password are used to gain access to a database. From that point, this same username has specific rights assigned to it. Just because a user can log on to a database does not mean that the user has free rein over all of the data. It's like your workplace—just because you were given a key to the office's front door doesn't mean you'll be able to open every door once you're inside. You're not supposed to be in the boss's office, so you're locked out. (Hopefully, he invites you in at least around annual pay-raise time.)

Letting People In

The first thing that you need to do for your database users is to let them in the front door. If you've been following along in the book so far, trying out the samples, you already have an idea what this security is about. Almost any database that you deal with will force you to log on to it before you can do anything else. Some come with default usernames and passwords; others have you set them up when the database is first installed. One notable exception is Microsoft Access. By default, Access lets you create a new database and work away as long as you want without password protection. You can go back later to set up passwords in Access whenever you are ready.

When it comes to creating new user accounts, each DBMS does things its own way. We'll show you examples of several in a few minutes. But first we want to talk about a couple of security options that are provided by the larger vendors.

Database Authentication

The first option is one that is provided by all database systems. This is the method where a person provides a username and password to the database for verification. The database software is in charge of validating this information and allowing or denying access. Passwords are stored and maintained by the database system, most likely encrypted within the database itself.

Operating System Authentication

Many of the large DBMSs offer the option of authenticating users at the operating system level. When this option is in place, once users are logged on to their operating system, network, or domain, they don't need to log on a second time to access the database. As long as their current username has been given permission in the database, they are free to go straight in.

This authentication model has some pros and cons to consider. One of the big advantages is that you'll be able to make your database applications more seamless. Users can just open the database application and begin working. The need for yet another username and password has been eliminated. The database will still know who the user is and be able to apply the correct privileges with regard to the data. Another advantage is that this introduces the opportunity to use more advanced security measures, such as card readers or fingerprint scanners. Devices like this can grant access to a network after which the authentication is passed automatically to the database.

Many people choose the database authentication instead because they want users to explicitly log on every time. Sometimes in an office environment there are shared workstations in use. Using operating system authentication would require that one user log off of a workstation and the other log on before starting the database application. An even more common reason for not letting the operating system authenticate is the problem of users who get up and leave their workstation unprotected. Because a database using this option does not require a password, this vacant workstation is leaving data vulnerable. Anyone who happens by and launches one of the database's applications will be seen by the database as this absent person. Any data that was meant for this person to see is now in the hands of someone else.

Creating User Accounts and Groups

Once you've decided on a method of authentication, you'll be ready to create the accounts. You'll take a look at creating both individual user accounts as well as groups. Using a group is a convenient way to assign privileges. Instead of assigning the same privileges over and over again to similar users, you can assign them one time to a group. You can then add and remove users from the group as often as you like.

As we said, user accounts and groups are created a different way on each DBMS. We'll cover several of them here so you can get a feel for them. We'll just show the basic syntax for each, so you'll want to check your documentation for any special options that might be available. One thing they all have in common is that in order to create user accounts and groups, you will have to be logged on as the system or database administrator.

Creating Server Logon Names and Roles in Microsoft

To create a new user logon name in Microsoft SQL Server, you'll use a system-stored procedure.

```
EXECUTE sp_addlogin logonname [, password] [, database];
```

This is one of many stored procedures that come preinstalled with the database system. The arguments to this procedure are a unique database logon name, an optional password, and an optional database name that the user will connect to by default. You'll use this procedure to create a server logon name for a new employee of the Slick Shop.

```
EXECUTE sp_addlogin 'JackieP', 'oillady', 'SlickShop';
```

If you want to use operating system authentication, just make sure the logon name is the same as the user's network logon name. After running this procedure, Jackie can now log on to the database server but can't do anything. Even though you've assigned her a default database, she is not yet a user in this database. Her logon name must be added as a user to each database that you want to grant her access into. This is done with another system-stored procedure.

```
USE dbname;
EXECUTE sp_adduser loginname;
```

First you need to get yourself into the correct database. Then on the procedure call, you specify the logon name that you created earlier.

```
USE slickshop;
GO
EXECUTE sp_adduser 'JackieP';
```

Now Jackie will be able to not only log on to the database server but also get into the SlickShop database. Sadly for her, though, this will still not do her any good. At this point she has no rights. She cannot view or edit any data. This will come later when we talk about granting permissions.

If you want to get rid of a logon account, you first must drop it as a user from each database that it's been added to.

```
USE slickshop;
GO
EXECUTE sp_dropuser 'JackieP';
```

Only after it's no longer a user in any database can its server logon name be dropped.

```
EXECUTE sp_droplogin 'JackieP';
```

NOTE Throughout the rest of this session you're going to use the JackieP logon account. So if you've just dropped it, you'll want to recreate it now.

Groups (or roles, as they are called in SQL Server) are very similar in that they are created with a system-stored procedure.

```
EXECUTE sp_addrole 'Accounting';
```

This new role that is created is different than a logon name because no one can use it to log on to the database server. Instead, it is available to accept members. Members can be added to the role with another procedure.

```
EXECUTE sp_addrolemember 'Accounting', 'JackieP';
```

Now any privileges that are given to the Accounting role are also automatically assigned to Jackie as well. Jackie can be removed from the group later with a similar command.

```
EXECUTE sp_droprolemember 'Accounting', 'JackieP';
```

In doing so, Jackie will lose all of the privileges that the Accounting role has. If she has any permissions that were specifically assigned to her, she will keep these. Finally, use this command to remove the entire role:

```
EXECUTE sp_droprole 'Accounting';
```

All users must be removed from the role before this command will be allowed.

Creating Server Logon Names and Groups in Sybase

Remember from the Friday Evening session that Sybase Adaptive Server and Microsoft SQL Server actually used to be the same product. Because of this, as we've already shown you several times, the two still share a lot of commands. In fact, the way user logon names are created is still the same. Refer to the preceding section on Microsoft for the following commands:

```
sp_addlogin
sp_adduser
sp_dropuser
sp_droplogin
```

Sybase, however, creates groups and roles differently. The syntax that we're going to show you is actually still supported by Microsoft, but the concept of the roles is now preferred. To create a new group, you'll use another system-stored procedure.

```
EXECUTE sp_addgroup 'Accounting';
```

Users can be added to the group like this:

```
EXECUTE sp_changegroup 'JackieP', 'Accounting';
```

This will put Jackie into the Accounting group. If she was already assigned to another group, she will be removed from it and placed in this group now. A user can be assigned to only one group at a time.

To drop a group, use this command:

```
EXECUTE sp_dropgroup 'Accounting';
```

A group cannot be dropped if it has any users still in it.

Roles are actually now the preferred method of grouping users in Sybase. A role is created with this command:

```
CREATE ROLE Marketing;
```

If you want to add Jackie to this role, you'd issue the following command:

```
GRANT ROLE Marketing TO JackieP;
```

You can even set up a hierarchy of roles within Sybase. You'd do this by granting one role access to another.

```
CREATE ROLE Finance;
GRANT ROLE Accounting TO Finance;
GRANT ROLE Payables TO Finance;
GRANT ROLE Receivables TO Finance;
```

This way you could have employees separated into their own roles such as `Payables` or `Receivables`. However, you could also have users in the `Finance` role that have access to everything that the other roles have.

To remove a role, you do not have to remove its members.

```
DROP ROLE Accounting;
```

All users within this role will lose their membership.

Creating Users and Roles in Oracle

If you use Oracle, the following syntax will allow you to create new users.

```
CREATE USER username
    IDENTIFIED BY password;
```

This is very similar to the commands that Sybase and Microsoft use. One difference is that this one command creates an account within the database, where Sybase and Microsoft needed two commands to do this. In this command you'll need to specify a new username and come up with a password. There are other options that you can use that will specify such things as the amount of disk space the logon name is limited to use and whether or not the password will expire in the future.

```
CREATE USER JackieP
    IDENTIFIED BY oillady;
```

Assuming this command is run from the SlickShop database, it will create Jackie as a database user. However, she will not be able to log on to the database until she has first been granted the CREATE SESSION privilege.

```
GRANT CREATE SESSION TO JackieP;
```

If Jackie quits the company, just use the following command to remove her account:

```
DROP USER JackieP;
```

Oracle also uses roles to group user accounts together. To create a new role, use the following syntax:

```
CREATE ROLE Accounting IDENTIFIED BY numbers;
```

Notice how the role has a password. This is one of many ways to create a new role. In this case, a user who wants to start using this role would need to supply the password with the SET ROLE command. User accounts can be added to the role with the following command:

```
GRANT Accounting TO JackieP;
```

Users can be removed from the role with this one:

```
REVOKE Accounting FROM JackieP;
```

And, finally, the role can be dropped. You can drop the role even if users are currently assigned to it. They will obviously not be in the role any more and will lose all privileges that the role had.

```
DROP ROLE Accounting;
```

Creating Users and Roles in Informix

With Informix, you will be using the operating system authentication that we talked about earlier. The user must first have a logon name created at the network. Informix will use this logon name. All you have to do is allow the user to connect to the database system. You do this with the GRANT command.

```
GRANT CONNECT TO JackieP;
```

Later, we'll show you the SQL GRANT command used by all databases. You'll use it to give people access to tables and other objects.

To remove Jackie as a user from the database, use the REVOKE command.

```
REVOKE CONNECT FROM JackieP;
```

A new role can be created with this command:

```
CREATE ROLE Accounting;
```

Next, users can be added to the role this way:

```
GRANT Accounting TO JackieP;
```

In order to make use of the role, after Jackie is logged in, she'll have to use this command:

```
SET ROLE Accounting;
```

This command will verify that she is indeed a member of this role and give her all access that has been previously granted to the role.

Creating Users in MySQL

In MySQL you use the GRANT command as follows to create Jackie's new account.

```
GRANT USAGE ON *.* TO JackieP@localhost IDENTIFIED BY oillady;
```

Like the other DBMSs, this just gets her into the database but doesn't give her access to any data yet.

Creating Users and Groups in Access

Microsoft Access is going to be the exception in the security discussion. Although Access has the same security features as the other database systems being discussed, it is not set up through commands. In Access, you manage all of the security through menu options and dialog boxes. For instance, to create a new user or group, select the Tools menu, and then Security, and then User and Group Accounts. The dialog box that opens will allow you to create a new user and assign a password.

Other dialog boxes allow groups to be created, users to be assigned to groups, and privileges to be assigned. It should be noted that many of the other DBMSs also have nice user interfaces like Access that let you do the same thing. However, because this is a SQL book, you'll continue to look at the commands to accomplish these tasks.

Granting Privileges

Now people have access to the database and they can log in. They might even be members of a group or be assigned to one or more roles. But unless they or their group is explicitly granted privileges, they are helpless. You'll be using the SQL GRANT and REVOKE commands to administer rights.

The most basic kind of database security that you can have is just to allow everyone to do everything. Don't laugh. Although this doesn't sound like security at all, it is actually a valid security model. In certain situations, the security measures that we're going to talk about are overkill. This is usually the case where there are a very limited number of users that are well trusted. Setting up and maintaining security on a table-by-table basis might actually be a waste of time. Remember, these users do need to have a valid database logon name in the first place. So there is some level of security.

Most of the time, however, you will want to set up restrictive security. There are many good reasons for this. It will help to prevent accidental modifications or deletions. It will prevent extraneous objects, like tables, views, and procedures, from being created. But probably most important, it will keep prying eyes off of data that shouldn't be seen.

Granting Table Privileges

You've already seen the GRANT command in action a few times. It's used by some of the database systems to create users. Standard SQL uses the GRANT command to give users access to the data in tables. Take a look at the syntax.

```
GRANT [ALL PRIVILEGES] |
      [SELECT | INSERT | UPDATE | DELETE | REFERENCES [, ...]]
      [(columns [, ...])] ON table_or_view
   TO user_or_role [, ...]
[WITH GRANT OPTION];
```

There are a lot of things to talk about in this command, so let's start with the basics. The main information you need to provide is what privileges you're granting, what table you're granting them on, and who you're granting them to. If you want to allow the user JackieP to view the Customer table but not add, change, or delete data, you use the following command:

```
GRANT SELECT
   ON Customer
   TO JackieP;
```

Now she can run all of the SELECT commands she wants on the Customer table. However, if she attempts an INSERT command, she will get an error. The same is true for UPDATE and DELETE. Now log in to the database with the JackieP logon account. With this account you'll be able to perform SELECT commands like the following:

```
SELECT LastName, Count(*)
  FROM Customer
 WHERE PostalCode IN ('50990', '50991', '50992')
 GROUP BY LastName;
```

Any SELECT command that involves the Customer table will now be valid for this user. The following command, however, will not be allowed.

```
SELECT c.LastName, v.Make, v.Model
  FROM Customer AS c
  JOIN Vehicle AS v ON c.CustomerID = v.CustomerID;
```

In order to run this command, the user will have to have the SELECT privilege granted on all tables involved in the query. In this case, that means both Customer and Vehicle.

More than one privilege can be granted at the same time.

```
GRANT SELECT, INSERT, UPDATE
    ON Customer
    TO JackieP;
```

This command will allow Jackie to do everything with the Customer table except delete rows from it.

Privileges can also be assigned to more than one user at the same time. This allows you to quickly set up the same rights for similar users.

```
GRANT SELECT, INSERT, UPDATE
    ON Customer
    TO JackieP, MarkB, LarryR;
```

NOTE This GRANT command includes two new users, Mark and Larry. In order to run the command you will first need to create logon accounts for them and grant them access to the SlickShop database.

So, using the GRANT command, you'll move through the database table by table, assigning the appropriate rights to each user. As you can imagine, you'll need to put some thought into this activity. For example, in the preceding code three users are given the rights to add, modify, and view customers. Let's say that these three people are employees at the Slick Shop. Will there be some other user then that has the ability to delete customers? Probably so. This will most likely be a manager or supervisor. This person will most likely be given all rights to the table.

```
GRANT ALL PRIVILEGES
    ON Customer
    TO GusT;
```

This is the same thing as granting Gus SELECT, INSERT, UPDATE, and DELETE. What other things will the three employees be allowed to do? In the Slick Shop database, they will probably be allowed to add and modify vehicles as well as job tickets. So they would be granted the following privileges:

```
GRANT SELECT, INSERT, UPDATE
    ON Vehicle
    TO JackieP, MarkB, LarryR;

GRANT SELECT, INSERT, UPDATE
    ON JobTicket
    TO JackieP, MarkB, LarryR;

GRANT SELECT, INSERT, UPDATE
    ON JobTicketDetail
    TO JackieP, MarkB, LarryR;

GRANT SELECT, INSERT, UPDATE
    ON PartUsed
    TO JackieP, MarkB, LarryR;
```

Again the shop manager Gus would be granted ALL PRIVILEGES to these four tables. This would allow him to log on to the database and perform any operation including deleting. Kind of reminds you of being at a department store, doesn't it? You know, the way a supervisor has to come over to the register and enter his or her password in order to perform an override.

For the three employees, however, this access is not good enough yet. If they are creating a job ticket, they will want to be able to pick parts and services from a list. This means that they will need to be able to select from these two tables. In the same way, they will need to be able to select from the `StateOrProvince` table so they can view the list of states.

```
GRANT SELECT
    ON Part
    TO JackieP, MarkB, LarryR;
```

```
GRANT SELECT
    ON Service
    TO JackieP, MarkB, LarryR;

GRANT SELECT
    ON StateOrProvince
    TO JackieP, MarkB, LarryR;
```

Tables like these might seem inconsequential because they are small and mainly just used for lookup information. However, security should not be taken lightly on tables such as these. Let us give you a couple of examples of what could happen if all employees were granted INSERT and UPDATE to these tables. First a dishonest employee could use it as a way to give his friends unauthorized discounts. Before creating a job ticket, he could update the Service table and reduce the labor cost. After the ticket is created, he could reset it. It doesn't have to be a dishonest person you have to worry about. A well-meaning employee could get into this table and add or change services and really make a mess out of things. Finally, you have the company joker to worry about. He might take advantage of his INSERT privileges on StateOrProvince to add Cuba and Iceland as new states.

ISN'T APPLICATION SECURITY GOOD ENOUGH?

Many times a front-end application will perform its own security. Applications will often recognize the user that has logged on and administer its own security. It might limit the menu options or screens that can be accessed. It will hide certain data from certain users. It will even remove certain options from the screen, such as a Delete button, for some users. Under this method, all database users are given all rights to all tables. The application's security, however, ensures that the right people are getting to the right data. You might be asking if this is good enough especially if this application is the only way the user has of accessing the database.

con.

As mentioned earlier, this security method is valid but has its pitfalls. Most often if someone feels that setting up security at the database level is too big of a pain, they will simply grant all rights to everyone. Then they will allow the application to handle the security. The reasoning is that otherwise there will be a duplication of effort. The same security will have to be controlled both in the database and in the application.

The biggest problem with relying on application security is the assumption that the front-end application is the only entry point into the database. There are a lot of software products available that allow anyone with a username and password to access a relational database. Microsoft Access is one such product. Even if your database is not Access, it is likely that it can still attach to your database. Once users connect this way, they will be limited only by database security. Third-party products such as this are easier to come by than you might think. Simply jump on the Internet and perform a search. It won't take you long to find several low-cost or even free software applications that can log on to a relational database and perform SQL commands.

Another problem can come from the application development staff. Unless you have excellent documentation procedures in place, it's possible that someone one day will misunderstand your security intentions. If they see that all users have full access to all tables, they might assume that there are no security restrictions. They might spend a lot of time developing an application that allows users to see and modify data that they shouldn't.

So unless you have a great deal of trust and control over all of the developers and users on your database, it's usually best to issue privileges at the database level in addition to the application.

The table security can be fine-tuned by going down to the column level. Sometimes you'll have tables that you want everyone to look at and maybe modify, but a few of the columns contain sensitive data. It might be an employee table where everyone in the company is allowed to see the names, job titles, and phone numbers. The table might have information that is not for everyone to see, such as salary, age, and home address. These columns can be protected with the GRANT command by explicitly naming the columns that users are allowed to view or modify.

Let's take the Slick Shop's Customer table as an example. The Slick Shop has decided that customer addresses and phone numbers should only be available to the store manager. If Gus is the manager and Jackie is the employee, the following GRANT commands will make this happen.

```
GRANT SELECT (CustomerID, FirstName, LastName)
    ON Customer
    TO JackieP;

GRANT SELECT
    ON Customer
    TO GusT;
```

Now when Jackie logs in, she will only be able to see three columns in the table, whereas Gus will be able to see all of them. If Jackie tries one of the following SELECT commands, she will get an error.

```
SELECT CustomerID, LastName, City, PhoneNumber
    FROM Customer;

SELECT *
    FROM Customer;
```

Both of these commands are trying to access columns that Jackie does not have permission to view. The only thing that's going to work for her is to write a SELECT that is limited to CustomerID, FirstName, and LastName. Because no column limitations have been specified for Gus, he will be able to select any or all columns from this table.

Limiting columns like this is sometimes called *vertically partitioned security*. Vertical refers to the way only certain columns can be accessed. It's important to note that all rows can still be accessed. Limiting the rows would be *horizontally partitioned security*. We'll be talking about this later in the chapter in the section "Creating and Using Views."

If the Slick Shop were using vertical security like this for SELECT on the Customer table, they would probably do the same for UPDATE.

```
GRANT SELECT (CustomerID, FirstName, LastName)
    ON Customer
    TO JackieP;

GRANT UPDATE (CustomerID, FirstName, LastName)
    ON Customer
    TO JackieP;

GRANT ALL PRIVILEGES
    ON Customer
    TO GusT;
```

Now Jackie is allowed to not only view these three columns but update them as well. Gus will be the only one who is allowed to insert new customers, delete customers, and update their address and phone information.

You're most likely starting to see the potential for a lot of work on your part. If there are dozens of employees and managers and dozens of tables, it could take all day to get these rights granted. That's where the groups or roles come in. By granting the rights to the role, you can set up a particular type of user one time and then simply assign the role to users. So far, for the database, you will have discovered two types of users, employees and managers. These are great candidates for roles.

To go about setting up this type of security, you would first create the roles the way we described at the beginning of this chapter. Let's say you've created a role called Employee and one called Manager. Next you'd create all of the user logon names but only give them enough rights to log on to the database. You will not assign them rights on any tables. Now you can start assigning privileges to the roles.

```
GRANT SELECT (CustomerID, FirstName, LastName)
    ON Customer
    TO Employee;

GRANT UPDATE (CustomerID, FirstName, LastName)
    ON Customer
    TO Employee;

GRANT SELECT, INSERT, UPDATE
    ON Vehicle
    TO Employee;

GRANT SELECT, INSERT, UPDATE
    ON JobTicket
    TO Employee;

GRANT SELECT, INSERT, UPDATE
    ON JobTicketDetail
    TO Employee;

GRANT SELECT, INSERT, UPDATE
    ON PartUsed
    TO Employee;

GRANT SELECT
    ON Part
    TO Employee;

GRANT SELECT
    ON Service
    TO Employee;

GRANT SELECT
    ON StateOrProvince
    TO Employee;
```

Now the Employee role is set up and you don't have to worry about granting these specific rights again. All you have to do is assign a user to this role and he's ready to go. We will not show the GRANT commands used to set up the Manager role, but for this one you would simply grant it ALL PRIVILEGES on every table.

If you're able to plan your groups or roles well, you might never need to grant anything to an individual user. All of their rights will come from the role. You might, however, need to make exceptions. The Slick Shop might find that parts need to be updated more frequently than they first thought. This is fine as long as a manager is available. If no managers are around, they'd want someone like Jackie to do it. You could solve this by granting the UPDATE privilege to JackieP. Now she will have all of the rights of the Employee role, plus the ability to update the Part table.

◆◆◆

Although making "one off" exceptions like this is perfectly fine, if you start making a lot of them, you'll lose the major benefit of roles. You could easily find yourself back in the business of managing privileges on a user-by-user basis. If possible, try to create another role to fill the need. In the preceding example, you could have created a new role called AssistManager and granted UPDATE on Part to this role. Then you could make Jackie a member of both roles, Employee and AssistManager.

◆◆◆

Another common practice is to share user logon names among several users. For example, instead of having Jackie, Larry, and Gus access the database with their own logon names, they would use generic usernames like SlickUser and SlickMgr. These logon names would be granted permissions the same way as we talked about before. In fact, this method is very similar to using roles or groups. Once a privilege is granted to the logon name, everyone who uses it benefits right away. The main advantage to this method is that it's easy. A handful of logon names can be created and granted access. That's all that has to be done. When new employees are hired, there's no need to create a new logon name—just tell them the username and password. No logon names have to be created, and no one has to be added to a group or role.

The problem is (you knew this was coming) there are a lot of drawbacks to this type of security. It can be summed up this way—you lose accountability. You won't know who is who. There are times where you will want your database to store information about which user performed an action and when it occurred. You might want to add columns to some tables that store the username of the last person who modified each row along with the time. This is still possible with this security method, but all you'll see are a bunch of rows modified by generic users like `SlickUser`. This really won't help much if you're trying to track down a problem. There are also times that you'll need to see who's logged on to the database right now and what they are doing. When you use your DBMS's feature to show everyone who's logged on at the moment, all you'll see are a bunch of users with the same name. What if something has gone wrong with one of those logon names? Maybe it's grabbed some locks on some tables and won't let go, causing all of the other users to wait on it. This would be a great time to know exactly who that person is so that you could do something about it. But with generic logon names, you'll only be able to narrow it down to a certain group of people.

Another problem is that it makes password management more difficult. Given that several people depend on the same password, it takes coordination between everyone involved just to change a password. As you can imagine, for this reason, the passwords tend to stay the same forever, which is a problem in itself. Why do people change passwords in the first place? To keep the bad guys guessing. If someone learns the password, at least it's only valid until the next time it's changed. A password like this one, however, which will probably never change, can be a security risk. People will come and go, and although most will forget all about that database and its password, there just might be that one guy who tucks that information away. A password that never changes can be like leaving a key under the doormat.

Finally, this security method takes away the ability to grant permission for the "one off" situations discussed earlier. Remember when Jackie, a member of the `Employee` role, needed access to update the `Part` table? Using the method of generic logon names, this would not be possible. One of two things would have to happen. You would either have to grant the permission to the generic logon name that she uses or let her borrow a manager logon name. Granting the permission to her generic logon name will of course grant it to everyone else who uses it. Letting her borrow the manager's logon name means that she now has too much access. Not to mention that she now knows the magic password that's not likely to change.

An option of the GRANT command that we haven't talked about yet is WITH GRANT OPTION. This is tacked on to the end of a GRANT statement. It not only gives the user the permission that you specified but also allows the user to grant that permission to someone else.

```
GRANT SELECT, UPDATE
    ON Customer
    TO GusT
 WITH GRANT OPTION;
```

Gus can now view and modify the customer data, plus he can also issue the GRANT command himself. However, he will only be able to grant SELECT and UPDATE permissions on the Customer table. Gus can log in to the database and run the following command:

```
GRANT UPDATE
    ON Customer
    TO JackieP;
```

Gus is not allowed to grant INSERT or DELETE, and he is not allowed to grant any kind of access to any other table. The WITH GRANT OPTION clause is a way of passing on some database management responsibility. This could be used as a nice way of taking care of those "one off" situations that we keep talking about. Let's say Gus is leaving for the day or going on vacation. He could grant the UPDATE permission on Customer to Jackie. When he returns he could take the permission away again. This could all be done without having to contact or bother you, the database administrator.

This option, of course, means that you trust the person to whom you grant access to do the right thing. Hopefully, that person won't just grant rights to everyone so as not to have to worry about it anymore. It can become easy for you to lose track of who has what permission. If several people have the WITH GRANT OPTION and each of them start mer-rily granting away, you might have a little mess on your hands. You, as the database administrator, will still be able to see which user has which permissions. However, if it ends up that every user has every privilege, what was the point of your carefully planned security in the first place?

Also, as the database administrator, you will always be able to revoke the rights that one user has granted to another. We'll be talking about revok-ing rights in a little bit. If you find that Gus has gone nuts and granted permissions to everyone, you can take them away again. Of course, that will not stop Gus from granting them back again. If you want to take away Gus's right to grant to other people, you'd have to revoke his per-mission and then grant it back, this time without the WITH GRANT OPTION. As long as we're talking about revoking, let us tell you what happens when you revoke a user's rights after they have granted to some-one else. The rights that are taken away from a user will cascade down to everyone else that the first user granted rights to. This will only happen, though, if you use the CASCADE option. So looking back to the last example, if you revoked Gus's UPDATE permission on the `Customer` table with the CASCADE option, Jackie would also lose that same permission. Later in this chapter, we'll talk about revoking users' rights and the use of this CASCADE option.

The final option of the GRANT command that we haven't talked about yet is the REFERENCES privilege. This is a privilege like SELECT or UPDATE that is granted on a table. When REFERENCES is granted, it allows the user to create a foreign key constraint that references that table. Now this is not going to be very useful to someone unless they have the ability to create their own table. That's what we'll tell you about in the next section.

Granting Database Privileges

All of the granting that we've talked about so far has been for tables. This covers a large percentage of the permissions that you'll be handing out. However, there are other tasks that you might want to allow users to perform, such as running stored procedures and creating tables.

Granting Permission to Create Tables

Let's start with giving users the rights to create their own tables. This allows them to create and maintain their own table structures side by side with the ones that you've created. They will even be able to create foreign key references from their tables to yours if they have the REFERENCES privilege granted on your tables.

The syntax for allowing users to create tables is very similar to what you've seen so far. It's just another privilege like SELECT and UPDATE. The difference is that you don't name a table like you've seen with the GRANT command so far. The following syntax works for most of the database systems.

```
GRANT CREATE TABLE TO GusT;
```

In the MySQL database, you grant the same way, only you're required to use the ON keyword. However, you're granting rights not to a specific table but rather to the database as a whole. You do this by specifying *.*.

```
GRANT CREATE ON *.* TO JackieP@localhost;
```

Working with User-Created Tables

Why would you want to let people create their own tables? Aren't the ones you created good enough? Don't get your feelings hurt! There are some very good reasons to allow users to create their own tables. Let's talk about the user first. Many times database users have the need to store additional information that either you didn't think about or don't have the time to set up for them. There are situations in which a user might only need the table for a short period of time. Giving users the right to create their own tables can be a convenience for both of you.

As an example, say that Gus the Slick Shop manager wants to store additional information about the vehicles that he services. If he had been granted the permission, he might log in and create the following table:

```
CREATE TABLE VehicleInfo
  (VehicleID              int,
   RepairNotes            varchar(1000),
   Odometer               int,
   SpecialInstructions    varchar(1000)
  );
```

Also if Gus is granted the REFERENCES permission on the Vehicle table, he will be able to create the table with a foreign key like this:

```
CREATE TABLE VehicleInfo
  (VehicleID              int  REFERENCES Vehicle (VehicleID),
   RepairNotes            varchar(1000),
   Odometer               int,
   SpecialInstructions    varchar(1000)
  );
```

This new VehicleInfo table lets Gus store notes, instructions, and odometer readings for the vehicles that come into his shop. It's important to note that Gus is now the owner of this table. He is the only user that has access to it. Gus automatically has all permissions on his own table. He also has the ability to grant rights to his table to any other user. Gus can run the following command to let Jackie see his data:

```
GRANT SELECT ON VehicleInfo TO JackieP;
```

Now here's the tricky part. After Gus grants Jackie this permission, she logs in and runs the following:

```
SELECT *
  FROM VehicleInfo;
```

Instead of seeing the data, she gets an error message telling her that VehicleInfo is an invalid table name! What's happening is that the database is looking for a VehicleInfo table that was created by the database owner (dbo). When you as the database administrator create tables, they are owned by dbo. Whenever a table is named in a SQL command, the database only considers tables owned by dbo. If you want the SQL command to use a table owned by another user, you must prefix the table name with that user's logon name. So Jackie should rewrite her SELECT command to look like this:

```
SELECT *
  FROM GusT.VehicleInfo;
```

This will return all the rows from Gus's table. The only user that does not have to do this is Gus himself. When Gus is logged on, he can issue commands like these:

```
SELECT *
  FROM VehicleInfo;

UPDATE VehicleInfo
   SET Odometer = 65099
 WHERE VehicleID = 3;
```

For Gus, these commands will work even though they are not prefixed with his logon name. The database knows that this is his table, and therefore the prefix is not required. All other users that Gus has granted permission, however, must use the prefix.

Another case where allowing users to create tables is during development. Allowing the development staff to create tables can give them some flexibility. Developers can create their own tables while working on a new project or system phase. This lets them play with various table designs until they find one that works best. Later they can have tables created by dbo.

Another useful strategy is for developers to create their own copy of an existing table. There can be more than one table with the same name in a database if they are owned by different users. As an example, let's say Becca, an application developer on the Slick Shop project, has been given the assignment to upgrade the system to collect some new vehicle information. She'll be adding two new columns to store the engine size, one by cylinders and one by cubic liters. Both of these columns will be required and so will use the NOT NULL constraint. While she is developing her front-end application, she will be working in a development database so she will not disrupt the end users. She does not, however, want to change the Vehicle table until all of her changes are complete. If she put her new required columns in the Vehicle table, none of the other developers would be able to use the Slick Shop application until Becca made her new application available. The old Slick Shop application would be attempting to insert rows into the Vehicle table without the two required columns, which would cause it to fail.

The method she should use is to create her own Vehicle table. Her table will sit side by side with the original Vehicle table. One will be owned by Becca, the other by dbo. When Becca modifies the SQL in her application, she will be able to write ordinary commands like this one:

```
INSERT INTO Vehicle
    (VehicleYear, Make, Model, Color, LicensePlate#,
        Cylinders, CubicLiters)
VALUES
    (2003, 'Volkswagen', 'Beetle', 'Yellow', 'BUGSME2', 4, 2.2);
```

Notice how she does not have to put a prefix in front of the table name. The database will see that she has her own Vehicle table and use that one. Other users, however, will still be directed to the Vehicle table that is owned by dbo. So they will be able to run the old application the same as always. If someone else wants access to Becca's table, she will have to grant them rights to it. When they use the table name in a SQL command, they must remember to prefix it with her logon name.

One final note about user tables. The database administrator or dbo always has all privileges on all tables. The only thing to remember is that even the dbo must prefix the tables with the owner's name if they belong to someone else.

Granting Permission to Run Stored Procedures

The other main privilege that you should be aware of is EXECUTE. If your database supports stored procedures, you'll need to use this privilege to allow users to run them.

```
GRANT EXECUTE ON CreateJobTicket TO JackieP;
```

Remember that you can do many things in a stored procedure. A single procedure might perform several inserts, updates, and deletes. The EXECUTE permission gives you a good way of securing powerful procedures. You'll be able to decide which users can run each stored procedure.

There's another feature of stored procedures that will let you secure your database even further. When a user runs a stored procedure, it has all of the rights of its creator. So when a user is executing a procedure that database owner created, the user will have all the rights of the dbo (which is full access to everything). Don't worry, though—only the owner of a procedure can change it. So anyone who runs it will only be performing the commands that are built into the procedure.

The user who runs a procedure is not required to have permissions on the tables that the procedure accesses. This is where the extra security measure comes in. You could actually build your database in such a way that all SQL commands are issued through stored procedures. If this is the case, none of the users would have to have permissions on the tables. They would only need the EXECUTE privilege on the appropriate procedures. Tightening down the security this way means that users can still access and modify data, but it is strictly controlled by your procedures. Without specific permissions on tables, they would not be able to execute SQL of their own.

Is this level of security really necessary? The answer will certainly depend on your situation. But if you're worried about people using third-party tools to modify data, this strategy will help. If the users have no permissions to any tables, these tools will be useless. Is it practical to lock down every single table and access them through stored procedures exclusively? Probably not. This can really hinder the user and put a burden on the stored procedure developer. Some tables are so easy to work with that a stored procedure might not be necessary. Take the Part table, for instance. You could write four stored procedures to access this table: one to select from it, one to insert a row, one to update a row, and another to delete a row. But the Part table is not very complicated and does not have a lot of difficult relationships with other tables. This might be a good table to hand out rights to appropriate users, allowing them to work with the table directly.

Other times you might feel that the tables are too cryptic for the average user or have delicate relationships that must be maintained. In cases like this, you could allow access via stored procedure only. In the Slick Shop database, you could make this case for the tables that store job ticket data. There are a handful of tables involved that relate to one another. You might want to create some stored procedures that manage this data and maintain its integrity properly. In the Sunday Morning session, we showed you a couple of procedures that do just that. If the thought of users poking around in these tables makes you nervous, maybe you'd want to take away permissions to these tables. A possible downside to this is that you might end up having to write more procedures in order to cover different scenarios.

Other Database Privileges

The CREATE TABLE and EXECUTE permissions are two of the most useful and widely supported privileges. However, your DBMS is likely to have many other database-level privileges that you want users to have. Following is a list of some of these privileges:

➤ Create databases
➤ Create logon names
➤ Create groups or roles
➤ Create indexes
➤ Create stored procedures
➤ Create views
➤ Create triggers
➤ Back up and restore databases

Although this is not a complete list and not every database system supports all of these privileges, this should give you an idea of what can be done. Using these plus the ones discussed earlier, you have a very large number of privilege combinations that you can set up.

Revoking Privileges

Finally, you've come to the part about taking rights away from someone. This won't take long because it's really the same as the GRANT command, only it uses the keyword REVOKE. The syntax for this command is as follows:

```
REVOKE [ALL PRIVILEGES] |
      [SELECT | INSERT | UPDATE | DELETE | REFERENCES [, ...]]
      [(columns [, ...])] ON table_or_view
 FROM user_or_role [, ...]
      [CASCADE];
```

You'll notice another difference in that it uses the keyword FROM instead of TO in order to make the command's English more proper. So when you decide that you want to take away some of Jackie's rights on the Customer table, you can use this command:

```
REVOKE INSERT, UPDATE, DELETE
    ON Customer
  FROM JackieP;
```

Now Jackie cannot modify data in this table anymore. However, if she previously had the SELECT permission, she will still be able to query this table. You could also get very specific and revoke access to just a few columns. Assume Jackie was given permission to update certain columns with this command:

```
GRANT UPDATE
    (Make, Model, Color, VehicleYear) ON Vehicle
    TO JackieP;
```

Later her access could be restricted a little with this command:

```
REVOKE UPDATE
    (Color, VehicleYear) ON Vehicle
  FROM JackieP;
```

Now Jackie can still update the `Vehicle` table, but only the `Make` and `Model` columns.

The other option is one that we mentioned before, CASCADE. Its purpose is to revoke the rights not only from the named user but also from anyone else that this user had granted the same rights. Remember earlier how you let Gus grant rights to others on the `Customer` table with this command:

```
GRANT SELECT, UPDATE
   ON Customer
   TO GusT
 WITH GRANT OPTION;
```

If you later decide to revoke his UPDATE privilege, you can use the CASCADE option to also revoke UPDATE from everyone that he gave it to.

```
REVOKE UPDATE
     ON Customer
   FROM GusT
CASCADE;
```

Take a Break!

Okay, it's break time! But don't reach for that bookmark yet! Being that it's Sunday afternoon, you're liable to turn on football or auto racing, and then you'll never come back! There's some good stuff ahead, so stick around.

While we're on the subject of security, we're reminded of a good story about computer hacking. If you're at all interested in this sort of thing, we'd recommend the book "Cuckoo's Egg: Tracking a Spy Through the Maze of Computer Espionage" by Clifford Stoll. Although it was written in 1989, it still holds up well. It's an interesting detailed account of how the author discovers someone is hacking into his company's mainframe.

He chronicles his efforts to not only stop but also track down the hacker. The whole saga begins when Stoll notices that a balance sheet is off by just 75 cents!

Creating and Using Views

Okay, let's get back to it with a new topic. In this section we'll introduce views. You'll see that a view is a lot like a table and how sometimes it's easy to forget that it's not. We've put it in this chapter because we're going to talk about one way views can be used to control security. But we're also going to talk about a few of its other uses as well.

A view is a saved query that can function in many of the ways a table does. The general syntax is pretty simple.

```
CREATE VIEW view_name
    AS
select_statement
```

You can create a view based on a select from the Customer table, as follows:

```
CREATE VIEW IndianaCustomers
    AS
SELECT CustomerID, FirstName, LastName, City, StateOrProvince,
    PostalCode
  FROM Customer
 WHERE StateOrProvince = 'IN'
```

You can put any valid SELECT command after the keyword AS. The view now works like a table. You can select from it like this:

```
SELECT *
  FROM IndianaCustomers;
```

The database will recognize that IndianaCustomers is a view, and it will actually run the SELECT command that is in the view's definition. The result of this query on the view is as follows:

Customer ID	FirstName	LastName	City	State-OrProvince	PostalCode
4	Bryce	Hatfield	Marion	IN	NULL
5	Kylee	Dicken	Upland	IN	46905
6	Alex	Thompson	NULL	IN	NULL
7	Davis	Thompson	Greensburg	IN	46514
8	Harrison	Thompson	Indianapolis	IN	46123

Pay attention to two things here. First, only the rows with customers who live in Indiana are returned. The WHERE clause in the view's definition was used. Second, even though you specified a SELECT *, you only got six of the table's eight columns back. This is because the view's definition determines which columns the view returns.

Views are dynamic in that while the view itself might never change, its results will. Because a view is simply executing a SELECT command, it will always display the latest data in the underlying table or tables.

Using Views for Security

Earlier in this chapter, you looked at a method of security called vertically partitioned. It was vertical because it used the GRANT command to limit the columns of a table that a given user could view or modify. This is useful if a table has certain columns that you want hidden, such as salary amounts or phone numbers. We also mentioned that we would show you how to horizontally partition a table for security.

Do you see how the view can be used to provide horizontally partitioned security? You grant a user SELECT access to the view only, not the table. This will force the user to query with the view, which can limit the rows that are returned. In fact, because a view's definition specifies the columns that are visible, it can be used for vertically partitioned security as well.

Users who have permission to query a view can choose their own columns and apply their own WHERE clause.

```
SELECT FirstName, StateOrProvince, PostalCode
  FROM IndianaCustomers
 WHERE PostalCode IS NOT NULL;
```

This query will return the following result set:

```
FirstName        StateOrProvince    PostalCode
-----------      -----------        ---------
Kylee            IN                 46905
Davis            IN                 46514
Harrison         IN                 46123
```

You asked for only three columns and rows where the postal codes are not NULL. This shows how you can filter a view rather than just accept all of its output. When you put a WHERE clause on a view as done here, you're actually instructing the database to process two WHERE clauses. In the example, it will first filter out just the Indiana customers, and then it will filter out the non-NULL postal codes.

NOTE Your DBMS's optimizer is actually smart enough to recognize what's going on here. Instead of processing two separate WHERE clauses, it has the ability to internally combine them. The optimizer will likely combine them into one WHERE clause that looks like this:

```
WHERE StateOrProvince = 'IN' AND PostalCode IS NOT NULL
```

A set of similar views can be created to let each user see the same data in a different way. For example, you might want to divide the customer base geographically, allowing the employees to see only their assigned customers. To do this you could create views like these:

```
CREATE VIEW NorthEastCust
    AS
SELECT *
  FROM Customer
 WHERE StateOrProvince IN ('CT', 'DE', 'ME', 'NH', 'RI', 'VA', 'WV')

CREATE VIEW MidwestCust
    AS
SELECT *
  FROM Customer
 WHERE StateOrProvince IN ('IL', 'IN', 'OH', 'MI', 'KY', 'MO')
```

```
CREATE VIEW CanadaCust
    AS
SELECT *
  FROM Customer
 WHERE StateOrProvince IN
  ('AB', 'BC', 'MBv, 'NB', 'NF', 'NS', 'NT', 'NU', 'ON', 'PE', 'QC',
       'SK', 'YT')
```

This way, employees can be granted the SELECT permission on just the view that applies to them. Then they don't have to worry about sifting through the entire list of customers.

NOTE Permissions are granted to views the same way as they are on tables. Use the GRANT command and place the name of the view where you would normally put the table name.

Using Views to Simplify Queries

You could even create a view that comprises more than one table. In this next example, the view will pull together all of the job ticket data. You're not going to put a WHERE clause in the view this time, though. This way it will return all the job tickets by default. If the user wants to filter the data, he can use his own WHERE clause on the view just as he would on a table.

```
CREATE VIEW JobTicketView
    AS
SELECT jt.JobTicketID,
       jt.StartDate,
       jtd.LineItemNumber,
       s.Description AS Service,
       p.Description AS Part,
       jt.CustomerID
  FROM JobTicket AS jt
  JOIN JobTicketDetail AS jtd ON jt.JobTicketID = jtd.JobTicketID
  JOIN PartUsed AS pu ON (jtd.JobTicketID = pu.JobTicketID
                          AND jtd.LineItemNumber = pu.LineItemNumber)
  JOIN Service AS s ON jtd.ServiceID = s.ServiceID
  JOIN Part AS p ON pu.PartID = p.PartID
```

A great advantage of a view like this is the way you can shield users from complex SQL. This view is fairly involved. It has five tables and four joins in it. The people who run this view don't have to know anything about the tables involved in the query. To them, `JobTicketView` will look like it's one big table with all of the job ticket details in it.

NOTE It's important for you to understand that views are not tables and do not contain any data themselves. The underlying tables will still hold all of the data. A view simply holds the query. Every time a view is used in a SQL command, the query within the view will be executed again.

This view can now be treated like a table in a query. You'll select some job ticket data using the view now. However, because you don't want all of the job tickets, you'll include a WHERE clause.

```
SELECT JobTicketID, LineItemNumber, Service, Part
  FROM JobTicketView
 WHERE StartDate >= '2002-1-30'
ORDER BY JobTicketID, LineItemNumber;
```

If you didn't know better, you'd look at this query and think it was using a table. Well, okay—the name of the view is a dead giveaway! Notice how the user of the view is able to write a simple query and not have to worry about joins and the five tables it takes to get this data. The results of this query are shown in the following:

```
JobTicket   LineItem    Service              Part
ID          Number
--------    ---------   ------               ------------
5           1           Replace Wiperblades  ACME Wiper Blades
5           2           Oil Change           Black Gold 10w-30 Oil
5           2           Oil Change           ACME Oil Filter
5           2           Oil Change           ACME Transmission Fluid
5           2           Oil Change           ACME Windshield Fluid
7           1           Oil Change           Protects 10w-30 Oil
7           1           Oil Change           ACME Oil Filter
7           1           Oil Change           ACME Transmission Fluid
```

```
7          1          Oil Change           ACME Windshield Fluid
7          2          Replace Air Filter   ACME Air Filter
7          3          Change PVC Valve      ACME PVC Valve
7          4          Change and Flush      ACME Differential Fluid
                      Differentia
7          5          Change and Flush      ACME Coolant
                      Cooling Sys
```

That's not to say that they can't do joins if they want to. Because a view works just like a table, it can be joined to other views or tables. In the JobTicketView, you've included the CustomerID column but none of the information from the Customer table. If you want to see some of that data, you'll have to join the view to that table.

```
SELECT jtv.JobTicketID,
       c.FirstName,
       c.LastName,
       c.City,
       jtv.Part
  FROM JobTicketView AS jtv
  JOIN Customer AS c ON jtv.CustomerID = c.CustomerID
 WHERE jtv.StartDate >= '2002-1-30';
```

Just use the view in a join like it was a table. The query will produce these results:

```
JobTicketID   FirstName   LastName   City     Part
---------     --------    -------    -------  ----------
5             Kylee       Dicken     Upland   ACME Wiper Blades
5             Kylee       Dicken     Upland   Black Gold 10w-30 Oil
5             Kylee       Dicken     Upland   ACME Oil Filter
5             Kylee       Dicken     Upland   ACME Transmission Fluid
5             Kylee       Dicken     Upland   ACME Windshield Fluid
7             Bryce       Hatfield   Marion   Protects 10w-30 Oil
7             Bryce       Hatfield   Marion   ACME Oil Filter
7             Bryce       Hatfield   Marion   ACME Transmission Fluid
7             Bryce       Hatfield   Marion   ACME Windshield Fluid
7             Bryce       Hatfield   Marion   ACME Air Filter
7             Bryce       Hatfield   Marion   ACME PVC Valve
7             Bryce       Hatfield   Marion   ACME Differential Fluid
7             Bryce       Hatfield   Marion   ACME Coolant
```

Look back at the code that created the view. Do you see how the keyword AS is used to rename two of the columns? This is done because there are two columns named Description, one from the Service table and one from Part. All of the other column names are left alone. The columns of a view will adopt the column names on the underlying tables unless you rename them. Another way you can use a view is for the purpose of giving columns better or more meaningful names. This next view is very simple. You're just going to select all of the rows and columns from the Customer table, but you'll give some of the columns new names.

```
CREATE VIEW CustView
     AS
SELECT CustomerID,
       FirstName + ' ' + LastName AS Name,
       Address,
       City,
       StateOrProvince AS State,
       PostalCode AS Zip,
       PhoneNumber
   FROM Customer
```

This view uses the keyword AS to rename a few of the columns. You've even combined the first and last names into one column called Name. Now, using the view, the query can be a little more user friendly.

```
SELECT Name, City, State, Zip
  FROM CustView
 WHERE State <> 'IN';
```

The results of this query are shown in the following. Notice how the column headers have the new names as well.

```
Name              City          State   Zip
----------        --------      ------  ------
John Smith        North Beach   VA      10234
Victoria Smithe   Huntington    WV      22211
```

A view could also be used to simplify queries that aggregate data. You might want to give the users a simple view that will show them the total number of parts used during each month.

```
CREATE VIEW PartsByMonth
AS
SELECT DATEPART(yyyy, jtd.DateComplete) AS Year,
       DATEPART(mm, jtd.DateComplete) AS Month,
       SUM(pu.Quantity) AS PartsUsed
  FROM JobTicketDetail AS jtd
  JOIN PartUsed AS pu ON (jtd.JobTicketID = pu.JobTicketID
                      AND jtd.LineItemNumber = pu.LineItemNumber)
 GROUP BY DATEPART(yyyy, jtd.DateComplete),
          DATEPART(mm, jtd.DateComplete)
```

Instead of having to deal with date functions, joins, and aggregate commands, the user can run a simple command,

```
SELECT * FROM PartsByMonth
ORDER BY Year, Month;
```

and get up-to-date results quickly and easily.

Year	Month	PartsUsed
2001	7	7
2001	8	1
2001	9	5
2002	1	12
2002	2	11
2002	5	8
2002	7	1

Views versus Stored Procedures

You might be thinking that views and stored procedures are similar. In a way they are. They both let you store a query in a nice little package and run it later without having to type the whole query again. However, that's where the similarity ends. A view can only contain the SELECT command, whereas procedures can have any SQL command as well as the DBMS's programming language. A view can have one and only one SELECT, whereas a procedure can have many. Now your view can use a UNION to combine more than one SELECT in a view, but this is still considered a single SQL command. In case you missed it, we introduced the UNION in the Saturday Afternoon session. By the way, you can use views within a stored procedure.

Updating Data with Views

Like its name implies, the main purpose of a view is to look at data. Your DBMS, however, might allow you to insert, update, or delete data with a view. You might want to use views in this way as an additional security feature. If you've already written views that limit the data that a user can see, you could have them use those same views to update the data.

Updating Data with Simple Views

Remember the views that you created that let employees see only the customers that are in their assigned region? One of them looked like this:

```
CREATE VIEW NorthEastCust
    AS
SELECT *
  FROM Customer
 WHERE StateOrProvince IN ('CT', 'DE', 'ME', 'NH', 'RI', 'VA', 'WV')
```

You might have granted Larry SELECT access to this view so that you would not have to grant it on `Customer`. You could also grant him INSERT, UPDATE, and DELETE permissions on this view. This gives Larry permission to work with his set of customers while not disturbing the others that don't belong to him.

Let's take a look at the steps involved. First assume that Larry does not have any permissions granted on the `Customer` table. Now grant him rights on his view `NorthEastCust`.

```
GRANT SELECT, INSERT, UPDATE, DELETE
    ON NorthEastCust
    TO LarryR;
```

Now when he logs in and selects the data from his view, he will see only his customers.

```
SELECT CustomerID, FirstName, LastName, StateOrProvince
  FROM NorthEastCust;
```

CustomerID	FirstName	LastName	StateOrProvince
1	John	Smith	VA
3	Victoria	Smithe	WV

Because he has been granted the ability to update the view, he can perform the following command:

```
UPDATE NorthEastCust
   SET FirstName = 'Roberto'
 WHERE CustomerID = 1;
```

This command will work and will actually change the data in the Customer table. What if Larry starts getting funny ideas about updating a customer that does not belong to him? The view will prevent him from doing it. Let's say he tries this command:

```
UPDATE NorthEastCust
   SET FirstName = 'Roberto'
 WHERE CustomerID = 5;
```

Customer number 5 is not one that is included in the NorthEastCust view. This customer is from Indiana. This UPDATE command will fail to update any data. So how does this view do this? By combining WHERE clauses. Look at the WHERE clause used to create the view and the one used in the UPDATE command. If you were to combine the two, you'd get a command that looks like this:

```
UPDATE Customer
  SET FirstName = 'Roberto'
 WHERE CustomerID = 5
   AND StateOrProvince IN ('CT', 'DE', 'ME', 'NH', 'RI', 'VA', 'WV');
```

When Larry tried to use the view to update customer 5, this is the command that the database's optimizer actually attempted. This command, however, doesn't find any rows to update because there is no row that has CustomerID of 5 and one of those seven states.

This same concept applies when using a view to delete rows. The WHERE clause from the view will be combined with the WHERE clause from the DELETE. So a user will only be able to delete rows that are contained within the view. Larry can try this delete:

```
DELETE FROM NorthEastCust
 WHERE CustomerID = 12;
```

The command will only work if customer number 12 is from one of the seven states that are in the NorthEastCust view. This prevents him from deleting customers that he couldn't even see in the first place.

The INSERT statement is the exception. Because the basic INSERT doesn't use a WHERE clause, it can't combine with a view's WHERE clause like you've seen before. You can insert rows with a view that are not contained within that view. This means that after the row is inserted, you might not be able to see it with the view. For example, Larry uses the following command:

```
INSERT INTO NorthEastCust
  (FirstName, LastName, City, StateOrProvince)
VALUES
  ('Natasha', 'Velk', 'Rome', 'GA');
```

This will work. However, because Georgia is not one of the states included in the view, Larry will never be able to see, update, or delete his new customer.

Because a view does not have to contain all of the columns from a table, you should be aware of how the INSERT command handles this type of view. The columns that are not included in the view will either be given a value of NULL or be set to the column's default. If a column outside of the view has the NOT NULL constraint and does not have a default, the INSERT will fail.

It's important to note that whenever you use a view to modify data, you are actually changing the data on the underlying table. There are no changes being made to the view since views themselves don't contain any data.

Updating Data with Complex Views

Earlier we showed you examples of views that involve more than one table. The purpose of these was to bring data together from several tables without the users having to make their own joins. Each DBMS handles data modification with complex views a little bit differently. In general, though, the modifications will be allowed as long as they are kept within a single table. Take a look at the following view that joins two tables together.

```
CREATE VIEW Jobs2002
    AS
SELECT jt.JobTicketID, jt.StartDate,
       jt.EndDate, jtd.LineItemNumber, jtd.HoursSpent
  FROM JobTicket jt
  JOIN JobTicketDetail jtd ON jt.JobTicketID = jtd.JobTicketID
 WHERE jt.StartDate BETWEEN '1-1-2002' AND '12-31-2002'
```

The view shows all job tickets created in 2002 along with some of the line item details. A simple update that you are allowed to perform through this view would be to change the start or end date of the job ticket.

```
UPDATE Jobs2002
   SET StartDate = '3-22-2002'
 WHERE JobTicketID = 7;
```

You can do this because it's fairly simple for the view to determine that the StartDate column comes from the JobTicket table and that you're using the primary key in the WHERE clause. Remember also that the WHERE clause of the UPDATE will be combined with the WHERE clause of the view. So the command will work as long as job ticket number 7 was started in the year 2002.

What if you tried to update the other table, JobTicketDetail?

```
UPDATE Jobs2002
   SET HoursSpent = 2.5
 WHERE JobTicketID = 7;
```

This might not work on your DBMS. It works in SQL Server, but Oracle will not accept it. Oracle has a requirement that in order to update a given table, each of its primary key columns must be included in the view. So in order for this update to work in Oracle, you'd have to have the `JobTicketID` column included as a column in the `Jobs2002` view.

None of the database systems are going to like this command:

```
UPDATE Jobs2002
   SET StartDate = '3-23-2002', HoursSpent = 1.5
 WHERE JobTicketID = 7;
```

Here you're attempting to update columns from two different tables at the same time. This is just one of the restrictions placed in multitable views that we're going to talk about next.

Restrictions on Joined Views

Before you start using views to update data, be sure that you're aware of the restrictions your DBMS has established. We'll talk about some of the most common or even obvious ones next.

A view cannot be used to modify data if it has any of the following characteristics:

➤ The view cannot contain aggregate functions such as GROUP BY, AVG, MIN, MAX, or SUM.

➤ The view cannot have a keyword (other than WHERE) that modifies the number of rows that are returned, such as DISTINCT, UNION, or TOP.

➤ The view must have at least one table. In other words, it cannot be built entirely from expressions.

➤ The view cannot involve computed or derived columns. It should just select simple column names.

➤ If the view contains a join, only one table can be modified.

➤ It is likely that your DBMS will require that the view contain all of the primary key columns from the table you are modifying, especially when inserting or deleting.

➤ Column names cannot be ambiguous. For example, if the view has two columns called `Description` from two different tables, it will not know what to do when you try to update a column called `Description`.

Again, be sure to check out your documentation on the view topic. Many DBMSs even have special options for the CREATE VIEW command if you know ahead of time that a view is going to be used to modify data. There is also a special trigger called INSTEAD OF that some DBMSs support, which makes updating with a view easier. In the next section, we'll introduce triggers and the wide variety of things they can do for you.

Using Triggers

Triggers are another powerful feature that you'll find on most database systems, such as Sybase, Microsoft, Oracle, Informix, and DB2. A trigger is very similar to a stored procedure. The biggest difference is that you must explicitly run a stored procedure, whereas a trigger is run automatically in response to a specific event. The events are either when a row is inserted, updated, or deleted. We'll be going into detail in this section, but in short some of the things you can do with triggers include:

➤ Write to an audit log when rows are changed.

➤ Synchronize changes to a backup database.

➤ Cascade changes and maintain referential integrity.

➤ Enforce complex data validation and business rules.

Using Triggers to Audit User Activity

A trigger can be defined to automatically "fire" whenever an INSERT, an UPDATE, or a DELETE command is issued on a particular table. You can create any one or all three of these triggers for each table in the database. You must be the owner of a table in order to create a trigger on it; however, anyone can cause the trigger to fire. For example, Jackie creates a table and therefore is the only one who can create triggers on it. So she creates an INSERT trigger. She then grants Larry the INSERT permission on her table. Now every time either she or Larry inserts a row into this table, the trigger will fire.

The basic syntax for a trigger is as follows:

```
CREATE TRIGGER trigger_name
   ON table_name
   {AFTER | BEFORE | INSTEAD OF} {[INSERT] [,] [UPDATE] [,] [DELETE]}
   AS
trigger_code
```

Although triggers can serve countless purposes, we'll just present a few practical ideas here and let your own creativity take over after that. The first idea that we'll talk about is to make an audit trail.

◄◄
An **audit trail** is a historical record of changes that are made to a set of data. The record can include the name of the person who made the changes, the date, the time, and specific details about the data that was inserted, updated, or deleted.
◄◄

As a part of your security plan you might want to use an audit trail to keep an eye on what the users are up to. Possibly even a more practical use of an audit trail is to be able to trace a table's history in case data one day gets lost, damaged, or overwritten. In some cases, audit trails are even required by law for certain types of data.

As an example, let's say you've decided that you'd like to start an audit trail on a few of your Slick Shop tables. You'll begin by creating a table that will hold the audit trail data.

```
CREATE TABLE AuditTrail
  (TableName  varchar(30),
   Action     char(6),
   Details    varchar(2000),
   LogDate    smalldatetime
  );
```

Because you will eventually store audit information from different tables, the first column, TableName, will tell where the change took place. Action will be either INSERT, UPDATE, or DELETE. The large Details column will contain whatever descriptive information you want to put, such as the data values that were involved. Finally, the LogDate column will store the date and time the row was entered into the audit trail.

Now you're ready to create your first trigger that will make an audit trail entry every time a new row is inserted into the Customer table.

```
CREATE TRIGGER tr_i_Customer
    ON Customer
  AFTER INSERT
    AS

  DECLARE @first varchar(20);
  DECLARE @last  varchar(30);

  SELECT @first = FirstName
    FROM inserted;

  SELECT @last = LastName
    FROM inserted;

  INSERT INTO AuditTrail
    (TableName, Action, Details, LogDate)
  VALUES
    ('Customer',
     'Insert',
     'New customer added: ' + @first + ' ' + @last,
        getdate());
```

Remember that triggers are very similar to stored procedures. Triggers can make heavy use of DBMS-specific languages. The trigger examples in this book are written in Transact-SQL, which is the language of Sybase and Microsoft. All of the concepts that we'll discuss, however, can be carried over to any other DBMS that supports triggers.

You begin this trigger by naming it `tr_i_Customer` (`tr` for trigger and `i` for insert). You then specify that the trigger be placed on the `Customer` table and that it should fire when an INSERT command is issued. Specifically, this trigger will start running after the row has been inserted. Following the keyword AS, you begin writing the trigger's code. For this trigger, there are just a few short commands. But like a stored procedure, it could have many commands and include things like loops and conditional statements.

NOTE

As you probably guessed, a trigger that uses the keyword BEFORE runs before the data is modified, whereas AFTER runs the trigger code after the data is modified.

Microsoft SQL Server and Sybase Adaptive Server do not support BEFORE triggers.

In the trigger, every time a new `Customer` row is inserted, you have it automatically insert a row into `AuditTrail`. That way, users don't have to worry about doing it themselves. In fact, users might not even know this is happening—maybe you don't want them to know. All the users will see is that the `Customer` they inserted got added like they expected.

Notice how the trigger performs two SELECT commands from a table called `inserted`. In Transact-SQL this is a special virtual table that is only available within a trigger. This virtual table will have the exact same column structure as the table on which the trigger is based. It will also contain the row or rows of data that are currently being inserted. In the trigger, you used this special table to look at the first and last names and store them into variables. You then took these two variables and put them together to form a string that shows the name of the new customer added. This string gets placed in the Details column of the AuditTrail table.

 NOTE Oracle and DB2 can also look at the new data being inserted—they just use a different syntax.

In DB2 you must give the virtual table a name with this command, REFERENCING NEW TABLE AS NewCust. Then columns can be accessed like NewCust.FirstName.

It's nearly the same in Oracle. The virtual table is named with REFERENCING NEW AS NewCust, and a colon must precede the table name as :NewCust.FirstName.

Now that the trigger is created, whenever someone inserts a row such as this one,

```
INSERT INTO Customer
  (FirstName, LastName, Address, City, StateOrProvince,
    PostalCode)
VALUES
  ('Paul', 'Trulock', '3340 Westwood Rd.', 'San Diego', 'CA',
    '20800');
```

you'll find the following row will be placed in the AuditTrail table.

```
TableName Action  Details                       LogDate
--------  ------  ---------                     ----------
Customer  Insert  New customer added: Paul Trulock 2003-7-19 17:25:32
```

If you were reading along carefully, you'll know that we said that the inserted table contains the row or rows that are currently being added. Normally, this will just be one row. But you'll recall that it's possible to insert more than one row at a time. Take, for example, the following command that copies customers from one table to another.

```
INSERT INTO Customer
  (FirstName, LastName, Address, City, StateOrProvince, PostalCode)
SELECT FirstName, LastName, Address, City, StateOrProvince,
    PostalCode
  FROM PeoriaCust
 WHERE CustomerID <= 300;
```

This command will insert 300 customers at the same time. This means that when the insert trigger fires, the inserted table will have 300 rows in it. The two SELECT commands in the trigger don't expect more than one row to be in the inserted table. Also the INSERT command that adds a row to AuditTrail is only designed to insert a single row. You should instead write the trigger like the one that follows:

```
CREATE TRIGGER tr_i_Customer
    ON Customer
 AFTER INSERT
    AS

INSERT INTO AuditTrail
    (TableName, Action, Details, LogDate)
  SELECT 'Customer', 'Insert',
         'New customer added: ' + FirstName + ' ' + LastName,
         getdate()
    FROM inserted;
```

This trigger inserts rows into the AuditTrail table based on a SELECT from the inserted table. This will ensure that all of the rows in the inserted table are seen and that corresponding entries are made in AuditTrail.

Maybe instead of logging every single action that takes place, you only want to note some of the more interesting things that happen. Say, for example, you want to make an audit trail entry only when a customer's phone number changes. For this you would need an update trigger. The update trigger will be fired whenever an UPDATE command is performed on the Customer table. It could be that the first name changed, or maybe the postal code, or maybe the phone number. You're only interested in making a log entry if the phone number actually changed.

Triggers have the ability to determine which columns have changed and which have not. The Transact-SQL command that you'll use to find this out is IF UPDATE.

```
CREATE TRIGGER tr_u_CustPhone
    ON Customer
 AFTER UPDATE
    AS
IF UPDATE(PhoneNumber)
  INSERT INTO AuditTrail
      (TableName, Action, Details, LogDate)
      SELECT 'Customer', 'Update',
             'Phone number change!',
             getdate();
```

Using Triggers to Synchronize Data

Another common use of triggers is to keep data synchronized between different tables, which might be on separate databases. This is sometimes used as a form of replication, so that two databases remain identical.

◄◄◄

Replication is the term used for copying or distributing data between two or more databases. It can involve creating identical copies of data, summarizing data, or storing a subset of the original.

◄◄◄

In the Saturday Evening session, we used an example where the Slick Shop had 1,800 stores nationally and there was a corporate office that wanted to keep track of all of the data. They would like to start by keeping a master customer table that holds all customers from all locations. Assuming the appropriate connections exist between the stores and the corporate office, triggers could be used to do this. You want the corporate database to receive a copy of each new customer inserted. Likewise you want updates and deletions to carry over as well. For this example, each Slick Shop location has a connection to the corporate database called SlickCorp.

The structure of the Customer table in the SlickCorp database will be the same as the stores use with a few differences. First, a new column called StoreID will identify which store the data originated from. Second, the CustomerID column will not be set up as an auto-numbered column. It will instead get the values directly from the stores. Finally, the primary key of this table will be StoreID and CustomerID.

The insert trigger is pretty similar to what you saw earlier. In this one, you will provide for the extra column, StoreID, by giving it the number of this particular Slick Shop, 1108.

```
CREATE TRIGGER tr_i_Customer
    ON Customer
 AFTER INSERT
    AS
INSERT INTO SlickCorp.dbo.Customer
    (StoreID, CustomerID, FirstName, LastName,
    Address, City, StateOrProvince,
    PostalCode, PhoneNumber)
SELECT 1108, CustomerID, FirstName, LastName,
    Address, City, StateOrProvince,
    PostalCode, PhoneNumber
  FROM inserted;
```

The delete trigger is a little more involved. It loops through a cursor of each row that was deleted and removes the corresponding row from the corporate database. Notice the use of the virtual table deleted. It's just like the inserted table, only it contains a copy of all rows that were removed by the DELETE command.

```
CREATE TRIGGER tr_d_Customer
    ON Customer
 AFTER DELETE
    AS
DECLARE @id int;
DECLARE c1 CURSOR FOR
 SELECT CustomerID
   FROM deleted;
```

```
OPEN c1;
FETCH c1 INTO @id;
WHILE @@FETCH_STATUS = 0
  BEGIN
    DELETE FROM SlickCorp.dbo.Customer
     WHERE CustomerID = @id
       AND StoreID = 1108;

    FETCH c1 INTO @id;
  END

CLOSE c1;
DEALLOCATE c1;
```

Finally, you need a trigger to handle any updates that modify a customer. Rather than try to figure out each and every column that has changed, you could instead just delete the customers that changed and then insert them with the new data. To do this, you'll perform the same actions that you did in the delete and insert triggers, one after the other.

```
CREATE TRIGGER tr_u_Customer
    ON Customer
 AFTER UPDATE
    AS
DECLARE @id int;
DECLARE c1 CURSOR FOR
 SELECT CustomerID
   FROM deleted;

OPEN c1;

FETCH c1 INTO @id;
WHILE @@FETCH_STATUS = 0
  BEGIN
    DELETE FROM SlickCorp.dbo.Customer
     WHERE CustomerID = @id
       AND StoreID = 1108;

    FETCH c1 INTO @id;
  END
```

```
CLOSE c1;
DEALLOCATE c1;

INSERT INTO SlickCorp.dbo.Customer
    (StoreID, CustomerID, FirstName, LastName,
     Address, City, StateOrProvince,
     PostalCode, PhoneNumber)
SELECT 1108, CustomerID, FirstName, LastName,
     Address, City, StateOrProvince,
     PostalCode, PhoneNumber
  FROM inserted;
```

Notice how this trigger is a combination of the prior two triggers, tr_d_Customer and tr_i_Customer. The first part of the trigger deletes all of the modified customers from the SlickCorp database. The last part of the trigger inserts the customers back in complete with its modified data.

Your database will not have an "updated" table or anything similar. Instead, inside an UPDATE trigger you will be able to see how the row looked before the update occurred and also see how it looks after. In Transact-SQL this means that you'll be looking at both the inserted and deleted tables.

A trigger can only be applied to one table within a single database. So each of these three triggers would have to be created on every Slick Shop database that you wanted to replicate. Before each trigger is created, the hard-coded store number would have to be changed to reflect the proper value.

There are many other variations of synchronization triggers like these. You could have triggers that synchronize data within the same database. You could send summarized data to another table. You could even have a trigger run some stored procedures for you.

Using Triggers to Maintain Referential Integrity

In the Saturday Evening session, we talked about a feature that some DBMSs have, called cascading updates and deletes. They automatically carry updates or deletes through to related tables in order to maintain referential integrity. For example, if a row from the Customer table were deleted, a cascading delete would automatically delete all of the related rows in the Vehicle table. This would help prevent *orphaned* rows in the Vehicle table—vehicles without related customers. If your database system does not support these kinds of cascading actions, you could accomplish the same thing with triggers.

The following is a delete trigger on the Customer table. It will delete all vehicles owned by the customer who was deleted.

```
CREATE TRIGGER tr_d_CustVehicle
    ON Customer
 AFTER DELETE
    AS
DELETE FROM Vehicle
 WHERE CustomerID IN (SELECT CustomerID
                        FROM deleted);
```

Now this trigger is set except for one thing, the foreign key that exists between Customer and Vehicle. If you attempt to delete a row from Customer while there is a related row in Vehicle, the command will fail. The foreign key relationship is tested before the trigger is executed. The only way for this trigger to do its job is to remove the foreign key definition from the Vehicle table.

You'll recall back in that Saturday Evening session the long discussion about the pros and cons of using foreign keys. If you have a database that you've decided you want to have foreign keys, this trigger doesn't look too attractive. There is, however, an alternative. In that session, we told you that in order to delete a row on the primary key side of the relationship, you'd first have to delete the foreign key side rows. In this case, you'd have to delete the Vehicle rows first; then you'd be able to delete the Customer. The problem with the trigger is that it's deleting the Customer row first. The INSTEAD OF trigger option allows you to bypass a command's normal action and run just the trigger's code instead.

Knowing this, you should rewrite the trigger so that it will delete the Vehicle rows first and then the Customer rows.

```
CREATE TRIGGER tr_d_CustVehicle
     ON Customer
INSTEAD OF DELETE
     AS
DELETE FROM Vehicle
  WHERE CustomerID IN (SELECT CustomerID
                          FROM deleted);


DELETE FROM Customer
  WHERE CustomerID IN (SELECT CustomerID
                          FROM deleted);
```

Now when someone issues a command like this,

```
DELETE FROM Customer WHERE CustomerID = 207;
```

the delete on the Customer table will not happen. Instead, the trigger code will run, which will first delete any vehicles owned by that customer. After that the trigger will go ahead and delete the customer. Notice how this trigger is also written to handle the case where several customers are deleted at the same time, as in the next command.

```
DELETE FROM Customer WHERE LastName = 'Wilson';
```

■ ■
TIP Try to make your triggers as concise and fast as possible. Remember that every time the user modifies data, your trigger now will cause more work to be done than before.
■ ■

Using Triggers on Views

A view cannot have BEFORE or AFTER triggers assigned to it the way a table can. However, if the view is capable of modifying data and the underlying table has a trigger, that trigger will fire even if the view was used in the SQL command. The only type of trigger that can be created directly on a view is an INSTEAD OF trigger. As we said earlier, there are many restrictions on views that determine whether or not a view can be used to modify data. The INSTEAD OF trigger option can be used to give a nonupdating view the ability to modify data. Truthfully, the view will have nothing to do with the data modification. The INSTEAD OF trigger will do all the work.

To demonstrate this type of trigger on a view, you'll create a nonupdatable view. This view will join two tables and aggregate some data.

```
CREATE VIEW JobSummaryView
    AS
SELECT j.JobTicketID, j.StartDate, j.EndDate, COUNT(*)
    AS 'NumOfLines'
  FROM JobTicket AS j
  JOIN JobTicketDetail AS jtd ON j.JobTicketID = jtd.JobTicketID
  GROUP BY j.JobTicketID, j.Startdate, j.EndDate
```

When you do a SELECT * on this view, you get the following:

JobTicketID	StartDate	EndDate	NumOfLines
1	2002-01-20 00:00:00	2002-01-20 00:00:00	1
2	2001-07-20 00:00:00	2001-07-20 00:00:00	3
3	2001-09-16 00:00:00	2001-09-16 00:00:00	1
4	2002-01-26 00:00:00	2002-01-26 00:00:00	1
5	2002-05-21 00:00:00	2002-05-21 00:00:00	2
6	2001-08-13 00:00:00	2001-08-13 00:00:00	1
7	2002-03-22 00:00:00	2002-02-17 00:00:00	5

It shows the start and end dates of every job ticket and how many line items there are for each. Because this view aggregates data with GROUP BY, it can't be used to update data. If you attempted to issue an UPDATE command on this view right now, you'd get an error. In order to allow updates, you'll create an INSTEAD OF trigger for this view.

```
CREATE TRIGGER tr_u_JobSummaryView
    ON JobSummaryView
INSTEAD OF UPDATE
    AS

 DECLARE @id    int;
 DECLARE @start smalldatetime;
 DECLARE @end   smalldatetime;
```

```
DECLARE c1 CURSOR FOR
 SELECT JobTicketID, StartDate, EndDate
   FROM inserted;

OPEN c1;

FETCH c1 INTO @id, @start, @end;
WHILE @@FETCH_STATUS = 0
  BEGIN
    UPDATE JobTicket
       SET StartDate = @start,
           EndDate   = @end
     WHERE JobTicketID = @id;

     FETCH c1 INTO @id, @start, @end;
  END

CLOSE c1;
DEALLOCATE c1;
```

Now you can write a command like the following:

```
UPDATE JobSummaryView
   SET StartDate = '2003-1-2', EndDate = '2003-1-3'
 WHERE JobTicketID = 1;
```

Remember that the INSTEAD OF trigger will cause the UPDATE to be ignored. Basically, all it will do is fire the trigger. This means that you'll have to do all of the work yourself in the code of the trigger. As before, you've written this one to loop through all of the rows that would be affected by the WHERE clause of the UPDATE command. The virtual tables that show inserted and deleted rows are available just like they are in regular table triggers.

As it loops through each row, the cursor puts the job ticket number and the new date values into variables. Then the trigger performs its own UPDATE command on the JobTicket table. This will all be seamless to users; they'll just execute an UPDATE command and it will run as expected.

Using Triggers to Enforce Business Rules

In the Saturday Evening session, when we talked about creating tables, we showed you how you can build some validation into a table. You can use the CHECK constraint on a column to perform some simple validation. Triggers are better suited for more complex validation or enforcement of business rules.

◄◄

A **business rule** defines or restricts data to meet a particular business practice rather than just a universally accepted fact. For example, this is a business rule: "License plate numbers are required for all vehicles except those from Canada." This is a rule that the database will allow you to break unless you somehow prevent it. It's also a rule that some companies will use and others will not. This is not a business rule: "Quantity values cannot contain any letters or special characters." This is a universally accepted fact.

◄◄

We'll give you a few examples of triggers that enforce business rules, starting with a simple one that ensures that each job ticket's end date does not come before the start date.

```
CREATE TRIGGER tr_iu_JobDates
    ON JobTicket
  AFTER INSERT, UPDATE
    AS
 IF EXISTS (SELECT * FROM inserted WHERE EndDate < StartDate)
   BEGIN
     RAISERROR ('The start date must be before the end date.', 16, 1);
     ROLLBACK TRANSACTION;
   END
```

Notice how this one trigger applies to both INSERT and UPDATE. It looks at the data in the inserted table, which holds both newly inserted rows and the new values of updated rows. Notice also that this trigger uses the ROLLBACK command to cancel the inserts or updates that took place. The insert or update that was executed was considered its own transaction even if there was not an explicit BEGIN TRANSACTION command. So any violation of this business rule will cause the inserted or updated rows to be cancelled. Also included is the Transact-SQL command RAISERROR, which returns an error message to the user. For more information on transactions, look back at the Sunday Morning session.

TIP ■■

Your DBMS might allow you to create more than one of the same type of trigger on the same table. For example, you might be able to create three different update triggers on the Customer table. If this feature is available, there will also be a command that will allow you to specify the order in which the triggers will be fired.

■■

Triggers can also enforce business rules by looking into other tables in the same database or even a separate database. Let's assume that the Slick Shop has a business rule that a certain part cannot be installed in older cars due to some government regulation. This next trigger watches the parts that are being used on job tickets. It will prevent vehicles built before 2000 from using part number 9.

```
CREATE TRIGGER tr_i_CheckPart9
    ON PartUsed
 AFTER INSERT
    AS
IF EXISTS (SELECT *
              FROM Vehicle AS v
              JOIN JobTicket AS j ON j.VehicleID = v.VehicleID
              JOIN inserted AS i ON i.JobTicketID = j.JobTicketID
             WHERE v.VehicleYear < 2000
               AND i.PartID = 9)
  BEGIN
    RAISERROR ('The ACME Oil Filter is not for use in cars
               built before 2000.', 16, 1);
    ROLLBACK TRANSACTION;
  END
```

This trigger joins the inserted table through JobTicket to Vehicle to find out if any of the parts being inserted are number 9, going on a pre-2000 car. If it finds a violation, it will raise an error message and roll back the changes.

Triggers and CHECK constraints are similar but have a few key differences. The trigger is much more powerful in that it has the ability to base decisions on other columns, tables, and databases. The trigger, however, can only validate data that is changed after the time that you create the trigger. It cannot validate data that was already sitting in the table before you applied the trigger. A CHECK constraint will go back and validate all data that is currently in a table.

A trigger can also be used to create or modify data, as the next example will demonstrate. For this one, you've received a request from the Slick Shop's marketing department to combine the city, state, and postal code fields. This will help them to format their mailing label more easily. You, of course, don't want to combine these three fields into one because you'd lose the ability to query these fields independently. What you will do, though, is create a new column that will fit their needs.

```
ALTER TABLE Customer
  ADD CityStateZip varchar(46);
```

This new column is big enough to hold the City, StateOrProvince, and PostalCode columns with a few extra bytes for a comma and some blank spaces. Next you'll create a trigger that will populate this column automatically every time customer data is inserted or updated.

```
CREATE TRIGGER tr_iu_CityStateZip
    ON Customer
 AFTER INSERT, UPDATE
    AS

 DECLARE @id    int;
 DECLARE @city  varchar(30);
 DECLARE @state char(2);
 DECLARE @zip   varchar(10);

 DECLARE c1 CURSOR FOR
  SELECT CustomerID, City, StateOrProvince, PostalCode
    FROM inserted;
```

```
OPEN c1;

FETCH c1 INTO @id, @city, @state, @zip;
WHILE @@FETCH_STATUS = 0
  BEGIN
    UPDATE Customer
        SET CityStateZip = @city + ', ' + @state + '  ' + @zip
      WHERE CustomerID = @id;

    FETCH c1 INTO @id, @city, @state, @zip;
  END

CLOSE c1;
DEALLOCATE c1;
```

As before, you're able to use the same trigger for both inserts and updates. Notice how this trigger actually updates the same table on which the trigger is built. So if an INSERT command is run on the Customer table, first the row will be inserted, the trigger will perform an UPDATE on that same row. Because a trigger and the command that fired the trigger run within their own transaction, other users cannot see any changes until the trigger is finished. In the case of the previous trigger, this means that if someone happens to run a SELECT in the split second between the INSERT and the trigger's UPDATE, they will not see the new customer at all. However, the instant that the trigger is done, the transaction is committed and everyone (with proper authority) can see the changes.

Remember also that all of the rows that existed before this trigger was created will have NULL values in the CityStateZip column. You would probably want to write a little stored procedure to get the existing values updated. You could use the trigger code as a basis for the procedure. You would only have to run it one time—from then on the trigger will keep the column synchronized.

Because this is a chapter on security, you'll finish with a trigger that updates column data in order to save audit information. This trigger is an alternative to the one presented in the section "Using Triggers to Audit User Activity." This one will update columns within the same table that is being modified. This is a technique that we have used with success on past projects. What you do is add two columns to the end of every table: one will store the last date and time a row was changed, the other will store the username of the last person who performed the change. Because you're probably tired using the Customer table for examples, you'll use Part this time. Following is the command to create the Part table with the two extra columns you need.

```
CREATE TABLE Part (
PartID          Integer  IDENTITY(1,1)  NOT NULL PRIMARY KEY CLUSTERED,
Description     Varchar(100)            NOT NULL,
Cost            Money                   NOT NULL,
UpdateDate      SmallDateTime           NULL,
UpdateUser      Varchar(30)             NULL
)
```

Notice that the two new columns must allow NULL values. This is because when a new row is added, the user will not include the date and username information. They will get inserted with NULL values, and the trigger will then update them right away. Now all you need is a trigger that will automatically update these columns whenever a row is inserted or updated. The trigger uses two Transact-SQL functions, getdate and suser_sname, to get the current date and the logged-in user, respectively. Other DBMSs will use different function names.

```
CREATE TRIGGER tr_iu_PartTracking
    ON Part
 AFTER INSERT, UPDATE
    AS
 UPDATE Part
    SET UpdateDate = getdate(),
        UpdateUser = suser_sname()
  WHERE PartID IN (SELECT PartID
                     FROM inserted);
```

So, when a row is inserted,

```
INSERT INTO Part
  (Description, Cost)
VALUES
  ('60 Month Battery', 65.99);
```

the last two columns will tell you who added the row and when.

```
PartID  Description       Cost     UpdateDate           UpdateUser
------  ---------         -------  ----------           ----------
15      60 Month Battery  65.9900  2002-06-03 11:43:00  GusT
```

And when someone later comes along and updates the row,

```
UPDATE Part
   SET Cost = 72.50
 WHERE PartID = 15;
```

the two columns will get automatically updated.

```
PartID  Description       Cost     UpdateDate           UpdateUser
-----   ----------        ------   ---------            ---------
15      60 Month Battery  72.5000  2002-12-18 15:27:00  JackieP
```

We've found this to be very useful, especially in databases with a large user base. Although it doesn't provide as much information as the audit trail presented earlier, it is another way to track down problems. We've had pretty good success with it when we've needed to find data that changed on a certain day or find out who last touched a particular row.

What's Next?

We're going to wrap up the book this evening by discussing application development languages. Although SQL can be placed in the hands of end users, this is not very common. Instead, developers usually write and compile applications that mask most if not all of the SQL. End users don't have to ever know what language or database is being used. As a developer, you have many choices of languages that can access your relational database.

In the next chapter, we'll show you a few of the most popular and widely available languages and how each of them deals with SQL.

SQL and the Application Developer

- ➤ Making Use of SQL with Office and Microsoft Query
- ➤ Building Database Applications with Visual Basic and Visual Basic .NET
- ➤ Getting Visual C++ and Visual C# .NET to Use SQL
- ➤ Making Data Driven Web Pages with ASP and ASP .NET
- ➤ Using SQL with PowerBuilder

ell, you're into the home stretch now! You've learned as much SQL as we're going to show you in this book. Now we'll move on to some of the ways that users and application developers interact with SQL. Users fall into three categories. The first type of users don't want to have to deal with SQL, tables, columns, or procedures. They just want an easy-to-use interface to their data. They want to do their job as quickly and accurately as possible. The application developer will support these users. The second type are somewhat more advanced users who don't mind dabbling with tools that will allow them to create their own reports. This is especially true if they have tools to use that will let them point-and-click instead of typing SQL commands. The user type is the power-user. Power-users are people who don't mind getting their hands dirty and typing some good old SQL.

Most users fall into the first category. They will rely on you to build them sophisticated database applications. In this evening's session, you'll see various ways that you'll be able to satisfy this type of user.

Making Use of SQL with Office and Microsoft Query

The products within Microsoft Office have very nice database query capabilities built into them. The applications such as Word and Excel can run live queries against a relational database and bring the results back into the document or spreadsheet. The queries can be saved so that the results can be refreshed later. One of the uses for this in Word is to use query results to make mail merge documents. As you read through this section, keep in mind that many other spreadsheet and word-processing programs offer similar data access capabilities.

The Office applications accomplish their query capabilities through another Office application called *Microsoft Query* (or just *Query*).

Using Microsoft Query

Query is an application that is often overlooked or even unknown to many people. One reason for this is that it's not installed with Office by default. Even if it is installed, a shortcut is not placed on the menu for you. In this section, we'll step you through the highlights of this application, starting with how to get it installed.

One way to tell whether Query is already installed is to start Excel and click Data, and then Get External Data, and then New Database Query. If Query is not installed, you'll be told now. The newer versions of Office will prompt you to insert your Office CD so that the installation can begin. After a very short installation process, you'll see the Choose Data Source dialog box, as shown in Figure 7.1. This is the same dialog box you'll see if Query was installed in the first place.

For now, just cancel this dialog box and either close or minimize Excel. You'll come back to it later. First we want to show you how to get Query on your Start menu. The reason that the install does not create a shortcut for you is because Microsoft considers it to be a second-tier application. This means that although it's a fully functional, supported application, its main purpose is to be executed from within other applications such Word and Excel. Query, however, is a worthwhile program that can be used to simplify database queries by writing SQL for you. Many times people who don't know about Query scour the Internet in search of a program

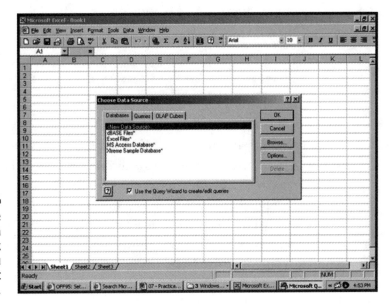

Figure 7.1

If you can get the Choose Data Source dialog box to appear, you know that Microsoft Query is installed.

that does the same thing. Sometimes they'll even purchase expensive packages with advanced capabilities that they don't need just in order to give users an easy way to look at their data.

Query can be given to your advanced users and power-users. They will need to deal with tables, columns, and some syntax rules, but not SQL. They will not have to learn syntax for the SELECT command, WHERE clause, or joins. For the most part they can just point-and-click and they'll have their results. The queries can be saved and the output can be copied and pasted somewhere else.

Okay then, time to get Microsoft Query on your Start menu. Once it's installed, all you need to do is locate the program and create a shortcut for it. Easier said than done! Each new version of Office likes to put programs in a different place. We've found that even if a PC has only had one version of Office installed on it, there can be as many as 10 subdirectories named "Office" or some variation thereof.

Anyway, here are a few places it's been known to hide:

```
C:\Program Files\Office2K\Office\MSQRY32.EXE
C:\Program Files\Microsoft Office\Office\MSQRY32.EXE
C:\Program Files\Common Files\Microsoft Shared\Msquery\MSQRY32.EXE
```

If you don't find it in one of these places, try searching your whole hard drive for MSQRY32.EXE. When you find it, create a new shortcut with this file as the target and name it "Microsoft Query". Now use the shortcut to start Query and we'll walk you through the product. After it starts, you'll be taken to a blank screen. Press the first button on the toolbar or select File, and then New from the menu. You'll see the Choose Data Source dialog box that's back in Figure 7.1. You may see some default data sources in this dialog box, but you'll want to create a new one to point to your own database. Make sure <New Data Source> is highlighted and click on OK. This will open the Create New Data Source dialog box, as shown in Figure 7.2. Type in any name for your data source and select the driver type that matches your DBMS, such as SQL Server, Oracle, or Informix.

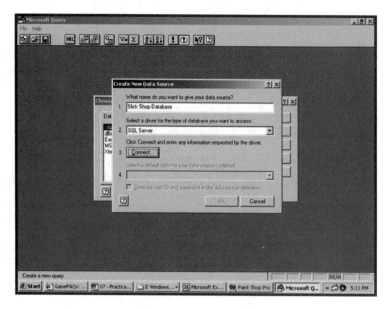

Figure 7.2

Start creating a new data source by giving it a name and indicating what DBMS your database lives in.

Next, press Connect to get to the Login dialog box. Here you'll tell it the name of your server first. The check box called Use Trusted Connection should be turned on only if you're using server authentication. Remember from the Sunday Afternoon session that this means your network logon is the same as your database logon. If you're not using database authentication, clear the check box and enter your login name and password. Don't press OK yet; first you'll want to click Options. This will let you choose the database that you want to connect to. You can just leave the other three options alone. The completed Login dialog box is shown in Figure 7.3.

Now you can press OK, after which you'll find yourself back at the Create New Data Source dialog box. The fourth option here asks you if you want to specify a default table. Don't select one. It's easier just to wait until later when you're ready to build a query. The last option is a check box that allows you to save your password along with the other data source information. If you check this box, right away you'll get a warning message. It will tell you that although this is a nice feature, it's going to

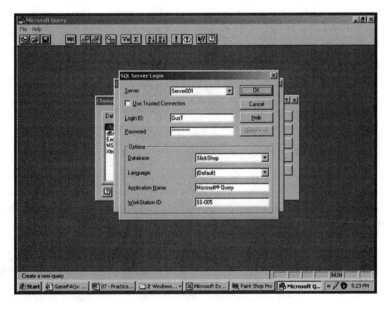

Figure 7.3

In the Login dialog box, you'll provide all the necessary information to connect to your database.

store your password in a plain text file that someone could find one day. They're not lying either. When you press OK, Query will create a text file with a .DSN extension that will simply show all the information you put in the last two dialog boxes (including your password). If you leave the check box cleared, you'll be prompted for your database password whenever you use this data source.

After you press OK, you'll be back to the Choose Data Source dialog box, and your new data source will be in the list. Select your data source, but before you press OK, clear the Use Query Wizard check box. The wizard is a nice little set of dialog boxes that step you through building a simple query. Let's be tough about it and go without the wizard's help. After clearing the check box, press OK and you'll enter the query interface. The Add Tables dialog box, as shown in Figure 7.4, will open on its own.

The permissions that you've granted to a user will take effect here. The user will only see tables for which he or she has SELECT permission. Remember when we discussed security in the Sunday Afternoon session? You may have users who find their way into Query on their own, so make

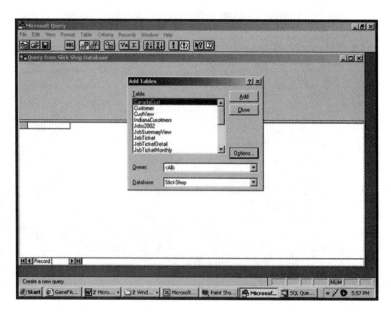

Figure 7.4

The Add Tables dialog box will display the tables and views that you have permission to query.

sure you have the permissions set up properly! Notice that in Figure 7.4 not only are tables listed but also the views created in the last session. Both the tables and the views are available for your new query.

TIP Unless you use some kind of naming convention to distinguish tables from views, this is an example of a place where you won't know which is which. Then again, maybe you don't want to confuse your users with tables versus views. It might be best to just let them think they're all tables.

Select the `Customer` table and press Add. The table is added to the query window behind the dialog box. You can keep adding as many tables as you need, but for now just press Close. If you need to, resize the panes inside the query window and resize the `Customer` table dialog box so you can see all of the columns. Figure 7.5 shows the query window.

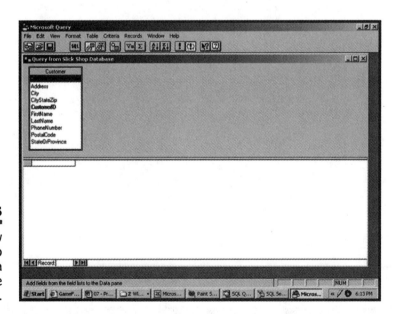

Figure 7.5

The query window is now ready to start building a new query with the `Customer` table.

NOTE
• •
If you skipped the Sunday Afternoon session, you might be wondering where the CityStateZip column came from. This is a column that you added in the last session. It is populated by a trigger and contains the combination of the City, StateOrProvince, and PostalCode columns.
• •

The pane in the lower half of the query window is where your query results will be displayed. There is nothing there yet because you haven't told it what columns you want to see. To get this done, just drag columns one-by-one from the table to the lower pane. You can also click the white rectangular box in the lower pane to drop down a list of columns to choose from. Figure 7.6 shows four of the columns from Customer selected.

Notice that at the top of the table there is an asterisk (*). If you want to see all of the columns, you can just drag this down to the results pane instead of dragging each column one by one. If you want to remove a column later, just click on the column name in the results pane and press the Delete key.

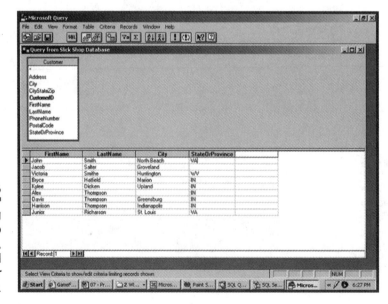

Figure 7.6

When you drag columns down to the results pane, the data will appear automatically.

You can sort the results by selecting a column and pressing the Sort Ascending or Sort Descending button. If you want to sort by more than one column, select Records, Sort from the menu. A sorting dialog box will let you add and remove sorting combinations.

Now press the Show/Hide Criteria button on the toolbar or choose View, Criteria from the menu. This will open the criteria pane in the middle of the query window. In the same way you did it in the results pane, you can drag or select columns in the criteria pane. Once you have a column in the criteria pane, you can then specify a comparison value below it. If the column is a character data type, you must put single quotes around the value. As soon as you click somewhere else or move the cursor out of the value box, the results will be filtered. The query window in Figure 7.7 indicates that only customers from Indiana should be displayed.

A nice feature of the criteria pane is that it can help you define the comparison value. Double-click the value rectangle directly below the column name. The Edit Criteria dialog box will open. This dialog box has several options for the operator such as, "equals", "does not equal", "is greater

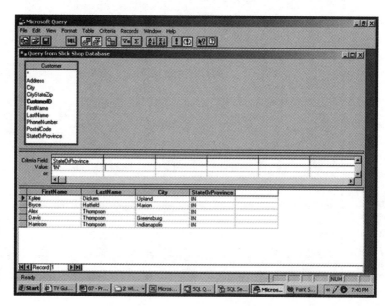

Figure 7.7

The middle pane allows you to specify criteria that will filter the query.

than", "is between", and "begins with", just to name a few. Select one of these operators, and then enter a value below it. In this particular value box, if you don't put quotes around character values, Query will do it for you. When you press OK, the filter will be applied. In Figure 7.8, the filter has been changed to show all customers that are not in Indiana.

Anything that the Edit Criteria dialog box enters in the value field you can do yourself if you know the proper syntax. For example, if you want to see all last names that start with the letter "S", you could open the dialog box, select Begins With, and type s in the value box. But if you know the syntax, you could skip the dialog box and just enter Like 'S%' in the query window's value box. There is one nice thing the Edit Criteria dialog box can do for you that you can't do on your own. Open the dialog box again and click on Values. This will open the Select Value(s) dialog box, which will show you all of the unique values that currently exist in that column. If you select a value, it will be returned to the previous dialog box. This is a nice way to take a look at the data that's available in a column, especially if you're not familiar with the table or column.

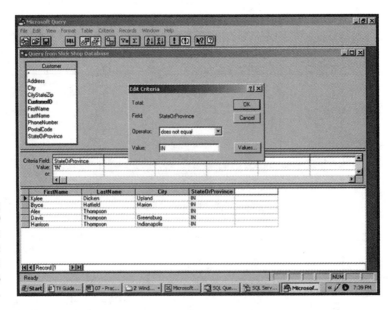

Figure 7.8

The Edit Criteria dialog box can be used to assist you with the various operators.

TIP

■■■■■■■■■■■■■■■■■■■■■■■■■■■■■■■■■■■■■■

Be careful with the Values button. If you're working with a very large table, it could take a long time to bring back the list. When it's pressed, it is running a SQL command similar to this:

```
SELECT DISTINCT StateOrProvince FROM Customer;
```

If the column is not indexed, you're asking for a table scan. The DISTINCT keyword will slow the query a bit more as well.

■■■■■■■■■■■■■■■■■■■■■■■■■■■■■■■■■■■■■■

Of course, what you're really doing in the criteria pane is having Query build a WHERE clause for you. You can view the SQL that Query is building any time during this process. Just press the View SQL button or select View and then SQL from the menu. The SQL dialog box, like the one in Figure 7.9, will show you the command that Query has built so far.

You can highlight and copy the SELECT command from this dialog box. This raises an interesting idea. Could you click and drag within Query to build a SELECT and then paste it into your stored procedure, trigger,

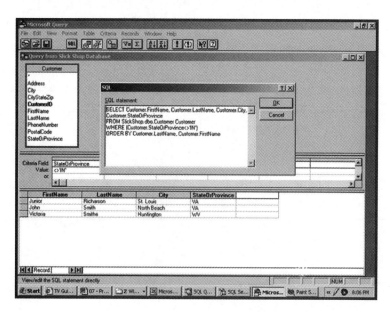

Figure 7.9

The SQL dialog box shows the command that Query has built.

view, or application code? Sure! If you find this to be an easier method of writing queries, go for it! It can also be a good way for someone to teach himself some SQL.

Microsoft Query is not limited to single-table queries, so let's get another table involved. Click the Add Table(s) button or select Table and then Add Tables on the menu. You'll get the Add Tables dialog box that you've seen before (see Figure 7.4). Select the Vehicle table and then press Add. Although the dialog box does not go away, you'll be able to see that the Vehicle table was added to the top pane. The dialog box stays open in case you need to add more tables. That's all we want you to add, so just press Close.

We want you to notice how the two tables, Customer and Vehicle, have a line between them. This shows the relationship between the two tables. Specifically, the ends of the line point to the CustomerID column of each table. How did Query know to do this? It read the foreign key that you created on the Vehicle table. Now what you can do is drag columns from this table into the results pane and the criteria pane. For Figure 7.10, three columns have been added from the Vehicle table to the results, and the VehicleYear has been used in the criteria.

Something else done in Figure 7.10 was to add another value to the criteria under the StateOrProvince column. Notice the word "or" on the second line below the column name. This means that values placed below the column will be an OR condition. Because 'IN' is on the first line and 'WV' is on the second, this is the same as

```
StateOrProvince = 'IN' OR StateOrProvince = 'WV'
```

To remove a table from a query, click on the table in the top pane and press the Delete key. Because the table is being removed from the query, all columns from that table will be removed from the results and criteria panes.

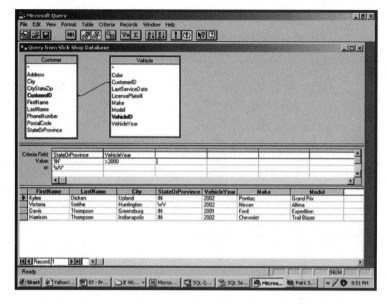

Figure 7.10

The query window with two tables joined.

So far, every time you've added a new column or changed criteria, the results pane has updated itself right away. Of course, what's happening here is that Query is sending a new SELECT command to the database each time. For a table as small as the ones you're using, that's not a problem. However, with tables of substantial size, this could be an annoyance. Even if the query takes just two seconds, you'll find Query delaying your progress often to rerun its command. Toggle the Auto Query button off or select Records and then Automatic Query to turn this feature off. You'll now be able to work on queries without the results updating. When you're ready to run the query, just press the Query Now button or select Records then Query Now on the menu.

You can use the Save button to name and save your query. Now it will be available for you to open and run later. You could use this feature to create some standard queries for your users. They could later open the queries and change the criteria to suit their needs. If you do this, keep in mind that your logon may have access to more tables than they do. If you save a query using tables that they don't have permission on, the query will not work for them. The users, of course, can always create and save their own queries.

Contrary to its name, Query will also allow you to edit the data in the results pane. By default, you cannot change anything. But you can turn on the edit mode by selecting the Records menu, and then Allow Editing. Now you'll be able to go down in the results pane and change the values. The database will get updated when you move off of the row. You cannot edit data if there is more than one table in the query.

Using Query within Excel

Now it's time to look back to the Office products to see how they integrate with Microsoft Query. If you still have Query open, go ahead and close it now. This is where you will see why Microsoft calls it a second-tier application. Open Excel now and start with a blank spreadsheet. Now you can access Query the same way we had you do at the beginning of this session. Select Data from the menu, and then Get External Data, and then New Database Query. You'll see the Choose Data Source dialog box now, just like you saw back in Figure 7.1. Select the data source you created earlier and press OK. Enter your database password if necessary. You'll now find yourself back in the query window that you worked through in the last section.

Go ahead and create a new query now by adding a table or two and several columns for the results. After you get the query all set up, you can save it if you want to. Now you're ready to send this data back to Excel. Choose the File menu, and then Return Data to Excel. You'll be sent back to Excel and given a dialog box called Returning External Data to Microsoft Excel, as shown in Figure 7.11.

You can see from this dialog box that Excel is giving you a choice of three places to put the results of the query. It can go in the current worksheet, a new worksheet, or a pivot table.

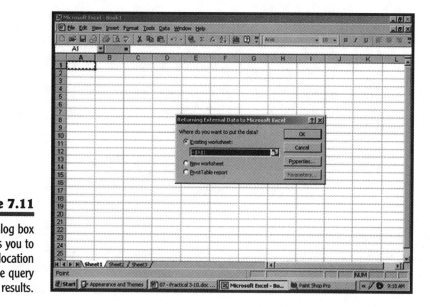

Figure 7.11

This dialog box prompts you to specify a location for the query results.

 TIP We don't have the space here to get into Excel pivot tables, but if you've never played with one, check it out sometime. Pivot tables allow you to place your data in a cross-tab layout. After that you can group data, drag columns around, and summarize different ways in order to analyze the results.

Just press OK and let the data start in cell A1. Now the results of your query are brought into Excel. Notice also that you'll have the External Data toolbar available now. Figure 7.12 shows the query results after they've been returned to Excel.

Query will feed Excel the column headers and all of the rows and columns of data in your result set. You are able to work with the data in these cells in all of the usual ways. You can format the cells, create formulas, and even change the data in the result set. You should note, however, that changing the values in Excel will not change the database values. Excel has a copy of the data.

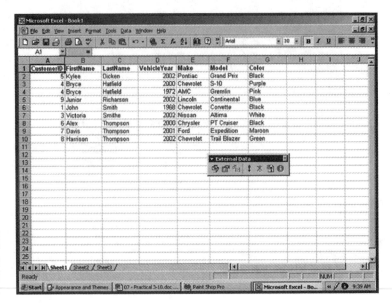

Figure 7.12

Results that have
been returned from
Query into Excel.

When you save the spreadsheet, the values and any of your modifications
will be saved as well. Excel also saves information about the source of the
data in the spreadsheet. This is so that you'll be able to refresh the data
later. The next time you open the spreadsheet, the data will be the same
as you last saved it. Excel will not automatically retrieve from your database. When you're ready to rerun your query, move to one of the cells
within your results. When you do this, the Refresh Data button on the
External Data toolbar will become available. This button has a picture of
a red exclamation point. Press this button to have Microsoft Query go
out and run your query again. The new result set will be brought back
into the same spot in the spreadsheet. You won't even see any of Query's
windows pop up, unless it encounters an error or has to ask you for a
password. Any changes that you've made to the data will be replaced with
the real values from the database. This goes for formatting changes too,
which revert back to their defaults. Everything else in the spreadsheet that
is outside of the result set's cells will remain untouched.

Using Query within Word

Another popular use of Microsoft Query that we'll show you is to get data into Word. This is similar to the way Excel does it, but there are some differences with the menus and the functionality. Finding Query when you're in Word can be a little tricky. First, you'll need to open the Database toolbar. From the View menu, select Toolbars, and then Database. This will give you a new toolbar with 10 buttons on it. Now you're ready to integrate some data into your documents.

The first sample we'll show you will just be a quick way to place query results into a Word document. After that you'll do a mail merge sample. Press the Insert Database button and you'll be given the Database dialog box, as shown in Figure 7.13.

This dialog box kind of works like a three-step wizard. The first thing you must do is press Get Data. This will give you a dialog box in which you can search for a file to open. Instead of selecting a file, press MS Query. This will open Microsoft Query and bring you to the Choose Data Source dialog box, just like Figure 7.1. Now that you're in Query, you can

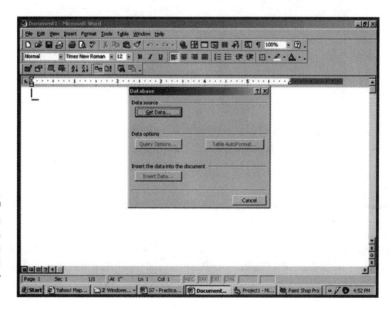

Figure 7.13

The Database dialog box steps you through the process of pulling data into your document.

either open a saved query or create a new one. Create a query the same way that you did earlier, and when you're finished, choose Return Data to Microsoft Word from the File menu. Now you'll be sent back to Word and the Database dialog box where three new options are available. Choose Query Options to go back to work on the query again. Clicking Table AutoFormat will let you define what the Word table is going to look like. After using these two options (or not), press Insert Data. This will put the query results into your document in a Word table.

Just like Excel, this data is just a copy, so you can modify it if you want. Your changes will not affect the database. Query was used to bring data into the document shown in Figure 7.14.

One of the most popular reasons for accessing a database via Word is to create mail merge documents. These are documents that have placeholders for data such as name and address. A single document can be created with these placeholders, and then when the addresses are pulled in it will generate a separate document for each row of data.

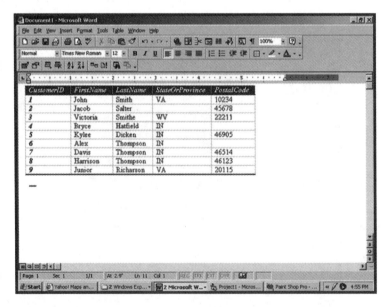

Figure 7.14

Query data that has been retrieved into a Word document.

The Customer table will work as an excellent source of mail merge data. To start a mail merge, open a new blank document and choose Mail Merge from the Tools menu. This will open another wizard-like dialog box, called Mail Merge Helper. This dialog box is shown in Figure 7.15.

For step one, press Create and notice that you have a few options here. For this sample choose Form Letters. Word will ask you if you want to create the form letter in the current document or a new one. Press Active Window. Now in step two, press Get Data and choose Open Data Source. Like before, this will give you the dialog box where you can search for a file to open. Also like before, click MS Query and you'll be sent to the Microsoft Query window. You know what to do here. Create a query that includes the customers' names and addresses. When you return the data to Word, you'll be shown a warning that there are no merge fields in your document yet. That's okay—you'll take care of that in a minute. Just press Edit Main Document and you'll be returned to your blank document.

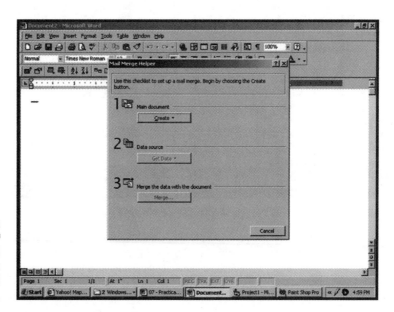

Figure 7.15

This dialog box will step you through creating a mail merge document.

You'll notice that the Mail Merge toolbar is now available. On this toolbar press the Insert Merge Field button, and a list of your columns will drop down. Select them one by one, placing them in the document at appropriate spots. You can intersperse these fields with your own text. Figure 7.16 shows your document after you've completed adding the fields and typing the text.

To see how real data will look in the form letter, press the View Merged Data button. You'll see the first name and address appear instead of the placeholders. You can now move back and forth through the data with the navigation buttons on the toolbar. There are many other mail merge features included in Word that we'll let you explore on your own.

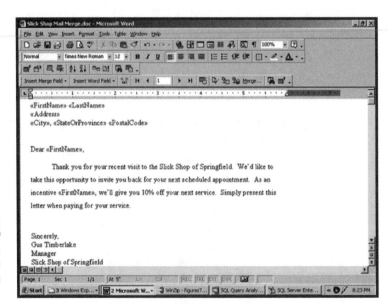

Figure 7.16

The merge fields in this document are noted by the double brackets.

Building Database Applications with Visual Basic and Visual Basic .NET

Users who do not want to work with SQL, even on a point-and-click level, often turn to application developers to help them out. Most users today prefer the ease of use that comes with graphical user interface (GUI) applications. One of the most popular GUI application development tools is Visual Basic. In addition to creating these applications, Visual Basic has strong capabilities for accessing relational databases. In this section, we'll split up the discussion between Visual Basic 6.0 and its newest release, Visual Basic .NET.

Using SQL with Visual Basic 6.0

Visual Basic 6.0 (VB6) has been a longtime mainstay in many development shops. There are still a considerable number of programs in VB6 and will be until they are either converted to the newer version or retired. Throughout the history of Visual Basic, there have been a few ways of accessing data, most notably Remote Data Objects (RDO) and Data Access Objects (DAO). When VB6 came along the preferred method became ActiveX Data Objects (ADO). When writing VB6 code you'll mostly deal with ADO, which we'll demonstrate later. In this first section, however, you'll see how to use ADO controls that let you build a database application with very little programming.

Data Bound Controls in VB6

In VB6 many of the controls that are available to you can be synchronized with a result set from a database. When you do this they become bound controls. Examples of some of these controls include text boxes, drop-down lists, check boxes, radio (or option) buttons, and grids. In this first demonstration, we'll show you how to get your relational data into a grid control.

Using the VB6 Grid Control

A grid control is very much like a spreadsheet. When it has data, you'll see columns and rows with a separate cell for each value. You can even use the grid control to update the database. To get started with this example, open VB6 and start a new Standard EXE project. When you do this you'll get a blank form (or window) to work with. Before you do anything else, you'll need to add a couple of components to this project. Select the Project menu, and then Components. As shown in Figure 7.17, in the Components dialog box, check both Microsoft ADO Data Control 6.0 and Microsoft DataGrid Control 6.0, and then press OK.

The toolbox with various controls should be available on the left side of the VB6 window. If it is not, select the View menu, and then Toolbox. In the toolbox, double-click the ADO Data Control button to add it to the form. The purpose of this control is to establish a connection to your database, run queries, and retrieve result sets. Right-click the control on the form and select ADODC Properties. This property page is where you will provide information about your database and how to get connected

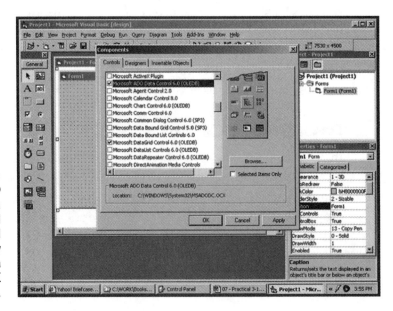

Figure 7.17

The ADO Data Control and DataGrid Control are not included by default in a Standard EXE project.

to it. Choose Use Connection String and press Build. This will open a dialog box that will guide you through the process of creating a connection string. Select your DBMS from the list of providers and press Next. Now enter the server name, username, and password and select your database. For this example, be sure to check Allow Saving Password. The completed dialog box is shown in Figure 7.18.

Press Test Connection to make sure you can successfully log in. When you press OK in the dialog box, you'll notice that back on the property page a long string has been entered for you. The string will look something like this:

```
Provider=SQLOLEDB.1; Persist Security Info=True;
    User ID=GusT;Password=oilman;Initial Catalog=SlickShop;
    Data Source=Server001
```

You could type this string in yourself instead of using the Data Link Properties dialog box. If you do, just make sure that you have it formatted correctly or you won't get connected to your database. Before you close this dialog box, set up a query that the data control will use. Click the Record-

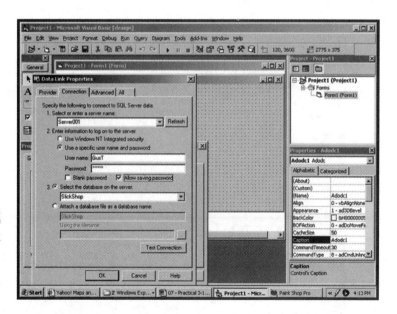

Figure 7.18

The Data Link Properties dialog box assists you in building a connection string.

Source tab, and then 1 - `adCmdText` from the drop-down list. This indicates that you want to write your own query. In the Command Text box you can type any SQL SELECT command. For this example, use the following command:

```
SELECT *
  FROM JobTicketDetail
 WHERE DateComplete > '2001-1-1';
```

Now double-click the DataGrid button in the toolbox to add a grid to the form. Resize the grid to fill up the form. Highlight the grid in the form and find its `DataSource` property in the property pane. In the drop-down next to the `DataSource` property, find and select the name of your ADO Data Control, which by default is `Adodc1`. By doing this, you have just bound the grid to the data control.

That's all you need to do! Click the Start button on the toolbar or press F5 to run the application. When the form opens, the data control will automatically connect to your database. Because the grid is bound to the data control, it displays the result set. Your sample application is shown in Figure 7.19.

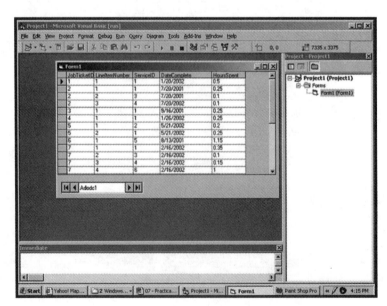

Figure 7.19

A data grid control that displays data from the `JobTicketDetail` table.

Notice that the data control has navigation arrows on it. You can press these to move through the next, previous, first, and last records. If you don't like it or don't have a use for it, you can set its `Visible` property to `False`. That way the control will still be there and do its job, but you'll only see the grid. You can move around the cells in the grid and change the data. The changes that you make will be saved immediately to the database. If you don't want people changing the data, you can set the grid's `AllowUpdate` property to `False`.

As with all controls in VB6, you can use code to change a grid's behavior at run-time. As a quick example of this, we'll show you how to modify this form so that you can dynamically change the SQL SELECT and reload the grid. If you haven't done so already, close your form and return to VB6. Now add two more controls to the form, a text box and a command button. Place both of them below the grid. Set the `MultiLine` property of the text box to `True` and set the `Caption` of the command button to `Run SQL`.

Double-click the command button to open the code window. You'll see that VB6 has created an empty subroutine for the `Click` event. Enter the following two lines in the `Click` event:

```
Private Sub Command1_Click()
    Adodc1.RecordSource = Text1.Text
    Adodc1.Refresh
End Sub
```

NOTE In this code `Adodc1` is the default name of the ADO data control. To find out the name of your data control, click on it and look at its `Name` property.

This code will take whatever you type into the text box and assign it as the new `RecordSource` for the data control. The `Refresh` method is then called to actually run the query and return the results to the bound grid. The modified form is shown in Figure 7.20.

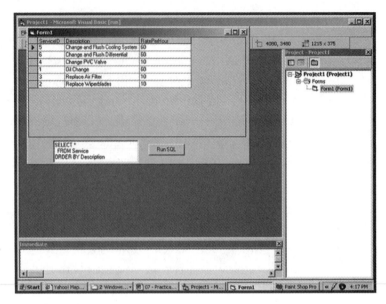

Figure 7.20

This form only needs two lines of code in order to allow users to enter their own queries.

Using Other VB6 Controls

As mentioned, many of the other controls can be bound to a data source as well. Binding text boxes, check boxes, and option buttons will let you further customize your applications. The idea is very much the same as binding a grid control. The major difference is that these other controls will each be bound to their own column.

We'll step you through an example like the one you did with the grid, only this time you'll use separate controls. Starting with the form from the last example, highlight and delete the grid control. You should be left with the data control, text box, and command button. Remember, the data control is already configured to connect to your database and has a SELECT command assigned to its RecordSource property. If the data control is not visible, set it back to True now. Add three labels and three text boxes to the form. Set the captions of the labels to say Job Ticket ID, Line Item #, and Date Complete. Size each control and arrange them as shown in Figure 7.21. Now set the Data Source property of all three text boxes to the name of your data control (which is Adodc1 unless you renamed it). Finally, you'll need to assign a column to each text box. Set the DataField property of the first text box to JobTicketID, the second to LineItemNumber, and the third to DateComplete. Now press the Start button on the VB6 toolbar and your form should look something like Figure 7.21.

Notice that with this method, you can only see one row of data at a time. You can use the navigation buttons on the data control to scroll forward and backward through the rows. Most developers, however, don't like the looks of the data control. You can get the same results by making your own navigation buttons. Set the Visible property of the data control back to False, and add two new command buttons. Set the caption of one to Next and the other to Previous. Now just write one line of code for the Click event of each.

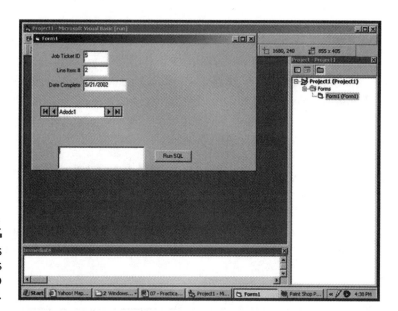

Figure 7.21

This form uses individual controls that are bound to the data control.

```
Private Sub cmdNext_Click()
    Adodc1.Recordset.MoveNext
End Sub

Private Sub cmdPrev_Click()
    Adodc1.Recordset.MovePrevious
End Sub
```

There's one more thing to notice about this sample. If you try to type a SELECT command in the text box and press the Run SQL button, you'll find that it doesn't work. The reason is that each text box is bound to a specific column. Unless the SELECT command you use has the same columns in the result set, it will not be able to bind it back to the text boxes. Of course, VB6 is a strong enough language that you could write code to determine the columns returned from the new query and change the DataField property for each text box.

Using SQL in VB6 Code

As you develop applications with VB6, you might find that you need more capabilities than bound controls can give you. By writing code, you'll have an almost unlimited capacity to deal with your relational database. In code, you can still use ADO objects, but you don't have to use the controls as you did before.

Begin a new Standard EXE project just as you did in the last example. To make sure the ADO objects are available, select References from the Project menu. In the References dialog box, check Microsoft ActiveX Data Objects 2.x Library. Because there have been many versions of this object library, you might see several to choose from. For this example, choose the latest version.

Now place two text boxes on the form and two command buttons. Name the text boxes txtFirst and txtLast. Name the command buttons cmdRetrieve and cmdNext. Also set their captions to Retrieve and Next, respectively. This little application will display the first and last names of customers one at a time and allow you to scroll through them.

Following is the code that will make it all work:

```
Dim conn As ADODB.Connection
Dim rs As ADODB.Recordset

Private Sub cmdRetrieve_Click()
  Set conn = New ADODB.Connection
  conn.ConnectionString = "Provider=SQLOLEDB.1; " & _
    "Persist Security Info=True;User ID=GusT; " & _
    "Password=oilman;Initial Catalog=SlickShop;Data Source=Server001"
  conn.Open
  Set rs = conn.Execute("SELECT CustomerID, FirstName, LastName " & _
                        " FROM Customer")
  txtFirst.Text = rs.Fields("FirstName")
  txtLast.Text = rs.Fields("LastName")
End Sub

Private Sub cmdNext_Click()
  rs.MoveNext
  txtFirst.Text = rs.Fields("FirstName")
  txtLast.Text = rs.Fields("LastName")
End Sub
```

The first line declares a variable called conn that is an ADO connection object. The next line declares rs to be an ADO recordset object. In the code for the Click event of the cmdRetrieve button, the first thing that's done is to create the connection object and assign it to conn. Next the connection object's ConnectionString property is set. You'll recognize the string that it's being set to from the grid control sample earlier. This ConnectionString has the same syntax. Now the Open method is called to actually connect to the database.

Now it's time to send a query. For this, use the Execute method of the connection object. As the argument to the method, send any SQL SELECT command. The result set that's returned from the Execute method will come back in the form of an ADO recordset object. So the rs variable is set to capture and store this recordset. At this point, the recordset object, rs, contains the entire set of rows and columns returned from the query. It is pointing to the first row of data. The last thing the Click event of cmdRetrieve does is to set the two text boxes to show the names. It uses the `Fields` property of the recordset object to set the text value of each box. Now when this event is done, it will show the name of the first customer. The sample application is shown in Figure 7.22.

The `Click` event of the `cmdNext` command button first needs to move the recordset object's pointer to the next row. It does this with the `MoveNext` method. All it has to do then is reset the values of the two text boxes the same way the code for the `cmdRetrieve` button did. Now as you click Next, the text boxes will change to display the name that matches the recordset's current row. If you press it enough times, you'll eventually get an error message stating, `"Either BOF or EOF is True."` BOF and EOF mean "Beginning of File" and "End of File," respectively. In your case, you've reached the end of file (the end of the result set). You'll want to add some error checking in your program to prevent users from getting this message. The `Click` event for `cmdNext` is shown here with this improvement.

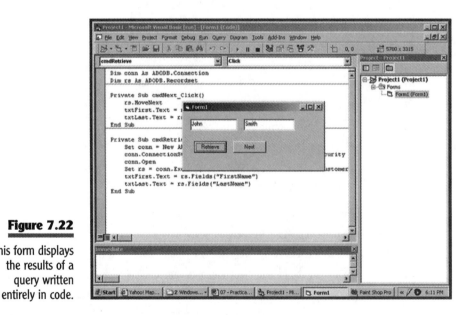

Figure 7.22

This form displays the results of a query written entirely in code.

```
Private Sub cmdNext_Click()
    rs.MoveNext
    If rs.EOF Then
        txtFirst.Text = ""
        txtLast.Text = ""
        cmdNext.Enabled = False
    Else
        txtFirst.Text = rs.Fields("FirstName")
        txtLast.Text = rs.Fields("LastName")
    End If
End Sub
```

After the recordset moves to its next row, the code looks at the EOF
property. If it is True this indicates that it just moved past its last row.
In this case the code blanks out the two text boxes and disables the Next
button so that it can't be pressed again. If the recordset is not at EOF,
it is pointing at a good row, so the first and last names can be displayed.

At this point, the form looks and acts a lot like the one you created with
bound text boxes. The difference is that although you have more control
over the way these text boxes behave, they do not yet have the capability
to update the database. Because this form accessed its data with code, it
will have to update it the same way. You'll do this by modifying the Click
event of cmdNext again to perform a SQL UPDATE command before it
moves to the next row. You'll have to construct your own UPDATE—
that's why you included the primary key column CustomerID in the query.

```
Private Sub cmdNext_Click()
    Dim cmd As ADODB.Command

    Set cmd = New ADODB.Command
    cmd.ActiveConnection = conn
    cmd.CommandType = adCmdText
    cmd.CommandText = "UPDATE Customer " & _
            "SET FirstName = '" & txtFirst.Text & "', " & _
            "    LastName = '" & txtLast.Text & "' " & _
            "WHERE CustomerID = " & rs.Fields("CustomerID")
    cmd.Execute
    Set cmd = Nothing
```

```
        rs.MoveNext
        If rs.EOF Then
            txtFirst.Text = ""
            txtLast.Text = ""
            cmdNext.Enabled = False
        Else
            txtFirst.Text = rs.Fields("FirstName")
            txtLast.Text = rs.Fields("LastName")
        End If
End Sub
```

At the beginning of the script you've declared a new variable cmd to be an ADO command object. The command object is useful for SQL that does not return result sets like the UPDATE command. First it creates a new instance of the command object, and then it sets three of its properties. The connection object that was established earlier is set to the ActiveConnection property. The CommandType is set to adCmdText to tell it to expect a text command, as opposed to a table name or stored procedure name. Finally, the CommandText property gets set to a string that contains the UPDATE command. Notice how this string is built using the values from the two text boxes. These values are the new data to be saved. Also notice that even though the CustomerID column is never displayed on the screen, it is still available in the recordset object. The code uses this value in the WHERE clause. Now the command can be run with the Execute method. The last new thing to happen is that the command object gets set to Nothing. This will destroy the object and free the memory that it was using.

NOTE   Destroying objects like this is an important step to ensure that your application does not consume memory without releasing it. To keep the example simple, we did not show the code that destroyed the connection and recordset objects. As a rule of thumb, be sure to destroy everything that you create.

This is where you'll leave this application. Although it functions and does its job, there is so much more that it could do. It could collect and display the full set of data, validate the information as it's being typed in, print out reports, and so on. Another important part of writing code for database access is error checking. Although your simple application will work most of the time, it probably won't take you long to break it. For example, try clicking Next before you click Retrieve. Also try entering a first name longer than 20 characters. Your database application needs to anticipate these kinds of errors and gracefully handle them. You'll need to write code that displays helpful messages to the users instead of just letting it crash and burn.

Using SQL in Visual Basic .NET

Visual Basic .NET (VB .NET) represents one of the product's largest leaps forward in its history. For the purposes of this book, one of the changes that you'll be looking at is the use of the next version of ADO. You should not be surprised to learn that this new version is called ADO.NET. In this section, you'll see that although the names of the objects have changed between ADO and ADO.NET, most of them function the same way.

As far as VB .NET itself is concerned, you'll see that there are similar ways to access your SQL database. We'll show you an example of binding a data grid control to a data source, similar to the VB6 sample you worked with in the last section.

To start your sample, open Visual Studio .NET and choose to begin a new Visual Basic project. Select Windows Application as the project template. This will put you into the VB .NET development environment and start you with a new blank form. The first thing you'll need to add to the form is a data adapter. The data adapter will contain the SQL command that you'll use later to populate a data set. Open the Toolbox menu by clicking or hovering your mouse pointer over the toolbox icon. On the menu choose the Data tab, and then drag OleDbDataAdapter onto the form. This will start the Data Adapter Configuration wizard. On the second page of this wizard you'll be asked to select a data connection to use. Unless you've created one before, there will not be any to choose from. Press New Connection to open the Data Link Properties dialog box. This is the same dialog box that you saw back in Figure 7.18. Fill in the connection information for your server and database, and then press OK.

Now back in the wizard you are asked if you'll be using SQL statements or stored procedures. Select SQL statements, and then press Next. Finally, you're asked for the SQL SELECT command that will be used to load the data set. You can use the familiar graphical query builder that you've seen a couple times before or just type the command yourself. For this sample, enter the same query that you used in the VB6 sample.

```
SELECT *
  FROM JobTicketDetail
 WHERE DateComplete > '2001-1-1'
```

Press Next to see the final wizard page, and then press Finish. You'll see that two objects have been placed in a pane below the form. The first is a connection, which VB .NET has named OleDbConnection1. It contains the information necessary to connect to your database. The other is the data adapter named OleDbDataAdapter1, which contains your SQL SELECT.

Another thing you'll need to add to the form is a DataSet object that will hold the query's results. A DataSet object is similar to the recordset you used in VB6. One of the major differences though is where a recordset can only hold data from one table, a DataSet can store rows from many tables. You can think of a DataSet as holding more than one recordset. To add the DataSet to the form, select the Data menu and then Generate Dataset. In the dialog box that opens, all you really need to do is choose to create a new DataSet and give it a name. Call it dsJobTicket. The rest should be done for you. Just make sure that there's a check next to the JobTicketDetail table and the option is checked that says "Add This Dataset to the Designer." After you press OK, the pane below the form will display the new DataSet object that you just created.

Now you're ready to place one or more controls on your form and bind them to the DataSet. In this example, you'll be using a grid control; however, just like the VB6 example before, you can also bind individual columns to controls such as text boxes and drop-down lists. VB .NET binding, in fact, is more powerful than VB6, where you could only bind data to one property (usually the Text property). In VB .NET you can bind a DataSet to any of a control's properties. For example, if you have a database column with color values or digital images, you can bind a control's foreground or background color properties or even set its images. This way certain properties as well as data can be displayed without having to explicitly set property values.

Now back in your project, click the Toolbox menu and then click the Windows Forms tab. Drag the data grid onto your form, and then reposition and size it. Go to the properties of the data grid and select DsJobTicket1 as the Data Source property. Next select JobTicketDetail as the DataMember property. Unlike VB6, if you run the application now, the grid will not display your data. You'll need one line of code to populate the grid. Double-click on an empty spot on the form to get into the form's Load event. Enter this one line of code that will fill the DataSet:

```
OleDbDataAdapter1.Fill(DsJobTicket1)
```

Figure 7.23 shows the VB .NET development environment with many of the features we've discussed. In it you can see the form with the data grid placed on it. Below that is a separate pane with the data adapter, connection, and data set objects. At the bottom, you can see the code for the form's Load event. Then on the right side, in the property pane you'll see the data grid's DataMember and Data Source properties that have been set.

Now you can click the Start button in the toolbar to run the application. After it compiles, the form will open and display the table's data. You can move freely around the grid and change data; however, in order to have it update the database, there is one more line of code you'll have to write.

Figure 7.23

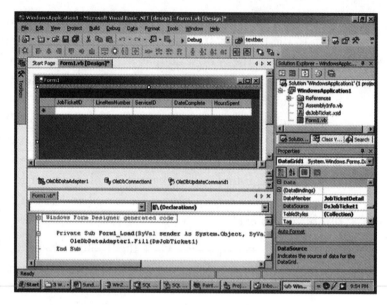

This is the Visual
Basic .NET
development
environment after
you have your data
grid application
ready to go.

Close the form to return to VB .NET. Add a command button to the
form and set its name to Save. Now double-click it to get into its Click
event and enter the following line:

```
OleDbDataAdapter1.Update(DsJobTicket1)
```

Now you can run the application, change some data, and use the Save
button to write the changes to the database.

Take a Break!

Well, there's not long to go now! We hope that you've already seen some
great ways to use SQL in everyday applications and that you're coming
up with some ideas of your own. We thought we'd take a minute to tell
you about a few ways that we've used SQL databases in the past.

One of the largest database applications that we've worked on was for a
large automobile auction company. The application collects real-time
data as the auction is taking place. It then serves as a cash register, col-

lecting payments and printing checks. We even wrote an application that runs on a touch-screen computer that can query the database and provide lookups for customers.

We've developed a Web site that takes orders for scouting troops' fund-raisers. Another of our projects accesses a relational database to provide dynamic content for more than 100 radio stations' Web sites. One of our GUI applications maintains environmental regulation data for the state government. Another prints product labels for a manufacturing company in different languages. We've also created a variety of programs to move data from one DBMS to another.

Nearly every project that we've been a part of in our careers has been based on a relational database. We've had to use several combinations of DBMSs and development languages. The nice thing about it was that once we had mastered the fundamentals of SQL, we were able to apply that knowledge from one database to the next.

Okay, hold on for the final stretch because you're going to start off with a little more complicated language, C++.

Getting Visual C++ and Visual C# .NET to Use SQL

C++ (pronounced "C Plus Plus") and C# (pronounced "C Sharp") are considered lower-level languages than Visual Basic, PowerBuilder, and Access. They give you greater control, more flexibility, and more access to the operating system, and they perform better than the other languages. This comes at a price though. C++ and C# are more difficult to learn and allow you to make more serious mistakes. Usually the result of such mistakes is crashing the operating system.

There are many C++ compilers available, and some even have an integrated development environment (IDE). In this section, you'll be taking a look at Microsoft's Visual C++ and Visual C# .NET. These IDEs assist you by letting you point and click to create forms and controls much the same way that Visual Basic does. As you do, the IDE will generate C++ or C# code behind the scenes. You'll be able to go in later and add to this code.

Retrieving SQL Data with Visual C++

Here, we'll step you through a small sample application that will retrieve rows from your database and display them in a list box control. To begin this exercise, start Visual C++ and choose New from the File menu. Select MFC AppWizard (exe) as the project type and enter SlickShopDemo as the project name. After you press OK, you'll see the MFC AppWizard. Select Dialog Based as the application type and press Next. Uncheck About Box and ActiveX Controls because you don't need support for these features. Now just press Next until you get to the end of the wizard and then press Finish. You'll be shown a summary of what the wizard is about to do. Press OK and the wizard will create a form and write some code for you. The new form has two command buttons, OK and Cancel, as well as a static text control that instructs you to place controls on the form. You will do that in a few minutes.

Your new form is on the right side, the workspace pane is on the left, and the toolbox containing the controls is floating near the form. Switch to the FileView tab in the workspace pane. This tab will show all of the files that are included in your project. If you click around a little you'll discover that Visual C++ has already created about 10 files. Expand the Header Files folder and double-click on StdAfx.h. This file defines other files that will be compiled into your application. Add the following two lines to the very end of this file:

```
#include <comdef.h>
#import "c:\program files\common files\system\ado\msado15.dll"
➡no_namespace rename ("EOF", "adoEOF")
```

◆ ◆

The second line is pretty long, but you must put it all on one line. If you don't, your program will not compile properly. The ➥ character you see on certain code lines indicates that these lines, although represented in the book on several lines due to page size, should in reality be one long line.

◆ ◆

◆ ◆

Pay special attention to the capitalization of the commands in this section. C++ is case sensitive and will not compile if you use the wrong case.

◆ ◆

These lines make sure your application has access to the ADO library. Now close and save this file. Next go to the ClassView tab in the workspace pane and expand the application class, CSlickShopDemoApp. Double-click the InitInstance method so that you can modify it. Notice how this method already has several lines of code. You are going to add two function calls to the beginning to initialize ADO. Add the commands as shown here immediately after the curly bracket.

```
/////////////////////////////////////////////////////////////////
// CSlickShopDemoApp initialization
BOOL CSlickShopDemoApp::InitInstance()
{
     AfxOleInit();
     AfxEnableControlContainer();
     // Standard initialization
  (several more lines appear here...)
}
```

Close and save this file. Now you'll place a list box control on the form that will display the query results. Do this by dragging the List Box button from the floating toolbox onto the form. Resize the list box to fill the empty space in the form. You can delete the static text control that Visual C++ placed there if you want. Right-click on the list box and select Properties to open its property dialog box. Notice that its ID (or name) is IDC_LIST1. Don't do anything here—just close the dialog box.

What you're going to do now is create a class variable that references your list box. Right-click anywhere in the form and choose ClassWizard. Go to the Member Variables tab and select IDC_LIST1 from the list of Control IDs. This indicates which control you will be associating the variable with. Now press Add Variable and you'll see the dialog box displayed in Figure 7.24.

Make the name of the new variable m_lbPart, choose Control for the category, and select CListBox for the variable type. Press OK and you'll see this information added to the list next to IDC_LIST1. Press OK again to exit the ClassWizard. In case you're wondering, what the wizard has just done is add a few lines of code to SlickShopDemoDlg.cpp and SlickShopDemoDlg.h.

All you have left to do now is write the code that will run a query and populate the list box. You'll have this action take place when the OK button on your form is pressed. Double-click the OK button and a small dialog box will open and ask you what you want to name the function for its Click event. It offers you the default name OnOK, which is fine. Press

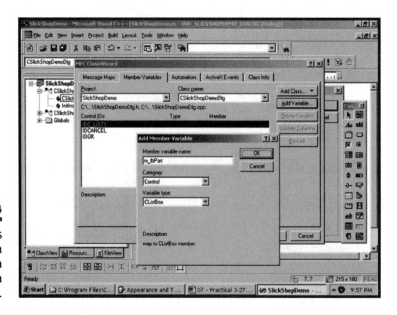

Figure 7.24

This dialog box is used to associate a new variable with a control that is on a form.

OK to accept it and you will be taken into the code for that function. In this function there is a comment and one line of code already there. Place two slashes in front of that line of code to comment it out. That is a function call that will close the form when OK is pressed, which you don't want to happen. Instead, you want it to run the query and fill the list box, so enter the code as follows:

```
void CSlickShopDemoDlg::OnOK()
{
    // CDialog::OnOK();

    _RecordsetPtr   pRecordSet;
    _variant_t  vRecordSetField;
    Cstring  sRecordSetField;

    _bstr_t  bConn("Provider=SQLOLEDB.1; Persist
        ➥Security Info=True;User ID=GusT;Password=oilman;
        ➥Initial Catalog=SlickShop;Data Source=Server001");
    _variant_t  vQuery("SELECT * FROM Part;");

pRecordSet.CreateInstance(__uuidof(Recordset));
    pRecordSet->Open(vQuery, bConn, adOpenDynamic,
        ➥adLockOptimistic, adCmdText);

    while (!pRecordSet->GetadoEOF())
    {
        vRecordSetField = pRecordSet->GetCollect(L"Description");
        sRecordSetField = vRecordSetField.bstrVal;

        m_lbPart.AddString(sRecordSetField);

        pRecordSet->MoveNext();
    }
}
```

Some of this code will remind you of the Visual Basic example that you worked on earlier. After the variables are declared, a connection string is assigned to bConn and a query string is assigned to vQuery. An instance of a recordset object is created, and then its Open method connects to the database, runs the query, and stores its results. After that a loop is run that moves through each row in the result set. In the loop the `Description` column is copied to a variable and added to the list box. By default, the list box will automatically sort the strings as they are added.

Now you're ready to try it out. Before you do, press the Save All button on the toolbar or select Save All from the File menu. To compile your application into an executable file, select `Build SlickShopDemo.exe` from the Build menu or just press F7. The output window will open at the bottom of the screen and display some compile messages. Any errors that are found will be displayed here. If all goes well, the output window will report the following:

```
SlickShopDemo.exe — 0 error(s), 0 warning(s)
```

If there are any errors or warnings, scroll up through the output window to see the details. You'll be told which file and line number has a problem. One of the most common errors is a misspelled variable or function name. Remember that case matters in C++. After you get a good compile, go back to the Build menu and select Execute SlickShopDemo.exe. Your form will open, and when you press OK, your list box will display the descriptions from the `Part` table. Your completed application will look something like Figure 7.25.

Retrieving SQL Data with Visual C# .NET

One of the nice innovations of Visual Studio .NET is that you can work within the same IDE no matter what language you choose. This means that everything you learn about the visual designers can be carried over from one language to the next. The only thing you'll find different is the syntax of the language itself.

To show you what we mean, turn back to the section called "Using SQL in Visual Basic .NET." Follow those instructions step by step to create a Visual C# application that retrieves data into a grid. There are only two minor differences that you need to note. First, when you choose to create a new project, select Visual C# Projects instead of Visual Basic Projects.

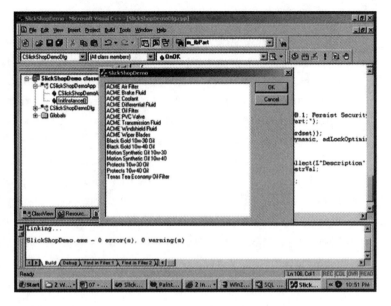

Figure 7.25

The completed
C++ demo
application.

The second is to pay careful attention to the case used in your code because C#, like C++, is case sensitive. The command you used in Visual Basic .NET remains the same but a couple of the letters have to change from uppercase to lowercase. The command that goes in the Form_Load event must look like this:

```
oleDbDataAdapter1.Fill(dsJobTicket1);
```

Note also that C# commands end with a semicolon. Other than that, everything you did in the Visual Basic .NET sample applies to Visual C# .NET the very same way.

Now we're going to have you try a C# program that involves a little more code. This one will allow you to search for customers by their state or province, display the rows found, and scroll through them.

To begin the sample, you should close your project if you currently have one open. Do this by selecting Close Solution from the File menu. Now start a new project in Visual Studio .NET. In the New Project dialog box select Visual C# Projects and choose Windows Application as the template. When you press OK a new blank form will be created for you. In the next few steps you'll be creating the data adapter and data set objects just like you did previously and back in the Visual Basic .NET sample. To create the data adapter, click on the toolbox icon, and then open the Data tab. `Drag OleDbDataAdapter` onto your form. This will open the Data Adapter Configuration wizard. Click Next and you will be asked to select a data connection. If you followed the Visual Basic .NET or the last C# sample, you will already have a data connection in the drop-down list. If not, you can create one by pressing New Connection. This will open the Data Link Properties dialog box shown previously in Figure 7.18. Fill out this dialog box with the server name, username, password, and database name.

Back in the Data Adapter Configuration wizard, press Next and you'll be asked to choose a query type. Select Use SQL Statements and press Next. Now you get to type your SQL SELECT command. Notice that there is a Query Builder button that you can use to graphically build the query if you'd like to. Enter the following query:

```
SELECT FirstName, LastName, Address, City, PhoneNumber
  FROM Customer
 WHERE (StateOrProvince = ?);
```

The question mark represents an argument that you will feed to the query at run-time. Now press Finish, and two new objects will be placed into the pane below the form, `oleDbDataAdapter1` and `oleDbConnection1`. Next you will create the data set object that will hold the rows returned from the query. Right-click on the data adapter object, `oleDbDataAdapter1`, and select Generate Dataset. In the Generate Dataset dialog box you'll be creating a new data set. Change its name from `DataSet1` to `dsCustomer`. Be sure to leave the check mark next to the `Customer` table and press OK. The new data set will appear in the pane below the form and be given the name `dsCustomer1`.

Now you're ready to add a few controls to the form. You're going to add six text boxes and three buttons. To add a text box, click on the toolbox icon, and then select the Windows Forms tab. Drag the TextBox icon onto the form, and then resize and position it. In the Properties pane, set its name to txtState and erase the Text property. Repeat this process for the next five text boxes. Name them txtFirstName, txtLastName, txtAddress, txtCity, and txtPhone. Now create the first button by dragging the Button icon from the toolbox onto the form. Set its Text property to Get Customers, and name it btnGetCust. Name the other two buttons btnNext and btnPrevious. Set their Text properties to Next and Previous, respectively.

Now for a little code that will use the state or province that you put in the text box to run your query. The code will put the results of the query into the data set dsCustomer1. Double-click the Get Customers button to open the code editor. It will place your cursor in the button's Click event. Enter the code as follows:

```
private void btnGetCust_Click(object sender, System.EventArgs e)
{
    oleDbDataAdapter1.SelectCommand.Parameters["StateOrProvince"].
    ➥Value = txtState.Text;
    dsCustomer1.Clear();
    oleDbDataAdapter1.Fill(dsCustomer1);
}
```

The first command takes the value from the txtState text box and assigns it as the parameter of the SQL query. The next command clears out any data that may be left in the data set. Finally, the Fill method runs the query and populates the data set.

You are now ready to bind the other five text boxes to the data set. Start by clicking on txtFirstName and going to the property pane. Find the DataBindings property and expand it. Under it click on the drop-down next to the Text property. In that drop-down box, click to expand dsCustomer1, expand Customer, and finally select FirstName. This binds the data set's FirstName column to the text box. Repeat this process with the other four text boxes, binding them to the appropriate columns.

You can try your application now by pressing F5 or clicking the Start button on the toolbar. Your form should look something like Figure 7.26.

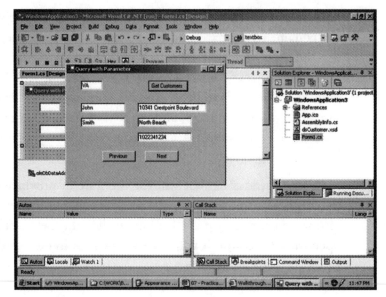

Figure 7.26

This C# application
runs a query with a
parameter.

Type a state or province abbreviation in the first text box and press Get
Customers. You'll see the first matching customer's data appear in the
other text boxes.

The last thing you'll do with this sample is to get the Next and Previous
buttons working. They will allow you to scroll through all of the rows in
the data set. Close your application form to return to Visual C# .NET.
Double-click on the Next button to open the code editor to its Click
event. Enter the following line of code in this event:

```
private void btnNext_Click(object sender, System.EventArgs e)
{
     this.BindingContext[dsCustomer1, "customer"].Position +=1 ;
}
```

Likewise, put the next line of code in the Click event for the Previous button:

```
private void btnPrevious_Click(object sender, System.EventArgs e)
{
     this.BindingContext[dsCustomer1, "customer"].Position -=1 ;
}
```

Now when you run your application, if your query returns more than one row, you'll be able to use these buttons to scroll forward and backward through the data set.

Making Data Driven Web Pages with ASP and ASP.NET

Active Server Pages (ASP) is one of Microsoft's most popular server-side development languages. All of the ASP code that you write runs on the server and returns a standard Hypertext Markup Language (HTML) page back to the user's Internet browser. This means that no special browser or operating system is required to view ASP pages. The only requirement is that the server be capable of processing ASP code. Microsoft's Internet Information Server (IIS) not surprisingly is one that can do this. Some other Web servers can be given this capability with add-on software.

Because all of your ASP code runs on your server, you have the luxury of full control over the environment. This includes connecting to your database, which can be located on either the same server or a different one. In this section, we will first talk about the ASP that has been widely used for the last several years. After that, we will take a look at the newest version, ASP.NET.

Web Page Data Access with ASP

When you program with ASP you have two choices for the language you use, VBScript or JScript. VBScript is a subset of Visual Basic. It uses the same syntax and commands, only there are fewer available. Most notably, you do not have access to anything visual such as text boxes and command buttons. JScript is similar to JavaScript. It doesn't matter too much which one you choose. Although there are slight differences in their capabilities, the choice is mostly a matter of preference. For this book, we'll use VBScript in our examples.

ASP can use the same objects as Visual Basic. In the first example,
you're going to use ADO and its recordset object in the same way VB
would. In this example, you're going to run a SELECT command on
the StateOrProvince table and display the results in an HTML table.
The way that ASP returns Web pages is to write out all the HTML,
essentially building the page piece by piece. Your ASP is going to return
to the user's browser HTML that looks something like this:

```
<HTML>
<HEAD><TITLE>SlickShop Demo</TITLE></HEAD>
<TABLE border=1>
<TR><TH>Abbr</TH><TH>State or Province</TH></TR>
<TR><TD>AB</TD><TD>Alberta</TD></TR>
<TR><TD>AK</TD><TD>Alaska</TD></TR>
<TR><TD>AL</TD><TD>Alabama</TD></TR>
<TR><TD>AR</TD><TD>Arkansas</TD></TR>
</TABLE>
</HTML>
```

ASP files are a mixture of HTML and code. When you want to write
VBScript code, place it between the brackets <% and %>. Everything
between these two brackets will run on the server. Everything outside
of the brackets will simply be returned to the browser. So all you have
to do to return HTML to a browser is type it in your ASP file outside
the brackets. To have VBScript return HTML, you'll use ASP's
Response object. Feed its Write method the strings you want to send
back to the browser. Use any simple file editor such as Notepad to
enter this ASP page:

```
<%@ language="VBScript" %>
<HTML>
<HEAD><TITLE>SlickShop Demo</TITLE></HEAD>
```

```
<TABLE border=1>
<TR><TH>Abbr</TH><TH>State or Province</TH></TR>
<%
  Dim rs
  Dim sSQL
  Dim sConnectString
  Const adOpenStatic = 3
  Const adLockReadOnly = 1
  Const adCmdText = &H0001

  sConnectString = "Provider=SQLOLEDB;Data Source=Server001;" _
      & "Initial Catalog=SlickShop;User Id=GusT;Password=oilman;" _
      & "Connect Timeout=15;Network Library=dbmssocn;"

  sSQL = "SELECT * FROM StateOrProvince ORDER BY StateOrProvince;"

  Set rs = Server.CreateObject("ADODB.Recordset")
  rs.Open sSQL, sConnectString, adOpenStatic,
  ➥adLockReadOnly, adCmdText

  If Not rs.EOF Then
     rs.MoveFirst
     Do While Not rs.EOF
           Response.Write "<TR><TD>"
           Response.Write rs.Fields("StateOrProvince")
           Response.Write "</TD><TD>"
           Response.Write rs.Fields("StateOrProvinceName")
           Response.Write "</TD></TR>" & vbCrL
           rs.MoveNext
     Loop
  End If

  rs.Close
  Set rs = Nothing
%>
</TABLE>
</HTML>
```

There are several similarities between this ASP page and the Visual Basic examples that you saw earlier. It uses a nearly identical connection string to provide the logon details. It also uses the ADO recordset object. In Visual Basic you declared this object with Dim; however, in ASP you bring it to life with Server.CreateObject. The recordset's Open method runs the query and returns the result set. A loop then goes through each row and writes the values out in HTML table format.

Save the file as GetStates.asp on your Web server. Now open your Web browser and enter the server, path, and file name to request your ASP page. Figure 7.27 shows the results in a browser.

In the next example, you'll create a simple page that will add a new row to the Part table. This is a lot like the last example. It uses the recordset object again, only this time you'll populate it with some data, and then use its Update method to perform the INSERT.

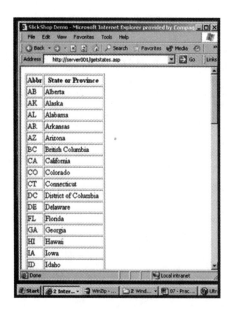

Figure 7.27

The HTML for this page was built on the server and returned to the browser.

Open a new file and enter the following ASP code:

```
<%@ language="VBScript" %>
<HTML>·
<HEAD><TITLE>SlickShop Insert Demo</TITLE></HEAD>
<%
    Dim sConnectString
    Dim rs
    Dim iPartID
    Const adOpenKeyset = 1
    Const adLockPessimistic = 2

    sConnectString = "Provider=SQLOLEDB;Data Source=server001;" _
        & "Initial Catalog=SlickShop;User Id=GusT;Password=oilman;" _
        & "Connect Timeout=15;Network Library=dbmssocn;"

    Set rs = Server.CreateObject("ADODB.Recordset")

    rs.Source = "Part"
    rs.ActiveConnection = sConnectString
    rs.CursorType       = adOpenKeyset
    rs.LockType         = adLockPessimistic
    rs.Open

    rs.AddNew

    rs.Fields("Description") = "Tiger skin seat covers"
    rs.Fields("Cost") = 45.95

    rs.Update

    ' Get the new autonumbered PartID
    iPartID = rs.Fields("PartID").Value

    Response.Write "<P>Part ID #" & iPartID & " was added</p>"

    rs.Close
    Set rs = Nothing
%>
</HTML>
```

Save this file as `AddPart.asp` in one of the Web server's directories. In this file the connect string is the same as before. This time, however, after creating the recordset object, you set its `Source` property to `Part`. This tells the recordset that you don't need it to retrieve any data, but to be prepared to interact with the `Part` table. You open the recordset and then add a new blank row to it. You only need to provide values for the `Description` and `Cost` columns; remember that the `PartID` is an auto-numbered column. The `Update` method takes care of generating and sending a SQL INSERT to the server. The recordset then automatically gets itself updated with the new `PartID` value that the server assigned. Your code stores this in a variable and writes it to the browser.

You could make browser output more interesting than we've done. All this page will display after it inserts the row is `"Part ID #17 was added"`. The other obvious enhancement to this ASP page would be to allow users to enter their own values instead of hard-coding them. ASP is an excellent language for building Web-based data entry forms. Many times an ASP page will provide the data entry controls such as text boxes and drop-down lists. This page will then call another ASP page like the one in the last example to perform the SQL.

Building Data Access Pages with ASP.NET

As you might expect, the newest version of Active Server Pages, ASP.NET, includes a lot of new features, scalability, performance, and strength. For example, where ASP gave you the choice to program only in VBScript or JScript, ASP.NET has dozens of choices. You can use languages such as VB .NET, C#, JScript .NET, and even FORTRAN and Cobol! Another one of its biggest advancements is its set of server controls. These are controls that appear in the browser, such as text boxes, drop-down lists, and calendars. ASP.NET server controls are much easier to work with, provide more capabilities, and require less code than HTML controls in ASP.

As with the first ASP.NET sample, you're going to build a page that returns an HTML table that contains all of the data from the `StateOrProvince` table. This ASP.NET page is going to produce the same results that the ASP sample in the last section did. This will give you the chance to compare the differences.

NOTE Again, as with ASP, in order to run this sample, you'll need to save it on a computer that can act as a Web server. This server must have the Microsoft .NET Framework installed. As before, the Web server can simply be your local computer.

FIND IT ▶
ONLINE
The .NET Framework is available as a free download from Microsoft at **http://msdn.microsoft.com**.

If you begin developing full-scale Web applications with ASP.NET, you'll want a nice development environment like Microsoft Visual Studio .NET. However, for this sample you can simply use a plain text editor to enter this code:

```
<%@ Page Language="VB"%>
<%@ Import Namespace="System.Data" %>
<%@ Import Namespace="System.Data.SqlClient" %>

<script language="VB" runat="server">
   Dim conn As SqlConnection

   Sub Page_Load(Sender As Object, E As EventArgs)
   conn = New SqlConnection("Data Source=server001;" _
      & "Initial Catalog=SlickShop;User Id=GusT;Password=oilman;" _
      & "Connect Timeout=15;Network Library=dbmssocn;")
   ShowDataGrid
    End Sub

   Sub ShowDataGrid()
   Dim comm As SqlCommand
   Dim sSQL As String

   sSQL = "SELECT * FROM StateOrProvince ORDER BY StateOrProvince;"
   comm = New SqlCommand(sSQL, conn)
   conn.Open()
```

```
        StateGrid.DataSource = comm.ExecuteReader _
            (System.Data.CommandBehavior.CloseConnection)
                StateGrid.DataBind()
conn.Close()
    End Sub
</script>
<HTML>
<HEAD><TITLE>ASP.NET Grid Sample</TITLE></HEAD>
<asp:DataGrid id="StateGrid" runat="server" />
</HTML>
```

NOTE This code sample and the next one use the objects that are specifically tuned for SQL Server. These objects include `SqlConnection`, `SqlCommand`, and `SqlParameter`. If you're using a different DBMS, you can use the equivalent objects `OleDbConnection`, `OleDbCommand`, and `OleDbParameter`, used in previous examples. You will also need to change the third code line to include the namespace `System.Data.OleDb`.

Save this file on the Web server as `GetStates_Net.aspx`. Notice that the file extension for ASP files is .asp, whereas ASP.NET uses .aspx. Now for a look at some of this file's highlights. The first line specifies that the language you'll be using in this file is VB (actually VB .NET). Because VB .NET is driven by events, so is this ASP.NET code. The first event you code for is `Page_Load`, which happens when the page is first called on. This event uses a connect string to create a connection object, and then calls the subroutine `ShowDataGrid`.

The `ShowDataGrid` routine sets up a SQL SELECT and uses it and the connection object to create a command object. When the connection object's `Open` method is executed, the query is run on the database server. Up until this point there have only been a few differences. The names of the objects and the order they're accessed are slightly different. But the two commands that come next show off one of ASP.NET's new data controls. You'll see that these two lines reference an object named `StateGrid`. If you look down to the next to the last line in the file, you'll see the definition of this object. An `asp` tag on that line places a `DataGrid` control on the page and names it `StateGrid`.

Back in the `ShowDataGrid` routine, the code is setting the `DataSource` property of `StateGrid` to the command object. It then binds the result set to the grid control. You will recall from earlier that this is very similar to the bound grid you used in Visual Basic. Also notice that there is no need to loop through the result set and build the HTML table the way you did in ASP. Here, once you bind the result set to the data grid, ASP.NET will take care of building the HTML. The `DataGrid` control has many properties and methods that you can access in your code to fine-tune its appearance and behavior.

One more thing to notice is the way that the program code is separated from the HTML. This is in contrast to ASP, where code and HTML are often interwoven. Now use your browser to call `GetStates_Net.aspx`. You'll see that the results are nearly identical to Figure 7.27.

NOTE   When you run an ASP.NET page through a browser for the first time, you'll notice that it is somewhat slower than an ASP page. Don't let this discourage you. The first time it runs, the server is compiling your script for you. Now every time this page is requested in the future, its compiled version can be used. It will actually perform much better than old ASP.

The next example will mimic the second ASP example where you wrote a page that added a row to the `Part` table. Begin another new file and type in this ASP.NET code:

```
<%@ Page Language="VB"%>
<%@ Import Namespace="System.Data" %>
<%@ Import Namespace="System.Data.SqlClient" %>

<script language="VB" runat="server">
   Dim conn As SqlConnection

   Sub Page_Load(Sender As Object, E As EventArgs)
   conn = New SqlConnection("Data Source=server001;" _
      & "Initial Catalog=SlickShop;User Id=GusT;Password=oilman;" _
      & "Connect Timeout=15;Network Library=dbmssocn;")
```

```
AddPart
 End Sub

Sub AddPart()
Dim comm As SqlCommand
Dim sSQL As String

sSQL = "INSERT INTO Part " _
    & "(Description, Cost) " _
    & "VALUES (@sDesc, @dCost)"

comm = New SqlCommand(sSQL, conn)

comm.Parameters.Add(New SqlParameter
➥("@sDesc", SqlDbType.VarChar, 80))
comm.Parameters.Add(New SqlParameter("@dCost", SqlDbType.Decimal))

comm.Parameters("@sDesc").Value = "Tire Chains"
comm.Parameters("@dCost").Value = 22.50

conn.Open()
comm.ExecuteNonQuery()
conn.Close()

PartLabel.Text = "A new part has been added!"
 End Sub
</script>

<HTML>
<HEAD><TITLE>ASP.NET Insert Sample</TITLE></HEAD>
<asp:Label id="PartLabel" runat="server" />
</HTML>
```

Save this file with the name AddPart_Net.aspx on your Web server. Again in this code sample, the Page_Load event creates a new connection object, and then calls a subroutine to do the work. In the AddPart routine, you've set up a string that will perform the insert. There are a couple of choices here. You could have built your values right into the string and saved a few lines of script. However, we're having you use parameters instead. You created two new parameter objects and added them to the command object. Each parameter has its own specific data type, VARCHAR, and decimal. After that you assigned a value to each parameter. Parameters can be helpful if you're dealing with large or complicated SQL commands or stored procedures. Sometimes it's easier for you to code it this way and understand it later rather than concatenating long strings.

Now at the bottom of the `AddPart` routine, you use the connection object's `Open` method to connect to the database. You then use the `ExecuteNonQuery` method to run the INSERT command. As its name indicates, this method is used because it is not returning any results. Now you use the `Close` method to disconnect from the database. Finally, you set the text of an ASP.NET label object that appears in the HTML at the bottom of the file.

Now you're ready to switch over to your browser and enter the server, path, and file name to see this page run. The page will just appear as a simple message stating that a part has been added. When you check your `Part` table, you'll see that indeed a new row has been inserted.

Using SQL with PowerBuilder

PowerBuilder is a well-established application development language that has been around for several years. It is a Sybase product that is a Visual Basic competitor. After its introduction it quickly became a developer favorite for creating GUI applications because of its ease of use and its strong relational database support. Although its popularity has declined recently, it is still alive within many businesses.

The PowerBuilder DataWindow

One of the reasons that PowerBuilder (PB) became such a widely used language was due to the DataWindow. The PB DataWindow is an object that can access databases for display and modification of data. It is similar to a Visual Basic grid control, but much more powerful. An entire interface can be designed with a DataWindow, allowing for complete data maintenance with very little code.

To begin your sample, start PowerBuilder and choose to create a new application. Give the application a name and choose a directory in which to store the PB Library file. Before you create anything, you'll need to establish a connection with your database. Press the DB Profile button on the toolbar, and you'll see the Database Profiles dialog box appear. In it you should see your DBMS listed under the Installed Database Interfaces. If not, then you'll have to install it from the PowerBuilder CD. Now highlight your DBMS and press New. You can see from Figure 7.28 that the information it asks for is the same as each of the other products has wanted: server name, login name, password, and database name.

Press OK to save the profile and close the Database Profile dialog box. Now when you create new DataWindows, they will automatically use this profile. To do this, press the New button on the toolbar and select the DataWindow tab in the dialog box. You are presented with several styles of DataWindows to choose from. Besides being a great data entry object, the DataWindow is also an excellent report writer. As you can see in Figure 7.29, many of the styles, such as Crosstab, Label, Group, and Graph, are oriented toward reporting.

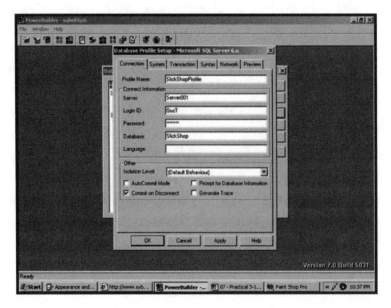

Figure 7.28

A profile like this one is used by PowerBuilder to make database connections.

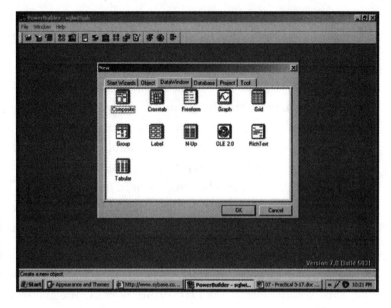

For this example, choose Freeform, which will allow you to place columns and labels anywhere on the form. You're now given a dialog box that asks which data source you'd like to use. Your choices include a SQL SELECT, a stored procedure, and external data. Choose the SQL SELECT option and you will be taken to a query building window. This window looks a little bit like the Microsoft Query interface. Hold down the Ctrl key and click both the Customer table and Vehicle. When you press Open, the two tables will be displayed with a line drawn between them to display the relationship.

Click the columns that you'd like to include in the DataWindow. Include columns that you need but don't want to show to the users, such as primary keys. For this example, click CustomerID, FirstName, LastName, StateOrProvince, VehicleYear, Make, and Model. There are many query options in the pane in the lower half of the window. We'll just have you set a couple of them. On the Sort tab, drag LastName, and then FirstName to the right side. The SQL command will use this for its ORDER BY clause. Now on the Where tab, select Vehicle.VehicleYear from the

Column drop-down. Select >= as the operator, and enter 2000 as the Value. This, of course, will help build the WHERE clause. At any time, as shown in Figure 7.30, you can click the Syntax tab to view the SQL that it has built so far.

When you're finished building the query, press the Return button on the toolbar. You'll be given some options about the colors of the text labels and data fields. Just accept the defaults and you will be taken to the DataWindow editor, what is called a painter. The painter is divided into several panes that can be sized or hidden as you need. The main one that you'll be working in is the design pane. This is where you can lay out the data fields and labels as well as other objects like lines and boxes.

Although a DataWindow can display data from more than one table at a time, it can only modify the data in one. Because you included two tables in the query, the DataWindow made the assumption that this is a read-only report. In doing so, it set the tab order of each field to 0 so that the cursor cannot enter any fields. Because you want the fields from the Customer table to be editable, you can turn the tab order back on.

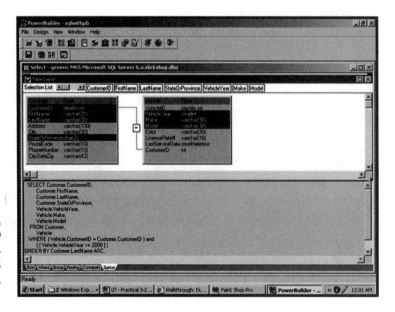

Figure 7.30

The DataWindow's query builder helps you build a SQL SELECT command.

Press the Tab Order button on the toolbar or select Tab Order from the Format menu. Little red numbers will appear near each field. Click on the number by the first name field and type the number 1. Next click on the number next to the last name field and type a 2. Finally, set the state field to 3. Now toggle the Tab Order feature off. Highlight and delete the CustomerID field and its related label. It will still be a part of the DataWindow, but the users don't need to see it. Now you can modify the text for the labels, fonts, and colors if you want.

As you're working in the design pane, you'll see the changes taking effect in the preview pane if it's open. If it isn't, select Preview from the View menu. This will show you what the DataWindow will look like with live data in it. You can even scroll through the rows.

Now an important step you'll need to take if this DataWindow is to be used to modify data is to set the update properties. Select the Rows menu, and then Update Properties. If your query had been from just one table, this dialog box would be completed for you. However, because you have two tables, everything is turned off. Because you want this DataWindow to handle data modifications, turn on the Allow Updates check box. Now choose the Customer table from the Tables To Update drop-down. Skip down to the Unique Key Column(s) list box. This is where you need to tell the DataWindow which column or columns make up the primary key of the table you want it to update. In this case, you'll click customer_customerid. Remember, even though this column is not displayed, the DataWindow still retrieves its data for later use. To the left of this list box you'll find another one, titled Updateable Columns. Click every column that you want the DataWindow to modify. In this case it will be customer_firstname, customer_lastname, and customer_stateorprovince. We won't talk about the rest of the dialog box. These are advanced options that pertain to multiuser concurrency. When your dialog box looks like Figure 7.31, press OK.

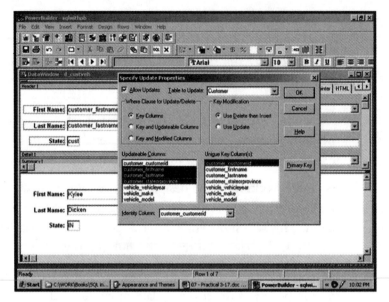

Figure 7.31

The Specify Update
Properties dialog
box must be
completed before a
DataWindow can
modify data.

The selections that you make in this dialog box tell the DataWindow how to build the SQL commands that it will send to your database. For example, in this dialog box you indicated that the primary key is CustomerID. The DataWindow will now build SQL UPDATE and DELETE commands with this column in the WHERE clause.

If you investigate the preview pane, you'll see that you can now modify data in the three customer fields. You can even scroll up and down in order to see and change other rows. However, unlike Visual Basic bound controls, your changes will not affect the database until you say so. The DataWindow is keeping track of every modification you make, as well as any new rows added or old rows deleted. If you want to make your changes permanent, press the Save Changes button on the toolbar, or select Update from the Rows menu. This will cause the DataWindow to build an UPDATE for each row changed, an INSERT for each new row, and a DELETE for every row deleted. These commands will be sent one by one to the database. The DataWindow does all of the work for you!

Although you can get your DataWindow looking pretty nice, you don't want your users to have to get into PowerBuilder to use it. Instead, you'll be creating a window to place the DataWindow into. First you'll need to save and name it. Press the Save button or select Save from the File menu and give it a name.

Now press the New button and you'll be taken back to the dialog box in Figure 7.29. Change to the Object tab and select Window. This will open a new blank window in PowerBuilder's window painter. Like the DataWindow painter, there are several panes to work with. The layout pane has your new window in it. On it you're going to place your DataWindow and two command buttons. Select the Insert menu, then Control, and then DataWindow. Now click somewhere on your blank window. This will create a small white box. With the box highlighted, go to the Properties pane and either type your DataWindow name into the DataObject property or search for it by pressing the ellipse button. As soon as you do, you'll see that the white box has changed to display your DataWindow. Resize the box so that you can see all of the DataWindow's contents. Next add a command button by selecting the Insert menu, then Control, and then CommandButton. Click somewhere below the DataWindow. Add a second one the same way. Set the Text property of the first one to Get Data and the second to Save Data.

PowerBuilder, like Visual Basic, lets you write code for several events of each control. To access the script-writing pane, double-click on your DataWindow control. The script pane will open, and you notice from one of the drop-down lists that you've been put into the itemchanged event. The event can be changed from here by choosing a new one from the drop-down. Change it to the constructor event now. Without going into too much detail, we're now going to show you the code involved with getting this window to retrieve data, allow modifications, and save data.

The following code goes in the constructor event of your DataWindow control. It makes a connection to the database and tells that DataWindow control to make use of that connection.

```
SQLCA.DBMS = "MSS Microsoft SQL Server"
SQLCA.Database = "SlickShop"
SQLCA.ServerName = "Server001"
SQLCA.LogId = "GusT"
SQLCA.LogPass = "oilman"
SQLCA.AutoCommit = False
SQLCA.DBParm = ""
CONNECT;
this.SetTransObject(SQLCA)
```

TIP Notice that a specific DBMS is referenced in the code. Yours will need to go in place of this if it's different. A quick way to build these first seven lines of code is to go back to the Database Profiles dialog box and edit the profile that you set up earlier. In the dialog box you saw back in Figure 7.28, select the Syntax tab. Here you will have the code written for you. You can simply copy it and paste in into the constructor event of your DataWindow control.

Put this next line of code in the Clicked event of the Get Data button. It will instruct the DataWindow to perform its SELECT command and return the data.

```
dw_1.Retrieve()
```

The next line goes in the Clicked event of the Save Data button. It tells the DataWindow to perform the INSERT, UPDATE, and DELETE commands that it has saved up.

```
dw_1.Update()
```

Now the window is done. You can save it and give it the name w_custveh. The only thing left is to tell your application what to do when it first starts. Press the Open button on the toolbar, and in the dialog box, choose Applications from the Object Type drop-down list.

There will only be one application found; choose it and press OK. You'll be taken into a script pane showing the application's Open event. Type this command:

```
Open(w_custveh)
```

This will tell the application that the first (and only) thing it should do when it's run is to open your window. That's all there is to it! Now when you click the Run button, your window will open. Clicking Get Data will display the customer and vehicle data. You can use the PageUp and Page-Down keys to scroll through the rows. You can make changes to any of the customer fields. Finally, if you want to save the changes to the data-base, press Save Data. The window is shown in Figure 7.32.

You can see that the DataWindow is a very powerful tool. The real-life PowerBuilder applications that we have written always make extensive use of DataWindows. It is not uncommon for a PowerBuilder project to actually use more DataWindows than regular user interface windows. Remember that not only is it used for data modification, but also it is a very strong and full-featured report writer. When you're dealing with

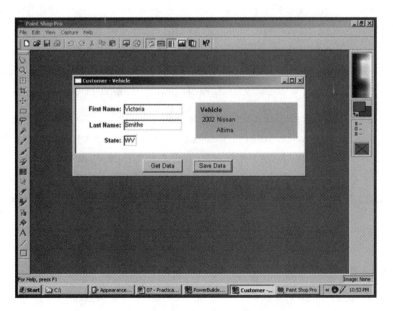

Figure 7.32

The functional PowerBuilder application took only a dozen lines of code.

databases, you should always try to utilize DataWindows first. If they don't meet your needs, then you always have the option to use SQL within PowerBuilder code.

Using SQL in PowerScript

PowerScript is the language of PowerBuilder. It is similar to Visual Basic, and if you know one, it's not hard to learn the other. PowerScript supports embedded SQL, meaning that you can mix SQL in with the regular PowerScript commands. For example, you can write code that uses a SQL INSERT command inside a PowerScript loop, as follows:

```
Integer i

For i = 1 To 5
    INSERT INTO Customer
      (FirstName, LastName, City, StateOrProvince)
    VALUES
      ("Hannah", "Yoder", "Madison", "WI");
Next
```

This is just a very simple script that declares an integer variable and uses it to loop five times. In the loop is an ordinary INSERT command. This command will be sent to the database to which the application is currently connected. Of course, this command is not very useful because it inserts the same person five times. Usually your embedded SQL commands will use variables in place of hard-coded data.

The next example will use embedded SQL to let a users provide the data for new customers instead of hard-coded values. To begin, create a new window the same way you did in the last section. Place four labels, three single-line edits, one drop-down list box, and one command button on the window. Name the controls and set their Text properties according to Table 7.1.

TABLE 7.1		
OBJECTS AND PROPERTIES FOR THE POWERBUILDER SAMPLE		
Control	**Property**	**Value**
Label	Name	st_1
	Text	First Name:
Label	Name	st_2
	Text	Last Name:
Label	Name	st_3
	Text	City:
Label	Name	st_4
	Text	State:
Single Line Edit	Name	sle_first
Single Line Edit	Name	sle_last
Single Line Edit	Name	sle_city
Drop-Down List Box	Name	ddlb_state
	VscrollBar	(checked)
Command Button	Name	cb_save
	Text	Save New
Window	Name	w_newcust
	Title	New Customer

Arrange the controls on the window as you see them in Figure 7.33. When you're done, save the window, but don't close it.

As you can see from Figure 7.33, you're going to be putting code into the Open event of the window (w_newcust). Go to the script pane now and select this event. A quick way to get there is to double-click a blank spot on the window. The following code goes in this event:

```
SQLCA.DBMS = "MSS Microsoft SQL Server"
SQLCA.Database = "SlickShop"
SQLCA.ServerName = "Server001"
SQLCA.LogId = "GusT"
SQLCA.LogPass = "oilman"
SQLCA.AutoCommit = False
SQLCA.DBParm = ""

CONNECT;

String lsState
```

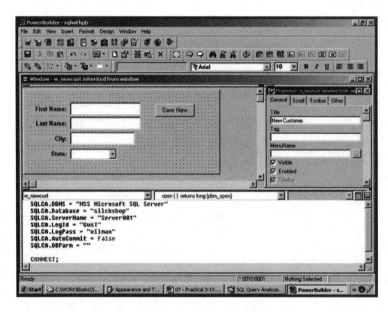

Figure 7.33

This is a window that uses embedded SQL to add new customers.

```
DECLARE c1 CURSOR FOR
 SELECT StateOrProvince
   FROM StateOrProvince
  ORDER BY StateOrProvince;

OPEN c1;

FETCH c1 INTO :lsState;

Do While SQLCA.SQLCode = 0
   ddlb_state.AddItem(lsState)

   FETCH c1 INTO :lsState;
Loop
```

You'll notice that the first several lines are the same as those you used in the last section. This code actually only needs to appear one time in an application in order to connect to a database. We're showing it again here to give a more complete example. Briefly, SQLCA is a transaction object that manages the connection to a database and is available globally to all scripts in an application.

After the connection is made, you'll see that a SQL cursor is being used to return a result set of all rows from the StateOrProvince table. The cursor works the same way as we showed you in the Sunday Morning session. Look at the FETCH commands. Here you're going to be mixing a PowerScript variable in with the SQL. The FETCH command places the column value into the variable. In PowerScript, whenever a variable is used inside of a SQL command, a colon must precede the variable's name. A Do While loop will continue fetching each value until the end of the result set is reached. Inside the loop, you'll use the drop-down list box's AddItem method to put the value in the list. The result is that the list box will contain a sorted list of all states and provinces.

If you want to test this out now, there's one thing you'll have to do first—write a line of code to open the window. Go back to the application's Open event and change the line of code you wrote in the last section to open this window instead.

```
Open (w_newcust)
```

Now when you press the Run button, your new window will open and the drop-down list of states and provinces will be fully populated. The only thing left to do now is to make the Save Now command button work. Close your window and go back to the window painter for w_newcust. Double-click the command button so that its Clicked event appears in the script pane. Place the following code in this script:

```
String lsFirst, lsLast, lsCity, lsState

lsFirst = sle_first.Text
lsLast = sle_last.Text
lsCity = sle_city.Text
lsState = ddlb_state.Text

INSERT INTO Customer
    (FirstName, LastName, City, StateOrProvince)
VALUES
    (:lsFirst, :lsLast, :lsCity, :lsState);

sle_first.Text = ""
sle_last.Text = ""
sle_city.Text = ""
ddlb_state.Text = ""
```

In this code you first declare four string variables to temporarily store the user's data. Then copy the data from the Text properties of each of the four controls into the variables. Then you can use an embedded SQL INSERT command. Use all four variables in this command. After the INSERT, clear out each of the controls to get ready for the next new customer.

TIP

As mentioned earlier, a good rule of thumb with PowerBuilder is to try to make use of the DataWindow before resorting to embedded SQL. This last example was a nice way to introduce you to embedded SQL, but it all could have been done with DataWindows. Even the drop-down list box of states and provinces could be its own little DataWindow.

What's Next?

Congratulations, you made it all the way through in a weekend! You now know enough about SQL to build a good solid relational database, tuned for performance and ready to support production applications.

The only things left in this book are the appendixes. In them you'll find DBMS-specific SQL commands to create the Slick Shop sample database. Also, for each DBMS we've included the INSERT commands to get the database loaded. Plus you'll find sample syntax for the different DBMSs for many of the commands covered in the book.

SQL Samples in SQL Server

Accessing SQL Server

SQL Server comes with several graphical tools allowing you to do everything from trace queries executing against the database, to managing the database servers, to executing SQL commands and obtaining results. For this book, we are interested in your learning how to use SQL to create queries and to create and modify database objects. SQL Server has graphical tools that help you build these objects and hide the SQL from you. Instead of using these tools, we are going to use the Query Analyzer during this book so you can learn the commands that perform these tasks.

Query Analyzer can be found on the Start menu under Programs, Microsoft SQL Server, Query Analyzer. It will ask you to log in, as seen in Figure A.1. If you have SQL Server installed locally, you can leave the SQL Server box empty or put a period in there. As for the authentication, you will need to know which scheme the SQL Server uses. Check with the administrator for the scheme, login name, and password. If you installed SQL Server locally and don't remember how you set it up, try Windows authentication. If that doesn't work, select SQL Server authentication and use sa for the user. Leave the password blank.

Once you are in Query Analyzer, you can run the script to set up the tables. If you cannot download the script, type them in as they are in the next section. To obtain the script, go to the Premier Press Web site (**www.premierpressbooks.com/**) and download the sample script for SQL Server. Select File, Open from the menu to load the script. Select Query, Execute from the menu or press F5 to execute the SQL in the script. If you create the tables using this script, you can skip the next section.

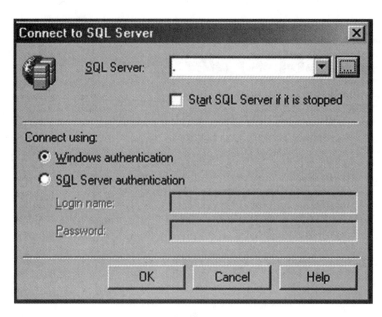

Figure A.1

The Query Analyzer login dialog box.

SQL for the Sample Database

This appendix will give you the SQL you need to create the database and tables for the Slick Shop sample database. This syntax can also be downloaded from the Premier Press Web site if you'd rather not type it in. The syntax covered here is in SQL Server. You can see the syntax for the other DBMSs covered here by accessing that vendor's specific appendix.

To create the database, open the Query Analyzer for SQL Server as described in the previous section. Type the command as you see it here and then click Execute:

```
CREATE DATABASE SlickShop
```

Now that the database is created, tell SQL Server that you'd like to use that newly created database. This command tells SQL Server which database to use for the commands that you will be executing next. Type the following and execute the command.

```
USE SlickShop
```

Now you can create the table structures for the sample database. If you'd like to see the graphical representation of those tables, please refer to Figure 1.3 in the Friday Evening session. Type in each code listing that follows and execute the command. Download the script from the Premier Press Web site, if you can, as an alternative to typing all this.

```
CREATE TABLE StateOrProvince (
StateOrProvince        Char(2)        NOT NULL PRIMARY KEY CLUSTERED,
StateOrProvinceName    Varchar(50)    NOT NULL
);

CREATE TABLE Customer (
CustomerID             Integer        IDENTITY NOT NULL
      PRIMARY KEY CLUSTERED,
FirstName              Varchar(20)    NULL,
LastName               Varchar(30)    NULL,
Address                Varchar(100)   NULL,
City                   Varchar(30)    NULL,
StateOrProvince        Char(2)        NULL REFERENCES
```

```
      StateOrProvince (StateOrProvince),
PostalCode              Varchar(10)       NULL,
PhoneNumber             Varchar(10)       NULL
);


CREATE TABLE Vehicle (
VehicleID               Integer           IDENTITY NOT NULL
      PRIMARY KEY CLUSTERED,
VehicleYear             SmallInt          NULL,
Make                    Varchar(30)       NULL,
Model                   Varchar(30)       NULL,
Color                   Varchar(30)       NULL,
LicensePlate#           Varchar(10)       NULL,
LastServiceDate         Smalldatetime     NULL,
CustomerID              Integer           NOT NULL
      REFERENCES Customer (CustomerID)
);


CREATE TABLE Service (
ServiceID               Integer           IDENTITY NOT NULL
      PRIMARY KEY CLUSTERED,
Description             Varchar(100)      NOT NULL,
RatePerHour             Money             NOT NULL
);


CREATE TABLE Part (
PartID                  Integer           IDENTITY NOT NULL
      PRIMARY KEY CLUSTERED,
Description             Varchar(100)      NOT NULL,
Cost                    Money             NOT NULL
);


CREATE TABLE JobTicket (
JobTicketID             Integer           IDENTITY NOT NULL
      PRIMARY KEY CLUSTERED,
CustomerID              Integer           NOT NULL
      REFERENCES Customer (CustomerID),
StartDate               Smalldatetime     NULL,
EndDate                 Smalldatetime     NULL,
VehicleID               Integer           NOT NULL
      REFERENCES Vehicle (VehicleID)
);
```

```
CREATE TABLE JobTicketDetail (
JobTicketID             Integer         NOT NULL
    REFERENCES JobTicket (JobTicketID),
LineItemNumber          TinyInt         NOT NULL,
ServiceID               Integer         NOT NULL
    REFERENCES Service (ServiceID),
DateComplete            Smalldatetime   NULL,
HoursSpent              Decimal(5,2)    NOT NULL DEFAULT 0,
CONSTRAINT PK_JobTicketDetail PRIMARY KEY (JobTicketID,
    LineItemNumber)
);

CREATE TABLE PartUsed (
JobTicketID             Integer         NOT NULL,
LineItemNumber          TinyInt         NOT NULL,
PartID                  Integer         NOT NULL REFERENCES Part (PartID),
Quantity                TinyInt         NOT NULL,
CONSTRAINT PK_PartUsed PRIMARY KEY (JobTicketID, LineItemNumber,
    PartID),
CONSTRAINT FK_JobTicketDetail_PartUsed FOREIGN KEY (JobTicketID,
    LineItemNumber)
REFERENCES JobTicketDetail (JobTicketID, LineItemNumber)
);
```

Now that the structures are in place, you can fill them up with the sample data. We've included the INSERT scripts in the following. Simply type them in and execute them, and you will have everything you need to get started. If you'd rather not type all these commands (and why would you?), you can download these statements from the Premier Press Web site.

```
INSERT INTO StateOrProvince VALUES('AB','Alberta');
INSERT INTO StateOrProvince VALUES('BC','British Columbia');
INSERT INTO StateOrProvince VALUES('MB','Manitoba');
INSERT INTO StateOrProvince VALUES('NB','New Brunswick');
INSERT INTO StateOrProvince VALUES('NF','Newfoundland');
INSERT INTO StateOrProvince VALUES('NT','Northwest Territories');
INSERT INTO StateOrProvince VALUES('NS','Nova Scotia');
INSERT INTO StateOrProvince VALUES('NU','Nunavut');
INSERT INTO StateOrProvince VALUES('ON','Ontario');
INSERT INTO StateOrProvince VALUES('PE','Prince Edward Island');
INSERT INTO StateOrProvince VALUES('QC','Quebec');
INSERT INTO StateOrProvince VALUES('SK','Saskatchewan');
```

```
INSERT INTO StateOrProvince VALUES('YT','Yukon Territory');
INSERT INTO StateOrProvince VALUES('AL','Alabama');
INSERT INTO StateOrProvince VALUES('AK','Alaska');
INSERT INTO StateOrProvince VALUES('AZ','Arizona');
INSERT INTO StateOrProvince VALUES('AR','Arkansas');
INSERT INTO StateOrProvince VALUES('CA','California');
INSERT INTO StateOrProvince VALUES('CO','Colorado');
INSERT INTO StateOrProvince VALUES('CT','Connecticut');
INSERT INTO StateOrProvince VALUES('DE','Delaware');
INSERT INTO StateOrProvince VALUES('DC','District of Columbia');
INSERT INTO StateOrProvince VALUES('FL','Florida');
INSERT INTO StateOrProvince VALUES('GA','Georgia');
INSERT INTO StateOrProvince VALUES('HI','Hawaii');
INSERT INTO StateOrProvince VALUES('ID','Idaho');
INSERT INTO StateOrProvince VALUES('IL','Illinois');
INSERT INTO StateOrProvince VALUES('IN','Indiana');
INSERT INTO StateOrProvince VALUES('IA','Iowa');
INSERT INTO StateOrProvince VALUES('KS','Kansas');
INSERT INTO StateOrProvince VALUES('KY','Kentucky');
INSERT INTO StateOrProvince VALUES('LA','Louisiana');
INSERT INTO StateOrProvince VALUES('ME','Maine');
INSERT INTO StateOrProvince VALUES('MD','Maryland');
INSERT INTO StateOrProvince VALUES('MA','Massachusetts');
INSERT INTO StateOrProvince VALUES('MI','Michigan');
INSERT INTO StateOrProvince VALUES('MN','Minnesota');
INSERT INTO StateOrProvince VALUES('MS','Mississippi');
INSERT INTO StateOrProvince VALUES('MO','Missouri');
INSERT INTO StateOrProvince VALUES('MT','Montana');
INSERT INTO StateOrProvince VALUES('NE','Nebraska');
INSERT INTO StateOrProvince VALUES('NV','Nevada');
INSERT INTO StateOrProvince VALUES('NH','New Hampshire');
INSERT INTO StateOrProvince VALUES('NJ','New Jersey');
INSERT INTO StateOrProvince VALUES('NM','New Mexico');
INSERT INTO StateOrProvince VALUES('NY','New York');
INSERT INTO StateOrProvince VALUES('NC','North Carolina');
INSERT INTO StateOrProvince VALUES('ND','North Dakota');
INSERT INTO StateOrProvince VALUES('OH','Ohio');
INSERT INTO StateOrProvince VALUES('OK','Oklahoma');
INSERT INTO StateOrProvince VALUES('OR','Oregon');
INSERT INTO StateOrProvince VALUES('PA','Pennsylvania');
INSERT INTO StateOrProvince VALUES('RI','Rhode Island');
INSERT INTO StateOrProvince VALUES('SC','South Carolina');
```

```
INSERT INTO StateOrProvince VALUES('SD','South Dakota');
INSERT INTO StateOrProvince VALUES('TN','Tennessee');
INSERT INTO StateOrProvince VALUES('TX','Texas');
INSERT INTO StateOrProvince VALUES('UT','Utah');
INSERT INTO StateOrProvince VALUES('VT','Vermont');
INSERT INTO StateOrProvince VALUES('VA','Virginia');
INSERT INTO StateOrProvince VALUES('WA','Washington');
INSERT INTO StateOrProvince VALUES('WV','West Virginia');
INSERT INTO StateOrProvince VALUES('WI','Wisconsin');
INSERT INTO StateOrProvince VALUES('WY','Wyoming');

INSERT INTO Customer (FirstName, LastName, Address, City,
                      StateOrProvince, PostalCode, PhoneNumber )
    VALUES ('John', 'Smith', '10341 Crestpoint Boulevard',
            'North Beach', 'VA', '10234', '1022341234');

INSERT INTO Customer (FirstName, LastName, Address, City,
                      StateOrProvince, PostalCode, PhoneNumber )
    VALUES ('Jacob', 'Salter', '234 North Main', 'Groveland',
            null, '45678', '7665554444');

INSERT INTO Customer (FirstName, LastName, Address, City,
                      StateOrProvince, PostalCode, PhoneNumber )
    VALUES ('Victoria', 'Smithe', '14301 Mountain Ridge Court',
            'Huntington', 'WV', '22211', '2175438679');

INSERT INTO Customer (FirstName, LastName, Address, City,
                      StateOrProvince, PostalCode, PhoneNumber )
    VALUES ('Bryce', 'Hatfield', '566 Pine Road', 'Marion',
            'IN', null, null);

INSERT INTO Customer (FirstName, LastName, Address, City,
                      StateOrProvince, PostalCode, PhoneNumber )
    VALUES ('Kylee', 'Dicken', null, 'Upland', 'IN', '46905',
            '7654321098');

INSERT INTO Customer (FirstName, LastName, Address, City,
                      StateOrProvince, PostalCode, PhoneNumber )
    VALUES ('Alex', 'Thompson', null, null, 'IN', null,
            '3175551213');
```

```
INSERT INTO Customer (FirstName, LastName, Address, City,
                      StateOrProvince, PostalCode, PhoneNumber )
    VALUES ('Davis', 'Thompson', '298 North Broadway', 'Greensburg',
            'IN', '46514', '3175551214');


INSERT INTO Customer (FirstName, LastName, Address, City,
                      StateOrProvince, PostalCode, PhoneNumber )
    VALUES ('Harrison', 'Thompson', '345 Hawks Point Drive Apt B',
            'Indianapolis', 'IN', '46123', '3175551215');
INSERT INTO Vehicle (VehicleYear, Make, Model, Color, LicensePlate#,
                     LastServiceDate, CustomerID)
    VALUES ('2000', 'Chevrolet', 'S-10', 'Purple', 'TROJANS',
            '8-13-2001', 4);


INSERT INTO Vehicle (VehicleYear, Make, Model, Color, LicensePlate#,
                     LastServiceDate, CustomerID)
    VALUES ('1998', 'Ford', 'Mustang', 'Red', 'HH7832',
            '9-16-2001', 2);


INSERT INTO Vehicle (VehicleYear, Make, Model, Color, LicensePlate#,
                     LastServiceDate, CustomerID)
    VALUES ('2002', 'Pontiac', 'Grand Prix', 'Black', 'GOPRDUE',
            '5-21-2002', 5);


INSERT INTO Vehicle (VehicleYear, Make, Model, Color, LicensePlate#,
                     LastServiceDate, CustomerID)
    VALUES ('1968', 'Chevrolet', 'Corvette', 'Black', 'KODIAK',
            '1-20-2002', 1);


INSERT INTO Vehicle (VehicleYear, Make, Model, Color, LicensePlate#,
                     LastServiceDate, CustomerID)
    VALUES ('2002', 'Nissan', 'Altima', 'White', 'HEYDARE',
            '1-26-2002', 3);


INSERT INTO Vehicle (VehicleYear, Make, Model, Color, LicensePlate#,
                     LastServiceDate, CustomerID)
    VALUES ('2000', 'Chrysler', 'PT Cruiser', 'Black', 'ALEX T',
            '5-15-2002', 6);


INSERT INTO Vehicle (VehicleYear, Make, Model, Color, LicensePlate#,
                     LastServiceDate, CustomerID)
    VALUES ('2002', 'Chevrolet', 'Trail Blazer', 'Green', 'I TRADE',
            '5-31-2001', 8);
```

```
INSERT INTO Vehicle (VehicleYear, Make, Model, Color, LicensePlate#,
                LastServiceDate, CustomerID)
    VALUES ('2001', 'Ford', 'Expedition', 'Maroon', 'DAVIS T',
            '5-31-2001', 7);

INSERT INTO Vehicle (VehicleYear, Make, Model, Color, LicensePlate#,
                LastServiceDate, CustomerID)
    VALUES ('1972', 'AMC', 'Gremlin', 'Pink', 'UGOGIRL',
            '2-17-2002', 4);

INSERT INTO Service (Description, RatePerHour)
    VALUES ('Oil Change', 60.00);

INSERT INTO Service (Description, RatePerHour)
    VALUES ('Replace Wiperblades', 10.00);

INSERT INTO Service (Description, RatePerHour)
    VALUES ('Replace Air Filter', 10.00);

INSERT INTO Service (Description, RatePerHour)
    VALUES ('Change PVC Valve', 10.00);

INSERT INTO Service (Description, RatePerHour)
    VALUES ('Change and Flush Cooling System', 60.00);

INSERT INTO Service (Description, RatePerHour)
    VALUES ('Change and Flush Differential', 60.00);

INSERT INTO Part (Description, Cost)
    VALUES ('Protects 10w-30 Oil', 7.49)

INSERT INTO Part (Description, Cost)
    VALUES ('Protects 10w-40 Oil', 7.49)

INSERT INTO Part (Description, Cost)
    VALUES ('Black Gold 10w-30 Oil', 7.99)

INSERT INTO Part (Description, Cost)
    VALUES ('Black Gold 10w-40 Oil', 7.99);

INSERT INTO Part (Description, Cost)
    VALUES ('Motion Synthetic Oil 10w-30', 13.99);
```

```
INSERT INTO Part (Description, Cost)
    VALUES ('Motion Synthetic Oil 10w-40', 13.99);

INSERT INTO Part (Description, Cost)
    VALUES ('Texas Tea Economy Oil Filter', 3.99);

INSERT INTO Part (Description, Cost)
    VALUES ('ACME Oil Filter', 4.99);

INSERT INTO Part (Description, Cost)
    VALUES ('ACME Air Filter', 8.99);

INSERT INTO Part (Description, Cost)
    VALUES ('ACME Wiper Blades', 9.99);

INSERT INTO Part (Description, Cost)
    VALUES ('ACME Brake Fluid', 0.00);

INSERT INTO Part (Description, Cost)
    VALUES ('ACME Transmission Fluid', 0.00);

INSERT INTO Part (Description, Cost)
    VALUES ('ACME Coolant', 0.00);

INSERT INTO Part (Description, Cost)
    VALUES ('ACME Windshield Fluid', 0.00);

INSERT INTO Part (Description, Cost)
    VALUES ('ACME Differential Fluid', 0.00);

INSERT INTO Part (Description, Cost)
    VALUES ('ACME PVC Valve', 12.99);

INSERT INTO JobTicket (CustomerID, StartDate, EndDate, VehicleID)
    VALUES (1, '1-20-2002', '1-20-2002', 4);

INSERT INTO JobTicket (CustomerID, StartDate, EndDate, VehicleID)
    VALUES (1, '7-20-2001', '7-20-2001', 4);

INSERT INTO JobTicket (CustomerID, StartDate, EndDate, VehicleID)
    VALUES (2, '9-16-2001', '9-16-2001', 2);
```

```
INSERT INTO JobTicket (CustomerID, StartDate, EndDate, VehicleID)
    VALUES (3, '1-26-2002', '1-26-2002', 5);

INSERT INTO JobTicket (CustomerID, StartDate, EndDate, VehicleID)
    VALUES (5, '5-21-2002', '5-21-2002', 3);

INSERT INTO JobTicket (CustomerID, StartDate, EndDate, VehicleID)
    VALUES (4, '8-13-2001', '8-13-2001', 1);

INSERT INTO JobTicket (CustomerID, StartDate, EndDate, VehicleID)
    VALUES (4, '2-16-2002', '2-17-2002', 9);

INSERT INTO JobTicketDetail (JobTicketID, LineItemNumber, ServiceID,
                            DateComplete, HoursSpent)
    VALUES (1, 1, 1, '1-20-2002', .5);

INSERT INTO JobTicketDetail (JobTicketID, LineItemNumber, ServiceID,
                            DateComplete, HoursSpent)
    VALUES (2, 1, 1, '7-20-2001', .25);

INSERT INTO JobTicketDetail (JobTicketID, LineItemNumber, ServiceID,
                            DateComplete, HoursSpent)
    VALUES (2, 2, 3, '7-20-2001', .1);

INSERT INTO JobTicketDetail (JobTicketID, LineItemNumber, ServiceID,
                            DateComplete, HoursSpent)
    VALUES (2, 3, 4, '7-20-2002', .1);

INSERT INTO JobTicketDetail (JobTicketID, LineItemNumber, ServiceID,
                            DateComplete, HoursSpent)
    VALUES (3, 1, 1, '9-16-2001', .25);

INSERT INTO JobTicketDetail (JobTicketID, LineItemNumber, ServiceID,
                            DateComplete, HoursSpent)
    VALUES (4, 1, 1, '1-26-2002', .25);

INSERT INTO JobTicketDetail (JobTicketID, LineItemNumber, ServiceID,
                            DateComplete, HoursSpent)
    VALUES (5, 1, 2, '5-21-2002', .2);

INSERT INTO JobTicketDetail (JobTicketID, LineItemNumber, ServiceID,
                            DateComplete, HoursSpent)
    VALUES (5, 2, 1, '5-21-2002', .25);
```

```
INSERT INTO JobTicketDetail (JobTicketID, LineItemNumber, ServiceID,
                             DateComplete, HoursSpent)
    VALUES (6, 1, 5, '8-13-2001', 1.15);

INSERT INTO JobTicketDetail (JobTicketID, LineItemNumber, ServiceID,
                             DateComplete, HoursSpent)
    VALUES (7, 1, 1, '2-16-2002', .35);

INSERT INTO JobTicketDetail (JobTicketID, LineItemNumber, ServiceID,
                             DateComplete, HoursSpent)
    VALUES (7, 2, 3, '2-16-2002', .1);

INSERT INTO JobTicketDetail (JobTicketID, LineItemNumber, ServiceID,
                             DateComplete, HoursSpent)
    VALUES (7, 3, 4, '2-16-2002', .15);

INSERT INTO JobTicketDetail (JobTicketID, LineItemNumber, ServiceID,
                             DateComplete, HoursSpent)
    VALUES (7, 4, 6, '2-16-2002', 1.0);

INSERT INTO JobTicketDetail (JobTicketID, LineItemNumber, ServiceID,
                             DateComplete, HoursSpent)
    VALUES (7, 5, 5, '2-17-2002', .5);

INSERT INTO PartUsed (JobTicketID, LineItemNumber, PartID, Quantity)
    VALUES (1, 1, 4, 4);

INSERT INTO PartUsed (JobTicketID, LineItemNumber, PartID, Quantity)
    VALUES (1, 1, 7, 1);

INSERT INTO PartUsed (JobTicketID, LineItemNumber, PartID, Quantity)
    VALUES (1, 1, 11, 1);

INSERT INTO PartUsed (JobTicketID, LineItemNumber, PartID, Quantity)
    VALUES (1, 1, 12, 1);

INSERT INTO PartUsed (JobTicketID, LineItemNumber, PartID, Quantity)
    VALUES (2, 1, 5, 4);

INSERT INTO PartUsed (JobTicketID, LineItemNumber, PartID, Quantity)
    VALUES (2, 1, 14, 1);
```

```
INSERT INTO PartUsed (JobTicketID, LineItemNumber, PartID, Quantity)
    VALUES (2, 1, 8, 1);

INSERT INTO PartUsed (JobTicketID, LineItemNumber, PartID, Quantity)
    VALUES (2, 2, 9, 1);

INSERT INTO PartUsed (JobTicketID, LineItemNumber, PartID, Quantity)
    VALUES (2, 3, 16, 1);

INSERT INTO PartUsed (JobTicketID, LineItemNumber, PartID, Quantity)
    VALUES (3, 1, 6, 4);

INSERT INTO PartUsed (JobTicketID, LineItemNumber, PartID, Quantity)
    VALUES (3, 1, 7, 1);

INSERT INTO PartUsed (JobTicketID, LineItemNumber, PartID, Quantity)
    VALUES (4, 1, 1, 4);

INSERT INTO PartUsed (JobTicketID, LineItemNumber, PartID, Quantity)
    VALUES (4, 1, 8, 1);

INSERT INTO PartUsed (JobTicketID, LineItemNumber, PartID, Quantity)
    VALUES (5, 1, 10, 1);

INSERT INTO PartUsed (JobTicketID, LineItemNumber, PartID, Quantity)
    VALUES (5, 2, 3, 4);

INSERT INTO PartUsed (JobTicketID, LineItemNumber, PartID, Quantity)
    VALUES (5, 2, 14, 1);

INSERT INTO PartUsed (JobTicketID, LineItemNumber, PartID, Quantity)
    VALUES (5, 2, 12, 1);

INSERT INTO PartUsed (JobTicketID, LineItemNumber, PartID, Quantity)
    VALUES (5, 2, 8, 1);

INSERT INTO PartUsed (JobTicketID, LineItemNumber, PartID, Quantity)
    VALUES (6, 1, 13, 1);

INSERT INTO PartUsed (JobTicketID, LineItemNumber, PartID, Quantity)
    VALUES (7, 1, 1, 4);
```

```
INSERT INTO PartUsed (JobTicketID, LineItemNumber, PartID, Quantity)
     VALUES (7, 1, 8, 1);

INSERT INTO PartUsed (JobTicketID, LineItemNumber, PartID, Quantity)
     VALUES (7, 1, 14, 1);

INSERT INTO PartUsed (JobTicketID, LineItemNumber, PartID, Quantity)
     VALUES (7, 1, 12, 1);

INSERT INTO PartUsed (JobTicketID, LineItemNumber, PartID, Quantity)
     VALUES (7, 2, 9, 1);

INSERT INTO PartUsed (JobTicketID, LineItemNumber, PartID, Quantity)
     VALUES (7, 3, 16, 1);

INSERT INTO PartUsed (JobTicketID, LineItemNumber, PartID, Quantity)
     VALUES (7, 4, 15, 1);

INSERT INTO PartUsed (JobTicketID, LineItemNumber, PartID, Quantity)
     VALUES (7, 5, 13, 1);
```

Your sample database is now ready to use. Enjoy!

Education, Training, and Certification

This book only covers SQL as a language and not specific information on the database management systems that use it. Should you decide to continue to use SQL Server, you may need a more specific book about the product. Following is a list of some of the books available on SQL Server:

Title: *Professional SQL Server 2000 Programming*
Author(s):   Rob Vieira
Publisher: Wrox Press
List Price: $59.99

Title: *Microsoft SQL Server 2000 Reference Library*
Author(s):   David Iseminger
Publisher: Microsoft Press
List Price: $179.99

Title:	*Teach Yourself SQL Server in 21 Days*
Author(s):	Richard Waymire and Rick Sawtell
Publisher:	Sams
List Price:	$39.99

Title:	*SQL Server 2000 Unleashed*
Author(s):	Ray Rankins, Paul Jensen, et al.
Publisher:	Sams
List Price:	$59.99

There is a magazine available on SQL Server as well. It has both hard copy and CD-ROM versions available. You can find out more or subscribe at **www.sqlmag.com/**.

Microsoft offers Web casts, online seminars, CD-ROMs, and instructor-led training. The classes are offered through Microsoft Certified Technical Education Centers (Microsoft CTECs). To find the training you need, check out **www.microsoft.com/sql/using/training/default.asp**.

Microsoft has a long list of certifications available. For SQL Server, you could get a simple Microsoft Certified Professional (MCP) certification, which can be obtained to denote proficiency in a particular Microsoft application. There is also Microsoft Certified Solution Developer (MCSD) or Microsoft Certified Application Developer (MCAD) certifications, which are more involved. They specify proficiency in Microsoft standards as well as both front-end and back-end technologies. These are primarily for the application developer. If you are more comfortable with the administrative side of things, you might look at the Microsoft Certified System Engineer (MCSE) or Microsoft Certified Database Administrator (MCDBA) certifications. MCSE is more for individuals who support and administer servers. If you want to be a database administrator, you may wish to seek the MCDBA certification. You can find the official curriculum for all these at **www.microsoft.com/traincert/mcp**.

SQL Samples in Oracle

Accessing Oracle

Oracle provides an editor called SQLPlus. SQLPlus allows you to execute SQL commands against the database. Once you have the client tools installed for Oracle, you can find SQLPlus on the Start menu under Programs, Oracle Application Tools.

When you start SQLPlus, you will be asked for a username, password, and host. If you don't already have a username and password assigned, type in SYSTEM for the username and MANAGER for the password. Leave host blank unless you are connecting to a remote database. When you bring up the editor, you will see a prompt, SQL>. This is where you type your commands. All commands in SQLPlus have to be terminated. Unlike SQL Server, where you do not have to have the semicolon at the end of each statement, SQLPlus will not execute the statement until a terminator is typed in (or Run is selected from the menu). In this case, you are going to use the semicolon. Once the semicolon is typed, terminating the command, and Return is pressed, the editor automatically runs the command. Should you need to cancel a command, type Ctrl+C. To exit, type EXIT.

The best way to enter in the commands needed to set up the sample database is to download the commands for Oracle from the Premier Press Web site (**www.premierpressbooks.com/**). You can copy the commands from the downloaded file and paste them into the editor.

If you can download the SQL, you can skip the next section. Should you need to type the commands in yourself, however, the next section will give you all the commands necessary to load up the sample database.

Should you make a mistake while entering the commands that you can't correct, type the following command and start over:

```
DROP DATABASE SlickShp;
```

SQL for the Sample Database

This section will give you the SQL you need to create the database and tables for the Slick Shop sample database. However, because Oracle does not allow database names longer than eight characters, you will have to name the database SlickShp instead.

This syntax can also be downloaded from the Premier Press Web site if you'd rather not type it in. The syntax covered here is for Oracle only.

To create the database, open SQLPlus as described. Type the command as you see it here and then press Enter on the keyboard:

```
CREATE DATABASE SlickShp;
```

Now you can create the table structures for the sample database. If you'd like to see the graphical representation of those tables, please refer to Figure 1.3 in the Friday Evening session. Type in each code listing as follows:

```
CREATE TABLE StateOrProvince (
StateOrProvince        Char(2)         NOT NULL PRIMARY KEY,
StateOrProvinceName    Varchar2(50)    NOT NULL
);

CREATE TABLE Customer (
CustomerID             Integer         NOT NULL PRIMARY KEY,
FirstName              Varchar2(20)    NULL,
LastName               Varchar2(30)    NULL,
Address                Varchar2(100)   NULL,
City                   Varchar2(30)    NULL,
StateOrProvince        Char(2)         NULL REFERENCES StateOrProvince
                                       (StateOrProvince),
PostalCode             Varchar2(10)    NULL,
PhoneNumber            Varchar2(10)    NULL
);

CREATE SEQUENCE CustomerSeq NOCACHE;

CREATE TABLE Vehicle (
VehicleID              Integer         NOT NULL PRIMARY KEY,
VehicleYear            SmallInt        NULL,
Make                   Varchar2(30)    NULL,
Model                  Varchar2(30)    NULL,
Color                  Varchar2(30)    NULL,
LicensePlate           Varchar2(10)    NULL,
LastServiceDate        Date            NULL,
CustomerID             Integer         NOT NULL
     REFERENCES Customer(CustomerID)
);

CREATE SEQUENCE VehicleSeq NOCACHE;

CREATE TABLE Service (
ServiceID              Integer         NOT NULL PRIMARY KEY,
Description            Varchar2(100)   NOT NULL,
RatePerHour            Number(5,2)     NOT NULL
);
```

```
CREATE SEQUENCE ServiceSeq NOCACHE;

CREATE TABLE Part (
PartID              Integer         NOT NULL PRIMARY KEY,
Description         Varchar2(100)   NOT NULL,
Cost                Number(5,2)     NOT NULL
);

CREATE SEQUENCE PartSeq NOCACHE;

CREATE TABLE JobTicket (
JobTicketID         Integer         NOT NULL PRIMARY KEY,
CustomerID          Integer         NOT NULL REFERENCES Customer
                                        (CustomerID),
StartDate           Date            NULL,
EndDate             Date            NULL,
VehicleID           Integer         NOT NULL REFERENCES Vehicle
                                        (VehicleID)
);

CREATE SEQUENCE JobTicketSeq NOCACHE;

CREATE TABLE JobTicketDetail (
JobTicketID         Integer         NOT NULL
    REFERENCES JobTicket (JobTicketID),
LineItemNumber      Number(3)       NOT NULL,
ServiceID           Integer         NOT NULL
    REFERENCES Service (ServiceID),
DateComplete        Date            NULL,
HoursSpent          Number(5,2)     DEFAULT 0 NOT NULL,
CONSTRAINT PK_JobTicketDetail PRIMARY KEY (JobTicketID,
    LineItemNumber)
);

CREATE TABLE PartUsed (
JobTicketID         Integer     NOT NULL,
LineItemNumber      Number(3)   NOT NULL,
PartID              Integer     NOT NULL REFERENCES Part (PartID),
Quantity            Number(3)   NOT NULL,
CONSTRAINT PK_PartUsed PRIMARY KEY (JobTicketID, LineItemNumber,
    PartID),
```

```
CONSTRAINT FK_JobTicketDetail_PartUsed FOREIGN KEY (JobTicketID,
    LineItemNumber) REFERENCES JobTicketDetail (JobTicketID,
    LineItemNumber)
);
```

Now that the structures are in place, you can fill them up with the sample data. We've included the INSERT scripts in the following. Simply type them in and execute them, and you will have everything you need to get started. If you'd rather not type all these commands (and why would you?), you can download these statements from the Premier Press Web site.

```
INSERT INTO StateOrProvince VALUES('AB','Alberta');
INSERT INTO StateOrProvince VALUES('BC','British Columbia');
INSERT INTO StateOrProvince VALUES('MB','Manitoba');
INSERT INTO StateOrProvince VALUES('NB','New Brunswick');
INSERT INTO StateOrProvince VALUES('NF','Newfoundland');
INSERT INTO StateOrProvince VALUES('NT','Northwest Territories');
INSERT INTO StateOrProvince VALUES('NS','Nova Scotia');
INSERT INTO StateOrProvince VALUES('NU','Nunavut');
INSERT INTO StateOrProvince VALUES('ON','Ontario');
INSERT INTO StateOrProvince VALUES('PE','Prince Edward Island');
INSERT INTO StateOrProvince VALUES('QC','Quebec');
INSERT INTO StateOrProvince VALUES('SK','Saskatchewan');
INSERT INTO StateOrProvince VALUES('YT','Yukon Territory');
INSERT INTO StateOrProvince VALUES('AL','Alabama');
INSERT INTO StateOrProvince VALUES('AK','Alaska');
INSERT INTO StateOrProvince VALUES('AZ','Arizona');
INSERT INTO StateOrProvince VALUES('AR','Arkansas');
INSERT INTO StateOrProvince VALUES('CA','California');
INSERT INTO StateOrProvince VALUES('CO','Colorado');
INSERT INTO StateOrProvince VALUES('CT','Connecticut');
INSERT INTO StateOrProvince VALUES('DE','Delaware');
INSERT INTO StateOrProvince VALUES('DC','District of Columbia');
INSERT INTO StateOrProvince VALUES('FL','Florida');
INSERT INTO StateOrProvince VALUES('GA','Georgia');
INSERT INTO StateOrProvince VALUES('HI','Hawaii');
INSERT INTO StateOrProvince VALUES('ID','Idaho');
INSERT INTO StateOrProvince VALUES('IL','Illinois');
INSERT INTO StateOrProvince VALUES('IN','Indiana');
INSERT INTO StateOrProvince VALUES('IA','Iowa');
INSERT INTO StateOrProvince VALUES('KS','Kansas');
INSERT INTO StateOrProvince VALUES('KY','Kentucky');
```

```
INSERT INTO StateOrProvince VALUES('LA','Louisiana');
INSERT INTO StateOrProvince VALUES('ME','Maine');
INSERT INTO StateOrProvince VALUES('MD','Maryland');
INSERT INTO StateOrProvince VALUES('MA','Massachusetts');
INSERT INTO StateOrProvince VALUES('MI','Michigan');
INSERT INTO StateOrProvince VALUES('MN','Minnesota');
INSERT INTO StateOrProvince VALUES('MS','Mississippi');
INSERT INTO StateOrProvince VALUES('MO','Missouri');
INSERT INTO StateOrProvince VALUES('MT','Montana');
INSERT INTO StateOrProvince VALUES('NE','Nebraska');
INSERT INTO StateOrProvince VALUES('NV','Nevada');
INSERT INTO StateOrProvince VALUES('NH','New Hampshire');
INSERT INTO StateOrProvince VALUES('NJ','New Jersey');
INSERT INTO StateOrProvince VALUES('NM','New Mexico');
INSERT INTO StateOrProvince VALUES('NY','New York');
INSERT INTO StateOrProvince VALUES('NC','North Carolina');
INSERT INTO StateOrProvince VALUES('ND','North Dakota');
INSERT INTO StateOrProvince VALUES('OH','Ohio');
INSERT INTO StateOrProvince VALUES('OK','Oklahoma');
INSERT INTO StateOrProvince VALUES('OR','Oregon');
INSERT INTO StateOrProvince VALUES('PA','Pennsylvania');
INSERT INTO StateOrProvince VALUES('RI','Rhode Island');
INSERT INTO StateOrProvince VALUES('SC','South Carolina');
INSERT INTO StateOrProvince VALUES('SD','South Dakota');
INSERT INTO StateOrProvince VALUES('TN','Tennessee');
INSERT INTO StateOrProvince VALUES('TX','Texas');
INSERT INTO StateOrProvince VALUES('UT','Utah');
INSERT INTO StateOrProvince VALUES('VT','Vermont');
INSERT INTO StateOrProvince VALUES('VA','Virginia');
INSERT INTO StateOrProvince VALUES('WA','Washington');
INSERT INTO StateOrProvince VALUES('WV','West Virginia');
INSERT INTO StateOrProvince VALUES('WI','Wisconsin');
INSERT INTO StateOrProvince VALUES('WY','Wyoming');
INSERT INTO Customer (CustomerID, FirstName, LastName, Address, City,
                      StateOrProvince, PostalCode, PhoneNumber )
    VALUES (CustomerSeq.NEXTVAL, 'John', 'Smith',
            '10341 Crestpoint Boulevard', 'North Beach', 'VA',
            '10234', '1022341234');
```

```
INSERT INTO Customer (CustomerID, FirstName, LastName, Address, City,
                      StateOrProvince, PostalCode, PhoneNumber )
    VALUES (CustomerSeq.NEXTVAL, 'Jacob', 'Salter',
            '234 North Main', 'Groveland', null, '45678',
            '7665554444');

INSERT INTO Customer (CustomerID, FirstName, LastName, Address, City,
                      StateOrProvince, PostalCode, PhoneNumber )
    VALUES (CustomerSeq.NEXTVAL, 'Victoria', 'Smithe',
            '14301 Mountain Ridge Court', 'Huntington', 'WV',
            '22211', '2175438679');

INSERT INTO Customer (CustomerID, FirstName, LastName, Address, City,
                      StateOrProvince, PostalCode, PhoneNumber )
    VALUES (CustomerSeq.NEXTVAL, 'Bryce', 'Hatfield',
            '566 Pine Road', 'Marion', 'IN', null, null);

INSERT INTO Customer (CustomerID, FirstName, LastName, Address, City,
                      StateOrProvince, PostalCode, PhoneNumber )
    VALUES (CustomerSeq.NEXTVAL, 'Kylee', 'Dicken', null, 'Upland',
            'IN', '46905', '7654321098');

INSERT INTO Customer (CustomerID, FirstName, LastName, Address, City,
                      StateOrProvince, PostalCode, PhoneNumber )
    VALUES (CustomerSeq.NEXTVAL, 'Alex', 'Thompson', null, null,
            'IN', null, '3175551213');

INSERT INTO Customer (CustomerID, FirstName, LastName, Address, City,
                      StateOrProvince, PostalCode, PhoneNumber )
    VALUES (CustomerSeq.NEXTVAL, 'Davis', 'Thompson', '298 North
            Broadway', 'Greensburg', 'IN', '46514', '3175551214');

INSERT INTO Customer (CustomerID, FirstName, LastName, Address, City,
                      StateOrProvince, PostalCode, PhoneNumber )
    VALUES (CustomerSeq.NEXTVAL, 'Harrison', 'Thompson',
            '345 Hawks Point Drive Apt B', 'Indianapolis', 'IN',
            '46123', '3175551215');

INSERT INTO Vehicle (VehicleID, VehicleYear, Make, Model, Color,
                     LicensePlate, LastServiceDate, CustomerID)
    VALUES (VehicleSeq.NEXTVAL, '2000', 'Chevrolet', 'S-10',
            'Purple', 'TROJANS', '13-AUG-01', 4);
```

```
INSERT INTO Vehicle (VehicleID, VehicleYear, Make, Model, Color,
                     LicensePlate, LastServiceDate, CustomerID)
     VALUES (VehicleSeq.NEXTVAL, '1998', 'Ford', 'Mustang', 'Red',
             'HH7832', '16-SEP-01', 2);

INSERT INTO Vehicle (VehicleID, VehicleYear, Make, Model, Color,
                     LicensePlate, LastServiceDate, CustomerID)
     VALUES (VehicleSeq.NEXTVAL, '2002', 'Pontiac', 'Grand Prix',
             'Black', 'GOPRDUE', '21-MAY-02', 5);

INSERT INTO Vehicle (VehicleID, VehicleYear, Make, Model, Color,
                     LicensePlate, LastServiceDate, CustomerID)
     VALUES (VehicleSeq.NEXTVAL, '1968', 'Chevrolet', 'Corvette',
             'Black', 'KODIAK', '20-JAN-02', 1);

INSERT INTO Vehicle (VehicleID, VehicleYear, Make, Model, Color,
                     LicensePlate, LastServiceDate, CustomerID)
     VALUES (VehicleSeq.NEXTVAL, '2002', 'Nissan', 'Altima', 'White',
             'HEYDARE', '26-JAN-02', 3);

INSERT INTO Vehicle (VehicleID, VehicleYear, Make, Model, Color,
                     LicensePlate, LastServiceDate, CustomerID)
     VALUES (VehicleSeq.NEXTVAL, '2000', 'Chrysler', 'PT Cruiser',
             'Black', 'ALEX T', '15-MAY-02', 6);

INSERT INTO Vehicle (VehicleID, VehicleYear, Make, Model, Color,
                     LicensePlate, LastServiceDate, CustomerID)
     VALUES (VehicleSeq.NEXTVAL, '2002', 'Chevrolet',
             'Trail Blazer', 'Green', 'I TRADE', '31-MAY-01', 8);

INSERT INTO Vehicle (VehicleID, VehicleYear, Make, Model, Color,
                     LicensePlate, LastServiceDate, CustomerID)
     VALUES (VehicleSeq.NEXTVAL, '2001', 'Ford', 'Expedition',
             'Maroon', 'DAVIS T', '31-MAY-01', 7);

INSERT INTO Vehicle (VehicleID, VehicleYear, Make, Model, Color,
                     LicensePlate, LastServiceDate, CustomerID)
     VALUES (VehicleSeq.NEXTVAL, '1972', 'AMC', 'Gremlin', 'Pink',
             'UGOGIRL', '17-FEB-02', 4);
```

```
INSERT INTO Service (ServiceID, Description, RatePerHour)
     VALUES (ServiceSeq.NEXTVAL, 'Oil Change', 60.00);

INSERT INTO Service (ServiceID, Description, RatePerHour)
     VALUES (ServiceSeq.NEXTVAL, 'Replace Wiperblades', 10.00);

INSERT INTO Service (ServiceID, Description, RatePerHour)
     VALUES (ServiceSeq.NEXTVAL, 'Replace Air Filter', 10.00);

INSERT INTO Service (ServiceID, Description, RatePerHour)
     VALUES (ServiceSeq.NEXTVAL, 'Change PVC Valve', 10.00);

INSERT INTO Service (ServiceID, Description, RatePerHour)
      VALUES (ServiceSeq.NEXTVAL, 'Change and Flush Cooling System',
           60.00);

INSERT INTO Service (ServiceID, Description, RatePerHour)
     VALUES (ServiceSeq.NEXTVAL, 'Change and Flush Differential',
           60.00);

INSERT INTO Part (PartID, Description, Cost)
     VALUES (PartSeq.NEXTVAL, 'Protects 10w-30 Oil', 7.49);

INSERT INTO Part (PartID, Description, Cost)
     VALUES (PartSeq.NEXTVAL, 'Protects 10w-40 Oil', 7.49);

INSERT INTO Part (PartID, Description, Cost)
     VALUES (PartSeq.NEXTVAL, 'Black Gold 10w-30 Oil', 7.99);

INSERT INTO Part (PartID, Description, Cost)
     VALUES (PartSeq.NEXTVAL, 'Black Gold 10w-40 Oil', 7.99);

INSERT INTO Part (PartID, Description, Cost)
      VALUES (PartSeq.NEXTVAL, 'Motion Synthetic Oil 10w-30', 13.99);

INSERT INTO Part (PartID, Description, Cost)
     VALUES (PartSeq.NEXTVAL, 'Motion Synthetic Oil 10w-40', 13.99);

INSERT INTO Part (PartID, Description, Cost)
     VALUES (PartSeq.NEXTVAL, 'Texas Tea Economy Oil Filter', 3.99);
```

```
INSERT INTO Part (PartID, Description, Cost)
     VALUES (PartSeq.NEXTVAL, 'ACME Oil Filter', 4.99);

INSERT INTO Part (PartID, Description, Cost)
     VALUES (PartSeq.NEXTVAL, 'ACME Air Filter', 8.99);

INSERT INTO Part (PartID, Description, Cost)
     VALUES (PartSeq.NEXTVAL, 'ACME Wiper Blades', 9.99);

INSERT INTO Part (PartID, Description, Cost)
     VALUES (PartSeq.NEXTVAL, 'ACME Brake Fluid', 0.00);

INSERT INTO Part (PartID, Description, Cost)
     VALUES (PartSeq.NEXTVAL, 'ACME Transmission Fluid', 0.00);

INSERT INTO Part (PartID, Description, Cost)
     VALUES (PartSeq.NEXTVAL, 'ACME Coolant', 0.00);

INSERT INTO Part (PartID, Description, Cost)
     VALUES (PartSeq.NEXTVAL, 'ACME Windshield Fluid', 0.00);

INSERT INTO Part (PartID, Description, Cost)
     VALUES (PartSeq.NEXTVAL, 'ACME Differential Fluid', 0.00);

INSERT INTO Part (PartID, Description, Cost)
     VALUES (PartSeq.NEXTVAL, 'ACME PVC Valve', 12.99);

INSERT INTO JobTicket (JobTicketID, CustomerID, StartDate, EndDate,
                       VehicleID)
     VALUES (JobTicketSeq.NEXTVAL, 1, '20-JAN-02', '20-JAN-02', 4);

INSERT INTO JobTicket (JobTicketID, CustomerID, StartDate, EndDate,
                       VehicleID)
     VALUES (JobTicketSeq.NEXTVAL, 1, '20-JUL-01', '20-JUL-01', 4);

INSERT INTO JobTicket (JobTicketID, CustomerID, StartDate, EndDate,
                       VehicleID)
     VALUES (JobTicketSeq.NEXTVAL, 2, '16-SEP-01', '16-SEP-01', 2);

INSERT INTO JobTicket (JobTicketID, CustomerID, StartDate, EndDate,
                       VehicleID)
     VALUES (JobTicketSeq.NEXTVAL, 3, '26-JAN-02', '26-JAN-02', 5);
```

```
INSERT INTO JobTicket (JobTicketID, CustomerID, StartDate, EndDate,
                       VehicleID)
    VALUES (JobTicketSeq.NEXTVAL, 5, '21-MAY-02', '21-MAY-02', 3);

INSERT INTO JobTicket (JobTicketID, CustomerID, StartDate, EndDate,
                       VehicleID)
    VALUES (JobTicketSeq.NEXTVAL, 4, '13-AUG-01', '13-AUG-01', 1);

INSERT INTO JobTicket (JobTicketID, CustomerID, StartDate, EndDate,
                       VehicleID)
    VALUES (JobTicketSeq.NEXTVAL, 4, '16-FEB-02', '17-FEB-02', 9);

INSERT INTO JobTicketDetail (JobTicketID, LineItemNumber, ServiceID,
                             DateComplete, HoursSpent)
    VALUES (1, 1, 1, '20-JAN-02', .5);

INSERT INTO JobTicketDetail (JobTicketID, LineItemNumber, ServiceID,
                             DateComplete, HoursSpent)
    VALUES (2, 1, 1, '20-JUL-01', .25);

INSERT INTO JobTicketDetail (JobTicketID, LineItemNumber, ServiceID,
                             DateComplete, HoursSpent)
    VALUES (2, 2, 3, '20-JUL-01', .1);

INSERT INTO JobTicketDetail (JobTicketID, LineItemNumber, ServiceID,
                             DateComplete, HoursSpent)
    VALUES (2, 3, 4, '20-JUL-01', .1);

INSERT INTO JobTicketDetail (JobTicketID, LineItemNumber, ServiceID,
                             DateComplete, HoursSpent)
    VALUES (3, 1, 1, '16-SEP-01', .25);

INSERT INTO JobTicketDetail (JobTicketID, LineItemNumber, ServiceID,
                             DateComplete, HoursSpent)
    VALUES (4, 1, 1, '26-JAN-02', .25);

INSERT INTO JobTicketDetail (JobTicketID, LineItemNumber, ServiceID,
                             DateComplete, HoursSpent)
    VALUES (5, 1, 2, '21-MAY-02', .2);
```

```
INSERT INTO JobTicketDetail (JobTicketID, LineItemNumber, ServiceID,
                             DateComplete, HoursSpent)
     VALUES (5, 2, 1, '21-MAY-02', .25);

INSERT INTO JobTicketDetail (JobTicketID, LineItemNumber, ServiceID,
                             DateComplete, HoursSpent)
     VALUES (6, 1, 5, '13-AUG-01', 1.15);

INSERT INTO JobTicketDetail (JobTicketID, LineItemNumber, ServiceID,
                             DateComplete, HoursSpent)
     VALUES (7, 1, 1, '16-FEB-02', .35);

INSERT INTO JobTicketDetail (JobTicketID, LineItemNumber, ServiceID,
                             DateComplete, HoursSpent)
     VALUES (7, 2, 3, '16-FEB-02', .1);

INSERT INTO JobTicketDetail (JobTicketID, LineItemNumber, ServiceID,
                             DateComplete, HoursSpent)
     VALUES (7, 3, 4, '16-FEB-02', .15);

INSERT INTO JobTicketDetail (JobTicketID, LineItemNumber, ServiceID,
                             DateComplete, HoursSpent)
     VALUES (7, 4, 6, '16-FEB-02', 1.0);

INSERT INTO JobTicketDetail (JobTicketID, LineItemNumber, ServiceID,
                             DateComplete, HoursSpent)
     VALUES (7, 5, 5, '17-FEB-02', .5);

INSERT INTO PartUsed (JobTicketID, LineItemNumber, PartID, Quantity)
     VALUES (1, 1, 4, 4);

INSERT INTO PartUsed (JobTicketID, LineItemNumber, PartID, Quantity)
     VALUES (1, 1, 7, 1);

INSERT INTO PartUsed (JobTicketID, LineItemNumber, PartID, Quantity)
     VALUES (1, 1, 11, 1);

INSERT INTO PartUsed (JobTicketID, LineItemNumber, PartID, Quantity)
     VALUES (1, 1, 12, 1);

INSERT INTO PartUsed (JobTicketID, LineItemNumber, PartID, Quantity)
     VALUES (2, 1, 5, 4);
```

```
INSERT INTO PartUsed (JobTicketID, LineItemNumber, PartID, Quantity)
    VALUES (2, 1, 14, 1);

INSERT INTO PartUsed (JobTicketID, LineItemNumber, PartID, Quantity)
    VALUES (2, 1, 8, 1);

INSERT INTO PartUsed (JobTicketID, LineItemNumber, PartID, Quantity)
    VALUES (2, 2, 9, 1);

INSERT INTO PartUsed (JobTicketID, LineItemNumber, PartID, Quantity)
    VALUES (2, 3, 16, 1);

INSERT INTO PartUsed (JobTicketID, LineItemNumber, PartID, Quantity)
    VALUES (3, 1, 6, 4);

INSERT INTO PartUsed (JobTicketID, LineItemNumber, PartID, Quantity)
    VALUES (3, 1, 7, 1);

INSERT INTO PartUsed (JobTicketID, LineItemNumber, PartID, Quantity)
    VALUES (4, 1, 1, 4);

INSERT INTO PartUsed (JobTicketID, LineItemNumber, PartID, Quantity)
    VALUES (4, 1, 8, 1);

INSERT INTO PartUsed (JobTicketID, LineItemNumber, PartID, Quantity)
    VALUES (5, 1, 10, 1);

INSERT INTO PartUsed (JobTicketID, LineItemNumber, PartID, Quantity)
    VALUES (5, 2, 3, 4);

INSERT INTO PartUsed (JobTicketID, LineItemNumber, PartID, Quantity)
    VALUES (5, 2, 14, 1);

INSERT INTO PartUsed (JobTicketID, LineItemNumber, PartID, Quantity)
    VALUES (5, 2, 12, 1);

INSERT INTO PartUsed (JobTicketID, LineItemNumber, PartID, Quantity)
    VALUES (5, 2, 8, 1);

INSERT INTO PartUsed (JobTicketID, LineItemNumber, PartID, Quantity)
    VALUES (6, 1, 13, 1);
```

```
INSERT INTO PartUsed (JobTicketID, LineItemNumber, PartID, Quantity)
    VALUES (7, 1, 1, 4);

INSERT INTO PartUsed (JobTicketID, LineItemNumber, PartID, Quantity)
    VALUES (7, 1, 8, 1);

INSERT INTO PartUsed (JobTicketID, LineItemNumber, PartID, Quantity)
    VALUES (7, 1, 14, 1);

INSERT INTO PartUsed (JobTicketID, LineItemNumber, PartID, Quantity)
    VALUES (7, 1, 12, 1);

INSERT INTO PartUsed (JobTicketID, LineItemNumber, PartID, Quantity)
    VALUES (7, 2, 9, 1);

INSERT INTO PartUsed (JobTicketID, LineItemNumber, PartID, Quantity)
    VALUES (7, 3, 16, 1);

INSERT INTO PartUsed (JobTicketID, LineItemNumber, PartID, Quantity)
    VALUES (7, 4, 15, 1);

INSERT INTO PartUsed (JobTicketID, LineItemNumber, PartID, Quantity)
    VALUES (7, 5, 13, 1);
```

Your sample database is now ready to use. Enjoy!

Differences in Oracle

Oracle is a different beast compared to other databases. It has its own unique approach to handling SQL. Because of this, several changes were made to the syntax used to create the sample database so that it could be created in Oracle.

Oracle has a more limited set of data types. The Money data type and the SmallDatetime data type mean nothing to Oracle. Money was changed to Number(5,2) for the RatePerHour column in the Service table and also the Cost column in the Part table. Varchar is an unused data type in Oracle. It uses Varchar2 instead. Several columns required this change. Oracle also does not recognize the data type Tinyint. TinyInt was changed to

Number(3) for the LineItemNumber in both JobTicketDetail and PartUsed. Similarly, the Quantity column of PartUsed was changed. The SmallDatetime data type was changed to just Date. This affected the DateComplete column in JobTicketDetail and the StartDate and EndDate columns of the JobTicket table. The LastServiceDate column in Vehicle also required this change. Oracle also prefers that dates be entered in a certain format. The default format for date entry and display in Oracle is dd-mon-yy (for example, 21-MAY-02).

You may have also noticed that there are new commands that must be issued, called CREATE SEQUENCE. This command creates an object in the database that is responsible for maintaining the last sequential number issued and issuing the next value available. Whereas with SQL Server you were able to identify a column as an IDENTITY (or auto-number), with Oracle the sequence object is instead used to fill in the next sequential value. This is done by using the statement sequencename.NEXTVAL in the INSERT statement.

For instance, the Customer table's CustomerID is an IDENTITY in SQL Server. It is given the next sequential value simply by inserting NULL into that column in the INSERT statement or eliminating the column from the INSERT altogether. With Oracle, however, the CREATE SEQUENCE command is used to create the sequence object CustomerSeq. When a row is inserted into the Customer table, the sequence provides the value for CustomerID by explicitly inserting CustomerSeq.NEXTVAL instead of NULL.

Another major difference between SQL Server and Oracle is in the way they extend SQL. SQL Server uses T-SQL (or Transact-SQL) and Oracle uses PL-SQL. Other DBMS vendors use T-SQL to extend SQL, but only Oracle utilizes PL-SQL. You'll need to know about PL-SQL if you have a need to do more advanced SQL programming, such as procedures, packages, and triggers in Oracle.

Education, Training, and Certification

This book only covers SQL as a language and not specific information on the database management systems that use it. Should you decide to continue to use Oracle, you may need a more specific book about the product. The following are just a few of the hundreds of books available on Oracle and its related technologies:

Title: *Expert One on One: Oracle*
Author(s):   Thomas Kyte
Publisher: Wrox Press
List Price: $59.99

Title: *Learning Oracle PL/SQL*
Author(s):   Bill Pribyl and Steven Feuerstein
Publisher: O'Reilly and Associates
List Price: $39.99

Title: *Beginning Oracle Programming*
Author(s):   Sean Dillon
Publisher: Wrox Press
List Price: $49.99

Title: *Practical Oracle 8: Building Efficient Databases*
Author(s):   Jonathan Lewis
Publisher: Addison-Wesley
List Price: $44.99

Oracle also publishes its own magazine. You can register for the magazine on the Oracle Web site at **www.oracle.com/oramag**.

There are also several training classes available for Oracle. These classes can be taken from Oracle or through an authorized Oracle training center. The Oracle Web site (**www.oracle.com/education/oln**) has all the information on their training and certification offerings. They have instructor-led online training, estudy seminars, and self-paced training available. You can even structure your training to meet your specific certification goals.

Currently, Oracle offers three levels of certification. The associate level requires taking two exams. The professional requires four exams. An on-site exam is required for master certification. The exam must be taken at an Oracle University Education Center. Find out more at **otn.oracle.com/training/content.html**.

SQL Samples in MySQL

Accessing MySQL

MySQL comes with a character-based editor that can be used to communicate with the database. Once MySQL has been installed, there will exist a file named mysql.exe. For the Windows version of MySQL, this file resides in the bin directory under the MySQL directory.

Because the `mysql` editor, or terminal, is character based, it is run from a command prompt. To bring up the editor in Windows, bring up Run from the Start menu and type `c:\MySQL\bin\mysql test`. This allows you into MySQL without needing a login. For other operating systems, please refer to the documentation that comes with the download. It can be found in the docs directory under MySQL.

FIND IT ▶
ONLINE The MySQL documentation can also be found on the MySQL Web site at **www.mysql.com/**. The online documentation is searchable. This makes it much easier to find the exact topic you need.

When you bring up the editor, you will see a prompt, `mysql>`. This is where you type your commands. All commands in MySQL have to be terminated. Unlike SQL Server, where you do not have to have the semicolon at the end of each statement, MySQL will not execute the statement until a terminator is typed in. Once the semicolon is typed, terminating the command, and Return is pressed, the editor automatically runs the command. Should you need to cancel a command, type `/c`.

The best way to enter in the commands needed to set up the sample database is to download the commands for MySQL from the Premier Press Web site (**www.premierpressbooks.com/**). You can copy the commands from the downloaded file and paste them into the editor. Because the editor is running in a shell, however, you will need to access the paste command from the drop-down menu on the title bar (use the far left icon).

If you can download the SQL, you can skip the next section. Should you need to type the commands in yourself, however, the next section will give you all the commands necessary to load up the sample database.

Should you make a mistake while entering the commands that you can't correct, type the following command and start over:

```
DROP DATABASE SlickShop;
```

SQL for the Sample Database

This section will give you the SQL you need to create the database and tables for the Slick Shop sample database. This syntax can also be downloaded from the Premier Press Web site if you'd rather not type it in. The syntax covered here is for MySQL.

To create the database, open the MySQL editor as described previously. Type the command as you see it here and then press Enter on the keyboard:

```
CREATE DATABASE SlickShop;
```

Now that the database is created, tell MySQL that you'd like to use that newly created database. This command tells MySQL which database to use for the commands that you will be executing next. Type the following and press Enter:

```
USE SlickShop;
```

Now you can create the table structures for the sample database. If you'd like to see the graphical representation of those tables, please refer to Figure 1.3 in the Friday Evening session. Type in each code listing as follows:

```
CREATE TABLE StateOrProvince (
StateOrProvince         Char(2)       NOT NULL PRIMARY KEY,
StateOrProvinceName     Varchar(50)   NOT NULL
);

CREATE TABLE Customer (
CustomerID         Integer      AUTO_INCREMENT NOT NULL PRIMARY KEY,
FirstName          Varchar(20)  NULL,
LastName           Varchar(30)  NULL,
Address            Varchar(100) NULL,
City               Varchar(30)  NULL,
StateOrProvince    Char(2)      NULL REFERENCES StateOrProvince
                                (StateOrProvince),
PostalCode         Varchar(10)  NULL,
PhoneNumber        Varchar(10)  NULL
);

CREATE TABLE Vehicle (
VehicleID          Integer      AUTO_INCREMENT NOT NULL PRIMARY KEY,
VehicleYear        SmallInt     NULL,
Make               Varchar(30)  NULL,
Model              Varchar(30)  NULL,
Color              Varchar(30)  NULL,
LicensePlate       Varchar(10)  NULL,
```

```
LastServiceDate    Datetime      NULL,
CustomerID         Integer       NOT NULL
     REFERENCES Customer(CustomerID)
);

CREATE TABLE Service (
ServiceID          Integer       AUTO_INCREMENT NOT NULL PRIMARY KEY,
Description        Varchar(100)  NOT NULL,
RatePerHour        Decimal(5,2)  NOT NULL
);

CREATE TABLE Part (
PartID             Integer       AUTO_INCREMENT NOT NULL PRIMARY KEY,
Description        Varchar(100)  NOT NULL,
Cost               Decimal(5,2)  NOT NULL
);

CREATE TABLE JobTicket (
JobTicketID        Integer       AUTO_INCREMENT NOT NULL PRIMARY KEY,
CustomerID         Integer       NOT NULL REFERENCES Customer
                                 (CustomerID),
StartDate          Datetime      NULL,
EndDate            Datetime      NULL,
VehicleID          Integer       NOT NULL REFERENCES Vehicle
                                 (VehicleID)
);

CREATE TABLE JobTicketDetail (
JobTicketID        Integer       NOT NULL
     REFERENCES JobTicket (JobTicketID),
LineItemNumber     TinyInt       NOT NULL,
ServiceID          Integer       NOT NULL
     REFERENCES Service (ServiceID),
DateComplete       Datetime      NULL,
HoursSpent         Decimal(5,2)  NOT NULL DEFAULT 0,
CONSTRAINT PK_JobTicketDetail PRIMARY KEY (JobTicketID,
     LineItemNumber)
);

CREATE TABLE PartUsed (
JobTicketID        Integer       NOT NULL,
LineItemNumber     TinyInt       NOT NULL,
```

```
PartID            Integer        NOT NULL REFERENCES Part (PartID),
Quantity          TinyInt        NOT NULL,
CONSTRAINT PK_PartUsed PRIMARY KEY (JobTicketID, LineItemNumber,
     PartID),
CONSTRAINT FK_JobTicketDetail_PartUsed FOREIGN KEY (JobTicketID,
     LineItemNumber) REFERENCES JobTicketDetail (JobTicketID,
     LineItemNumber)
);
```

Now that the structures are in place, you can fill them up with the sample data. We've included the INSERT scripts in the following. Simply type them in and execute them, and you will have everything you need to get started. If you'd rather not type all these commands (and why would you?), you can download these statements from the Premier Press Web site.

```
INSERT INTO StateOrProvince VALUES('AB','Alberta');
INSERT INTO StateOrProvince VALUES('BC','British Columbia');
INSERT INTO StateOrProvince VALUES('MB','Manitoba');
INSERT INTO StateOrProvince VALUES('NB','New Brunswick');
INSERT INTO StateOrProvince VALUES('NF','Newfoundland');
INSERT INTO StateOrProvince VALUES('NT','Northwest Territories');
INSERT INTO StateOrProvince VALUES('NS','Nova Scotia');
INSERT INTO StateOrProvince VALUES('NU','Nunavut');
INSERT INTO StateOrProvince VALUES('ON','Ontario');
INSERT INTO StateOrProvince VALUES('PE','Prince Edward Island');
INSERT INTO StateOrProvince VALUES('QC','Quebec');
INSERT INTO StateOrProvince VALUES('SK','Saskatchewan');
INSERT INTO StateOrProvince VALUES('YT','Yukon Territory');
INSERT INTO StateOrProvince VALUES('AL','Alabama');
INSERT INTO StateOrProvince VALUES('AK','Alaska');
INSERT INTO StateOrProvince VALUES('AZ','Arizona');
INSERT INTO StateOrProvince VALUES('AR','Arkansas');
INSERT INTO StateOrProvince VALUES('CA','California');
INSERT INTO StateOrProvince VALUES('CO','Colorado');
INSERT INTO StateOrProvince VALUES('CT','Connecticut');
INSERT INTO StateOrProvince VALUES('DE','Delaware');
INSERT INTO StateOrProvince VALUES('DC','District of Columbia');
INSERT INTO StateOrProvince VALUES('FL','Florida');
INSERT INTO StateOrProvince VALUES('GA','Georgia');
INSERT INTO StateOrProvince VALUES('HI','Hawaii');
INSERT INTO StateOrProvince VALUES('ID','Idaho');
INSERT INTO StateOrProvince VALUES('IL','Illinois');
```

```
INSERT INTO StateOrProvince VALUES('IN','Indiana');
INSERT INTO StateOrProvince VALUES('IA','Iowa');
INSERT INTO StateOrProvince VALUES('KS','Kansas');
INSERT INTO StateOrProvince VALUES('KY','Kentucky');
INSERT INTO StateOrProvince VALUES('LA','Louisiana');
INSERT INTO StateOrProvince VALUES('ME','Maine');
INSERT INTO StateOrProvince VALUES('MD','Maryland');
INSERT INTO StateOrProvince VALUES('MA','Massachusetts');
INSERT INTO StateOrProvince VALUES('MI','Michigan');
INSERT INTO StateOrProvince VALUES('MN','Minnesota');
INSERT INTO StateOrProvince VALUES('MS','Mississippi');
INSERT INTO StateOrProvince VALUES('MO','Missouri');
INSERT INTO StateOrProvince VALUES('MT','Montana');
INSERT INTO StateOrProvince VALUES('NE','Nebraska');
INSERT INTO StateOrProvince VALUES('NV','Nevada');
INSERT INTO StateOrProvince VALUES('NH','New Hampshire');
INSERT INTO StateOrProvince VALUES('NJ','New Jersey');
INSERT INTO StateOrProvince VALUES('NM','New Mexico');
INSERT INTO StateOrProvince VALUES('NY','New York');
INSERT INTO StateOrProvince VALUES('NC','North Carolina');
INSERT INTO StateOrProvince VALUES('ND','North Dakota');
INSERT INTO StateOrProvince VALUES('OH','Ohio');
INSERT INTO StateOrProvince VALUES('OK','Oklahoma');
INSERT INTO StateOrProvince VALUES('OR','Oregon');
INSERT INTO StateOrProvince VALUES('PA','Pennsylvania');
INSERT INTO StateOrProvince VALUES('RI','Rhode Island');
INSERT INTO StateOrProvince VALUES('SC','South Carolina');
INSERT INTO StateOrProvince VALUES('SD','South Dakota');
INSERT INTO StateOrProvince VALUES('TN','Tennessee');
INSERT INTO StateOrProvince VALUES('TX','Texas');
INSERT INTO StateOrProvince VALUES('UT','Utah');
INSERT INTO StateOrProvince VALUES('VT','Vermont');
INSERT INTO StateOrProvince VALUES('VA','Virginia');
INSERT INTO StateOrProvince VALUES('WA','Washington');
INSERT INTO StateOrProvince VALUES('WV','West Virginia');
INSERT INTO StateOrProvince VALUES('WI','Wisconsin');
INSERT INTO StateOrProvince VALUES('WY','Wyoming');
INSERT INTO Customer (FirstName, LastName, Address, City,
                      StateOrProvince, PostalCode, PhoneNumber )
      VALUES ('John', 'Smith', '10341 Crestpoint Boulevard',
              'North Beach', 'VA', '10234', '1022341234');
```

```
INSERT INTO Customer (FirstName, LastName, Address, City,
                      StateOrProvince, PostalCode, PhoneNumber )
    VALUES ('Jacob', 'Salter', '234 North Main', 'Groveland', null,
            '45678', '7665554444');

INSERT INTO Customer (FirstName, LastName, Address, City,
                      StateOrProvince, PostalCode, PhoneNumber )
    VALUES ('Victoria', 'Smithe', '14301 Mountain Ridge Court',
            'Huntington', 'WV', '22211', '2175438679');

INSERT INTO Customer (FirstName, LastName, Address, City,
                      StateOrProvince, PostalCode, PhoneNumber )
    VALUES ('Bryce', 'Hatfield', '566 Pine Road', 'Marion', 'IN',
            null, null);

INSERT INTO Customer (FirstName, LastName, Address, City,
                      StateOrProvince, PostalCode, PhoneNumber )
    VALUES ('Kylee', 'Dicken', null, 'Upland', 'IN', '46905',
            '7654321098');

INSERT INTO Customer (FirstName, LastName, Address, City,
                      StateOrProvince, PostalCode, PhoneNumber )
    VALUES ('Alex', 'Thompson', null, null, 'IN', null,
            '3175551213');

INSERT INTO Customer (FirstName, LastName, Address, City,
                      StateOrProvince, PostalCode, PhoneNumber )
    VALUES ('Davis', 'Thompson', '298 North Broadway', 'Greensburg',
            'IN', '46514', '3175551214');

INSERT INTO Customer (FirstName, LastName, Address, City,
                      StateOrProvince, PostalCode, PhoneNumber )
    VALUES ('Harrison', 'Thompson', '345 Hawks Point Drive Apt B',
            'Indianapolis', 'IN', '46123', '3175551215');

INSERT INTO Vehicle (VehicleYear, Make, Model, Color,
                     LicensePlate, LastServiceDate, CustomerID)
    VALUES ('2000', 'Chevrolet', 'S-10', 'Purple', 'TROJANS',
            '2001-8-13', 4);
```

```
INSERT INTO Vehicle (VehicleYear, Make, Model, Color,
                     LicensePlate, LastServiceDate, CustomerID)
     VALUES ('1998', 'Ford', 'Mustang', 'Red', 'HH7832',
             '2001-9-16', 2);

INSERT INTO Vehicle (VehicleYear, Make, Model, Color,
                     LicensePlate, LastServiceDate, CustomerID)
     VALUES ('2002', 'Pontiac', 'Grand Prix', 'Black', 'GOPRDUE',
             '2002-5-21', 5);

INSERT INTO Vehicle (VehicleYear, Make, Model, Color,
                     LicensePlate, LastServiceDate, CustomerID)
     VALUES ('1968', 'Chevrolet', 'Corvette', 'Black', 'KODIAK',
             '2002-1-20', 1);

INSERT INTO Vehicle (VehicleYear, Make, Model, Color,
                     LicensePlate, LastServiceDate, CustomerID)
     VALUES ('2002', 'Nissan', 'Altima', 'White', 'HEYDARE',
             '2002-1-26', 3);

INSERT INTO Vehicle (VehicleYear, Make, Model, Color,
                     LicensePlate, LastServiceDate, CustomerID)
     VALUES ('2000', 'Chrysler', 'PT Cruiser', 'Black', 'ALEX T',
             '2002-5-15', 6);

INSERT INTO Vehicle (VehicleYear, Make, Model, Color,
                     LicensePlate, LastServiceDate, CustomerID)
     VALUES ('2002', 'Chevrolet', 'Trail Blazer', 'Green', 'I TRADE',
             '2001-5-31', 8);

INSERT INTO Vehicle (VehicleYear, Make, Model, Color,
                     LicensePlate, LastServiceDate, CustomerID)
     VALUES ('2001', 'Ford', 'Expedition', 'Maroon', 'DAVIS T',
             '2001-5-31', 7);

INSERT INTO Vehicle (VehicleYear, Make, Model, Color,
                     LicensePlate, LastServiceDate, CustomerID)
     VALUES ('1972', 'AMC', 'Gremlin', 'Pink', 'UGOGIRL',
             '2002-2-17', 4);

INSERT INTO Service (Description, RatePerHour)
     VALUES ('Oil Change', 60.00);
```

```
INSERT INTO Service (Description, RatePerHour)
    VALUES ('Replace Wiperblades', 10.00);

INSERT INTO Service (Description, RatePerHour)
    VALUES ('Replace Air Filter', 10.00);

INSERT INTO Service (Description, RatePerHour)
    VALUES ('Change PVC Valve', 10.00);

INSERT INTO Service (Description, RatePerHour)
    VALUES ('Change and Flush Cooling System', 60.00);

INSERT INTO Service (Description, RatePerHour)
    VALUES ('Change and Flush Differential', 60.00);

INSERT INTO Part (Description, Cost)
    VALUES ('Protects 10w-30 Oil', 7.49);

INSERT INTO Part (Description, Cost)
    VALUES ('Protects 10w-40 Oil', 7.49);

INSERT INTO Part (Description, Cost)
    VALUES ('Black Gold 10w-30 Oil', 7.99);

INSERT INTO Part (Description, Cost)
    VALUES ('Black Gold 10w-40 Oil', 7.99);

INSERT INTO Part (Description, Cost)
    VALUES ('Motion Synthetic Oil 10w-30', 13.99);

INSERT INTO Part (Description, Cost)
    VALUES ('Motion Synthetic Oil 10w-40', 13.99);

INSERT INTO Part (Description, Cost)
    VALUES ('Texas Tea Economy Oil Filter', 3.99);

INSERT INTO Part (Description, Cost)
    VALUES ('ACME Oil Filter', 4.99);

INSERT INTO Part (Description, Cost)
    VALUES ('ACME Air Filter', 8.99);
```

```
INSERT INTO Part (Description, Cost)
    VALUES ('ACME Wiper Blades', 9.99);

INSERT INTO Part (Description, Cost)
    VALUES ('ACME Brake Fluid', 0.00);

INSERT INTO Part (Description, Cost)
    VALUES ('ACME Transmission Fluid', 0.00);

INSERT INTO Part (Description, Cost)
    VALUES ('ACME Coolant', 0.00);

INSERT INTO Part (Description, Cost)
    VALUES ('ACME Windshield Fluid', 0.00);

INSERT INTO Part (Description, Cost)
    VALUES ('ACME Differential Fluid', 0.00);

INSERT INTO Part (Description, Cost)
    VALUES ('ACME PVC Valve', 12.99);

INSERT INTO JobTicket (CustomerID, StartDate, EndDate, VehicleID)
    VALUES (1, '2002-1-20', '2002-1-20', 4);

INSERT INTO JobTicket (CustomerID, StartDate, EndDate, VehicleID)
    VALUES (1, '2001-7-20', '2001-7-20', 4);

INSERT INTO JobTicket (CustomerID, StartDate, EndDate, VehicleID)
    VALUES (2, '2001-9-16', '2001-9-16', 2);

INSERT INTO JobTicket (CustomerID, StartDate, EndDate, VehicleID)
    VALUES (3, '2002-1-26', '2002-1-26', 5);

INSERT INTO JobTicket (CustomerID, StartDate, EndDate, VehicleID)
    VALUES (5, '2002-5-21', '2002-5-21', 3);

INSERT INTO JobTicket (CustomerID, StartDate, EndDate, VehicleID)
    VALUES (4, '2001-8-13', '2001-8-13', 1);

INSERT INTO JobTicket (CustomerID, StartDate, EndDate, VehicleID)
    VALUES (4, '2002-2-16', '2002-2-17', 9);
```

```
INSERT INTO JobTicketDetail (JobTicketID, LineItemNumber, ServiceID,
                             DateComplete, HoursSpent)
    VALUES (1, 1, 1, '2002-1-20', .5);

INSERT INTO JobTicketDetail (JobTicketID, LineItemNumber, ServiceID,
                             DateComplete, HoursSpent)
    VALUES (2, 1, 1, '2001-7-20', .25);

INSERT INTO JobTicketDetail (JobTicketID, LineItemNumber, ServiceID,
                             DateComplete, HoursSpent)
    VALUES (2, 2, 3, '2001-7-20', .1);

INSERT INTO JobTicketDetail (JobTicketID, LineItemNumber, ServiceID,
                             DateComplete, HoursSpent)
    VALUES (2, 3, 4, '2001-7-20', .1);

INSERT INTO JobTicketDetail (JobTicketID, LineItemNumber, ServiceID,
                             DateComplete, HoursSpent)
    VALUES (3, 1, 1, '2001-9-16', .25);

INSERT INTO JobTicketDetail (JobTicketID, LineItemNumber, ServiceID,
                             DateComplete, HoursSpent)
    VALUES (4, 1, 1, '2002-1-26', .25);

INSERT INTO JobTicketDetail (JobTicketID, LineItemNumber, ServiceID,
                             DateComplete, HoursSpent)
    VALUES (5, 1, 2, '2002-5-21', .2);

INSERT INTO JobTicketDetail (JobTicketID, LineItemNumber, ServiceID,
                             DateComplete, HoursSpent)
    VALUES (5, 2, 1, '2002-5-21', .25);

INSERT INTO JobTicketDetail (JobTicketID, LineItemNumber, ServiceID,
                             DateComplete, HoursSpent)
    VALUES (6, 1, 5, '2001-8-13', 1.15);

INSERT INTO JobTicketDetail (JobTicketID, LineItemNumber, ServiceID,
                             DateComplete, HoursSpent)
    VALUES (7, 1, 1, '2002-2-16', .35);
```

```
INSERT INTO JobTicketDetail (JobTicketID, LineItemNumber, ServiceID,
                             DateComplete, HoursSpent)
     VALUES (7, 2, 3, '2002-2-16', .1);

INSERT INTO JobTicketDetail (JobTicketID, LineItemNumber, ServiceID,
                             DateComplete, HoursSpent)
     VALUES (7, 3, 4, '2002-2-16', .15);

INSERT INTO JobTicketDetail (JobTicketID, LineItemNumber, ServiceID,
                             DateComplete, HoursSpent)
     VALUES (7, 4, 6, '2002-2-16', 1.0);

INSERT INTO JobTicketDetail (JobTicketID, LineItemNumber, ServiceID,
                             DateComplete, HoursSpent)
     VALUES (7, 5, 5, '2002-2-17', .5);

INSERT INTO PartUsed (JobTicketID, LineItemNumber, PartID, Quantity)
     VALUES (1, 1, 4, 4);

INSERT INTO PartUsed (JobTicketID, LineItemNumber, PartID, Quantity)
     VALUES (1, 1, 7, 1);

INSERT INTO PartUsed (JobTicketID, LineItemNumber, PartID, Quantity)
     VALUES (1, 1, 11, 1);

INSERT INTO PartUsed (JobTicketID, LineItemNumber, PartID, Quantity)
     VALUES (1, 1, 12, 1);

INSERT INTO PartUsed (JobTicketID, LineItemNumber, PartID, Quantity)
     VALUES (2, 1, 5, 4);

INSERT INTO PartUsed (JobTicketID, LineItemNumber, PartID, Quantity)
     VALUES (2, 1, 14, 1);

INSERT INTO PartUsed (JobTicketID, LineItemNumber, PartID, Quantity)
     VALUES (2, 1, 8, 1);

INSERT INTO PartUsed (JobTicketID, LineItemNumber, PartID, Quantity)
     VALUES (2, 2, 9, 1);

INSERT INTO PartUsed (JobTicketID, LineItemNumber, PartID, Quantity)
     VALUES (2, 3, 16, 1);
```

```
INSERT INTO PartUsed (JobTicketID, LineItemNumber, PartID, Quantity)
    VALUES (3, 1, 6, 4);

INSERT INTO PartUsed (JobTicketID, LineItemNumber, PartID, Quantity)
    VALUES (3, 1, 7, 1);

INSERT INTO PartUsed (JobTicketID, LineItemNumber, PartID, Quantity)
    VALUES (4, 1, 1, 4);

INSERT INTO PartUsed (JobTicketID, LineItemNumber, PartID, Quantity)
    VALUES (4, 1, 8, 1);

INSERT INTO PartUsed (JobTicketID, LineItemNumber, PartID, Quantity)
    VALUES (5, 1, 10, 1);

INSERT INTO PartUsed (JobTicketID, LineItemNumber, PartID, Quantity)
    VALUES (5, 2, 3, 4);

INSERT INTO PartUsed (JobTicketID, LineItemNumber, PartID, Quantity)
    VALUES (5, 2, 14, 1);

INSERT INTO PartUsed (JobTicketID, LineItemNumber, PartID, Quantity)
    VALUES (5, 2, 12, 1);

INSERT INTO PartUsed (JobTicketID, LineItemNumber, PartID, Quantity)
    VALUES (5, 2, 8, 1);

INSERT INTO PartUsed (JobTicketID, LineItemNumber, PartID, Quantity)
    VALUES (6, 1, 13, 1);

INSERT INTO PartUsed (JobTicketID, LineItemNumber, PartID, Quantity)
    VALUES (7, 1, 1, 4);

INSERT INTO PartUsed (JobTicketID, LineItemNumber, PartID, Quantity)
    VALUES (7, 1, 8, 1);

INSERT INTO PartUsed (JobTicketID, LineItemNumber, PartID, Quantity)
    VALUES (7, 1, 14, 1);

INSERT INTO PartUsed (JobTicketID, LineItemNumber, PartID, Quantity)
    VALUES (7, 1, 12, 1);
```

```
INSERT INTO PartUsed (JobTicketID, LineItemNumber, PartID, Quantity)
    VALUES (7, 2, 9, 1);

INSERT INTO PartUsed (JobTicketID, LineItemNumber, PartID, Quantity)
    VALUES (7, 3, 16, 1);

INSERT INTO PartUsed (JobTicketID, LineItemNumber, PartID, Quantity)
    VALUES (7, 4, 15, 1);

INSERT INTO PartUsed (JobTicketID, LineItemNumber, PartID, Quantity)
    VALUES (7, 5, 13, 1);
```

Your sample database is now ready to use. Enjoy!

Differences in MySQL

There are a few things we had to change in the syntax for the sample database so it could be used in MySQL. We would like to highlight those changes so you can be aware of the differences as you go through the text in the book.

MySQL has a more limited set of data types. The Money data type and the SmallDatetime data type mean nothing to MySQL. Money was changed to Decimal(5,2) for the RatePerHour column in the Service table and also the Cost column in the Part table. The SmallDatetime data type was changed to just Datetime. This affected the DateComplete column in JobTicketDetail and the StartDate and EndDate columns of the JobTicket table. The LastServiceDate column in Vehicle also required this change. In addition, the pound sign had to be removed from the end of the LicensePlate# column in Vehicle. MySQL does not like this special character in the column name.

There are some topics covered in this book that MySQL does not support. The makers of MySQL plan to support some in the future. Others, they feel they do not need to provide support for at all. You can check the MySQL Web site for the current status of their plans on each of these items.

The following is a list of the unsupported items in MySQL to date:

➤ Subqueries

➤ Stored procedures

➤ Triggers

➤ Foreign keys

➤ Views

Education, Training, and Certification

This book only covers SQL as a language and not specific information on the database management systems that use it. Should you decide to continue to use MySQL, you may need a more specific book about the product. Following is a list of some of the books available on MySQL:

Title:	*PHP and MySQL Web Development*
Author(s):	Luke Welling and Laura Thomson
Publisher:	Sams
List Price:	$49.99

Title:	*MySQL*
Author(s):	Paul Dubois and Michael Widenius
Publisher:	New Riders
List Price:	$49.99

Title:	*MySQL and mSQL*
Author(s):	Randy Jay Yager, George Reese, Tim King, and Andy Oram
Publisher:	O'Reilly
List Price:	$34.99

Title:	*Sams' Teach Yourself MySQL in 21 Days*
Author(s):	Mark Maslakowski and Tony Butcher
Publisher:	Sams
List Price:	$39.99

Title: *MySQL*
Author(s):   Michael Kofler
Publisher: APress
List Price: $39.95

The MySQL Web site contains a list of articles aimed at all levels of developers. The list of articles can be found at **www.mysql.com/articles/**. If you are looking for something more structured or detailed, there is online, CD-ROM, and instructor-led training available for MySQL. Classes are held at Authorized MySQL Training Centers. You can also request in-house training should this be necessary. Check out **www.mysql.com/training/index.html** for more information.

MySQL is in the process of offering a certification path. They plan to release the curriculum later this year (2002). The proposed certifications are Certified MySQL Database Administrator and Certified MySQL Database Developer.

SQL Samples in Sybase SQL Anywhere

Accessing SQL Anywhere

SQL Anywhere comes with a graphical editor called Interactive SQL (or ISQL). It is used to execute commands or view data in the database. You can find it on the Start menu under Programs, Sybase SQL Anywhere 7, Adaptive Anywhere 7, Interactive SQL.

When ISQL starts, it asks you to log in. By default it has installed a sample database, so you can log in to that database by typing in dba for the username and sql for the password. You can select the ODBC Data Source Name from the list. Pick either data source. This is demonstrated in Figure D.1.

Once logged in to ISQL, you will see a three-pane window as in Figure D.2. The top pane allows you to enter SQL commands. The middle pane is used to display messages, and the bottom pane is for output.

In ISQL, you execute commands by typing them in the top pane and clicking the Execute button on the toolbar (or by selecting SQL, Execute from the menu). You can also load in a script by selecting File, Open from the menu. Should you need to stop the execution of a statement or script, click the Interrupt button on the toolbar.

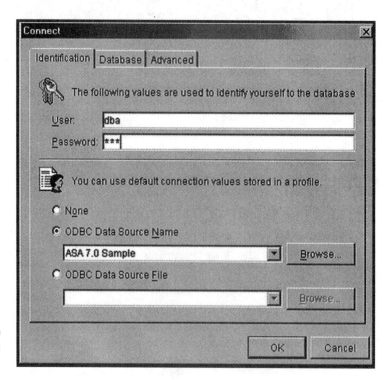

Figure D.1

The ISQL Connect dialog box.

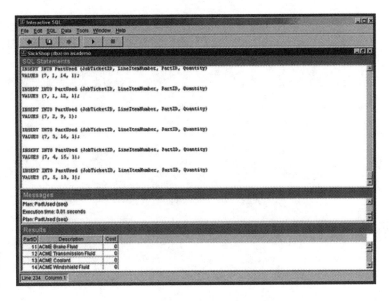

Figure D.2

The ISQL window.

The best way to enter in the commands needed to set up the sample database is to download the commands for SQL Anywhere from the Premier Press Web site (**www.premierpressbooks.com/**). You can open the file in ISQL as just described. Click on Execute and the sample database is ready.

First, however, you have to create the database in ISQL. This is very different, so you'll have to do this separate from the rest of the statements. In the top pane, type the following and click Execute on the toolbar:

```
CREATE DATABASE 'C:\\SlickShop'
```

You have to connect to the Slick Shop database to execute the rest of the statements. On the menu, select File, New Window. The Connect dialog box displays. Type in DBA for the username and SQL for the password. Instead of selecting an ODBC data source, you need to select a database. Click on the Database tab. For Database Filename, type in C:\SlickShop.db or click on Browse to select it from the Open File dialog box. The Database tab is shown in Figure D.3. Now click on OK. The title over the panes shows that you are now connected to the Slick Shop database.

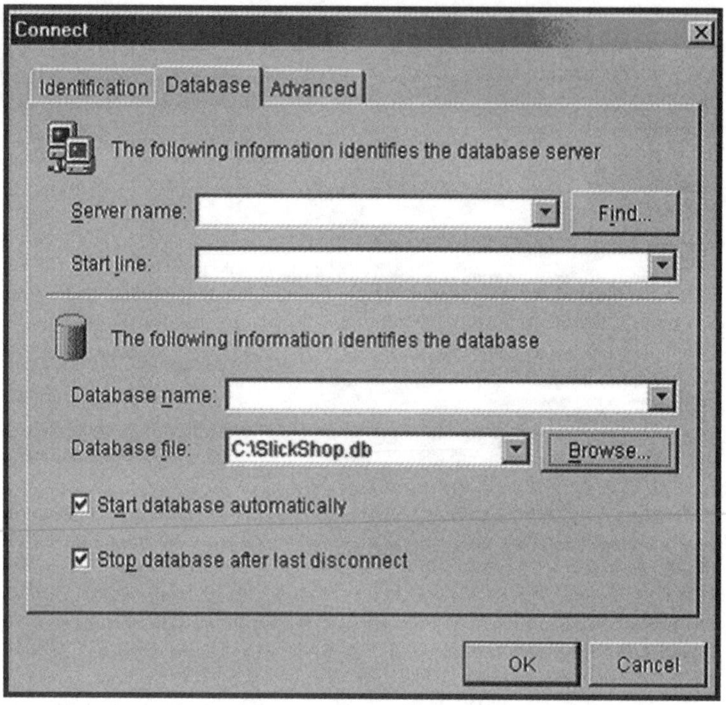

Figure D.3

The Database tab
on the Connect
dialog box.

If you can download the SQL, you can skip the next section. Should you need to type the commands in yourself, however, the next section will give you all the commands necessary to load up the sample database.

Should you make a mistake while entering the commands that you can't correct, type the following command and start over:

```
DROP DATABASE SlickShop;
```

SQL for the Sample Database

This section will give you the SQL you need to create the database and tables for the Slick Shop sample database. This syntax can also be downloaded from the Premier Press Web site if you'd rather not type it. The syntax covered here is for Sybase SQL Anywhere; however, this should work fine in Sybase as well.

If you haven't already created the database, do so now. The steps are described in the previous section.

Now you can create the table structures for the sample database. If you'd like to see the graphical representation of those tables, please refer to Figure 1.3 in the Friday Evening session. Type in each code listing as follows:

```
CREATE TABLE StateOrProvince (
StateOrProvince        Char(2)      NOT NULL PRIMARY KEY CLUSTERED,
StateOrProvinceName    Varchar(50)  NOT NULL
);


CREATE TABLE Customer (
CustomerID             Integer      IDENTITY NOT NULL
       PRIMARY KEY CLUSTERED,
FirstName              Varchar(20)  NULL,
LastName               Varchar(30)  NULL,
Address                Varchar(100) NULL,
City                   Varchar(30)  NULL,
StateOrProvince        Char(2)      NULL
       REFERENCES StateOrProvince (StateOrProvince),
PostalCode             Varchar(10)  NULL,
PhoneNumber            Varchar(10   NULL
);


CREATE TABLE Vehicle (
VehicleID              Integer      IDENTITY NOT NULL
       PRIMARY KEY CLUSTERED,
VehicleYear            SmallInt     NULL,
Make                   Varchar(30)  NULL,
Model                  Varchar(30)  NULL,
Color                  Varchar(30)  NULL,
LicensePlate#          Varchar(10)  NULL,
LastServiceDate        Smalldatetime NULL,
CustomerID             Integer      NOT NULL
       REFERENCES Customer (CustomerID)
);


CREATE TABLE Service (
ServiceID              Integer      IDENTITY NOT NULL
       PRIMARY KEY CLUSTERED,
```

```
Description             Varchar(100)     NOT NULL,
RatePerHour             Money            NOT NULL
);

CREATE TABLE Part (
PartID                  Integer          IDENTITY NOT NULL
     PRIMARY KEY CLUSTERED,
Description             Varchar(100)     NOT NULL,
Cost                    Money            NOT NULL
);

CREATE TABLE JobTicket (
JobTicketID             Integer          IDENTITY NOT NULL
     PRIMARY KEY CLUSTERED,
CustomerID              Integer          NOT NULL
     REFERENCES Customer (CustomerID),
StartDate               Smalldatetime    NULL,
EndDate                 Smalldatetime    NULL,
VehicleID               Integer          NOT NULL
     REFERENCES Vehicle (VehicleID)
);

CREATE TABLE JobTicketDetail (
JobTicketID             Integer          NOT NULL
     REFERENCES JobTicket (JobTicketID),
LineItemNumber          TinyInt          NOT NULL,
ServiceID               Integer          NOT NULL
     REFERENCES Service (ServiceID),
DateComplete            Smalldatetime    NULL,
HoursSpent              Decimal(5,2)     NOT NULL DEFAULT 0,
CONSTRAINT PK_JobTicketDetail PRIMARY KEY (JobTicketID,
     LineItemNumber)
);

CREATE TABLE PartUsed (
JobTicketID             Integer          NOT NULL,
LineItemNumber          TinyInt          NOT NULL,
PartID                  Integer          NOT NULL REFERENCES Part (PartID),
Quantity                TinyInt          NOT NULL,
CONSTRAINT PK_PartUsed PRIMARY KEY (JobTicketID, LineItemNumber,
     PartID),
```

```
CONSTRAINT FK_JobTicketDetail_PartUsed FOREIGN KEY (JobTicketID,
     LineItemNumber)
REFERENCES JobTicketDetail (JobTicketID, LineItemNumber)
);
```

Now that the structures are in place, you can fill them up with the sample data. We've included the INSERT scripts in the following. Simply type them in and execute them, and you will have everything you need to get started. If you'd rather not type all these commands (and why would you?), you can download these statements from the Premier Press Web site.

```
INSERT INTO StateOrProvince VALUES('AB','Alberta');
INSERT INTO StateOrProvince VALUES('BC','British Columbia');
INSERT INTO StateOrProvince VALUES('MB','Manitoba');
INSERT INTO StateOrProvince VALUES('NB','New Brunswick');
INSERT INTO StateOrProvince VALUES('NF','Newfoundland');
INSERT INTO StateOrProvince VALUES('NT','Northwest Territories');
INSERT INTO StateOrProvince VALUES('NS','Nova Scotia');
INSERT INTO StateOrProvince VALUES('NU','Nunavut');
INSERT INTO StateOrProvince VALUES('ON','Ontario');
INSERT INTO StateOrProvince VALUES('PE','Prince Edward Island');
INSERT INTO StateOrProvince VALUES('QC','Quebec');
INSERT INTO StateOrProvince VALUES('SK','Saskatchewan');
INSERT INTO StateOrProvince VALUES('YT','Yukon Territory');
INSERT INTO StateOrProvince VALUES('AL','Alabama');
INSERT INTO StateOrProvince VALUES('AK','Alaska');
INSERT INTO StateOrProvince VALUES('AZ','Arizona');
INSERT INTO StateOrProvince VALUES('AR','Arkansas');
INSERT INTO StateOrProvince VALUES('CA','California');
INSERT INTO StateOrProvince VALUES('CO','Colorado');
INSERT INTO StateOrProvince VALUES('CT','Connecticut');
INSERT INTO StateOrProvince VALUES('DE','Delaware');
INSERT INTO StateOrProvince VALUES('DC','District of Columbia');
INSERT INTO StateOrProvince VALUES('FL','Florida');
INSERT INTO StateOrProvince VALUES('GA','Georgia');
INSERT INTO StateOrProvince VALUES('HI','Hawaii');
INSERT INTO StateOrProvince VALUES('ID','Idaho');
INSERT INTO StateOrProvince VALUES('IL','Illinois');
INSERT INTO StateOrProvince VALUES('IN','Indiana');
INSERT INTO StateOrProvince VALUES('IA','Iowa');
INSERT INTO StateOrProvince VALUES('KS','Kansas');
INSERT INTO StateOrProvince VALUES('KY','Kentucky');
```

```
INSERT INTO StateOrProvince VALUES('LA','Louisiana');
INSERT INTO StateOrProvince VALUES('ME','Maine');
INSERT INTO StateOrProvince VALUES('MD','Maryland');
INSERT INTO StateOrProvince VALUES('MA','Massachusetts');
INSERT INTO StateOrProvince VALUES('MI','Michigan');
INSERT INTO StateOrProvince VALUES('MN','Minnesota');
INSERT INTO StateOrProvince VALUES('MS','Mississippi');
INSERT INTO StateOrProvince VALUES('MO','Missouri');
INSERT INTO StateOrProvince VALUES('MT','Montana');
INSERT INTO StateOrProvince VALUES('NE','Nebraska');
INSERT INTO StateOrProvince VALUES('NV','Nevada');
INSERT INTO StateOrProvince VALUES('NH','New Hampshire');
INSERT INTO StateOrProvince VALUES('NJ','New Jersey');
INSERT INTO StateOrProvince VALUES('NM','New Mexico');
INSERT INTO StateOrProvince VALUES('NY','New York');
INSERT INTO StateOrProvince VALUES('NC','North Carolina');
INSERT INTO StateOrProvince VALUES('ND','North Dakota');
INSERT INTO StateOrProvince VALUES('OH','Ohio');
INSERT INTO StateOrProvince VALUES('OK','Oklahoma');
INSERT INTO StateOrProvince VALUES('OR','Oregon');
INSERT INTO StateOrProvince VALUES('PA','Pennsylvania');
INSERT INTO StateOrProvince VALUES('RI','Rhode Island');
INSERT INTO StateOrProvince VALUES('SC','South Carolina');
INSERT INTO StateOrProvince VALUES('SD','South Dakota');
INSERT INTO StateOrProvince VALUES('TN','Tennessee');
INSERT INTO StateOrProvince VALUES('TX','Texas');
INSERT INTO StateOrProvince VALUES('UT','Utah');
INSERT INTO StateOrProvince VALUES('VT','Vermont');
INSERT INTO StateOrProvince VALUES('VA','Virginia');
INSERT INTO StateOrProvince VALUES('WA','Washington');
INSERT INTO StateOrProvince VALUES('WV','West Virginia');
INSERT INTO StateOrProvince VALUES('WI','Wisconsin');
INSERT INTO StateOrProvince VALUES('WY','Wyoming');
INSERT INTO Customer (FirstName, LastName, Address, City,
                     StateOrProvince, PostalCode, PhoneNumber )
     VALUES ('John', 'Smith', '10341 Crestpoint Boulevard',
             'North Beach', 'VA', '10234', '1022341234');

INSERT INTO Customer (FirstName, LastName, Address, City,
                     StateOrProvince, PostalCode, PhoneNumber )
     VALUES ('Jacob', 'Salter', '234 North Main', 'Groveland',
             null, '45678', '7665554444');
```

```
INSERT INTO Customer (FirstName, LastName, Address, City,
                      StateOrProvince, PostalCode, PhoneNumber )
   VALUES ('Victoria', 'Smithe', '14301 Mountain Ridge
           Court', 'Huntington', 'WV', '22211', '2175438679');

INSERT INTO Customer (FirstName, LastName, Address, City,
                      StateOrProvince, PostalCode, PhoneNumber )
   VALUES ('Bryce', 'Hatfield', '566 Pine Road', 'Marion',
           'IN', null, null);

INSERT INTO Customer (FirstName, LastName, Address, City,
                      StateOrProvince, PostalCode, PhoneNumber )
   VALUES ('Kylee', 'Dicken', null, 'Upland', 'IN', '46905',
           '7654321098');

INSERT INTO Customer (FirstName, LastName, Address, City,
                      StateOrProvince, PostalCode, PhoneNumber )
   VALUES ('Alex', 'Thompson', null, null, 'IN', null,
           '3175551213');

INSERT INTO Customer (FirstName, LastName, Address, City,
                      StateOrProvince, PostalCode, PhoneNumber )
   VALUES ('Davis', 'Thompson', '298 North Broadway',
           'Greensburg', 'IN', '46514', '3175551214');

INSERT INTO Customer (FirstName, LastName, Address, City,
                      StateOrProvince, PostalCode, PhoneNumber )
   VALUES ('Harrison', 'Thompson', '345 Hawks Point Drive
           Apt B', 'Indianapolis', 'IN', '46123', '3175551215');

INSERT INTO Vehicle (VehicleYear, Make, Model, Color,
                     LicensePlate#, LastServiceDate, CustomerID)
   VALUES ('2000', 'Chevrolet', 'S-10', 'Purple', 'TROJANS',
           '2001-8-13', 4);

INSERT INTO Vehicle (VehicleYear, Make, Model, Color,
                     LicensePlate#, LastServiceDate, CustomerID)
   VALUES ('1998', 'Ford', 'Mustang', 'Red', 'HH7832',
           '2001-9-16', 2);
```

```
INSERT INTO Vehicle (VehicleYear, Make, Model, Color,
                     LicensePlate#, LastServiceDate, CustomerID)
     VALUES ('2002', 'Pontiac', 'Grand Prix', 'Black', 'GOPRDUE',
             '2002-5-21', 5);

INSERT INTO Vehicle (VehicleYear, Make, Model, Color,
                     LicensePlate#, LastServiceDate, CustomerID)
     VALUES ('1968', 'Chevrolet', 'Corvette', 'Black', 'KODIAK',
             '2002-1-20', 1);

INSERT INTO Vehicle (VehicleYear, Make, Model, Color,
                     LicensePlate#, LastServiceDate, CustomerID)
     VALUES ('2002', 'Nissan', 'Altima', 'White', 'HEYDARE',
             '2002-1-26', 3);

INSERT INTO Vehicle (VehicleYear, Make, Model, Color,
                     LicensePlate#, LastServiceDate, CustomerID)
     VALUES ('2000', 'Chrysler', 'PT Cruiser', 'Black', 'ALEX T',
             '2002-5-15', 6);

INSERT INTO Vehicle (VehicleYear, Make, Model, Color,
                     LicensePlate#, LastServiceDate, CustomerID)
     VALUES ('2002', 'Chevrolet', 'Trail Blazer', 'Green',
             'I TRADE', '2001-5-31', 8);

INSERT INTO Vehicle (VehicleYear, Make, Model, Color,
                     LicensePlate#, LastServiceDate, CustomerID)
     VALUES ('2001', 'Ford', 'Expedition', 'Maroon', 'DAVIS T',
             '2001-5-31', 7);

INSERT INTO Vehicle (VehicleYear, Make, Model, Color,
                     LicensePlate#, LastServiceDate, CustomerID)
     VALUES ('1972', 'AMC', 'Gremlin', 'Pink', 'UGOGIRL',
             '2002-2-17', 4);

INSERT INTO Service (Description, RatePerHour)
     VALUES ('Oil Change', 60.00);

INSERT INTO Service (Description, RatePerHour)
     VALUES ('Replace Wiperblades', 10.00);
```

```
INSERT INTO Service (Description, RatePerHour)
    VALUES ('Replace Air Filter', 10.00);

INSERT INTO Service (Description, RatePerHour)
    VALUES ('Change PVC Valve', 10.00);

INSERT INTO Service (Description, RatePerHour)
    VALUES ('Change and Flush Cooling System', 60.00);

INSERT INTO Service (Description, RatePerHour)
    VALUES ('Change and Flush Differential', 60.00);

INSERT INTO Part (Description, Cost)
    VALUES ('Protects 10w-30 Oil', 7.49);

INSERT INTO Part (Description, Cost)
    VALUES ('Protects 10w-40 Oil', 7.49);

INSERT INTO Part (Description, Cost)
    VALUES ('Black Gold 10w-30 Oil', 7.99);

INSERT INTO Part (Description, Cost)
    VALUES ('Black Gold 10w-40 Oil', 7.99);

INSERT INTO Part (Description, Cost)
    VALUES ('Motion Synthetic Oil 10w-30', 13.99);
INSERT INTO Part (Description, Cost)
    VALUES ('Motion Synthetic Oil 10w-40', 13.99);

INSERT INTO Part (Description, Cost)
    VALUES ('Texas Tea Economy Oil Filter', 3.99);

INSERT INTO Part (Description, Cost)
    VALUES ('ACME Oil Filter', 4.99);

INSERT INTO Part (Description, Cost)
    VALUES ('ACME Air Filter', 8.99);

INSERT INTO Part (Description, Cost)
    VALUES ('ACME Wiper Blades', 9.99);
```

```
INSERT INTO Part (Description, Cost)
     VALUES ('ACME Brake Fluid', 0.00);

INSERT INTO Part (Description, Cost)
     VALUES ('ACME Transmission Fluid', 0.00);

INSERT INTO Part (Description, Cost)
     VALUES ('ACME Coolant', 0.00);

INSERT INTO Part (Description, Cost)
     VALUES ('ACME Windshield Fluid', 0.00);

INSERT INTO Part (Description, Cost)
     VALUES ('ACME Differential Fluid', 0.00);

INSERT INTO Part (Description, Cost)
     VALUES ('ACME PVC Valve', 12.99);

INSERT INTO JobTicket (CustomerID, StartDate, EndDate, VehicleID)
     VALUES (1, '2002-1-20', '2002-1-20', 4);

INSERT INTO JobTicket (CustomerID, StartDate, EndDate, VehicleID)
     VALUES (1, '2001-7-20', '2001-7-20', 4);

INSERT INTO JobTicket (CustomerID, StartDate, EndDate, VehicleID)
     VALUES (2, '2001-9-16', '2001-9-16', 2);

INSERT INTO JobTicket (CustomerID, StartDate, EndDate, VehicleID)
     VALUES (3, '2002-1-26', '2002-1-26', 5);

INSERT INTO JobTicket (CustomerID, StartDate, EndDate, VehicleID)
     VALUES (5, '2002-5-21', '2002-5-21', 3);

INSERT INTO JobTicket (CustomerID, StartDate, EndDate, VehicleID)
     VALUES (4, '2001-8-13', '2001-8-13', 1);

INSERT INTO JobTicket (CustomerID, StartDate, EndDate, VehicleID)
     VALUES (4, '2002-2-16', '2002-2-17', 9);

INSERT INTO JobTicketDetail (JobTicketID, LineItemNumber, ServiceID,
                             DateComplete, HoursSpent)
     VALUES (1, 1, 1, '2002-1-20', .5);
```

```
INSERT INTO JobTicketDetail (JobTicketID, LineItemNumber, ServiceID,
                             DateComplete, HoursSpent)
    VALUES (2, 1, 1, '2001-7-20', .25);

INSERT INTO JobTicketDetail (JobTicketID, LineItemNumber, ServiceID,
                             DateComplete, HoursSpent)
    VALUES (2, 2, 3, '2001-7-20', .1);

INSERT INTO JobTicketDetail (JobTicketID, LineItemNumber, ServiceID,
                             DateComplete, HoursSpent)
    VALUES (2, 3, 4, '2001-7-20', .1);

INSERT INTO JobTicketDetail (JobTicketID, LineItemNumber, ServiceID,
                             DateComplete, HoursSpent)
    VALUES (3, 1, 1, '2001-9-16', .25);

INSERT INTO JobTicketDetail (JobTicketID, LineItemNumber, ServiceID,
                             DateComplete, HoursSpent)
    VALUES (4, 1, 1, '2002-1-26', .25);

INSERT INTO JobTicketDetail (JobTicketID, LineItemNumber, ServiceID,
                             DateComplete, HoursSpent)
    VALUES (5, 1, 2, '2002-5-21', .2);

INSERT INTO JobTicketDetail (JobTicketID, LineItemNumber, ServiceID,
                             DateComplete, HoursSpent)
    VALUES (5, 2, 1, '2002-5-21', .25);

INSERT INTO JobTicketDetail (JobTicketID, LineItemNumber, ServiceID,
                             DateComplete, HoursSpent)
    VALUES (6, 1, 5, '2001-8-13', 1.15);

INSERT INTO JobTicketDetail (JobTicketID, LineItemNumber, ServiceID,
                             DateComplete, HoursSpent)
    VALUES (7, 1, 1, '2002-2-16', .35);

INSERT INTO JobTicketDetail (JobTicketID, LineItemNumber, ServiceID,
                             DateComplete, HoursSpent)
    VALUES (7, 2, 3, '2002-2-16', .1);

INSERT INTO JobTicketDetail (JobTicketID, LineItemNumber, ServiceID,
                             DateComplete, HoursSpent)
    VALUES (7, 3, 4, '2002-2-16', .15);
```

```
INSERT INTO JobTicketDetail (JobTicketID, LineItemNumber, ServiceID,
                            DateComplete, HoursSpent)
    VALUES (7, 4, 6, '2002-2-16', 1.0);

INSERT INTO JobTicketDetail (JobTicketID, LineItemNumber, ServiceID,
                            DateComplete, HoursSpent)
    VALUES (7, 5, 5, '2002-2-17', .5);

INSERT INTO PartUsed (JobTicketID, LineItemNumber, PartID, Quantity)
    VALUES (1, 1, 4, 4);

INSERT INTO PartUsed (JobTicketID, LineItemNumber, PartID, Quantity)
    VALUES (1, 1, 7, 1);

INSERT INTO PartUsed (JobTicketID, LineItemNumber, PartID, Quantity)
    VALUES (1, 1, 11, 1);

INSERT INTO PartUsed (JobTicketID, LineItemNumber, PartID, Quantity)
    VALUES (1, 1, 12, 1);

INSERT INTO PartUsed (JobTicketID, LineItemNumber, PartID, Quantity)
    VALUES (2, 1, 5, 4);
INSERT INTO PartUsed (JobTicketID, LineItemNumber, PartID, Quantity)
    VALUES (2, 1, 14, 1);

INSERT INTO PartUsed (JobTicketID, LineItemNumber, PartID, Quantity)
    VALUES (2, 1, 8, 1);

INSERT INTO PartUsed (JobTicketID, LineItemNumber, PartID, Quantity)
    VALUES (2, 2, 9, 1);

INSERT INTO PartUsed (JobTicketID, LineItemNumber, PartID, Quantity)
    VALUES (2, 3, 16, 1);

INSERT INTO PartUsed (JobTicketID, LineItemNumber, PartID, Quantity)
    VALUES (3, 1, 6, 4);

INSERT INTO PartUsed (JobTicketID, LineItemNumber, PartID, Quantity)
    VALUES (3, 1, 7, 1);

INSERT INTO PartUsed (JobTicketID, LineItemNumber, PartID, Quantity)
    VALUES (4, 1, 1, 4);
```

```
INSERT INTO PartUsed (JobTicketID, LineItemNumber, PartID, Quantity)
    VALUES (4, 1, 8, 1);

INSERT INTO PartUsed (JobTicketID, LineItemNumber, PartID, Quantity)
    VALUES (5, 1, 10, 1);

INSERT INTO PartUsed (JobTicketID, LineItemNumber, PartID, Quantity)
    VALUES (5, 2, 3, 4);

INSERT INTO PartUsed (JobTicketID, LineItemNumber, PartID, Quantity)
    VALUES (5, 2, 14, 1);

INSERT INTO PartUsed (JobTicketID, LineItemNumber, PartID, Quantity)
    VALUES (5, 2, 12, 1);

INSERT INTO PartUsed (JobTicketID, LineItemNumber, PartID, Quantity)
    VALUES (5, 2, 8, 1);

INSERT INTO PartUsed (JobTicketID, LineItemNumber, PartID, Quantity)
    VALUES (6, 1, 13, 1);

INSERT INTO PartUsed (JobTicketID, LineItemNumber, PartID, Quantity)
    VALUES (7, 1, 1, 4);

INSERT INTO PartUsed (JobTicketID, LineItemNumber, PartID, Quantity)
    VALUES (7, 1, 8, 1);

INSERT INTO PartUsed (JobTicketID, LineItemNumber, PartID, Quantity)
    VALUES (7, 1, 14, 1);

INSERT INTO PartUsed (JobTicketID, LineItemNumber, PartID, Quantity)
    VALUES (7, 1, 12, 1);

INSERT INTO PartUsed (JobTicketID, LineItemNumber, PartID, Quantity)
    VALUES (7, 2, 9, 1);

INSERT INTO PartUsed (JobTicketID, LineItemNumber, PartID, Quantity)
    VALUES (7, 3, 16, 1);

INSERT INTO PartUsed (JobTicketID, LineItemNumber, PartID, Quantity)
    VALUES (7, 4, 15, 1);
```

```
INSERT INTO PartUsed (JobTicketID, LineItemNumber, PartID, Quantity)
       VALUES (7, 5, 13, 1);
```

Your sample database is now ready to use. Enjoy!

Differences in Sybase SQL Anywhere

There are very few differences between SQL Server and Sybase at a basic level. The only change we had to make to the SQL that creates the sample database is the format of the dates that are inserted. Sybase expects the dates to be in the format yyyy-mm-dd. So instead of typing 05-21-2002, you have to type 2002-05-21, for instance.

You will see more differences between the two RDBMSs as you perform more advanced tasks. SQL Server and Sybase are, in our experience, the easiest databases to switch between.

Education, Training, and Certification

This book only covers SQL as a language and not specific information on the database management systems that use it. Should you decide to continue to use a Sybase RDBMS, you might need a more specific book about the product. Following is a list of some of the books available on Sybase Adaptive Server, Sybase SQL Server 11, and SQL Anywhere:

Title: *Sybase ASE 12.5 Performance and Tuning*
Author(s): Jeff Garbus
Publisher: Wordware Publishing
List Price: $59.95

Title: *Guide to Sybase and SQL Server*
Author(s): D. McGoveran and C.J. Date
Publisher: Addison-Wesley
List Price: $59.99

Title: *Sybase SQL Server 11 Unleashed*
Author(s): Ray Rankins et al.
Publisher: Sams
List Price: $59.99

Title: *SQL Anywhere Studio*
Author(s): Jose A. Ramalho and Cloyde Brown
Publisher: Wordware Publishing
List Price: $12.95

Sybase offers both online and instructor-led training. Sybase has several authorized training partners. These are training centers that are certified to teach Sybase technologies. Check the Sybase Web site at **www.sybase.com/education** for a listing of classes and training centers.

Sybase also offers a couple different levels of certification for their database products: Adaptive Server Administrator (Associate or Professional), SQL Anywhere, and SQL Developer. You can find out more about these certifications at **www.sybase.com/education/profcert**.

GLOSSARY

A

ABS—A SQL mathematical function that takes a value and returns the absolute value.

ALTER DATABASE—A SQL command used to change the properties of a database from a DBMS such as the character set, caching, and backup characteristics.

ALTER TABLE—A SQL statement that is used to change the properties of a table such as the columns it contains or the constraints that apply to it.

ANY—A SQL keyword that allows you to perform a comparison against a list of values—ANY is used in combination with the SQL comparison operators.

AS—A SQL keyword used to alias a column name, an expression, or a table name.

ASCII—A SQL function that provides the numeric ASCII value for a character.

Audit trail—A historical record of changes that are made to a set of data. The record may include the name of the person who made the changes, the date, the time, and specific details about the data that was inserted, updated, or deleted.

AUTO_INCREMENT—A column whose value automatically increments by a set value whenever a row is inserted with a NULL in the column. SQL Server and Sybase use IDENTITY.

AVG—A SQL aggregate function that takes a set of data (a column or an expression) and averages the values in the set.

B

BETWEEN—A SQL operator that determines if a value is within the specified range.

Business rule—Defines or restricts data to meet a particular business practice rather than just a universally accepted fact.

C

Cartesian product—Occurs when at least two tables are not properly joined together. Every row from the first table is joined with every row in the second table and so forth until every possible combination is presented.

Cascading delete—Handles the situation where a primary key row is deleted. The cascading delete will automatically delete the related foreign key rows in other tables. An alternative action may also be available to update the foreign key values to NULL instead of deleting the row.

Cascading update—Handles the situation where a primary key value is updated. The cascading update will automatically update any related foreign key values in other tables to match the new value.

CASE—A SQL function that is used to evaluate a value or an expression to determine the appropriate result. It can be used to compare values to a column or to evaluate several Boolean expressions.

CAST—A SQL function used to convert a column or an expression from one data type to another.

CEIL—*See* CEILING.

CEILING—A SQL function that returns the nearest integer greater than the value specified.

CHAR—A SQL function that returns the character associated with an ASCII value.

Clause—A portion of a statement. In the case of SQL, each clause is identified by a keyword such as FROM or WHERE.

Clustered index—An index that specifies the physical order of the data. A table may have only one clustered index.

Column—A piece of information in a table, such as the address of your customer.

Composite index—An index made up of two or more columns.

Computed columns—Columns in your result set that are made up of one or more columns from the tables in the FROM clause of the query. They are also referred to as *expressions*.

CONCAT—A SQL function that combines two strings together.

Constraint—An option that further defines a table or a column. It will either add more information to or put certain restrictions on the table or column.

CONVERT—A SQL function used to convert a column or an expression from one data type to another. It is similar to CAST, only CONVERT allows a format to be specified as well.

Correlated subquery—A subquery that references the tables of the outer query. Because of this reference, the subquery must be reevaluated for every row examined by the outer query.

COUNT—A SQL aggregate function that takes a set of data and counts the number of items in the set.

CREATE DATABASE—A SQL command used to create a database.

CREATE INDEX—A SQL command used to create an index on a table.

CREATE ROLE—A SQL command used to create a role in the database.

CREATE SESSION—A privilege that must be granted to each user in an Oracle database before the user can access the database.

CREATE TABLE—A SQL command used to create a table in the database.

CREATE TRIGGER—A SQL command used to create a trigger on a table.

CREATE USER—A SQL command used to create a user in the database.

CREATE VIEW—A SQL command used to create a view in the database.

CROSS JOIN—Used to join each row from the first table to each row of the second table. When used without a WHERE clause, it results in a Cartesian product. When used with a WHERE clause, it acts like an INNER JOIN.

D

Database—A container for related tables. It acts like a file cabinet containing many folders.

DATALENGTH—*See* LEN.

DATEADD—A SQL function used to add a particular value to part of the date. For instance, you could use it to add two days to the original date, or maybe you would like to add 32 weeks.

DATEDIFF—A SQL function used to find the interval between two dates. The interval can be expressed in any one of a list of units such as days, weeks, quarters, or many other units.

DATENAME—A SQL function that allows you to obtain the value of a specific piece of the DATE-TIME value. It is similar to DATEPART, except that this function will show you the name of the value instead of the number.

DATEPART—A SQL function that allows you to obtain the value of a specific piece of the DATE-TIME value.

DAY—A SQL function that returns the day portion of a date value.

DELETE—A SQL command used to remove rows of data from a table.

DIFFERENCE—A SQL function used to find out how closely two strings sound. A number from 0 to 4 is returned, with 4 being the best possible match.

DISTINCT—A SQL keyword that filters duplicates from a result set.

DROP DATABASE—A SQL command used to delete a database from a DBMS.

DROP INDEX—A SQL command used to delete an index from a table.

DROP ROLE—An Oracle command used to delete a role from the database.

DROP TABLE—A SQL command used to delete a table from the database.

DROP USER—An Oracle command that deletes a user from the database.

E

EXECUTE—A SQL command used to run a stored procedure or function.

EXISTS—A SQL command used to test for the existence of a result set returned from a subquery.

Explicit conversion—A conversion that requires the user to tell the DBMS that the value needs converted and what data type it needs to be.

F

FLOOR—A SQL function that returns the nearest integer lesser than the value specified.

Foreign key—A column in the table used to point to the primary key of another table.

FROM—A SQL clause used to specify the tables involved in a SELECT, an INSERT, an UPDATE, or a DELETE statement.

FULL OUTER JOIN—*See* OUTER JOIN.

G

GETDATE—A SQL function that returns the current date and time from the database server. SYSDATE is used instead of GETDATE by some DBMSs.

GRANT—A SQL command used to grant a privilege to a user, role, or group.

GRANT ROLE—A Sybase command used to grant a role to a user.

GROUP BY—A SQL clause used to group the rows in a result set by the specified columns.

H

HAVING—A SQL clause used to filter the groups in a result set. It is used with the GROUP BY clause.

I

IDENTITY—*See* AUTO_INCREMENT.

Implicit conversion—A conversion that the DBMS can perform without specific instruction to do so. For example, SQL Server will automatically convert an integer value to a string if it is used in a string function. SQL Server cannot convert a `smallint` to a string without being told to, however.

IN—A SQL operator that allows you to match a column or an expression against a list of values.

Index—An index provides the DBMS with the logical or physical order of the data in the table. When the DBMS has an index to tell it the order of the data, it can access the data in the table much faster.

INNER JOIN—A type of join in SQL. An inner join is used when the tables being joined must have a matching value in the other table.

INSERT—A SQL statement used to insert data into a table.

ISNULL—A SQL function that allows you to replace NULLs found in a column or an expression with a value of your choosing.

L

LEFT—A SQL function that removes the specified number of characters from the left side of a supplied string.

LEFT OUTER JOIN—*See* OUTER JOIN.

LEN—A SQL function that returns the length of a column or an expression.

LENGTH—*See* LEN.

LIKE—A SQL operator used to compare a column or an expression to a match expression.

LOWER—A SQL function that returns the supplied string in all lowercase characters.

LTRIM—A SQL function that trims spaces from the left side of the supplied string.

M

MAX—A SQL aggregate function that takes a set of data (a column or an expression) and returns the largest value in that set.

MIN—A SQL aggregate function that takes a set of data (a column or an expression) and returns the smallest value in that set.

MONTH—A SQL function that returns the month portion of a date value.

N

Naming convention—An agreed-upon standard for giving names to all objects within a database. The standard may dictate the case, tense, punctuation, and abbreviations that should be used when naming new objects.

Nonclustered index—An index that specifies a logical order for the data. A table may have many nonclustered indexes.

NULL—Means the value is unknown. It is not the same as an empty string.

NVL—*See* ISNULL.

O

Optimizer—Programming logic that is built into the DBMS. Its purpose is to investigate SQL commands before they are executed and determine the best and fastest way to execute the command.

ORDER BY—A SQL clause used to sort the result set on the columns specified.

Orphaned data—Data that cannot be traced back to its parent. It is data in a foreign key column that should exist as a primary key in another table, but does not. This is often the result of the row in the primary key table being deleted.

OUTER JOIN—A type of join in SQL. An OUTER JOIN is used when all the rows from one table should be returned regardless of a matching row being found in the other table. A RIGHT OUTER JOIN means all rows from the right table should be returned. A LEFT OUTER JOIN means all rows from the left table should be returned.

P

PL-SQL—Oracle's extension to ANSI SQL.

Primary key—A column or set of columns that uniquely identify each row in the table.

R

RDBMS—*See* Relational Database Management System.

Referential integrity—The concept of keeping a database's tables properly related to one another. If two tables are related in a database, then there should not be missing or undefined data in any of the columns that make up the relationship.

Relational Database Management System—Also known as RDBMS or just DBMS, the software that contains databases and provides an interface to those databases.

REPLACE—A SQL function that is used to replace a portion of a string with another value.

Replication—A term used for copying or distributing data between two or more databases. It can involve creating identical copies of data, summarizing data, or storing a subset of the original.

REVOKE—A SQL command used to remove a privilege previously granted to a user, role, or group.

RIGHT—A SQL function that removes the specified number of characters from the right side of a supplied string.

RIGHT OUTER JOIN—*See* OUTER JOIN.

ROUND—A SQL function used to round a value to the precision specified.

Row—Represents a single entry within a table.

RTRIM—A SQL function that trims spaces from the right side of the supplied string.

S

SELECT—A SQL command used to retrieve data from an RDBMS.

SET—A SQL command used to set various database environment variables.

SET ROLE—A SQL command Oracle users must issue before they can use a role they have been assigned.

SIGN—A SQL function that returns 1 if the specified value is positive, −1 if it is negative, or 0 if the value is zero.

SOUNDEX—A SQL function that converts the string into a number representing its sound value. When the SOUNDEX value of one string is equal to the SOUNDEX value of another string, it means the two strings sound alike even if they are spelled differently.

sp_addlogin—A SQL Server stored procedure used to add a login to the database.

sp_addgroup—A Sybase stored procedure used to add a group to the database.

sp_addrole—A SQL Server stored procedure used to add a role to the database.

sp_addrolemember—A SQL Server stored procedure used to add a user to a role in the database.

sp_adduser—A SQL Server stored procedure used to add a user to the database.

sp_changegroup—A Sybase stored procedure used to add a member to a group in the database.

sp_dropgroup—A Sybase stored procedure used to delete a group from the database.

sp_droplogin—A SQL Server stored procedure used to delete a login from the database.

sp_droprole—A SQL Server stored procedure used to drop a role from the database.

sp_dropuser—A SQL Server stored procedure used to delete a user from the database.

SPACE—A SQL function that returns a string containing the specified number of spaces.

SQL—An ANSI standard language used to communicate with relational database management systems.

SQRT—A SQL function that returns the square root of the value specified.

SQUARE—A SQL function that returns the square of the value specified.

STDEV—A SQL aggregate function that takes a set of data (a column name or an expression) and returns the standard deviation of the values in that set.

Stored procedures—A set of one or more queries or commands that are saved and can be executed later.

Subquery—A SELECT statement nested inside another query. It returns a value to the containing query for evaluation. The query containing the subquery is referred to as the *outer query*. Subqueries are often referred as an *inner query*, an *inner select*, a *subselect*, or a *nested query*.

SUBSTRING—A SQL function that returns the portion of the supplied string starting with the supplied beginning position and ending with the supplied ending position.

SUM—A SQL aggregate function that takes a set of data (a column name or an expression) and returns the sum of the values in that set.

Surrogate key—Data that by itself has no meaning, like a name or an address does. This data is used to uniquely identify each row in a table. A sequentially increasing number is an example of a surrogate key.

SYSDATE—*See* GETDATE.

T

Table—Stores pieces of related information like a folder in a file cabinet would. An example of a table would be a customer table that would hold things like customer name, address, and phone number.

Table scan—The process of a SQL command looking at every row in a table one by one in order to test the values of one or more columns.

TO_CHAR—An Oracle function that converts a value to a char data type.

TO_DATE—An Oracle function that converts a value to a date data type.

TO_NUMBER—An Oracle function that converts a value to a number data type.

Transact-SQL—An extension to ANSI SQL used by SQL Server and Sybase. It is also called T-SQL. Transact-SQL does not have the exact same capabilities between vendors, but the basis is similar.

Triggers—A set of SQL commands that runs automatically. A trigger is associated with a certain table and only executes when the specified action takes place on that table.

U

UNION—A SQL operator that allows you to combine the results of two or more similar SELECT statements.

Unique index—An index created on a column or set of columns to prevent duplicate entries. One is most often found on a primary key column.

UPDATE—A SQL statement used to modify the data in one or more columns of a table.

UPPER—A SQL function that returns the supplied string in all uppercase characters.

USER_NAME—A SQL function that returns the name of the current user, or the name associated with the supplied user ID.

V

VAR—A SQL aggregate function that takes a set of data (a column name or an expression) and returns the variance of the values in that set.

W

WHERE—A SQL clause used to filter the result set.

Y

YEAR—A SQL function that returns the year portion of a date value.

INDEX

Symbols

+ (addition operator), 75–76
* (asterisk), 338
/ (division operator), 75–76
= (Equal operator), 47
> (greater than operator), 47
>= (greater than or equal operator), 47
< (less than operator), 47
<=(less than or equal to operator), 47–48
* (multiplication operator), 75–76
<>(Not equal operator), 47
% (remainder of division operator), 75–76
[ ] (square brackets), 55
|| (string concatenation), 97
– (subtraction operator), 75–76
_ (underscore character), 54–55
% (wildcard character), 54

A

ABS function, 88
Access, creating user accounts and groups in, 274
accessing
    MySQL, 437–438
    Oracle, 419–420
    SQL Anywhere, 453–456
    SQL Server, 403–404
ACOS function, 88
Active Server Pages (ASP), Web page data access with, 377–382
ActiveX Data Objects (ADO), 351
Adaptive Server Enterprise (ASE), 6
Add Tables dialog box (Microsoft Query), 336, 342
adding
    columns to tables, 176
    Microsoft Query to Start menu, 332
addition operator (+), 75–76
ADO (ActiveX Data Objects), 351
ADO Control button (Visual Basic 6.0), 352